Joseph Smith Jr.

Joseph Smith Jr.

Reappraisals after Two Centuries

EDITED BY

REID L. NEILSON AND TERRYL L. GIVENS

OXFORD
UNIVERSITY PRESS

2009

OXFORD
UNIVERSITY PRESS

Oxford University Press, Inc., publishes works that further
Oxford University's objective of excellence
in research, scholarship, and education.

Oxford   New York
Auckland   Cape Town   Dar es Salaam   Hong Kong   Karachi
Kuala Lumpur   Madrid   Melbourne   Mexico City   Nairobi
New Delhi   Shanghai   Taipei   Toronto

With offices in
Argentina   Austria   Brazil   Chile   Czech Republic   France   Greece
Guatemala   Hungary   Italy   Japan   Poland   Portugal   Singapore
South Korea   Switzerland   Thailand   Turkey   Ukraine   Vietnam

Published by Oxford University Press, Inc.
198 Madison Avenue, New York, New York 10016

www.oup.com

Oxford is a registered trademark of Oxford University Press

Library of Congress Cataloging-in-Publication Data
Joseph Smith, Jr. : reappraisals after two centuries / edited
by Reid L. Neilson, Terryl L. Givens.
    p. cm.
Includes bibliographical references and index.
ISBN 978-0-19-536978-6; 978-0-19-536976-2 (pbk.)
1. Smith, Joseph, 1805–1844.   I. Neilson, Reid Larkin.   II. Givens, Terryl L.
BX8695.S6J665 2008
289.3092—dc22   2008012895

9 8 7 6 5 4 3 2 1
Printed in the United States of America
on acid-free paper

To Richard Lyman Bushman
scholar, gentleman, friend

Contents

Contributors

Catherine L. Albanese is Chair of the Department of Religious Studies and J. F. Rowny Professor of Comparative Religions at the University of California at Santa Barbara. Her books include *America: Religions and Religion; Nature Religion in America: From the Algonkian Indians to the New Age;* and *A Republic of Mind and Spirit: A Cultural History of American Metaphysical Religion.*

James B. Allen is Lemuel Harrison Redd Jr. Professor of Western American History Emeritus at Brigham Young University. His books include *The Story of the Latter-day Saints; Trials of Discipleship: The Story of William Clayton, a Mormon;* and *The Company Town in the American West.*

Margaret Barker is a past scholar at the University of Cambridge and a former president of the Society for Old Testament Study. Her books include *The Older Testament; The Great Angel;* and *The Great High Priest.*

Richard H. Brodhead is President and Professor of English at Duke University. His books include *Hawthorne, Melville, and the Novel; Cultures of Letters: Scenes of Reading and Writing in Nineteenth-Century America;* and *The Good of This Place: Values and Challenges in College Education.*

Richard Lyman Bushman is Gouverneur Morris Professor of History Emeritus at Columbia University. His books include *From Puritan to Yankee: Character and the Social Order in Connecticut, 1690–1765; The*

Refinement of America: Persons, Houses, and Cities; and *Joseph Smith: Rough Stone Rolling.*

Kevin Christensen is a professional technical writer for the Ansoft Corporation. His writing has appeared in *Dialogue: A Journal of Mormon Thought; Sunstone;* and various Foundation for Ancient Research and Mormon Studies publications.

Douglas J. Davies is Professor of Theology and Religion at Durham University (England). He is the author and editor of several books including *The Mormon Culture of Salvation; Anthropology and Theology;* and *An Introduction to Mormonism.*

Terryl L. Givens holds the James A. Bostwick Chair of English and is Professor of Literature and Religion at the University of Richmond. His books include *The Viper on the Hearth: Mormons, Myths, and the Construction of Heresy; By the Hand of Mormon: The American Scripture That Launched a New World Religion;* and *People of Paradox: A History of Mormon Culture.*

Klaus J. Hansen is Professor of History Emeritus at Queen's University (Kingston, Ontario). His two books are *Quest for Empire: The Political Kingdom of God and the Council of Fifty in Mormon History;* and *Mormonism and the American Experience.*

Wayne Hudson is Professor of Humanities at Griffith University (Australia). His books include *Constructivism and History Teaching; The Reform of Utopia;* and *Restructuring Australia.*

Laurie F. Maffly-Kipp is Associate Professor of Religious Studies at the University of North Carolina at Chapel Hill. Her works include *Religion and Society in Frontier California; Practicing Protestants: Studies in American Christian History;* and *Proclamation to the People: Nineteenth-century Mormonism and the Pacific Basin Frontier.*

Richard J. Mouw is President and Professor of Christian Philosophy at Fuller Theological Seminary. He is the author of several books including *The God Who Commands; Uncommon Decency: Christian Civility in an Uncivil World;* and *He Shines in All That's Fair: Culture and Common Grace.*

Reid L. Neilson is Assistant Professor of Church History and Doctrine at Brigham Young University. He is the author and editor of several books, including *The Mormon History Association's Tanner Lectures: The First Twenty Years; The Rise of Mormonism;* and *Believing History: Latter-day Saint Essays.*

Richard Dilworth Rust is Professor of English Emeritus at the University of North Carolina at Chapel Hill. He has written *Feasting on the Word: The Literary*

Testimony of the Book of Mormon and edited *Astoria, or Anecdotes of an Enterprize beyond the Rocky Mountains* and *The Pathfinder, or the Inland Sea.*

David J. Whittaker is Associate Professor of History and Curator of Nineteenth-century Western and Mormon Americana of the Harold B. Lee Library at Brigham Young University. His publications include *Mormon Americana: A Guide to Sources and Collections in the United States; Studies in Mormon History, 1830–1997;* and *Mormon History.*

PART I

American Prophet

I

Introduction

Reid L. Neilson and Terryl L. Givens

"Joe Smith," as he is commonly called, will soon find that America is not another Arabia, nor he another Mohammed; and his hope of founding a vast empire in the Western hemisphere must soon vanish away.

—Robert Baird, 1843

The Prophet, Joseph Smith Jr., is unquestionably the most important reformer and innovator in American religious history.

—Robert V. Remini, 2002

In August 2005, we sat among a group of academics and scattered spectators, listening to a series of papers at a scholarly conference at the National Taiwan University in Taipei. Arun Joshi, a respected Hindu journalist from India, was speaking on the relevance of the Mormon prophet Joseph Smith's 1820 First Vision to the conflicts in Kashmir and the Middle East. The confluence of setting, speaker, and subject was more improbable than Joshi's conclusion: "The message of Joseph Smith is more relevant . . . today than ever before."[1]

The occasion in this instance was commemorative. Joseph Smith's bicentennial observance, during 2005 and 2006, and a series of conferences around the world attended by scholars both from within and outside the LDS tradition (i.e., the traditions of The Church of Jesus Christ of Latter-day Saints), explored Smith's life and legacy. At sites ranging from Claremont, California, and Washington,

D.C., to Sydney, Australia, and Taipei, Taiwan, presenters weighed in on the impact of this controversial religious figure. Two hundred years should be ample time to assess the accuracy of Josiah Quincy Jr.'s famed prediction: "It is by no means improbable that some future text-book, for the use of generations yet unborn, will contain a question something like this: What historical American of the 19th century has exerted the most powerful influence upon the destinies of his countrymen? And it is by no means impossible that the answer to the interrogatory may thus be written: Joseph Smith, the Mormon prophet."[2]

Who was Joseph Smith? He burst into the American spotlight as a twenty-four-year-old youth in 1830 with the publication of a book claiming, all in one, to be new scripture, ancient history, and evidence of his call from God. He aroused only local notice at first, as just another one of New York's countless "humbugs of religion," although in his case, he quickly developed a Mormon print culture to spread his message and invite examination of his claims. Angels, gold plates, and mysterious "interpreters" sometimes overshadowed in the public mind the particulars of the message his Book of Mormon and of the revelations he conveyed, just as the size of the cohesive communities he inaugurated in late 1830 alarmed people not attuned to the purported spiritual significance of these latter-day gatherings of what they claimed to be remnants of a scattered Israel. Many people were converted, and many were outraged, but even from the beginning a few dispassionate observers wonderingly pondered the undeniable charisma of this prophet in pantaloons, who was as adept, noted one editor, at "prophecying [and] preaching" as he was at "building . . . temples[s], and regulating his empire."[3]

Smith's religion was a curious mix of old and new. He claimed to be recuperating a gospel and ordinances as old as Adam, with temples that invited comparison with Solomon's. Even plural marriage, rumors of which circulated as early as the 1830s, was but a restoration of a practice of the Patriarchs, he insisted. But from the perspective of orthodox Christianity, new scripture—half again the size of the entire Christian Bible—was sufficient departure from *sola scriptura* to warrant condemnation. Republican ideals, as well, were violated in Smith's apparent merging of church and state, and he flouted the public perception of the prophetic vocation in everything—from his name to his earthy deportment to his political aspirations. He was murdered before the last and most daring of his theological pronouncements—those involving an evolved God, human theosis, and marriage for the eternities—ever made it into the court of religious opinion.

But how has the story of Joseph Smith and the religious movement he founded been told since his assassination in 1844? The historical approach has traditionally governed the study of religion in America, although, religious studies scholar Catherine L. Albanese argues, this has changed in recent decades as sociologists, anthropologists, literary scholars, philosophers, and theologians have joined the field. Moreover, three major methodologies—the *consensus, conflict,* and *contact* models—have shaped the guild of American religious history.[4] As a result, past historians have written about Joseph Smith and Mormonism in predictable ways when making general surveys of the American religious landscape.[5] But that is beginning to change.

Speaking of the consensus approach, Albanese explains, "Consensus historiography writes the Anglo-Protestant past at the center of U.S. religious history. It sees processes of religious and ethnic blending—the proverbial 'melting pot'—strongly at work in the nation's history, and it minimizes any narrative of religious pluralism. . . . Likewise, it minimizes the impact of social, cultural, and religious change over time and stresses a religious culture of continuity with Anglo-Protestantism." The consensus model began when Robert Baird published *Religion in America* in 1843.[6] Because Mormonism challenged the Protestant establishment (the very thing Baird was trying to glorify), Baird was not at all sympathetic to Joseph Smith and his followers. "The annals of modern times furnish few more remarkable examples of cunning in the leaders, and delusion in their dupes, than is presented by what is called Mormonism," Baird wrote. "'Joe Smith,' as he is commonly called ["an ignorant but ambitious person" as Baird characterizes elsewhere], will soon find that America is not another Arabia, nor he another Mohammed; and his hope of founding a vast empire in the Western hemisphere must soon vanish away."[7]

A decade later, in 1855, Philip Schaff's *America: A Sketch of Its Political, Social, and Religious Character* was translated from German and made available in America. Like Baird, this German historian was antagonistic toward those groups, particularly the Mormons, who seemed to be thwarting or challenging the continued hegemony of European Protestantism in America.[8] "I confess, I would fain pass over this sect in silence. It really lies out of the pale of Christianity and the church," Schaff writes. "Nor has it exerted the slightest influence on the general character and religious life of the American people, but has rather been repelled by it, even by force, as an element altogether foreign and infernal." He dismissed Joseph Smith as "an uneducated but cunning Yankee" to his readers back in Germany, yet despaired over what the growth of Mormonism says about the United States: "I must only beg, in the name of my adopted fatherland, that you will not judge America in any way by this irregular growth."[9]

Two other authors of major surveys of religion in America followed in the same consensus footsteps.[10] Daniel Dorchester suggested that "Mormonism grew out of popular superstitions for a time quite prevalent among the more ignorant classes, about one hundred years ago," in *Christianity in the United States* (1888). He spent the next five pages of his book pillorying Joseph Smith, Brigham Young, and all things Mormon.[11] In *A History of American Christianity* (1897), Leonard Bacon likewise described Mormonism as "a system of gross, palpable imposture contrived by a disreputable adventurer, Joe Smith." Bacon continued:

> It is a shame to human nature that the silly lies put forth by this precious gang should have found believers. But the solemn pretensions to divine revelation, mixed with elements borrowed from the prevalent revivalism, and from the immediate adventism which so easily captivates excitable imaginations, drew a number of honest dupes into the train of knavish leaders, and made possible the pitiable history which followed.[12]

It is important to note, however, that Baird, Schaff, Dorchester, and Bacon were not professional historians of religion. William Sweet, holder of the inaugural chair in American church history at the University of Chicago, helped professionalize the discipline through his historical publications during the early decades of the twentieth century.[13] He offered a more sympathetic treatment of Joseph Smith and Mormonism in his well-known text *The Story of Religion in America* (1930).[14] One of Sweet's protégés, Sidney E. Mead, in *The Lively Experiment* (1963), put Joseph Smith in the company of antebellum religious leaders like Peter Cartwright, Charles G. Finney, and Henry Ward Beecher, who supplanted more traditional religious figures such as Timothy Dwight, John Witherspoon, and William White.[15] The closing bookend to the consensus historiography was Sydney E. Ahlstrom's tome, *A Religious History of the American People* (1972). The late dean of American religious history makes it clear "that the entire saga of Joseph Smith and Mormonism is a vital episode in American history," yet he struggles to articulate Smith's significance and legacy.[16]

During the past three decades, two avant-garde methods have challenged and, in many cases, supplanted the traditional consensus approach: the conflict and contact models. "By the time Ahlstrom's work appeared, . . . especially among younger scholars influenced by postmodernism, postcolonialism, and general critical-studies concerns, there was a general suspicion of grand narratives," Albanese explains. The conflict model "emphasizes contentiousness and contests for recognition, status, and a fair share of the benefits accorded to the various religious traditions and groups in the United States. . . . By definition, conflict historiography does not produce comprehensive narratives." The more recent contact model "seeks to encompass the conflict model but also to include more. Its argument is that conflict has been only one of a series of exchanges between religious peoples and religious goods when they have met in the United States and that, therefore, any comprehensive narrative of religion in America must examine and explore all of these exchanges."[17]

These recent historiographical evolutions have freed up space in scholarship for the Mormons and have leveled the rhetorical playing field. As scholars of the American religious past and present continue to move away from the consensus model, in which the upstart Latter-day Saint tradition had no real fit, and embrace conflict, contact, and other methodologies, Joseph Smith is beginning to get a new hearing in scholarly surveys, monographs, textbooks, and articles.

The rationale behind this collection is that the day has come when the founder of Mormonism and his prominent role in American history and religious thought cannot be denied. The attention paid to Smith's teachings, charismatic ministry, and religion-making imagination now comes from scholars in American history, religious studies, sociology, biblical studies, Christian philosophy, literature, and the humanities—all of whose areas of concentration are represented in this collection. It is our intent to reflect in these pages the wide-ranging interest in Joseph Smith that the commemorative conferences only suggested.

One challenge in assessing the historical importance and relevance of Joseph Smith's thought has been related to the difficulty of moving beyond the question that arrests all conversation—the question that asks whether Smith was a prophet or fraud. These essays are rich evidence that a variety of interpretive strategies can bypass this question in order to explore Smith's influence, historical impact, parallels with literary figures, and situatedness in new religious contexts. In addition, at least three of the essays directly address the challenge of transcending the insider/outsider schism in Joseph Smith studies (Maffly-Kipp, Mouw, and Hudson); their authors propose their own solutions.

Together, we have selected fourteen essays for this publication, the majority being previously unpublished papers, which we have organized into three sections: "American Prophet," "Sacred Encounters," and "Prophetic Legacy."[18] In part I, "American Prophet," five scholars situate Joseph Smith within an American setting in particular. In the opening essay, "Prophets in America circa 1830: Ralph Waldo Emerson, Nat Turner, Joseph Smith," literary scholar Richard H. Brodhead finds that by contextualizing Smith's history as "prophetic autobiography" alongside Nat Turner's, "uncannily similar" aspects emerge. As a result, what Brodhead calls a history of prophetism takes shape that delineates some of the forms and tragic consequences of prophetic self-assertion. The implications may be translatable across a spectrum of times and cultures.[19]

Historian Klaus J. Hansen, in "Joseph Smith, American Culture, and the Origins of Mormonism," argues why the Mormon prophet's contributions must be seen as the intersecting of American culture with Smith's own particular religious imagination. Comparing Smith to Samuel Johnson and Abraham Lincoln, Hansen uses the question of Smith's relationship to his father as a suggestive illustration of how personal loss becomes religious restoration, and a private experience taps universal appeal.

In "'I Love All Men Who Dive': Herman Melville and Joseph Smith," literary scholar Richard Dilworth Rust illuminates Smith's religion-making imagination by juxtaposing him with America's greatest myth-making novelist of the nineteenth century, Herman Melville. Melville revealed a recurrent interest in things Mormon, and the most telling preoccupation that unites him with Smith, Rust finds, is not so much the heights they both achieved as successful creators of epic systems, but the depths they plumb as "thought-divers," exploring the "darkest abysses" of human experience and of the tragic universe.[20]

Next, religious studies scholar Catherine L. Albanese examines "The Metaphysical Joseph Smith." Noting that American religious history has too often limited itself to mainstream denominationalism and evangelicalism, Albanese has worked to limn the contours of metaphysical religion. This tradition emphasizes the world and human beings as ontologically parallel to, and deriving a stream of spiritual energy from, a higher reality. The consequent worldview "as above, so below" is characteristic of hermeticism and modern mystics like Emanuel Swedenborg. Exploiting Richard Bushman's suggestion that Smith is a protean figure amenable to any number of religious agendas, Albanese finds he fits the bill perfectly as a proto-metaphysician. Extending the arguments of Harold Bloom and John L. Brooke, Albanese argues that in addition to exploring occult antecedents and their influence on Joseph Smith, it is time for American historians "to take account of the debt" that metaphysical religion owes to Joseph Smith.[21]

Historian James B. Allen begins his essay, "Joseph Smith vs. John C. Calhoun: The States' Rights Dilemma and Early Mormon History," with a discussion of the 1832 secession crisis involving South Carolina, reminding us that the popular violence enacted against the Mormons occurred in the immediate context of national debates and crisis over the states' rights question. Constitutional interpretation unfolded against—and under the influence of—this backdrop. The same prevailing views favoring state autonomy over federalism that facilitated eventual civil war also facilitated Mormon oppression. Allen thus offers a rare political and constitutional context for understanding the Mormons' difficulties, the development of Joseph Smith's political views, and Smith's own involvement in the national presidential campaign of 1844.[22]

Part II, "Sacred Encounters," addresses more directly the religion-making imagination of Joseph Smith. In "Joseph Smith and Creation of the Sacred," historian Richard Lyman Bushman proposes a simple fundamental in his accounting for Joseph Smith's religious appeal: Smith "met a human need for the sacred." So, of course, do all religions, but Smith was different, Bushman argues, in constructing the LDS faith around two potent loci: new sacred words, and new sacred places. His additions to scripture blend audacity and a self-effacing quality. The sacred words summarily annihilate the principle of *sola scriptura*, even as the personality delivering this coup de grâce, for Mormons, is subsumed in the voice of God. As for place, Smith literalized the concept of Zion and introduced into Christian worship the concept—and physical reality—of the temple. In the process, he became the first American religious figure to exploit the power of sacred space.[23]

Literary scholar Terryl L. Givens, in "Joseph Smith: Prophecy, Process, and Plenitude," connects Joseph Smith's religion making, in both its scope and its method, to the intellectual revolution called Romanticism. Like all intellectual revolutionaries of that era, from Thomas Malthus to Karl Marx to Charles Darwin, Joseph Smith rearticulated the fundamental vision of his field of influence in terms of contestation, struggle, and dynamism. His collapsing of sacred distance, his rupturing of the canon, his doctrines of preexistence and theosis, and his gestures toward a comprehensive, scriptural Urtext—all betoken an emphasis on process over product and a precarious tension between the searching and certainty that characterized both his personality and the faith he founded.[24]

Applying the analytical insights of Paul Tillich and William Whyte to the revelatory production of Joseph Smith is sociologist Douglas J. Davies in "Visions, Revelations, and Courage in Joseph Smith." His choices are intended to further the project of an interdisciplinary, rather than a provincial or academically ghettoized, approach to Mormon studies. Specifically, Davies considers the traumas of the young Smith, the psychodrama of his First Vision, and echoes of both in the Gethsemane theology Smith developed. The courage that is revealed in these contexts is embodied by Joseph Smith, personally, and institutionally in such forms as vicarious baptism and countercultural practices like plural marriage. Finally, Davies explores the paradox of the LDS emphasis on both courageous individualism and membership in a church that makes corporate belonging and corporate rites salvifically indispensable.[25]

Biblical scholar Margaret Barker, in "Seeking the Face of the Lord: Joseph Smith and the First Temple Tradition," comes to Mormonism as something only tangentially related to her own work in radically reformulating our understanding of ancient Jewish religion. She has elsewhere assessed the Book of Mormon in the context of preexilic Israelite religion. For this collection, she extends that interest by considering the temple worldview of early Israel before the reforms of King Josiah. Noting the primacy of this same temple-dominated vision in the prophetic career of Joseph Smith, she writes the first of a two-part essay on that subject, leaving to Kevin Christensen the job of more fully elaborating the specifics of Smith's visionary production. Specifically, Christensen applies to the Mormon case Barker's claim that "the rise of Christianity can only be understood if we recognize that Jesus' own visions drew upon and exemplified the First Temple tradition." From his translation of the Book of Mormon through the corpus of his own visions, Joseph Smith similarly established continuity with the Bible as text and Jerusalem as sacred space. Equally important is Smith's pattern of both chronicling sacred theophanies and urging their possibility in contemporary religious practice. That is why Christensen can argue that "Joseph Smith's restoration converges on the key time, place, institutions, and issues involved in Barker's reconstruction."

Part III, "Prophetic Legacy," our final section, expands the discussion to a consideration of Joseph Smith in a global context. Religious studies scholar Laurie F. Maffly-Kipp, in "Tracking the Sincere Believer: 'Authentic' Religion and the Enduring Legacy of Joseph Smith Jr.," furthers the project of an intellectually rich account of Mormonism by offering a critique of the centrality of sympathy in the polemics that have engulfed Mormon historical studies from their inception, and proposing an alternative. Her critique is situated in a largely postmodern, antiessentialist conception of identity as a malleable and fluid concept. At the same time, she sees, in Smith's own turn to ritual, a validation of appearances over essence, of doing over being. A focus on the epic of Mormonism's narrative rather than its characters, on popular rather than elite Mormon history, and on the geographical varieties of Mormonism, with their correspondingly different accounts—all are presented here as powerful antidotes to the snares of an approach that links, and therefore reduces, Joseph Smith and the religion he founded to an irresolvable debate over human motives.[26]

"The Possibility of Joseph Smith: Some Evangelical Probings" is Christian philosopher Richard J. Mouw's contribution. The interest of evangelical scholars in Mormonism has tended to be in the context of apologetics rather than scholarly inquiry. Mouw breaks new ground in this regard by responding to Richard Bushman's probing question "Is Joseph Smith *possible* for you?" Like Maffly-Kipp, Mouw stakes out an alternative to the facile either/or approaches that refuse to relinquish the burden of judgment. Turning the study of Joseph Smith in the direction of reception theory enables both a richer dialogue and the possibility of real insight into the religious yearnings and preoccupations of religious communities. As a tentative gesture in this direction, rather than a full examination of the subject, Mouw's essay makes history in a modest way.[27]

It would be hard to imagine a solution more different in tone from Mouw's than the argument advanced by humanities scholar Wayne Hudson in "The Prophethood of Joseph Smith." His premise, flatly stated, is that Joseph Smith is "a genuine prophet of world historical importance." In a bold reversal (for a non-Mormon), he takes such status for Smith as a historical given and as a starting point that can enrich our study of various prophethoods, rather than as a laurel to be disputed in religiously provincial and self-serving ways. Hudson takes a position based largely on the enduring consequences of Smith's pro-phetic output, and then turns to analyze the constituent elements of Smith's prophetic vocation: intelligibility, sincerity, charismatic force, cognitive com-plexity, and effectiveness. Hudson's main contribution in this regard is to probe the possibilities of taking prophecy seriously as an aspect of religious experi-ence and of cultural import, an aspect both "objective and culturally mediated," but to do so without lapsing into "irrationalism."[28]

In "Joseph Smith and Nineteenth-century Mormon Mappings of Asian Re-ligions," historian Reid L. Neilson turns to the subject of what Joseph Smith himself had to say about Mormonism's relationship to other religions, and ways of accommodating religious pluralism. Neilson traces the trajectories of Mormon thought on Eastern religious traditions, following the death of Smith, during the balance of the nineteenth century. Rather than fitting neatly into conventional religious studies paradigms, Neilson argues that the Latter-day Saints warrant their own categorization as "restoration inclusivists."[29]

Lastly, archivist David J. Whittaker provides an invaluable bicentennial bibliographical essay of the Mormon founder in "Studying Joseph Smith Jr.: A Guide to the Sources." Thankfully, he divides the voluminous manuscript sources on Smith into the various categories of journals, sermons and dis-courses, revelations, correspondence, personal history, administrative records, legal documents and judicial history, early Mormon publications, the papers of Smith's associates, and accounts of Smith's contemporaries. Whittaker also separates the hundreds of published sources on Smith into sections on bibliographical guides and sources, diaries and personal writings, sermons and discourses and writings, personal history, revelations, and biographical studies.[30]

It is our hope to provide between these two covers an assemblage of state-ments on the place of Joseph Smith in American history and religious thought that is more wide-ranging than any collection previously available. The most important consequence of this effort is simply a retrospective assessment of his legacy, but the cumulative weight of the evidence here presented suggests that greater attention to his contributions will enrich those fields and disciplines that are beginning to write him into their respective histories.

We appreciate our editor, Cynthia Read, and the board of Oxford University Press for sensing that there is more to Joseph Smith than the stories that have been told. We also thank Gwen Colvin of Oxford University Press for guiding the book through production.

2

Prophets in America circa 1830: Ralph Waldo Emerson, Nat Turner, Joseph Smith

Richard H. Brodhead

In Southampton County, Virginia, on August 21, 1831, a group of black slaves massacred their masters and surrounding white families, killing fifty-five people in the most potent slave revolt in U.S. history. Two months later, on October 30, the rebellion's elusive leader, Nat Turner, was caught; and in the days that followed, from prison, he told his story to a lawyer, Thomas Ruffin Gray. Read in court, this narrative led to Turner's conviction and his execution on November 11. When his story was published, as it was soon thereafter, it supplied missing antecedents for an event that had seemed as enigmatic as it was horrid. This book was *The Confessions of Nat Turner*, one of the most remarkable pieces of writing from the American 1830s.

The genre of *The Confessions of Nat Turner* is prophetic autobiography. This is the story, not of a person's life, but of those parts of a life that gave him a special identity as one divinely chosen for a holy work. A precocious child, the speaker recalls that the folk culture surrounding him read his precocity as a sign that he had the gift of second sight, causing "them to say in my hearing, I surely would be a prophet" (306).[1] Later, Turner learned to play toward his reputation for "divine inspiration," acting the prophet to this communal reception: "Having soon discovered [that] to be great, I must appear so, . . . [I] wrapped myself in mystery, devoting my time to fasting and prayer" (307). But at this point, what began in part as pretense suddenly literalized itself into a new mode of experience. Turner recalls that, in early manhood, he was struck by the scriptural passage: "Seek ye the kingdom of Heaven and all things shall be added unto you" (repetition in original). Then, later, "as I was praying one day at my plough, the spirit spoke to me, saying 'Seek ye the kingdom of Heaven and all things shall be added unto you.'" The astounded Gray asks at this point of *The Confessions*, "What do you mean by the Spirit?" Turner replies, with contempt for Gray's ignorance, "The Spirit that spoke to the prophets in former days" (307–8).

This revelation gave Turner the conviction that he had been "ordained for some great purpose in the hands of the Almighty," and this certainty was reinforced when, a few years later, the experience of revelation was renewed. In 1825, by Turner's account, "I had a vision—and I saw white spirits and black spirits engaged in battle, and the sun was darkened—the thunder rolled in the Heavens, and blood flowed in streams—and I heard a voice saying, 'Such is your luck, such you are called to see, and let it come rough or come smooth, you must surely bear it'" (308–9). In this vision, what would seem to be a fantasy or a premonition of a this-worldly race war is fused with the drama of an other-worldly biblical apocalypse, a conflation that later revelations make ever more powerful. Turner next had a vision in which the lights in the night sky become the hands of the crucified Christ, after which he discovered "drops of blood on the corn as though it were dew from heaven" and bloody hieroglyphs imprinted on forest leaves "representing the figures I had seen before in the heavens." The message of this fusion of observed natural and visionary spiritual realities is clear: "It was plain to me that the Saviour was about to lay down the yoke he had borne for the sins of men, and the great day of judgement was at hand" (309).

At this point, Turner recounts, he told his vision to a white man, Etheldred T. Brantley, who was first physically afflicted and then miraculously healed by Turner's prophetic message. Then "the Spirit appeared to me again, and said, as the Saviour had been baptised so should we be also—and when the white people would not let us be baptised in the church, we went down into the water together, in the sight of many who reviled us, and were baptised by the Spirit— After this I rejoiced greatly, and gave thanks to God" (310).

With no transition, Turner moves straight from this highly charged cross-racial baptism to the vision that brings the whole series to its climax: "And on the 12th of May, 1828, I heard a loud noise in the heavens, and the Spirit instantly appeared to me and said the Serpent was loosened, and Christ had laid down the yoke he had borne for the sins of men, and that I should take it on and fight against the Serpent, for the time was fast approaching when the first should be last and the last should be first" (310).

Informed that he was to be the agent of apocalypse, the man whose "fight against the Serpent" would bring about history's final inversionary turn, Turner learned that heavenly signs would tell him when he should "commence the great work" of racial insurgency and apocalyptic violence. The appearance of a sign, the startling solar eclipse of February 1831, instructed Turner that the time had come when "I should arise and prepare myself, and slay my enemies with their own weapons" (310). When he delayed, the sign reappeared yet more insistently in August 1831. At this point, according his narrative, Turner gathered his apostolic crew, staged a sacramental meal, and unleashed "the work of death" (312)—the massacre for which he was executed.

I recount *The Confessions of Nat Turner* at some length because, although this is a work everyone has heard of, it is a book few have actually read. I also retell the story with the thought that an audience of Mormon historians might recognize strange likenesses in Nat Turner's tale. I have never seen Joseph Smith mentioned in any study of Nat Turner, and I have never seen Turner alluded to in the voluminous work on Joseph Smith. It is easy to see why. Our way of conceptualizing the fields these figures appear in has the effect of locating them in mutually insulated categories: Turner in African American history or the history of slavery, Smith in Mormon studies or the history of American religion. But if we dissolve the partly fictitious structures that separate them and draw them into a common field, we find startling resemblances between these distant and unlikely doubles.

To begin, Nat Turner and Joseph Smith were near contemporaries, Turner having been born in 1800, Smith in 1805. The visionary experiences that lifted them out of historical anonymity were perhaps even more closely contemporaneous. Turner speaks of having had his first direct encounter with the Spirit after he had "arrived to man's estate" (307). If this means when he was twenty, a not implausible guess, then Turner would have had his inaugural vision in 1820, the same year as Joseph Smith's First Vision of the Father and the Son. Smith's next major manifestation, his first visit from the Angel Moroni, took place on September 21, 1823, an interesting numerical coincidence with Turner's August 21. (The number 21 is a date whose place in the horoscope may have given it occult significance for both Turner and Smith.[2]) After visits to the designated hill on this same date for four consecutive years, Smith received the golden plates on September 21, 1827, his probationary period having exactly bracketed Turner's 1825 vision. Smith had begun the translation of the Book of Mormon with Martin Harris as his scribe when Nat Turner had his May 1828 revelation. Smith was at work translating the Book of Mormon from 1825 through 1829, during the interval between Turner's call to fight the Serpent and the appearance of his final sign.

As they overlap in time, these bodies of experience take uncannily similar forms at a number of crucial points. In Joseph Smith's narrative of his First Vision (I am using the 1838 recital published in 1842) this experience involves an abrupt intrusion of transcendence, a moment in which divine or supernatural realities become directly present to a natural, human consciousness. (The Methodist minister who assured Joseph Smith that he could not have had a vision because the age of revelation was over was Smith's version of Turner's skeptical Thomas Gray.) This crossing of orders is a commonplace of vision; but in Smith's explanation, as in Turner's narrative, the vision springs from a similar type of prior event, an almost magical fixation on a passage from scripture. Smith recalls that, while in religious perplexity, he "was one day reading the Epistle of James, First Chapter and fifth verse which reads, 'If any of you lack wisdom, let him ask of God, that giveth to all men liberally and upbraideth not, and it shall be given him.' "³ (The message is virtually identical to that of Turner's fetishized text, "Seek and you shall find.") "Never did any passage of scripture come with more power to the heart of man than this did at this time to mine," Smith concludes—and here as with Turner, obsessional concentration on the divine word in its mediated, printed form promotes an unmediated contact in which the Spirit appears and speaks. Ushered into vision in this way, Smith, too, entered on a series of renewals of visionary privilege during which he too was given access to divinely encoded "caricters [sic] exactly like the ancient"⁴ and called by the Spirit to be baptized. In May 1829, while Smith and his new scribe, Oliver Cowdery, were brooding on the emptiness of sacraments in modern times, "on a sudden, as from the midst of eternity," in Cowdery's words, "the voice of the redeemer spake peace to us, while the vail was parted and the angel of God came down clothed with glory, and delivered the anxiously looked for message, and the keys of the gospel of repentance."⁵ In Smith's narrative of this event, the angel, whom he identifies as John the Baptist, "commanded us to go and be baptized, and gave us directions that I should baptize Oliver Cowdery, and afterward that he should baptize me."⁶ Smith and Cowdery thus performed in the Susquehanna the rite that Turner and Brantley had performed in the warmer waters of Virginia.

It goes without saying that neither *The Confessions of Nat Turner* nor Smith's account of his visions is taken at face value on all sides. Did the Spirit speak to either of them as, and when, they reported? The asserted events being inward, spiritual, and by their nature not available to those not comparably elected, there is no knowing them other than from the prophets' narratives. These narratives were both produced a considerable length of time after the incidents they describe, which raises the possibility that they may be retrospective reelaborations of what they record, or even late inventions of episodes that never "happened" as events at all. James B. Allen has established that Smith's First Vision was a relatively late addition to Smith's self-narrative and it only later became installed as the inaugural event of Mormon history. Recent work on Nat Turner has questioned the extent to which "his" narrative may be the work of his enforced collaborator, Thomas Gray. (We do not want to forget that, as an imprisoned slave, Turner was doubly denied the power to tell a free story.) New scholarship has also questioned the extent to which *The Confessions* may have been used as a cover story to hide the reality of a very different kind of rebellion—a mass uprising of the angry and rebellious, not the work of a solo prophetic leader.[7]

This is not the place to debate the question of these narratives' authenticity; and in any case, this question is in some crucial sense beside the point. For whatever their degree of truth or fictionality (which, precisely, we can never know), it is the nature of Smith's and Turner's stories that they succeeded in fusing themselves with real episodes in the world. From 1831 virtually until the present day, what some have proposed to call the Southampton Slave Revolt has been far more generally known as Nat Turner's Rebellion. The event has become known together with, and through, the published narrative, which has almost completely circumscribed its meaning. In similar fashion, since the moment of its publication, the Book of Mormon has been so thoroughly bound up with Smith's claim to divine powers that there has been virtually no reaction to this book that is not a reaction to that story. In this sense, at least, the prophetic narratives of Nat Turner and Joseph Smith have become historical facts, circulating in real history and determining responses to real historical events. Those who thought Turner sincere in his account of his visions, but deluded or demented, called him a fanatic, and those who suspected that he faked his visions and hieroglyphics to fool the naïve called him an impostor—"fanatic" and "impostor" being names prophets are called by those unpersuaded of their prophetic authority. These same names dogged the career of Joseph Smith, which tells us that the response to Smith, too, was a response to his prophetic self-assertion.

The differences between Smith and Turner are so clear as scarcely to require mention. One was a white, free man, one was a black slave; one led a bloody uprising, one founded a church. But as I hope to have suggested, once we begin to attend to them, the similarities in their careers become almost uncanny—and all the more haunting because they occur across such deep lines of social difference. How are we to understand these likenesses? Clearly, they are not products of direct interaction or mutual influence. Though the Book of Mormon was published in 1830 and Mormonism received considerable press from that time on, there is no evidence that Nat Turner heard of

Joseph Smith; the Smith narratives that I cited appeared only after Turner's death. Similarly, though he could scarcely have failed to hear of the August 1831 massacre, there is no evidence that Joseph Smith read or knew *The Confessions of Nat Turner*. (I do assume that Nat Turner's rebellion and the specter of race war that it unleashed lie behind Smith's December 1832 prophecy on the crisis of the South Carolina nullification crisis: "And it shall come to pass, after many days, slaves shall rise up against their masters." (Doctrine and Covenants 87:4). As I understand it, the ground of the likeness between these figures lies not in any relation between them but in their common involvement in an overlooked history: the history of prophetism in their time.

The history of prophetism is the story of how actual men and women have asserted themselves as bearers of prophetic privilege and of the consequences of these self-assertions. A prophet is a person singled out to enjoy special knowledge of ultimate reality and to give others mediated access to that otherwise unavailable truth. A prophet is also a man with a mission, one whose relation to a deep truth both requires and entitles him to enact that knowledge against the grain of worldly understandings. To say this is not to declare that some figures actually are this rare, super-entitled kind of self. Though religious belief will confer the status of true prophet on some figures and deny it to others (the decision that a Jesus, or a Muhammad, or a Joseph Smith was God's earthly messenger lies at the core of the choice of faith), the history of prophetism must include everyone who has envisioned and asserted himself on these terms. Apart from the designations of a faith, the prophet is never just something a person *is* but also something a person *takes himself to be* and *demands to be taken as*. This means that in the prehistory of any act of prophetic identification, a person must have access to some concept of "the prophet," an image that circulates in the cultural repertoire of identities as one idea of what a self can be. When people "become" prophets, they identify with some concept of the prophetic self, project themselves into this concept, and use it to tell themselves and others who they are.

To speak of the prophetic as a transaction (in part) between actual selves and the concepts of selfhood that people find around them is to recognize that prophetism has been available on different terms at different times and places. Clearly, this phenomenon has not been an American monopoly, as China's recent preoccupation with the Falun Gong sect and Afghanistan's recent experience with Mullah Omar can attest. But stretching down from Christopher Columbus to the 1630s antinomian prophetess Anne Hutchinson and the Quaker prophets executed in Boston around 1660 to prophetical self-asserters of more modern times—Elijah Muhammad, Martin Luther King Jr., David Koresh, the Unabomber Theodore Kaczynski, to name only a few—this country has hosted an unusually lively and variegated amalgam of prophetic traditions. The Nat Turner–Joseph Smith years form one particularly vigorous moment in this long-running history.

I began by trying to project these two prophets onto the same picture plane. But if we were to focus them on the larger ground of American prophetism, we would see that they form two points in a far larger display of prophetic activity, bearing likenesses and differences not just to one another but to a host of prophetic contemporaries. It has long been recognized that the early Mormons lived near the New York base of Jemima Wilkinson, the Publick Universal Friend, who had received her vision and commission on the eve of the Revolutionary War. Jemima Wilkinson shared territory with Handsome Lake, the prophet of the Seneca people, who delivered his own version of scripture: the Gaiwiio, or Code of Handsome Lake. In both New York and Ohio, the Mormons lived near communities formed around the prophetic career of Mother Ann Lee—the Shakers being a sufficiently proximate threat that Smith had a revelation in March 1831 denouncing their prophetic lore on sexual abstinence and the gender of the new Messiah (Doctrine and Covenants 49). After moving to Kirtland, Ohio, the Mormons could be coupled with Joseph Dylks, the self-appointed messiah whose contemporaneous Ohio cult was confused with Smith's Mormons in early newspaper reports.[8] Not far from Kirtland, having just returned from their Indiana base in New Harmony to the town of Economy in western Pennsylvania, was the Harmony Society, followers of the prophet George Rapp. (It was Rapp who proclaimed, "I am a prophet, and I am called to be one.") Rapp, whose prophetic authority established a community of goods, a belief in alchemy and magic stones, and a sense of end-time expectation— all with clear analogies to early Mormonism—predicted that the new age would be inaugurated on September 15, 1829, the high season of Smith's and Nat Turner's prophetic activities. Having sent letters to world rulers summoning the faithful to gather in America (Rapp, like Smith and Ann Lee, worked to gather in those to be included in the New World Zion), Rapp drew to Economy one Bernhard Müller, the illegitimate son of a German baron who "had become convinced, though reluctantly, that he himself was the reincarnated Messiah who would lead the world in the millennium." Rapp greeted Müller, who had rechristened himself with the prophetic name Count de Leon, as "the Anointed One," and presented him in this role to the community in Economy. This event occurred on October 18, 1831, while Smith was busy collecting his revelations and Turner was still twelve days from his capture.[9]

In August 1831, Father William Miller, the eventual leader of the largest millenarian movement in American history (the Millerites), stepped forth from shy silence in northern New York to begin his prophetic career. In June 1830 at virtually the same spot on the New York–Vermont border, the ne'er-do-well Robert Matthews came to the knowledge that "God was about to dissolve the institutions of man" and that he was God's new emissary, "Matthias"—a knowledge that moved him, too, to baptize his wife "in the Holy Spirit." (Either the Spirit is particularly insistent on this point or prophetism has cultural conventions.) Visiting New York in his new prophetic capacity, Matthias experienced a reciprocal confirmation of prophetic identity with the former investment banker Elijah Pearson, who had discovered himself to be the reincarnation of the prophet Elijah. Matthias and the now subjugated Elijah set up their prophetic community Holy Zion at Ossining, New York; but after a criminal inquiry, Matthias fled to Ohio, among other places, and called on the Mormons at Kirtland in 1835. Matthews, aka Matthias, is the "Joshua, the Jewish Minister" to whom Joseph Smith gave one of the earliest accounts of his first visions, a fact that permits us to recognize a dimension of prophetic sharing—or, perhaps, of prophetic competition—in that far fuller expansion on Smith's visionary history.[10]

The founder of a more enduring prophetic community than Holy Zion, the Oneida Community in upstate New York, John Humphrey Noyes, experienced the ecstatic conviction of his perfection in New Haven in 1832. Like Smith and like Turner (as I say: prophecy has its conventions), Noyes came to his vision by a quasi-magical biblical encounter. "As I sat brooding over my difficulties and prospects, I listlessly opened my Bible and my eye fell upon these words: 'The Holy Ghost shall come upon thee, and the power of the Highest shall overshadow thee; therefore also that holy thing which shall be born of thee shall be called the Son of God.' The words seemed to glow upon the page, and my spirit heard a voice from heaven through them promising me the baptism of the Holy Spirit and the second birth."[11] William Lloyd Garrison never formed a community in the sense of Oneida or Nauvoo, Illinois (where Mormons settled after being driven from Ohio and Missouri), but he created a community of opinion behind a radical abolitionism that, when it was first broached, seemed almost as unthinkable as Noyes's communalization of private property and sexual relations. Garrison did not claim immediate experience of the supernatural, but he clearly modeled his moral politics and his indignant, fulminative rhetoric on the Old Testament prophets. (Thomas Wentworth Higginson said that the typical Garrison speech or editorial sounded "like a newly discovered chapter of Ezekiel."[12]) Garrison's The Liberator made its debut in January 1831. Not far from Garrison's Boston base, Ralph Waldo Emerson began to put forth his eccentric and influential version of prophetism a short time later.

This rush of prophetic activity suggests that the years around 1830 were a time when the category of the prophetic was unusually accessible in America and when special pressures drove the recourse to this identity. Each of these new self-inventions bears the marks of its specific social origins. As is now widely recognized, in his early career, Joseph Smith fused a prophetism derived from biblical models with divination or folk magic elements drawn from his local culture. In *The Confessions*, Nat Turner brings almost unbearable intensity to a millenarianism widespread across social groups at this time, but African-derived folk elements help inflect his otherwise generic apocalypticism. Each of these figures can also help us identify local urgencies that sought release or resolution through prophetic assertion. Current historiography is fond of tracing the prophetism of the 1830s to anxieties bred by this time's rapid, dislocating social transformations.[13] This point is not unhelpful, but the exhibits just mentioned help identify a wider spectrum of motive forces. Turner fuses religious fantasies with the bloody rage bred in one 1830s social situation: the harsh subordination of blacks in slavery. John Humphrey Noyes was spared the degradations of status that Turner, Smith, Robert Matthews, and many of their fellows suffered. As I read it, Noyes was drawn to prophetism by the superior pleasure it afforded: he founded a society based on the improvement of pleasure that gave extraordinary scope to his fantasies of personal prerogative.

The embrace of prophetic identity typically unleashes a flooding of the self with a sense of authority, a sense that makes it feel compelled and entitled to announce a new right way against the authority of worldly customs. The meaning of antebellum prophetism is thus found partly in the careers it sponsored, but partly, too, in the ideas it put into social circulation. The self-assertions of prophetic individuals gave what authority they had to many of the counter-ethics and divergent practices of the United States of the 1830s and 1840s: alternatives to competitive economic individualism and private property (America's indigenous socialisms are mostly prophetic socialisms), alternative sexual regimes, alternative dietary regimes, and so on. But American antislavery is no less a product of antebellum prophetic identification. Garrison's powerfully seized prophetic stance gave force to the view that a higher law, God's law, required people to break their merely social laws in order to enact true righteousness. Sojourner Truth, another major antislavery orator, emerged from and drew upon a number of prophetic cultures: Truth was a follower of the prophet Matthias, then of William Miller, before she found the antislavery cause. She had a vision on June 4, 1827.[14] Both Garrison and Truth began by promoting a nonviolent form of resistance; but when slavery became the object of direct, violent physical assault, prophetism helped make violence a thinkable course. Turner's supernatural visions required and justified a violence that his ordinary ethics would have condemned. When John Brown took up his work as a holy instrument in the antislavery cause, prophetic fantasies licensed his paramilitary tactics.

(We know that Brown had Nat Turner on his mind when he first conceived the Harper's Ferry raid.[15])

But if the embrace of this identity helped authorize social forces of enduring importance, as another of its by-products, 1830s prophetism generated new versions of the prophetic itself. Emerson would be an example of a Nat Turner and Joseph Smith contemporary who engaged this same conception but realized it on different terms. Emerson has long been recognized as the spiritual father of American individualism, but it is less often observed that Emerson defines the idea of individualism in explicitly prophetic terms. In his 1838 address to Harvard Divinity School seniors, Emerson told the graduates that they were mispreparing themselves for spiritual careers. The heart of his message, built up to through a series of graceful and blandly uncontroversial paragraphs, is this:

> Jesus Christ belonged to the true race of prophets. . . . He saw that God incarnates himself in man, and evermore goes forth anew to take possession of his world. He said, in this jubilee of sublime emotion, "I am divine. Through me, God acts; through me, speaks. Would you see God, see me; or see thee, when thou also thinkest as I now think." But what a distortion did his doctrine and memory suffer in the same, in the next, and the following ages! . . . The understanding caught this high chant from the poet's lips, and said, in the next age, "This was Jehovah come down out of heaven. I will kill you, if you say he was a man." The idioms of his language and the figures of his rhetoric, have usurped the place of his truth; and churches are not built on his principles, but on his tropes.[16]

Jesus' claim to be the Christ or Messiah was never meant to be exclusionary, Emerson asserts. The idea that Jesus alone was the Son of God is a piece of retrospective mythmaking, an assertion made after the fact as part of the institutionalization of a Christian church. Before he was made a cult figure and his followers made subordinate to his alleged unique divinity, the message of the living Jesus was just the opposite: that he found God to be in himself, and he found himself to be God—and so can others, when they are in a state of parallel spiritual exaltation. "Would you see God, see me; or see thee, when thou thinkest as I now think." Once he is understood to have announced not his exclusive but our collective potential divinity, Emerson said, then Jesus invites his followers to a profoundly altered career. He invites them not to the role of minister, holder of an official position in an institutional church, but rather to the role of preacher-prophet: a proud enjoyer of access to the divine who awakens others to their own comparable powers. "Yourself a newborn bard of the

Holy Ghost,—cast behind you all conformity, and acquaint men at first hand with Deity" (89).

Emerson's Divinity School address proclaims that the function of the great prophets of the past is to call us to our own prophetic careers: "The divine bards are the friends of *my* virtue, of *my* intellect, of *my* strength. They admonish me, that the gleams which flash across my mind, are not mine, but God's; that they had the like, and were not disobedient to the heavenly vision" (81–82; emphasis added). Emerson's great 1841 essay "Self-Reliance" expands on this message with the difference that, while the Divinity School address still spoke of the opening of the self to a domain of spirit, that domain was now fully identified with the self. "Nothing is at last sacred but the integrity of your own mind" (261) is the central assertion of "Self-Reliance." Integrity here does not mean honesty or uprightness but something more like individuality, the traits that establish a person as one self—an integer—rather than another self. Emerson finds such integrity in a force of personal perception unshaped by the internalized opinions of others, a force that expresses itself spontaneously, inescapably, through the enactment of one's particular being. To say that "nothing is at last *sacred* but the integrity of your own mind" is to do more than praise this integrity as a good thing. It is to proclaim that such selfhood is the seat of the holiness that other men have located in the divine. In Exodus, God called to Moses from the burning bush, but in Emerson He reveals himself in any strong display of self: "Bid the invaders take the shoes from off their feet, for God is here within" (272).

Emerson's work in his Divinity School address and in "Self-Reliance" is to revive a prophetic conception of selfhood and rethink it in such a way that prophetic identity becomes virtually synonymous with selfhood itself. Personal identity is elevated in this process, made identical with the elect selfhood previously reserved for the prophets. But in a less noticed but more interesting development, prophecy itself is also radically diffused through this reconceptualization, removed from the category of rarity and made widely available and familiar. No longer the special province of a spiritual elite, the selfhood that is in touch with the sacred is reimagined by Emerson as something completely democratic, something open to each of us to the extent that we have an identity or *are someone*. As he dissolves the barrier to admission to the ranks of prophethood, Emerson also blurs the boundaries of the prophetic in a second way, broadening it to the point where it ceases to be limited to religious experience. Since, for Emerson, the prophetic displays itself wherever a distinctive self puts itself forth, the prophetic manifests itself in every act of individuality in every creative domain. In a verbal formula that enforces this message in "Self-Reliance," Emerson lists Moses as one more undifferentiated item in the list of "Moses, Plato and Milton" (259) and gives Jesus only third billing in the list that includes Pythagoras, Socrates, Jesus, Luther, Copernicus, Galileo, and Newton (265).

Emerson sought no converts but he did exert a powerful influence, and the figures he affected most deeply bear a clear prophetic cast. I am thinking of Thoreau, our great literary witness-bearer, reviver of the prophetic message "I know, as you obviously do not know, the truth that you should live by"; or Whitman, whose "Song of Myself" is both a poem and a newer testament, an annunciation of where the divine is to be found. (Guess where? In Myself.) But the point of Emerson is that his message was not heard only by those who tried to live it. Having made the prophetic a modality of ordinary experience, Emerson created a message that could be found inspiring without requiring to be "believed" in the hard sense. (No one ever called Emerson either a fanatic or an impostor.) This version of prophecy could be absorbed into the literature of national uplift and thence into American civic religion (or nonreligion), that distinctive ethic in which being oneself takes on the character of a personal mission and high moral obligation.

Joseph Smith, too, took the materials of prophetic self-conception and realized them in a new way. Smith and Emerson were another pair of contemporaries (Emerson was born in 1803); and from a distance, their careers have important aspects in common. Both begin by being called out of institutional religion. In his 1820 vision Joseph Smith goes to the woods to try to learn which of the churches of early nineteenth-century Protestantism is the true one, only to have it revealed that God is in no established church. "I asked the personages who stood above me in the light, which of all the sects was right . . . and which I should join. I was answered that I must join none of them, for they were all wrong, and . . . all their Creeds were an abomination in his sight."[17] Emerson was ordained a Unitarian minister in 1829 but resigned his ministry in 1832, and the 1838 Divinity School address is his classic statement of the emptiness of spirit he found in the church. Institutional religion is an empty form, Emerson maintains, because it worships or commemorates a divine incarnation it claims happened long ago. What Emerson calls the "assumption that the age of inspiration is passed" (88) is what Joseph Smith encounters in the Methodist minister who rebuffs his claim to vision: "He treated my communication not only lightly but with great contempt," Smith writes, "saying it was all of the Devil, that there was no such thing as visions or revelations in these days, that all such things had ceased with the apostles and that there would never be any more of them."[18]

Over against this historiography, and in massive resistance to the weight of official truth that attends it, Smith and Emerson propel themselves to the identities we know by claiming that revelation is not dead, that direct access to divinity is still available in the present, and that the experience of spirit in other times can be lived again, here, now, by me. Jesus "felt respect for Moses and the prophets; but no unfit tenderness at postponing their initial revelations to the hour and the man that now is," Emerson writes (80). In his right worship, Jesus will provoke us to the recognition that "God is, not was; that He speaketh, not spake" (88); and that "the gleams which flash across *my* mind" (82; emphasis added) are contemporary revelation. You say that there is no longer such an experience as "visions or revelations," Smith tells his skeptic, but guess what? I just had one. Though apparently the lowest of the low, "an obscure boy of a little over fourteen years of age and one too who was doomed to the necessity of obtaining a scanty maintenance by his daily labor, . . . it was nevertheless a fact, that I had had a vision."[19]

The great moves that Smith and Emerson make in common are what might be called the presencing and the appropriation of prophecy, the conversion of revelation from past to present tense and from the experience of others to something I can have. Smith's difference is that he couples these moves with a powerful gesture of literalization.[20] The early church took Jesus' sayings literally, Emerson writes, but to grasp their truth is to recover them as figures of speech. Emerson's strategy is to assert that Jesus, Moses, and the prophets are important, not as real historical individuals, but as images of the power that could be mine: "The divine bards are the friends of my virtue, of my intellect, of my strength. They admonish me that the gleams which flash across my mind are not mine, but God's; they had the like, and were not disobedient to the heavenly vision" (81–82). Joseph Smith, at the same conceptual pass, affirms that those who were elected to know God at firsthand are the very individuals scripture mentions (Smith saw Moses, Elijah, and John the Baptist but *not* Socrates, Copernicus, or Galileo) and that they had just that rare, unshared power that tradition assigns them. Smith refuses to be imaginative about the canonical prophets, we could say—or we could say that his imaginative act is to take them as literally, actually real. When he then appropriates what they were for himself and his present time, the result is that he thinks himself—the living, actual Joseph Smith—into a figure in the same elect line. The Book of Mormon announces this modern Joseph as a "choice seer" who shall be "great like unto Moses"; and though many Americans have presented themselves as Moses figures,[21] Smith asserted (as the literal truth) that he was God's elect intermediary. The result was to concentrate in his special person the privilege Emerson had opened to all. "Verily, verily I say unto thee, No one shall be appointed to receive commandments and revelations in this church excepting my servant Joseph Smith, Jr., for he receiveth them even as Moses" (Doctrine and Covenants 28:2), a revelation of September 1830 announced. When the Mormons arrived at Kirtland and a Mrs. Hubble was spurred by Smith's visions to have visions of her own, he let her know—or God let her know through him—that revelations were to come only "through him whom I have appointed unto you" and that "none else shall be appointed unto this gift except it be through him" (Doctrine and Covenants 43:1–2).[22]

Nat Turner's prophetic work was holy massacre. Joseph Smith's first prophetic work was holy translation. Here again Smith made his special difference through literalizing his claims. Treating divinely inspired speech as a figure for inspired speech of any sort, Emerson dissolves the boundary between scripture and imaginative literature such that Jesus' words can be called a "high chant from the poet's lips" (80), and the terms *Muse* and *Holy Ghost* become interchangeable "quaint names" for "unbounded substance" (485). At this same conceptual point, Joseph Smith asserts that some writing is indeed absolutely different from other writing and that the difference is that some is literally revealed by God. This strong traditionalism is the prelude to Smith's innovative act. For when he then claims such writing for his own, present self, the consequence is to make him the privileged bearer of this long-lost revelatory power. Smith's claim was that God literally spoke through him in the translation of the Book of Mormon, his Inspired Version of the scriptures, and in the continuing revelations printed in the Doctrines and Covenants, and Smith compelled others to respond to these works on those terms. Terryl Givens has reminded us of the peculiar extent to which Smith fused this claim with his writing, making it virtually impossible to read the Book of Mormon except in relation to Smith's claims to literal inspiration.[23] Readers have either accepted it as authentic scripture or rejected it as scriptural sham, but almost no one (Fawn Brodie is one exception) has read it as a piece of ordinary creative writing.

In Emerson, restored access to the spirit in "the hour and the man that now is" causes the dissolution of everything institutional, returning religion from the ritual and formal to a living, spiritual pulse. Smith is another great restorationist; but in his version of prophecy, recovering unmediated access to the Spirit leads to the re-establishment of religious institutions, not to their dissolution. The relation of these figures to the traditional sacraments is especially instructive here. Emerson was ordained in March 1829 but resigned his ministry three years later over his refusal to administer the Last Supper. In his final sermon, Emerson mounts many ingenious scholarly arguments against the notion that Christ actually meant later people to repeat this ritual, but he has another argument that counts as much as these: this ritual does not suit me. Having removed religious authority from what is now made a mere form, Emerson resigns the office of minister—now conceived as a purely bureaucratic role—the better to perform this role's "highest functions" (1140). Having founded his career on the refusal of received rites, the last thing Emerson has in mind is the creation of new ones. Toward the end of his Divinity School address he writes, "All attempts to project and establish a Cultus with new rites and forms, seem to me vain. . . . All attempts to contrive a system are as cold as the new worship introduced by the French to the goddess of Reason,—today, pasteboard and filigree, and ending tomorrow in madness and murder" (91).

Smith's prophetic career also begins with renegotiation of a sacrament, with baptism playing the role that the Last Supper played for Emerson. As usual, where Emerson worked to find a freeing figurative meaning for "Do this in remembrance of me," Smith's move is to literalize this practice back to a strong historical origin. In the May 1829 episode on the shores of the Susquehanna, Smith and Oliver Cowdery have been anxiously musing on the prophecy they had translated that spiritual darkness would cover the earth "and gross darkness the mind of the people." This provokes the thought that contemporary sacraments are without consecrating or redeeming power, since they lack the ground they possessed in apostolic times. In Cowdery's words, "On reflecting further, it was as easily to be seen, that amid the great strife and noise concerning religeon [sic], none had authority from God to administer the ordinances of the gospel[.] For, the question might be asked, have men authority to administer in the name of Christ, who deny revelation? when his testamony [sic] is no less then the spirit of prophecy?"[24] In this highly Emersonian passage, the modern church, having declared that immediate contact with the Spirit is a reality confined to a vanished age, in effect consigns its sacraments to the category of empty customs, since it denies the ongoing relation to divinity that would give men "authority from God to administer the ordinances of the Gospel."[25]

But having contrasted modern sacraments with their full, authoritative originals, Smith and Cowdery then see that exact original brought back to life—here, now, in the present, in them. In Smith's narrative:

> On a certain day [we] went into the woods to pray and inquire of the
> Lord respecting baptism for the remission of sins. . . . While we were
> thus employed praying and calling upon the Lord, a Messenger from
> heaven, descended in a cloud of light, and having laid his hands upon
> us, he ordained us, saying unto us, "Upon you my fellow servants in
> the name of the Messiah I confer the priesthood of Aaron, which
> holds the keys of the ministering of angels and the gospel of

repentance, and of baptism by immersion for the remission of sins, and that this shall never be taken again from the earth."[26]

This messenger identifies himself as "John, the same that is called John the Baptist in the New Testament." Smith goes on to say that the messenger commanded them "to go and be baptized, and gave us directions that I should baptize Oliver Cowdery, and afterward, that he should baptize me."[27]

Smith here embraces the sort of rite that Emerson refused to perform, but that is the least of what is going on. To catch the force of this episode is to realize that Smith is not just doing a baptism; he is also claiming to reinstitute the sacrament of baptism, restoring the value it had in the days of John the Baptist by recovering the power that gave it force. In Smith's wonderfully presumptuous assertion, on a spring day in 1829, in the middle of nowhere in northern Pennsylvania, God restored to actual, living men the authority to administer in his name and restored it as an ongoing historical presence. He restored it by reinstituting, through Joseph Smith's renewed prophetic authority, the sacrament of baptism and the divinely commissioned priesthood.[28]

As Smith's First Vision gave him his first prophetic role as seer and hearer of the Spirit, and as his 1823 vision gave him an augmented role as deliverer of a new scripture, the May 1829 vision or self-envisioning gives Smith his expanded prophetic role of church founder and institution builder. The rite of baptism reinstituted here would be followed by other rites he would give for those who accepted his prophetic claims—the temple endowments, the baptism of the dead, and so on. The recovery of the Aaronic priesthood would be followed by the panoply of administrative roles and structures he invented: the Melchizedek priesthood, the Quorum of the Twelve Apostles, the Council of Seventy, and more. Emerson's version of prophecy dissolved religious institutions to reopen access to the Spirit; Smith's reinstituted them as the vehicles through which the Spirit performs its saving work.

I have spoken of Smith's visualizations of his prophetic self, but the point is that they became more than that. Smith put forth his prophetic authority as a real-world fact and demanded that real others accept it on those terms. Emerson, so to speak, mentalized the prophetic, taking it out of the realm of persons, places, and things and making it available as a fiction of self-empowerment, a freely circulating, nondenominational thought that individuals could entertain with intermittently inspiring results with no continuing commitment to its truth. Smith insisted that he in his actual person was the bearer of the new dispensation, that his writings were divine revelations, that salvation was available through the exact forms, rites, and offices that he designated—and thousands of people accepted those claims as the truth. These were the converts to Joseph Smith's new church, whose numbers had reached 18,000 by the year of Emerson's Divinity School address. (When Emerson there wrote, "Where shall I hear words such as in elder ages drew men to leave all and follow,—father and mother, house and land, wife and child?" [84], he was not mindful of contemporary Mormon missionary activity.)

This essay began by surveying forms of prophetism in the American 1830s and the various consequences they gave rise to: slave revolts, the ethical and rhetorical style of the radical antislavery movement, and other countercultural ethics as well. To this list, two more consequences can now be added. After the 1830s, by virtue of the way one person engaged the matrix of prophetic thought, this country had in circulation a concept of selfhood that helped structure and legitimate the ethic of American individualism; and after 1830, by virtue of another such act, it had a new church that gathered in and helped produce a distinctive social community—the Mormons. These very different realities were products of a parallel act: the way two contemporaries realized the possibilities of a shared matrix of thought.

3

Joseph Smith, American Culture, and the Origins of Mormonism

Klaus J. Hansen

In *The Great Transformation: The Beginning of Our Religious Traditions* (a sequel to her celebrated *A History of God*), Karen Armstrong describes and analyzes the evolution of major world religions in an era known as the Axial Age, a term first used by German philosopher Karl Jaspers in 1948. —The Axial Age roughly encompasses the centuries from 900 B.C.E. to 200 B.C.E., which saw the birth of Buddhism, Confucianism, Taoism, and Judaism.[1] Both Jaspers and Armstrong argue that Axial Age religions were born in a cauldron of violence, disruption, and intolerance that characterized these societies—though I should emphasize that Armstrong, especially, does not see the rise of these religions in a mechanical, reductionist way, as a response to social problems, as is so common in much modern sociohistorical literature. (The influence of Max Weber, especially, comes to mind—with the concession that his followers have been more guilty here than the master himself.[2]) In the case of Joseph Smith, I tend to agree with Harold Bloom's argument that "the Prophet Joseph has proved . . . that economic and social forces do not determine human destiny. Religious history, like literary or any cultural history, is made by genius, by the mystery of rare human personalities," and like Bloom, "I am not persuaded by sociological and anthropological studies of Mormon history."[3]

My qualification is that as a historian I find it difficult to believe that ideas are born ex nihilo. For example, Albert Einstein did not arrive at the Special Theory of Relativity in 1905 (the *annus mirabilis* in which he published five monumental contributions to modern physics) in a vacuum.⁴ He had to address several major questions—for example, James Clerk Maxwell's counterintuitive observation that the speed of light must be a constant (confirmed by the Special Theory), the all but axiomatic belief that the transmission of electromagnetic forces required the medium of an "aether" (disconfirmed), and numerous related issues that had been floating around for some time and that were occupying many of the brightest minds in physics. Yet the world had to wait for the young employee of the Swiss patent office to resolve some of the most challenging scientific questions of the time in a solution of sheer brilliance that has defied attempts at explanation by psychologists or sociologists.

Although an analogy between physics and religion may at first appear far-fetched, a comparison of the so-called genius of Einstein with that of Joseph Smith may be valid, if genius is viewed as a generic quality rather than a quality associated with a specific discipline and talent. One encounters not infrequent references attributing the quality of religious genius to Joseph Smith, whereas Einstein is seen as a genius in physics. Einstein was also a person with deep religious insights, however, as well as a remarkably talented violinist. Perhaps he should be called a universal genius, a term historically applied to Leonardo da Vinci. My point is that there is a tendency to use the term *genius* too loosely. Rather than calling Smith a religious genius, I would prefer to call him simply a genius who applied his gift to the creation of a new religion. Both Smith and Einstein (as well as others in history who are referred to as geniuses) processed enormous amounts of information, insights, and inspiration into new and coherent forms, systems, works of art, and so on. Jan Shipps made an analogy between Joseph Smith and Mozart.⁵ I went so far as to compare him with Darwin and Marx: "Like them, Smith cast a vast body of knowledge and belief into a new mold."⁶ Harold Bloom "can think of not another American, except for Emerson and Whitman, who so moves and alters my own imagination" (as Joseph Smith does).⁷ Perhaps most apropos in the case of Joseph Smith is the poetic imagination of Thomas Carlyle: "The Great Man was always lightning out of Heaven; the rest of men waited for him like fuel, and then they too would flame."⁸

Shortly after the publication of the Book of Mormon, Alexander Campbell attacked the work by claiming that it was a hodgepodge addressing all the major theological questions of the times: "infant baptism, ordination, the trinity, regeneration, repentance, justification, the fall of man, the atonement, transubstantiation, fasting, penance, church government, religious experience, the call to the ministry, the general resurrection, eternal punishment, who may baptize, and even the question of freemasonry, republican government, and the rights of man."[9] Joseph Smith biographer Fawn Brodie used such charges in support of her own environmental interpretation.[10] Yet in the case of both Einstein and Smith, the necessary antecedents do not add up to a sufficient explanation of their genius. Nevertheless, even though their innermost thoughts and inspirations may not be determined solely by their environment, the historical context helps us understand more about the unique contribution of great individuals. Literary scholar Terryl Givens put it well by saying that "there is a dimension to 'the Great Man' and his influence that is to be understood historically. And there is a dimension that transcends history in its evocation of that which is universal. Both elements are present in Joseph Smith's case."[11] I, however, as a historian, rather than attempting to explain what is considered genius, must be content with the more humble task of chronicling "the Joseph of history."[12]

Indeed, in the case of Joseph Smith, it is his human weaknesses rather than his genius that has been a major source of controversy. In fact, so the argument goes, it was his brilliance that motivated him to commit religious fraud because lack of education and social standing prevented him from advancing in the normal channels open to members of the rising middle class. Crude and simplistic accusations common in nineteenth-century anti-Mormon literature were replaced by more sophisticated secular explanations, such as Fawn Brodie's in modern scholarship—though even Brodie was caught in the "truth or fraud" paradigm that was part of her Mormon upbringing. This mold was not broken until Jan Shipps introduced her religious studies approach into the Mormon scholarly community, bypassing the truth question in favour of a nonjudgmental investigation into just what made Joseph Smith tick.[13]

Returning now to Karen Armstrong, I pick up her argument that the two great world religions following the Axial Age chronologically—Christianity and Islam—likewise arose in periods of intense conflict and instability. If, as has been argued, Mormonism is an emerging world religion, it should not be surprising that its rise also occurred at a period of major change—especially in the United States, but also in the larger transatlantic region of which it was an integral part. The Smith family—Joseph Sr., his wife, Lucy, and their nine children (including young Joseph Jr.)—was part of a migration that helped transform western New York from sporadic clearings in the wilderness into a booming society urbanizing along the Erie Canal. That canal was completed in 1825, five years after Joseph's "First Vision" and five years before the official founding of Joseph's "Church of Christ" in 1830. During those same years, Rochester, New York, was transformed from a mere village into America's newest city, with a population of 10,000 that was providing prosperity, or at least optimistic visions of a better future, for many of the new arrivals in the region; it also led to disappointment and despair for some, including the Smith family.

The specific, unique nature of Joseph Smith's visions and the founding of a new religion may not have been caused by social and economic factors, but the questions he raised grew out of Joseph's environment. At the risk of simplifying a complex issue—having to paint in bold strokes in a short essay such as this one—I take my cue from the magisterial study of Marvin S. Hill, *Quest for Refuge: The Mormon Flight from American Pluralism*, which makes a persuasive case that Joseph Smith's response to the rapid social, political, and economic changes of the period was driven by a search for alternatives to a world driven by individualism, competition, and pluralism.[14] Methodologically, I am also guided by the example of Jay Fliegelman, whose explorations into American thought and culture recognize that "the relationship between idea and event is intractably complex," and that seemingly unrelated "events and texts reflect the same overarching preoccupations of their culture."[15]

The changes in the social, economic, political, and religious views and institutions of the age of Jackson had their origins in the colonial period, where perhaps their most dramatic impact was on the American Revolution. Richard Bushman's pioneering case study—*From Puritan to Yankee*—of the transformation of character and the social order in Connecticut, from 1690 through 1765, became a model for studies that link changes in society and culture across broad boundaries.[16] My own attempt to chart the complex interactions between religion and culture in *Mormonism and the American Experience* is greatly indebted to the insights of Bushman and those he inspired. In his conclusion to *Puritan and Yankee*, he states that the transformation of Connecticut life was for the most part positive: "In the century after the Revolution Yankee society produced a flowering of individualism, a magnificent display of economic and artistic virtuosity." Yet he acknowledges a negative side as well: "Yankees also learned the sorrows of rootlessness—fear, guilt, and loneliness. The light and the dark both were fruits of the liberty wrested in the eighteenth century from the Puritan social order."[17] I am reminded of a famous quotation from Alexis de Tocqueville:

> The woof of time is every instant broken, and the track of generations effaced. Those who went before are soon forgotten; of those who will come after, no one has any idea. . . . Thus not only does democracy make every man forget his ancestors, but it hides his descendants and separates his contemporaries from him; it throws him back forever upon himself alone and threatens in the end to confine him to the solitude of his own heart.[18]

As I see it, someone like Joseph Smith and those who became his followers had a vision of democracy and of the promise of American life that was different from the vision of the movers and shakers of what was to become mainstream America.

The latter, seeing opportunities in political and social change, welcomed the transformation, even dissolution, of traditional institutions. While the Revolution had already destroyed the traditional political order, by the early nineteenth century the privatization of the economy, the disestablishment of the churches, and major changes in family relations were well along their way. The Federalists had clung to patrician notions of government and society for the better part of a generation, but the election of Andrew Jackson in 1828 signalled both a substantive and symbolic passing of the torch to a new generation, greatly extending male franchise, loosening economic strings, and increasing social mobility. Although it is true that government continued to play an important role in the economy, the Jacksonian ideology proclaimed the arrival of the modern, negative state. Traditional, paternalistic conceptions of government regulation were rapidly making way for the principle of laissez-faire, exchanging the visible hand of government for the invisible hand of Adam Smith. The natural world of equality of opportunity, in the minds of most Jacksonians, was self-regulating, in distinction from the old and rapidly declining world of special privilege, deference, and monopolies. The Federalists had enjoyed a status based on inheritance and ascription; the Jacksonians had persuaded themselves that they had risen through their own efforts. By the 1830s institutional restraints in America had loosened dramatically.[19]

In the opinion of some scholars, this transformation led to major changes in public and private attitudes toward individualistic behaviour and competition. Richard Bushman has already identified such attitudes in the eighteenth century, describing them as a shift in the locus of authority in government, in religion, and in the family. While "stern fathers" had presided over individuals and families in colonial or Puritan society, both physically and symbolically, exercising externally sanctioned authority, Yankees and their nineteenth-century descendants were self-directed, having internalized the ethical and social demands imposed upon them. In the opinion of some historians, this shift in authority, both institutional and psychological, was an essential element in the creation of the new capitalist, urban, competitive order.[20]

Perhaps no institution played a more formative role in this transformation than religion. Richard Bushman sees its central role revealed in the First Great Awakening of the eighteenth century (1725–65). Strengthening as it did the relationship between the individual and God, it had the unintended consequence of loosening ties to traditional authorities of the state, the church, and the patriarchal family. Jay Fliegelman has followed the currents of these developments into the second half of the eighteenth century, seeing the American Revolution "as the most important expression" of a broader cultural revolution that separated a younger generation from its ancestors. Having broken with their literal fathers, the rebels were psychologically prepared to break with their king.[21]

Historian William McLoughlin has followed the logic of these events into the nineteenth century, arguing that the Revolution was but the first stage in a long and arduous process through which Americans established their national identity. The First Great Awakening had resulted in the external separation of the colonies from their mother country. A second awakening was required to "provide the internal ideology which every new nation needs but which America's founding fathers purposely omitted from the Constitution." Therefore, according to McLoughlin, the Second Great Awakening, which convulsed the American nation in several waves between the 1790s and 1860, was "the most central, the most pivotal event in the formation of the American national character or culture."[22]

Believing in the power of analogy to help explain such a drastic transformation, McLoughlin introduces the work of anthropologist Kenelm Burridge, whose influential study *New Heaven, New Earth* reports on a number of prophetic, millennial movements of the third world. In spite of profound specific differences among these various cults he has discovered remarkably similar patterns of social and cultural transformation. As the prophetic movement gains momentum, the old rules of society are jettisoned, followed by a period of "no rules"—a time of intense, even frenzied experimentations with new social forms and rituals. By its very nature, the intensity of this stage soon leads to exhaustion. It does not take long before the participants consolidate and stabilize the rules of the "new heaven and the new earth." At this point, the society has adopted "new rules," which in time may well become regarded as the old rules of yet another prophetic movement.[23]

The waning Federalist era may be identified as a period of old rules; the age of revivalism—of "freedom's ferment," as Alice Felt Tyler called it—can be seen as a period of no rules; and the era of the consolidation of corporate capitalism as an age of new rules (John Higham wrote of a transformation "from boundlessness to consolidation").[24] Another scholar attracted by the explanatory power of analogy is Lawrence Foster, who likewise sees revivalism as the central cultural expression of an age of transition, one in which individuals were suspended between two worlds, "between an old order that is dying and a new order that is yet to be born." Foster shares the opinion of several scholars who see this period in American history as a time when, to some creative individuals, "all things are possible."[25]

Joseph Smith was one of these. I agree with Harold Bloom that, like most geniuses, Joseph lacked the herd instinct that made other so-called leaders follow the temper of his times. I also believe that sociologists and anthropologists, and even historians, may be helpful in identifying necessary causes of genius, even if the sufficient causes explaining genius elude them. I am particularly impressed by Gordon Wood's brilliant inaugural Tanner Lecture at the Mormon History Association's sesquicentennial commemoration of the founding of the Mormon Church, at Canandaigua, New York, in April 1980—a veritable tour de force that recapped the culture of the New Republic. Wood concluded with the bold assertion that [Mormonism] "was born at a peculiar moment in the history of the United States, and it bears the marks of that birth. Only the culture of early-nineteenth-century evangelical America could have produced it. And through it we can begin to understand the complicated nature of that culture."[26] Wood's reading of Mormonism's relationship with the evangelical world was based on a sophisticated and deep reading of the relevant literature. To quote his summation:

> The Church of Jesus Christ of Latter-day Saints, for all its uniqueness, was very much a product of its time, but not in any simple or obvious way. Mormonism was undeniably the most original and persecuted religion of this period or of any period in American history. It defied as no other religion did both the orthodox culture and evangelical counterculture. Yet at the same time it drew heavily on both these cultures. It combined within itself different tendencies of thought. From the outset it was a religion in tension, poised like a steel spring by the contradictory forces pulling within it.[27]

This internal tension also led to external conflict.

Perhaps the greatest source of tension, both internal and external, was that generated by Joseph's most audacious and radical, even revolutionary, innovation—plural marriage, or celestial marriage as its author called it. I am particularly indebted to Lawrence Foster for my understanding of this complicated story. Foster attempts to explain Joseph's radical reordering of family relationships in the larger context of what he calls "the crisis of the family" in antebellum America. On the margins of response to this crisis were the Shakers, advocating celibacy; John Humphrey Noyes's Oneida Perfectionists, practicing religiously-sanctioned and -controlled multiple liaisons; and the Mormons, whose principle of plural marriage was seen as the most controversial of all social experiments in the nineteenth century. To all but devout Mormons, on one end of the cultural spectrum, and antipolygamy crusaders on the other end, plural marriage presented a perplexing and intriguing historical problem. The Saints, of course, simply accepted it as a commandment of God, justified for the reasons Joseph provided by revelation. The anti-Mormons had an equally simple explanation: a lecherous Joseph Smith and some of his lecherous associates had to devise a system that would provide religious sanction for their sexual appetites. Perhaps the most notorious version out of this so-called lecher school is Fawn Brodie's charge, which argues that, although Joseph had deep affection and love for his wife Emma, "monogamy seemed to him an intolerably circumscribed way of life." At the same time, "there was too much of the Puritan in him" to allow him to be content with clandestine affairs. To calm his own conscience "he could not rest until he had redefined the nature of sin and erected a stupendous theological edifice to support his new theories on marriage."[28]

Rejecting Brodie's simplistic interpretation, Foster sees plural marriage "as part of a larger effort to re-establish social cohesion and kinship ties in a socially and intellectually disordered environment,"[29] even as American society was moving rapidly toward the privatization of the economy, of the family, of religion, and even of politics, all accompanied by new rules ensuring stability. When Joseph Smith began to have his visions and revelations, this transformation was by no means complete. To him, the churches were speaking in a Babel-like babble of competing voices. In the 1820s and 1830s many Americans still lacked those internal gyroscopes that eventually—compliments of movements like evangelical religion—would stabilize Americans on their course toward progress and success. The perception of social disorder was still widespread in American society. For example, modern research has confirmed that the breakdown of external authority in the wake of the Revolution resulted in a dramatic rise of premarital pregnancies and drunkenness. Marital conflict led to an increasing number of wives leaving their husbands. Both slavery and the presence of free blacks in the northern cities were seen by many whites as causes of disorder and social unrest. The paternalistic reform movements of the early nineteenth century were virtually powerless to deal with these problems. The lower classes no longer listened to the exhortations of such reformists for sobriety, while colonization of emancipated slaves was seen as, at best, a feeble effort beyond the powers of paternalistic initiatives. Reforms toward both temperance and antislavery became successful only after they appealed to the individual directly, as evangelical religion did, without intermediaries, in keeping with Ralph Waldo Emerson's dictum that "an institution is the lengthened shadow of one man."[30]

Ironically, a statement like Emerson's cuts both ways—as an expression of the trend toward modernizing values of antebellum America, and as a motto of those leaders, such as Joseph Smith, who were resisting this trend, suggesting that, even in our post-Derrida world, the reading of texts can be a complicated business. In his recent biography, Richard Bushman argues that Joseph's reconstruction of the family "did not grow out of a diagnosis of social ills." If he is right (and he is certainly consistent in decoupling Joseph's prophetic genius from social context), it is also true that Joseph's "new and everlasting covenant" was not born in a vacuum. Many of the kind of people who became Mormons or Shakers or Oneida Perfectionists found themselves at sea in a rapidly changing society. Joseph convinced his followers that the old rules no longer applied in this time, when the new rules of the dominant culture had not yet been clearly defined and many new rules were not to the liking of the kind of people attracted to new movements. Change was a real possibility for many. In the words of Lawrence Foster, "Smith was attempting to demolish an old way of life and to build a new social order from the ground up." The message of the "new and everlasting covenant" illustrates this point forcefully: "All covenants, contracts, bonds, obligations, oaths, vows, performances, connections, associations, or expectations, that are not made and entered into and sealed by the Holy Spirit of promise . . . are of no efficacy, virtue, or force in and after the resurrection from the dead; for all contracts that are not made unto this end have an end when men are dead."[31]

In the opinions of William McLoughlin and Perry Miller, the Second Great Awakening was like a tidal wave—a tsunami that swept away the last vestiges of an old order and made possible the creation of the modern capitalist American empire founded on the bedrock of religious, political, and economic pluralism. According to Gordon Wood, "there was nothing like it on this popular scale since the religious turbulence of seventeenth-century England or perhaps the Reformation."[32] Those who regard these works as too speculative may turn to a number of case studies corroborating the importance of evangelical religion in the formation of the cultural values of modern America. In an influential study of Rochester, New York, from 1815 to 1837, Paul E. Johnson, not without some ingenuity, has extrapolated evidence from a wide range of data supporting his argument that Charles Finney's revivals in Rochester were an essential linchpin in the legitimation of the ideology of free labor among the entrepreneurs in that city and, by extension, in other industrializing communities affected by revivals.[33] Anthropologist Anthony F. C. Wallace's ambitious and detailed study *Rockdale* carefully and convincingly traces the formative role of evangelical religion in the establishment of the capitalist order in the cotton mill communities along the Delaware River in southern Pennsylvania.[34] In their examination of precisely how the modern order was born, showing the contingency of the process, these scholars have corrected the impression of historical inevitability implicit in the works of Miller and McLoughlin, by injecting a dialectical dimension into their narratives that shows precisely how the new order was born out of a conflict whose outcomes were not at all apparent to the participants at the time. Not surprisingly, the evangelical entrepreneurs and employers seen in these studies encountered strong resistance from traditionally oriented workers, who attempted to shape a separate identity and consciousness out of their own experiences of class and culture. The fact that, in the long run, even the most strong-willed or recalcitrant were forced to capitulate before the overwhelming force of the evangelical-capitalist ethos does not negate the intensity and historical significance of a struggle in which many workers ended up on the losing side.

There were, of course, many such losers other than these workers. It is only to be expected that in a country as large and diverse as the United States significant ethnic, cultural, or religious minorities would fail to share this evangelical fervor and its values, which did not necessarily reflect, and in some cases were in opposition to, these minorities' values. Some attempted to establish revitalization movements of their own. The old Calvinist Federalist establishment did not give in to the emerging democratic, pluralist middle-class society without a fight. For different reasons, various outsiders who had not shared in the power of the old order also opposed the atomistic individualism of a society that seemed to thrive on competition and conflict. Catholicism, separated into various ethnic components, is a major example. And other groups of Americans who stood outside the evangelical pale were those who founded or joined a collection of dissenting movements that attracted many who were physically or psychologically uprooted by the emerging new order. Many of these individuals found homes among Mother Ann Lee's Shakers, John Humphrey Noyes's Oneida Perfectionists, and Joseph Smith's Mormons.

Of all these movements, Mormonism came to be seen as the most serious threat to the hegemony of the evangelicals. Catholics were, of course, numerous and came in for their share of persecution.[35] But on a percentage basis, the persecution of the Mormons exceeded that of any other group of white Americans (though paling in comparison to the slaughter of Indians and the lynchings and race riots inflicted on African Americans). In the case of Catholicism, there could be cultural differences with Protestants that were absent vis-à-vis early Mormon converts, most of whom had Protestant New England or Mid-Atlantic roots. Moreover, Joseph Smith had always insisted on the peculiarly American nature of the origin and the doctrines of Mormonism. To Joseph, Mormonism was American to its very core, making it potentially subversive to those who saw such language as rhetoric that only masked a deep cultural divide. Mormonism presented itself not merely as another variant of American Protestant pluralism, but as an articulate and sophisticated counterideology that attempted to establish a "new heaven and a new earth" intended as an alternative to the Protestant evangelical millennium.

Although the relatively open, evangelically enthusiastic period of American history provided fertile soil for the rise of Mormonism, the new religion was largely untouched by the fires of the revivals. For the most part, the kind of people attracted to Mormonism were either confused by revivals, as was Joseph Smith himself, or were left cold by enthusiastic religion, like Brigham Young. The intensity of anti-Mormon persecution was, in its way, a backhanded compliment to a movement that became one of the most articulate, and the best-organized, in its rejection of the values and practices of the evangelicals. Even more than Shakers and Oneida Perfectionists, Mormons actively attempted to change the world through their all-encompassing vision of a kingdom of God that presented a challenge not only to the evangelical religious values but also to the closely related political, economic, and social values of antebellum America. When Mormonism was labelled the Islam of America by its opponents, the most obvious reason was plural marriage, but a more profound explanation must be sought in the fact that Joseph Smith, in the words of Harold Bloom, "intended a religious reform as total as the birth of Islam," one that would obviate distinctions between the secular and the religious, between church and state, between heaven and earth, and create a seamless web encompassing the entirety of existence, past, present, and future.[36] Even if Joseph's opponents may have perceived this grandest of visions only dimly, they knew enough to realize that Mormonism could be included in a pluralistic society only with great difficulty—an observation Alexis de Tocqueville underscored in his comparison between American Christianity and Islam, writing that "religions ought to keep themselves discreetly within the bounds that are proper to them and not seek to leave them, for in wishing to extend their power further than religious matters, they risk no longer being believed in any matter. They ought therefore to trace carefully the sphere within which they claim to fix the human mind, and beyond that to leave it entirely free to be abandoned to itself." Of course, had Joseph been familiar with Tocqueville's observations he would have rejected them.[37]

If, to repeat McLoughlin, it was the Second Great Awakening that provided the internal ideology that consolidated the American national character and culture, and the Awakening was thus "the most pivotal" movement in antebellum American history, then it stands to reason that a movement such as Mormonism, which attempted to follow a different drummer in the formation of American values, must be resisted. When it is further understood that the Mormon challenge occurred at a time when American values were still very much in the process of being formed, at a time when the national identity was far from secure—at a time, in fact, when the evangelical crusade, in the opinion of scholars such as McLoughlin and Miller, was the manifestation of a national identity crisis—then, perhaps, what is surprising about the anti-Mormon crusade is not that it happened, but that the tales of mob violence, arson, pillage, and murder do not fill an even larger volume.

Yet if McLoughlin is correct in his assertion that the Founding Fathers had purposely omitted the internal ideology of the American Republic from the Constitution and that this ideology was, in fact, in the process of being formed at the very time that Mormonism attempted its own definition of the meaning of America, then the label un-American, so freely attached to the Mormons in the nineteenth century, has merely propaganda value. In the light of this discussion, then, the extensive debate among historians on the question of whether or not nineteenth-century Mormons were "American" turns out to be a nonquestion. It is only by looking in the rearview mirror—after evangelical, pluralistic, and capitalist values were victorious in helping define an American identity—that certain historians have felt confident in settling the question with any degree of finality. Because the Mormons (along with other antievangelical dissenters) appeared to be on the losing side (at least until around the time of World War I), the propaganda of the victors seemed to have prevailed. Clearly, this is an American version of what Herbert Butterfield has called the Whig interpretation of history—from hindsight.[38]

An ideal alternative, of course, would be to write the history of the birth of Mormonism through the eyes of the participants—Richard Bushman's biography of Joseph might serve as a model.[39] Instead, I will attempt to illustrate in a brief postscript how I see "culture" and the religious imagination intersecting in the life of Joseph and his family. Plagued by economic hard times in Connecticut and Vermont that led to the loss of their farm, the Smiths moved their family seven times in fourteen years. Having Puritan origins on both sides, the family had internalized many of the values and habits of Yankees. Father Joseph's investment in a risky ginseng venture was a gamble he lost—according to Tocqueville a rather typical activity of many Americans in this period, driven by rising expectations of the early market revolution[40]—expectations that were dashed once again after the Smith family's move to western New York. Any hopes of providing for their children's future and their own old age evaporated for good after Joseph's parents, now both in their fifties, lost another farm. Such misfortunes appear to have left Joseph Sr. a broken man, and after the death of the eldest son, Alvin, the family leadership devolved on Joseph Jr.—a drama leading me to translate the abstract language of academia, such as the "shift in the locus of authority" into the vernacular of lived reality that, in the case of Joseph, was touched by the divine. The crisis might have become a tragedy but it found a religious resolution—though it was not inevitable, as the following two stories will illustrate.

The father of Samuel Johnson was a bookseller who had fallen on hard times, a broken man—physically and emotionally. One day, when Samuel was a young man of twenty-two, he refused to attend his father's bookstall, perhaps ashamed of the old man. "My pride prevented me," he wrote. "I gave my father a refusal." Fifty years later, on a rainy day, Samuel wrote that he took "a postchaise to Uttoxeter, and going into the market at the time of high business, uncovered my head, and stood with it bare an hour before the stall which my father had formerly used, exposed to the sneers of the standersby and the inclemency of the weather."[41] By that time Samuel had become "Doctor" Johnson of dictionary fame.

Closer to home is the story of Abraham Lincoln. Lincoln was three years younger than Joseph Smith Jr. Both boys grew up in families battered by economic hardships. In their struggles for economic security, both fathers moved their families westward—the Smiths to western New York, the Lincolns to the Indiana frontier (incidentally, in the same year—1816). Both boys had strong mothers (after Nancy's premature death, Lincoln had a supportive stepmother). Both had somewhat troubled relationships with their fathers (Lincoln more than Joseph). But whereas Joseph "reinvented" his father as a revered patriarch, Lincoln forged a successful life without his father, Thomas. In fact, it could be argued that it was only because of breaking with his father that Abraham Lincoln saw himself as being able to succeed in the competitive, individualistic world of the market revolution. Lincoln's illiterate father resented his son's attachment to books, which the young boy seems to have recognized as the means of escaping to a better world. The father saw no alternative to physical labour—which, to young Abe, perhaps, seemed a form of slavery. (Without naysaying Lincoln's deep ethical convictions, historians have suggested that the man instrumental in the abolition of slavery also saw the "peculiar institution" as a major impediment to free-market economics).[42] When Thomas Lincoln died, his son refused to attend the funeral of his father. If the son felt any remorse, the record is silent. According to biographer Doris Kearns Goodwin, "such conflict between father and son was played out in thousands of homes as the 'self-made men' of Lincoln's generation sought to pursue ambitions beyond the cramped lives of their fathers."[43]

These two stories project into bolder relief the relationship Joseph had with his father. As Richard Bushman tells it, the leadership of the Smith family devolved on Joseph because Joseph Sr. was seen as "not fully adequate. He was a gentle, disappointed man with an inclination to compensate for his failures with magic and drink. . . . Joseph Jr. eventually restored his father's dignity by giving him an honoured place in the church. If there was any childhood dynamic at work in Joseph Jr.'s life, it was the desire to redeem his flawed, loving father." Bushman then questions rhetorically, "But was this enough to make him a prophet?"[44] Probably not! But early in Joseph's prophetic career the Angel Moroni revealed to him Malachi's prediction that the prophet Elijah would "plant in the hearts of the children the promises made to their fathers, and the returning of the hearts of the children to their fathers." Joseph was then in his eighteenth year, about the same time that he seemingly had usurped his father's role as "patriarch" of the family. This was in 1823. After the restoration of the priesthood predicted by Moroni, and after the founding of the Mormon Church, Joseph ordained his father as patriarch (it is unclear whether in 1833 or 1834). Joseph Jr. predicted that his father, like Adam, would assemble his children. "His seed shall rise up and call him blessed. . . . his name shall be had in remembrance to the end."[45] Brought down by the ravages of the market revolution, the father had been redeemed by his son—a story that might have had several different outcomes: Oedipus killed his father and married his mother—a story that became iconic in the symbolic drama of a modern secular religion. Samuel Johnson could only do penance. Lincoln, seemingly without regret, refused to attend the funeral of his father.

In the case of Joseph, religion and culture did intersect. If, in the shift in the locus of authority, it is the loss of the father that is central, then the restoration of the father is likewise central. For Joseph, that restoration was religious. And it intersects with virtually all the other principles of the Mormon Restoration: priesthood, the temple, marriage, life before birth and after death, salvation and exaltation, cosmology. . . . So in the end, perhaps, the answer to Richard Bushman's question is—No! Joseph's desire to redeem his father wasn't enough to make him a prophet. To put it into the context of this essay, "culture" wasn't enough. But without that desire, what kind of a prophet would Joseph have become? Would Mormonism be alive today? And if so, how different would it be from the Mormonism we know—rooted as it is in Malachi's admonition and promise? As missionaries are spreading the message of Joseph Smith across the world, it becomes apparent that the appeal of the message in no small part derives from the bond Joseph established—not only with his father, but with many other fathers and their children—a theme that (though finding expression in a particular culture at a particular time) is universal.

Of course, it is not the only universal theme. For Joseph Smith, "the eternal feminine" was a necessary corollary. In the "new and everlasting covenant," exaltation could be achieved only by the eternal union of a man and a woman— not necessarily in a polygamous relationship (redefined after the "manifesto" of 1890). As Richard Bushman put it, "Before the marriage revelation, women were in the shadows in Joseph's theology, implied but rarely recognized. Now they moved to the center."[46] (In regard to this, some Mormon feminists argue that Bushman's is an insight that has been slow in coming, with the benefit of hindsight). Making a stronger case for Joseph's "feminism" is Clyde Forsberg, who argues that by the 1840s the Mormon prophet's views had already evolved into a theological middle ground between Masonic patriarchy (which excluded women from the lodge) and evangelical feminism, which many patriarchs saw as a threat to their manhood. Joseph's granting of equality to women in the temple, then, can be seen as a radical step that offended camps on both sides.[47] Feminists, who have been less than successful in mobilizing Mormon women, tend not to be impressed by the explanation that, in the eternal scheme of things, Mormon women see themselves as having achieved a degree of equality with their spouses that puts them ahead of most males outside the Church. It is true, however, that at the present time such promises (marriages, sealing promises, covenants) are "solemnized" in more than a hundred temples throughout the world.

Arguably, a future Karen Armstrong may well include Mormonism as a subject for another book on world religions, perhaps even linking its origins to a modern counterpart of the Axial Age.

Finally, for what I see as my personal conundrum vis-à-vis the Joseph of culture and the one who is God's mouthpiece, I take refuge in William Butler Yeats: "How can we know the dancer from the dance?"[48]

4

"I Love All Men Who Dive": Herman Melville and Joseph Smith

Richard Dilworth Rust

"I love all men who *dive*," wrote Herman Melville to a friend. "Any fish can swim near the surface, but it takes a great whale to go down stairs five miles or more; & if he dont attain the bottom, why, all the lead in Galena can't fashion the plummet that will. I'm not talking of Mr Emerson now—but of the whole corps of thought-divers, that have been diving & coming up again with blood-shot eyes since the world began."[1] Although Herman Melville probably never met Joseph Smith, he would probably have loved him as a "thought-diver." Melville said in his 1850 review of Nathaniel Hawthorne's *Mosses from an Old Manse* (1846), "For genius, all over the world, stands hand in hand, and one shock of recognition runs the whole circle around."[2]

Why might one want to consider Herman Melville and Joseph Smith together? This juxtaposition helps illuminate striking similarities as well as significant differences in the lives and responses to life of two of the nineteenth century's most remarkable men, both pioneers in their respective fields. What editor James G. Bennett of the *New York Herald* wrote about Joseph Smith could apply to Herman Melville as well: he was "undoubtedly one of the greatest characters of the age."[3] Future generations, observed Josiah Quincy Jr., the mayor of Boston, might well identify Joseph Smith as the American of the nineteenth century who "has exerted the most powerful influence upon the destinies of his countrymen."[4]

Likewise, Melville's place today as one of the greatest writers of American literature is undisputed. These two contemporaries have given to the world enduring works in the Book of Mormon (1830) and *Moby-Dick* (1851).

Both Melville and Smith pondered the deep questions of existence, such as the relationship of man to God, the nature and degree of human agency, and the purpose of life. Their writings range widely in examining problems of mortality and immortality, the brotherhood of man, self-realization, response to either earthly or heavenly authority, deception and hypocrisy, and good and evil. (By writings, I am considering all that came from these men: the translations and revelations of Joseph Smith as well as his letters, journals, and recorded sayings; and Herman Melville's letters and literary works.) They both grew up in New York State—Melville in Albany and Smith in Palmyra, locations separated by more than two hundred miles but connected by the Erie Canal. And while they were misunderstood and harshly judged during their lifetimes, their fame has increased during the last hundred years.

Herman Melville, according to noted literary critic R. W. B. Lewis, was "the one novelist in nineteenth-century America gifted with a genuinely myth-making imagination."[5] Joseph Smith similarly has been considered by the distinguished literary critic Harold Bloom to be "an authentic religious genius [who] surpassed all Americans, before or since, in the possession and expression of what could be called the religion-making imagination."[6] Yet Melville belonged to what Lewis called the party of Irony, while Smith could be considered to belong to the party of Hope. Melville had deeply probing questions; Smith, thinking as deeply but also calling on revelation, had answers to many of the very questions Melville posed. Both were willing to examine the questions thoroughly and honestly. Melville surely had himself as well as Hawthorne in mind when he said, "We think that into no recorded mind has the intense feeling of the visible truth ever entered more deeply than into this man's. By visible truth, we mean the apprehension of the absolute condition of present things as they strike the eye of the man who fears them not, though they do their worst to him."[7] Melville engaged, as critic Stan Goldman puts it, in "the painful struggle between the human and the divine. As Jacob wrestled with the angel, as Job wrestled with God—'but I will maintain mine own ways before him' (Job 13:15)—Melville also wrestled with 'contraries.'"[8] On his part, Smith believed that "'by proving contraries,' 'truth is made manifest,' and a wise man can search out 'old paths,['] wherein righteous men held communion with Jehovah, and were exalted through obedience."[9]

Melville and the Mormons

While there is no record that he and Joseph Smith ever met, Melville was aware of the Book of Mormon and was informed (or misinformed) about the Latter-day Saints. Probably the nearest Melville ever came to Smith was in 1840, when a twenty-one-year-old Melville took a steamboat from Galena to Cairo, both in Illinois, passing the fledgling Mormon settlement at Nauvoo, Illinois, where Smith then resided.[10] Melville's one overt reference to the Book of Mormon is in his novel *Pierre* (1852), where he puts the volume in a packet of great books a wealthy admirer has delivered to Plotinus Plinlimmon. This foreign scholar has sent Plinlimmon "a very fine set of volumes—Cardan, Epictetus, the Book of Mormon, Abraham Tucker, Condorcet and the Zend-Avesta."[11] As Robert Rees has pointed out, one characteristic these books have in common is their emphasis on benevolence.[12] But selfish Plinlimmon leaves the books untouched. Rather than accepting the wine contained in the new bottle of the Book of Mormon, Plinlimmon tells the scholar he would have preferred "some choice Curaçoa from a nobleman like you." After the scholar probes him, saying, "I thought that the society of which you are the head, excluded all things of that sort," Plinlimmon responds hypocritically, "Dear Count, so they do; but Mohammed hath his own dispensation."[13]

That Melville found something commendatory in the Book of Mormon is also suggested, as Rees argues quite persuasively, by his use of the name Alma for his prophet-Christ figure in *Mardi* (1849). Melville's Alma "was an illustrious prophet, and teacher divine" who came to instruct the Mardians "in the ways of truth, virtue, and happiness; to allure them to good by promises of beatitude hereafter; and to restrain them from evil by denunciations of woe."[14] Melville also identified his misunderstood novel *Mardi* with Mormons.

> Again: (as the divines say) political republics should be the asylum
> for the persecuted of all nations; so, if Mardi be admitted to your
> shelves, your bibliographical Republic of Letters may find some
> contentment in the thought, that it has afforded refuge to a work,
> which almost everywhere else has been driven forth like a wild,
> mystic Mormon into shelterless exile.[15]

Melville alluded to Mormons again in *The Confidence-Man: His Masquerade* (1857). One of the passengers on the steamboat *Fidèle* supposes that the lamblike man in cream colors is a "green prophet from Utah."[16] At one point in the novel, the swindling confidence man tries to interest a collegian in the New Jerusalem, which he says is "'the new and thriving city, so called, in northern Minnesota. It was originally founded by certain fugitive Mormons. Hence the name.'"[17] This "new and thriving" city founded by the Mormons calls to mind Nauvoo, although the northerly location and the reference to "fugitive" Mormons may also have reference to an apostate colony at Beaver Island, Wisconsin, once designated the New Jerusalem by colony leader James J. Strang, whose assassination in 1856 received national attention. The narrator of the novel implies skepticism about the city's "perpetual fountain" and "lignum-vitae rostrums"—that is, "the fountain of the water of life" and the tree of life in the New Jerusalem as described in the book of Revelation (see Rev. 21:1–6). Melville might have had in mind, as well, the New Jerusalem and the tree of life described in the Book of Mormon. And the narrator includes "Mormons and Papists" in his catalog of the "Anacharsis Cloots congress of all kinds of that multiform pilgrim species, man." After listing "happiness-hunters" and "truth-hunters," he probably thought of himself as belonging to the category of "still keener hunters after all these hunters."[18]

Backgrounds

There was much about the backgrounds of Melville and Smith that significantly colored their approaches to life. "Call me Ishmael," Melville begins his most famous novel, *Moby-Dick* (1851), presenting a character with a number of parallels to himself, just as he had previously done in the title characters of his novels *Redburn* (1849) and *White Jacket* (1850). An orphan (one who, judging by his name, had been cast out by his father), Ishmael goes to sea as a substitute for suicide. Even then, conditioned by his Calvinistic training, he considers his voyage fated. The writer behind the character was also bereft of his father, who had died raving when Melville was twelve. One analysis of Melville supposes that he first knew the punitive Calvinist God "chiefly through the image of his own father."[19] Melville had a difficult relationship with his mother, Marie Gansevoort Melville, a member of the neo-Calvinist Dutch Reformed Church. In fact, Herman Melville said that she hated him.[20]

The opening of the Book of Mormon, which Joseph Smith translated, is both roughly parallel to "Call me Ishmael" and significantly different from it. It starts, "I, Nephi, having been born of goodly parents . . ." (1 Nephi 1:1), declaring that Nephi is the narrator's real name and not just a name to be used on the occasion, and emphasizing the closeness of parents and son. Joseph Smith continually affirmed that he, too, had been born of goodly parents. His father, Joseph Smith Sr., was his confidant and friend, and his mother, Lucy Mack Smith, provided the constant support of love and belief. "Blessed of the Lord is my father," said Joseph,

> for he shall stand in the midst of his posterity and shall be comforted by their blessings when he is old and bowed down with years, and shall be called a prince over them, and shall be numbered among those who hold the right of Patriarchal Priesthood. . . .
>
> And blessed also, is my mother, . . .
>
> . . . for her soul is ever filled with benevolence and philanthropy: and notwithstanding her age, she shall yet receive strength and be comforted in the midst of her house: and thus saith the Lord. She shall have eternal life.[21]

Heavenly knowledge began for Joseph Smith at age fourteen, when he earnestly prayed vocally for the first time to ask God for wisdom—and received it directly from the Deity. When he was fourteen, the boy Melville worked in a bank in Albany and then briefly on his uncle's farm in Pittsfield, Massachusetts. But his major learning experiences came later. "Until I was twenty-five, I had no development at all," Melville confided to Hawthorne. "From my twenty-fifth year I date my life. Three weeks have scarcely passed, at any time between then and now, that I have not unfolded within myself."[22] At that point he had just returned from the sea with a store of whaling and naval experiences that he would use in his fiction and poetry to the end of his life. As with Ishmael, the whaling ship had been his "Yale College and [his] Harvard."[23] In his twenty-fifth year, Joseph Smith published the Book of Mormon and organized The Church of Jesus Christ of Latter-day Saints. One could say that Joseph Smith's most important "Harvard" experience was the instruction he received from heavenly visitants.

By age thirty, Melville was writing *Moby-Dick*; at that age, Smith had organized the Quorum of the Twelve Apostles and dedicated the Kirtland temple, among other accomplishments. Just eight years later, Joseph Smith was cruelly cut down at the height of his creativity. With the appearance of his skeptical work *The Confidence-Man*, in his thirty-eighth year Melville ended his career of writing fiction for publication.

During that year, 1857, with the support of his family, Melville went abroad to the Mediterranean and the Holy Land to restore his health and to see if he could regain some faith. The book-length poem *Clarel: A Poem and Pilgrimage in the Holy Land* (1876) is an imaginative account of that experience, featuring a variety of characters expressing diverse views on religion and other topics. Though no single character fully represents Melville, Clarel's question seems to be at the heart of Melville's quest: " 'Christ lived a Jew: and in Judaea / May linger any breath of Him?' "[24] Subsequently, thinking of the disciples on the road to Emmaus, Clarel expresses a longing for divine counsel: "I too, I too; could *I* but meet / Some stranger of a lore replete, / Who, marking how my looks betray / The dumb thoughts clogging here my feet, / Would question me, expound and prove, / And make my heart to burn with love—/ Emmaus were no dream to-day!"[25]

On his way to the Holy Land, Melville told Hawthorne of his "noble doubts" and desires. In his journal account of their visit near Liverpool in November 1856, Hawthorne muses:

> Melville, as he always does, began to reason of Providence and fu-
> turity, and of everything that lies beyond human ken, and informed
> me that he had "pretty much made up his mind to be annihilated";
> but still he does not seem to rest in that anticipation; and, I think,
> will never rest until he gets hold of a definite belief. It is strange how
> he persists—and has persisted ever since I knew him, and probably
> long before—in wandering to-and-fro over these deserts, as dismal
> and monotonous as the sand hills amid which we were sitting. He
> can neither believe, nor be comfortable in his unbelief; and he is too
> honest and courageous not to try to do one or the other. If he were a
> religious man, he would be one of the most truly religious and
> reverential; he has a very high and noble nature, and better worth
> immortality than most of us.[26]

Also an honest and courageous person, Joseph Smith at age thirty-eight was solidly sure in his belief. As he announced in his masterful King Follett discourse, he intended to edify his audience "with the simple truths from heaven."[27]

While their family relations and backgrounds were different, Herman Melville and Joseph Smith were alike in their thirst for knowledge. Merton M. Sealts's *Melville's Reading* and Mary K. Bercaw's *Melville's Sources* show that Melville, like Ishmael, "swam through libraries."[28] The journals of Joseph Smith transcribed in the *History of the Church* and *Personal Writings of Joseph Smith* show a man who, despite enormous demands on his time, was constantly learning new languages (such as German, Greek, and Hebrew), engaging in extended discussions such as those that took place in the School of the Prophets, and receiving revelation upon revelation. In their desire for truth, both men gained ever-expanding knowledge.[29]

The search for truth is a theme found throughout Melville's writings. "You must have plenty of sea-room to tell the Truth in," he said in his review of Hawthorne's *Mosses*, and in that review he implicitly includes himself with Hawthorne and Shakespeare as a master "of the great Art of Telling the

Truth,—even though it be covertly, and by snatches."[30] Identifying Hawthorne in that review as "a seeker, not a finder yet," Melville allies with him, proclaiming, "I seek for Truth."[31] Nearly the same age as Melville's friend Hawthorne, Joseph Smith, too, prized truth. He subscribed to the prophet Jacob's view in the Book of Mormon: The righteous "love the truth and are not shaken" (2 Nephi 9:40).

Diving out of Sight and Coming into View

Both during and after their lives, these forthright and genuine men were seriously misunderstood, their true characters unknown to many. One review of Melville's novel *Pierre* bore the bold headline "HERMAN MELVILLE CRAZY"![32] In *The Confidence-Man*, Melville acknowledged that "the acutest sage [is] often at his wits' ends to understand living character."[33] Only the most eagle-eyed readers, Melville said, could come close to understanding him. Even his family hardly knew his inner life. This point is made somewhat humorously in the sketch "I and My Chimney" (1856), in which the narrator protects the base of his chimney—symbolically, his ego—from being threatened or exposed.[34] Isabel's last words concerning Pierre could well apply to Melville: " 'All's o'er, and ye know him not!' "[35] Similarly, Joseph Smith stated, "You don't know me; you never knew my heart. No man knows my history. I cannot tell it: I shall never undertake it. I don't blame any one for not believing my history. If I had not experienced what I have, I could not have believed it myself."[36] Nor could he tell it all. "I have handled, heard, seen and known things which I have not yet told," he revealed.[37] Melville lamented, "What a madness & anguish it is, that an author can never—under no conceivable circumstances—be at all frank with his readers."[38]

Yet both Melville and Smith left significant bodies of writings from which one can approach their personal histories. I grant that Melville is complex and ambiguous and that no one character in his fiction represents him in any direct way. I also acknowledge that during his lifetime he stated or implied changing and sometimes conflicting views on religious and other matters. Still, it could be said that Melville wrote out his life in his works, from his Polynesian adventures in *Typee* (1846) and *Omoo* (1847), through his anguished experiences as an author in *Pierre*, to his examination of the relationships of a father and son in *Billy Budd* (1924; posthumous). As noted frequently, Melville's works involve some form of a journey with a quest—for beauty in *Mardi*, for truth in *Moby-Dick*, for virtue in *Pierre*.

To learn about Joseph Smith's life, one turns primarily to his journals and sermons; indeed, his 1839 history, with its account of his First Vision, is the core story of his life—which, as he put it, is inextricably related to "the rise and progress of the Church of Jesus Christ of Latter-day Saints." (Joseph Smith–History 1:1). As with Melville's life story, Smith's is a repeated account of journeys that include the migrations of the Smith family and the Latter-day Saints as a people. These journeys replicate those found within the Book of Mormon: the journeys of the Jaredites, of the people of Lehi, and of Alma's people. Experiencing and writing about the journey archetype, both Melville and Smith could consider themselves wanderers.

In regard to his journeying, Smith could affirm, "Go forward and not backward. Courage, brethren; and on, on to the victory!" (Doctrine and Covenants 128:22). Melville, though, wrote about a series of incomplete or failed journeys and placed elements of himself in the character Redburn, who felt "in early youth . . . the pangs which should be reserved for the stout time of manhood," and in Ishmael, who at times had "a damp, drizzly November" in his soul.[39]

Experiencing Darkness and Light

The emotional cloud over Melville is often represented as blackness. What Melville found in Hawthorne certainly was true of himself: "This great power of blackness in him derives its force from its appeals to that Calvinistic sense of Innate Depravity and Original Sin."[40] As Melville's biographer Edwin Haviland Miller believes:

> Only a man who himself had experienced the despair that accompanies the blackness of depressions, where grievances or hurts are magnified against the background of overwhelming feelings of helplessness, could have created Ahab, Pierre, and Bartleby. These characters, in overwrought rhetoric or in its opposite, silence, are imprisoned in despair, feelings of ineffectuality, self-destructive rages, teetering on the brink of complete loss of control. If they are poised perilously at the abyss, Melville had preceded them there.[41]

Yet Melville found that "profoundest gloom" sometimes allows one to discover "deeper truths in man." "Utter darkness is then his light," he says, "and cat-like he distinctly sees all objects through a medium which is mere blindness to common vision."[42] "Every night, when the curtain falls," he says in "The Piazza" (1856), "truth comes in with darkness."[43] As with the tortoise of the Enchanted Isles with its bright yellow underside and dark back, Melville believed that one should "enjoy the bright, keep it turned up perpetually if you can, but be honest and don't deny the black."[44]

Joseph Smith knew darkness. Regarding the Sacred Grove experience, he wrote, "Thick darkness gathered around me, and it seemed to me for a time as if I were doomed to sudden destruction" (Joseph Smith–History 1:15). Yet Satan's darkness was superseded in Smith's first vision by "a pillar of light . . . above the brightness of the sun" (Joseph Smith–History 1:16). As there is a power of darkness in Melville, there could be called a power of light in Smith. Despite his persecutions, Joseph Smith prophesied that he would "stand and shine like the sun in the firmament."[45] He was like Gazelem's stone, "which shall shine forth in darkness unto light" (Alma 37:23). "That which is of God is light," he wrote, "and he that receiveth light, and continueth in God, receiveth more light; and that light groweth brighter and brighter until the perfect day" (Doctrine and Covenants 50:24). Conversely, "He that will not receive the greater light, must have taken away from him all the light which he hath; and if the light which is in you become darkness, behold, how great is that darkness!"[46]

These perspectives of Melville and Smith regarding darkness and light correlate with their views on human agency. The blighted Melville, with his early Calvinistic training, struggled with matters of fate and free will. Surely there were times in his life when he felt the plight of a Pierre who "was not arguing Fixed Fate and Free Will, now; Fixed Fate and Free Will were arguing him, and Fixed Fate got the better in the debate."[47] Acknowledging a parallel between Melville and Ishmael, literary scholar Paul Brodtkorb says, "Whenever Ishmael contemplates time, fatality is the aspect of it that is most apt to concern him."[48] In contrast, Joseph Smith's position was that of Lehi in the Book of Mormon, who said:

> And because . . . [the children of men] are redeemed from the fall
> they have become free forever, knowing good from evil; to act for
> themselves and not to be acted upon. . . . And they are free to choose
> liberty and eternal life, through the great Mediator of all men, or to
> choose captivity and death, according to the captivity and power of
> the devil. (2 Nephi 2:26–27)

Smith found through divine instruction that Presbyterianism, with its Calvinistic base, was wrong. And while living in the world of time, Smith "let the solemnities of eternity" rest upon his mind (Doctrine and Covenants 43:34).

Whether they were dominantly pessimistic or optimistic, both men understood evil. Melville describes Ishmael at the tiller at night, perceiving that "the rushing Pequod, freighted with savages, and laden with fire, and burning a corpse, and plunging into that blackness of darkness, seemed the material counterpart of her monomaniac commander's soul."[49] Transfixed into a doze in which he nearly capsizes the vessel, Ishmael gives himself this admonition,

"Look not too long in the face of the fire, O man!"[50] Smith, too, had a sight of what Ishmael calls "fiend shapes."[51] An angel showed him "the prince of darkness, surrounded by his innumerable train of associates." The heavenly messenger then said, " 'All this is shown, the good and the evill [*sic*], the holy and impure, the glory of God and the power of darkness, that you may know hereafter the two powers and never be influenced or overcome by that wicked one.' "[52] At another time, Smith beheld "Satan, that old serpent," and saw "a vision of the sufferings of those with whom he made war and overcame" (Doctrine and Covenants 76:28–30). In the Book of Moses, translated by Joseph Smith, Enoch had a similar experience: He "beheld Satan; and he had a great chain in his hand, and it veiled the whole face of the earth with darkness; and he looked up and laughed, and his angels rejoiced" (Moses 7:26).

In discerning the good and the evil, both men were exceptionally honest; they were maskless men in a world too often appearing as a masquerade.[53] As such, they were totally committed to seeking for, and speaking, the truth. "I mean to give the truth of the thing, spite of this," Melville wrote to a friend.[54] Yet he knew only too well how little the world rewarded truth-tellers: "Try to get a living by the Truth—and go to the Soup Societies," Melville commented to Hawthorne.[55] For his part, Smith affirmed, "Water, fire, truth and God are all realities. Truth is 'Mormonism.' God is the author of it."[56]

Doubt and Faith

While seeking for the truth, Melville pondered how one can be sure of it, especially as pertains to the unseen world. The degree to which he worked out his own questionings and grapplings in his fiction is evident in his novels. He has Pierre lamenting "the everlasting elusiveness of Truth."[57] In varying degrees through his life, Melville struggled with questions of doubt and faith.[58] " 'Own, own with me, and spare to feign,' " he has Clarel say; " 'Doubt bleeds, nor Faith is free from pain!' "[59] "Doubts of all things earthly, and intuitions of some things heavenly; this combination . . . makes a man who regards them both with equal eye," Melville's narrator says in *Moby-Dick*.[60] One can easily see Melville's alignment with this position expressed in *Mardi*: " 'I am dumb with doubt; yet, 'tis not doubt, but worse: I doubt my doubt. . . . Would, would that mine were a settled doubt, like that wild boy's, who without faith, seems full of it. The undoubting doubter believes the most. Oh! that I were he.' "[61] Doubting his doubt, Melville was never bound to just one position. As he puts it in *Moby-Dick*:

> There is no steady unretracing progress in this life; we do not advance through fixed gradations, and at the last one pause:—through

infancy's unconscious spell, boyhood's thoughtless faith, adolescence' doubt (the common doom), then skepticism, then disbelief, resting at last in manhood's pondering repose of If. But once gone through, we trace the round again; and are infants, boys, and men, and Ifs eternally. Where lies the final harbor, whence we unmoor no more?[62]

A critical difference in Joseph Smith's life was personal revelation. For him, revelation was new wine in new bottles. To objections about Latter-day Saints not admitting the validity of sectarian baptism, Smith responded that

> to do otherwise would be like putting new wine into old bottles, and putting old wine into new bottles. What! new revelations in the old churches? New revelations would knock out the bottom of their bottomless pit. New wine into old bottles! The bottles burst and the wine runs out![63]

As for the benefit of new revelations, he said, "Could you gaze into heaven five minutes, you would know more than you would by reading all that ever was written on the subject [of a future state]."[64] And he spoke from experience. "The heavens were opened upon us," he testified on another occasion, "and I beheld the celestial kingdom of God, and the glory thereof, whether in the body or out I cannot tell."[65]

Heights and Depths

This searching out the things of God is often presented in images of descent and ascent. For instance, Smith said:

> A fanciful and flowery and heated imagination beware of; because the things of God are of deep import; and time, and experience, and careful and ponderous and solemn thoughts can only find them out. Thy mind, O man! if thou wilt lead a soul unto salvation, must stretch as high as the utmost heavens, and search into and contemplate the darkest abyss, and the broad expanse of eternity—thou must commune with God.[66]

Joseph experienced the abyss in the jail at Liberty, Missouri, where, in his anguish, he was told by the Lord:

> And if thou shouldst be cast into the pit, or into the hands of murderers, and the sentence of death passed upon thee; if thou be cast into the deep; if the billowing surge conspire against thee; if fierce winds

become thine enemy: if the heavens gather blackness, and all the elements combine to hedge up the way; and above all, if the very jaws of hell shall gape open the mouth wide after thee, know thou, my son, that all these things shall give thee experience, and shall be for thy good. The Son of Man hath descended below them all. Art thou greater than he? (Doctrine and Covenants 122:7–8)

Melville experienced and described adversity, too. Like Wellingborough Redburn, Melville lamented that "there is no misanthrope like a boy disappointed; and such was I, with the warm soul of me flogged out by adversity."[67] Through his character Babbalanja in *Mardi* he says, "He knows himself, and all that's in him, who knows adversity. To scale great heights, we must come out of lowermost depths. The way to heaven is through hell. We need fiery baptisms in the fiercest flames of our own bosoms."[68] In *Mardi* Melville further affirms, "If after all these fearful, fainting trances, the verdict be, the golden haven was not gained;—yet in bold quest thereof, better to sink in boundless deeps, than float on vulgar shoals."[69]

Melville's movement through heights and depths is perhaps best illustrated in *Moby-Dick* by the "Catskill eagle in some souls that can alike dive down into the blackest gorges, and soar out of them again and become invisible in the sunny spaces. And even if he for ever flies within the gorge, that gorge is in the mountains; so that even in his lowest swoop the mountain eagle is still higher than other birds upon the plain, even though they soar."[70] "All truth is profound," he further expounds in the same novel. "Winding far down from within the very heart of this spiked Hotel de Cluny where we here stand. . . . Wind ye down there, ye prouder, sadder souls! question that proud, sad king!"[71] In its extreme, this plunging into the depths takes a person from sanity to insanity: witness Pip, the black boy aboard the *Pequod*, who, left alone on the sea, has his soul

> carried down alive to wondrous depths, where strange shapes of the unwarped primal world glided to and fro before his passive eyes; and the miser-merman, Wisdom, revealed his hoarded heaps; and among the joyous, heartless, ever juvenile eternities, Pip saw the multitudinous, God-omnipresent, coral insects, that out of the firmament of waters heaved the colossal orbs. He saw God's foot upon the treadle of the loom, and spoke it; and therefore his shipmates called him mad. So man's insanity is heaven's sense; and wandering from all mortal reason, man comes at last to that celestial thought, which, to reason, is absurd and frantic; and weal or woe, feels then uncompromised, indifferent as his God.[72]

Melville's spiritual quest to see "God's foot upon the treadle of the loom" is most fully developed in his poem *Clarel*, which follows the pattern of his excursion to the Holy Land and culminates—to that point—a lifetime of questioning. As Stan Goldman shows, Melville's religious outlook in *Clarel* paradoxically combines doubt and faith, despair and hope, anger and love, seriousness and scathing irony, in an attempt to find or to establish the limits within which faith is possible, within which life endures and has meaning. Melville's characters in the poem have a full range of views on these matters. One character, the Anglican churchman Derwent, thinks that Clarel struggles with these issues too much. "'Alas, too deep you dive,'" he says. "'But hear me yet for little space: / This shaft you sink shall strike no bloom: / The surface, ah, heaven keeps *that* green; / Green, sunny: nature's active scene, / For man appointed, man's true home.'"[73]

Voyaging in Deep Water

Yet Melville finally had little sympathy with surfaces or land-based security. In *Mardi* he identifies himself as one who has "chartless voyaged" and who says, "Those who boldly launch, cast off all cables; and turning from the common breeze, that's fair for all, with their own breath, fill their own sails."[74] In *Moby-Dick* he admires Bulkington, who sees "that mortally intolerable truth; that all deep, earnest thinking is but the intrepid effort of the soul to keep the open independence of her sea."[75] "'Of all divers,'" Ahab soliloquizes, the whale "'hast dived the deepest. That head upon which the upper sun now gleams has moved amid this world's foundations.'"[76] The end of that great novel is about descent with no compensating ascent: The ship and all but one of its crew sink to "one common pool."[77] And Ishmael—with Melville standing behind him—sees himself as a bereft Job, the one "who wrote the first account of our Leviathan."[78] The epigraph to the epilogue of *Moby-Dick* is the sad message repeatedly brought to Job by the four persons announcing the loss of his possessions and family: "'And I only am escaped alone to tell thee.'"[79]

Joseph Smith, too, kept the open independence of his sea. "Deep water is what I am wont to swim in," he said.[80] He was familiar with sea stories from the Book of Mormon's accounts of the voyages of the Lehites and the Jaredites. The latter of these two narratives even records the potential danger of a destructive whale:

> And it came to pass that they were many times buried in the depths
> of the sea, because of the mountain waves which broke upon them,
> and also the great and terrible tempests which were caused by the
> fierceness of the wind. . . . And thus they were driven forth; and no

> monster of the sea could break them, neither whale that could mar
> them; and they did have light continually, whether it was above the
> water or under the water. (Ether 6:6, 10)

The significant difference between the *Pequod* and the Jaredite barges is that the latter emerge unscathed. As well, in contrast to Ahab's fire-ship plunging into a "blackness of darkness,"[81] divine help to the Jaredites includes light for their vessels when they are "swallowed up in the depths of the sea" (Ether 2:25).

Melville and Smith differ in their comprehensions of Job, however. When the prophet cries in anguish, "O God, where art thou? And where is the pavilion that covereth thy hiding place?" (Doctrine and Covenants 121:1), he is comforted with the following revelation.

> My son, peace be unto thy soul; thine adversity and thine afflictions
> shall be but a small moment. . . . Thy friends do stand by thee, and
> they shall hail thee again with warm hearts and friendly hands. Thou
> art not yet as Job; thy friends do not contend against thee, neither
> charge thee with transgression, as they did Job. (Doctrine and Cov-
> enants 121:7, 9–10)

Smith's suffering is not useless, for God speaks with and comforts mankind. Melville's Ishmael, alone, emerges to tell his lonely tale of plummeting to Job's depths. Smith's loneliness is arrested in the voice of God, foreshortening his suffering.

A Voice Out of Silence?

A "thought-diver" along with Melville, Smith nevertheless affirmed much more the clear path to ascent—which, in Smith's writings and thought, invariably comes after the descent. This is often paradoxically so, as in the repeated accounts in the Book of Mormon of the condescension of the Savior in coming down to the level of humanity and then suffering ignomiy on the cross so that his people could be lifted up. "My Father sent me," Jesus says, "that I might be lifted up upon the cross; and after that I had been lifted up upon the cross, that I might draw all men unto me, that as I have been lifted up by men even so should men be lifted up by the Father, to stand before me, to be judged of their works" (3 Nephi 27:14; see also 1 Nephi 11:16–33).

As far as the narrator in *Pierre* represents the author, Melville holds a bleaker view of communications with God. "Silence," the narrator says, "is the general consecration of the universe. Silence is the invisible laying on of the Divine Pontiff's hands upon the world. Silence is at once the most harmless and the most awful thing in all nature. It speaks of the Reserved Forces of Fate. Silence is the only Voice of our God."[82] "How can a man get a Voice out of Silence?" he asks later.[83] Yet, written scripture had great importance for *Pierre's* narrator. The Bible, he says, is "the truest book in the world" and the Sermon on the Mount the "greatest real miracle of all religions. . . . This is of God! cries the heart, and in that cry ceases all inquisition."[84]

Silence is found in Joseph Smith's world, too, but with this profound difference: A divine voice emerged from that silence.[85] In a grove of trees near his father's farm, Joseph heard, as did John the Baptist, the voice of God the Father testifying, "This is My Beloved Son" (Joseph Smith–History 1:17). Subsequently, he is commanded to "listen to the voice of Jesus Christ, your Lord, your God, and your Redeemer, whose word is quick and powerful" (Doctrine and Covenants 27:1). Reflecting back on the early history of the Latter-day Church, Smith affirmed, "Now, what do we hear in the gospel which we have received? A voice of gladness!—A voice of mercy from heaven; and a voice of truth out of the earth; glad tidings for the dead; a voice of gladness for the living and the dead; glad tidings of great joy" (Doctrine and Covenants 128:19)!

Again, this response from heaven points to the most essential difference in the outlook of Melville, with his noble doubts, and that of Smith, who knew what he had seen of heavenly matters—and who knew that God knew that Smith had seen it (see Joseph Smith–History 1:25).

Melville's fullest exploration of matters of faith is in *Clarel*, discussed earlier. The epilogue to that poem merits some attention in an examination of Herman Melville's religious explorations, especially as defined by juxtaposition with Joseph Smith's. Responding in part to Charles Darwin's *The Origin of Species* (1859), which came out two years after Melville returned from the Holy Land, Melville says:

If Luther's day expand to Darwin's year,
Shall that exclude the hope—foreclose the fear?
     Unmoved by all the claims our times avow,
The ancient Sphinx still keeps the porch of shade;
And comes Despair, whom not her calm may cow,
And coldly on that adamantine brow
Scrawls undeterred his bitter pasquinade.
But Faith (who from the scrawl indignant turns)
With blood warm oozing from her wounded trust,
Inscribes even on her shards of broken urns
The sign o' the cross—*the spirit above the dust!*

> Yea, ape and angel, strife and old debate—
> The harps of heaven and dreary gongs of hell;
> Science the feud can only aggravate—
> No umpire she betwixt the chimes and knell:
> The running battle of the star and clod
> Shall run forever—if there be no God.[86]

Yet with all his questionings, Melville here expresses his belief that there is a God and that

> Even death may prove unreal at the last,
> And stoics be astounded into heaven.
>   Then keep thy heart, though yet but ill-resigned—
> Clarel, thy heart, the issues there but mind;
> That like the crocus budding through the snow—
> That like a swimmer rising from the deep—
> That like a burning secret which doth go
> Even from the bosom that would hoard and keep;
> Emerge thou mayst from the last whelming sea,
> And prove that death but routs life into victory.[87]

Seeking the Ultimate

"I love all men who *dive*," Melville said, and dive he did. "Deep, deep, and still deep and deeper must we go," he writes in *Pierre*, "if we would find out the heart of a man; descending into which is as descending a spiral stair in a shaft, without any end, and where that endlessness is only concealed by the spiralness of the stair, and the blackness of the shaft."[88] Again, speaking in the review of *Mosses*, Melville says, "There is no man in whom humor and love are developed in that high form called genius; no such man can exist without also possessing, as the indispensable complement of these, a great, deep intellect, which drops down into the universe like a plummet."[89] "A seeker, not a finder yet," Melville thought deeply about the divinity of man, marking scriptures on the subject in his Bible. He annotated Jesus' response to the unbelieving Jews, "Is it not written in your law, I said, Ye are gods?" (John 10:34), with the following thought for which he gives no author: "In our idea of man there can be no inconsistency with our idea of God: and if we often feel a certain disagreement with Him and remoteness from Him, it is but the more on that account our duty . . . to seek out every property and beauty, by which our pretension to a similarity with the Divinity may be made good."[90]

Joseph Smith had an absolute conviction of humanity's connection with divinity. Speaking of a potential ultimate ascension, he taught:

We consider that God has created man with a mind capable of instruction, and a faculty which may be enlarged in proportion to the heed and diligence given to the light communicated from heaven to the intellect; and that the nearer man approaches perfection, the clearer are his views, and the greater his enjoyments, till he has overcome the evils of his life and lost every desire for sin; and like the ancients, arrives at that point of faith where he is wrapped in the power and glory of his Maker and is caught up to dwell with Him.[91]

Finally, near the close of his life, this diver, seeker, and finder affirmed in the King Follett discourse his understanding of an upward heavenly movement:

Here, then, is eternal life—to know the only wise and true God; and you have got to learn how to be Gods yourselves, and to be kings and priests to God, the same as all Gods have done before you, namely, by going from one small degree to another, and from a small capacity to a great one; from grace to grace, from exaltation to exaltation, until you attain to the resurrection of the dead, and are able to dwell in everlasting burnings, and to sit in glory, as do those who sit enthroned in everlasting power.[92]

5

The Metaphysical Joseph Smith

Catherine L. Albanese

One of the central interpretive questions surrounding Joseph Smith has been the character and connections of his own religiosity. Was he a latter-day Puritan reexpressing the impulses of the older English reform movement that had succeeded so spectacularly in early America? Or was he an evangelical Christian, essentially, who built on the sectarian Christian choices available in the famed Burnt-over District of upstate New York to reproduce it in new guise? Still again, should he be read, instead, as the founder of a new religious movement? And one more time, might we find some combination of these choices in his religious makeup and persona? These are all interpretive moves that are arguable and make considerable religious sense as we explore the cases that scholars have advanced in support of them. My own way of making religious sense of Joseph Smith, though, moves in a direction that certainly overlaps these views at different intersections but also inserts the Latter-day founder in yet another frame. Taking my cue from Richard Bushman, who once suggested that we should devise a "usable Joseph Smith" as a "protean figure" who could function "for our own purposes," I propose here another way of exploring what Smith means as a religious figure.[1]

In Joseph Smith, I am convinced, we can find an early and clearly identifiable case of the meeting in one person—and a major leader, at that—of the combined strands of belief and practice that came together later as mature metaphysical religion. In short, the

Joseph Smith that has excited me as a historian is a culture broker for American metaphysical religion and, as such, himself a proto-metaphysician.

Here I need to be clear on what constitutes metaphysical religion in an American context. It is easy to cite mid-nineteenth-century and later séance spiritualism, post–Civil War Theosophy, New Thought, and Christian Science, and, by the later twentieth century, the New Age movement and the "new spirituality" of the present. The components of American metaphysical religion, however, may be tracked from a time far earlier—beginning in the European Renaissance with the high culture rediscovery of Hermes Trismegistus and the growth, on the Continent and in England, of esotericism. It can also be tracked in European traditions of folk and country magic and in American colonial versions of the same, but with Native American and African American materials added to the synthesis. By the nineteenth century, an augmented ingredient list would include cultural manifestations as different as Freemasonry, Universalism (the denomination and the theology), and New England Transcendentalism. In this vernacular mix of actors and acts (of thought, of practice), the commonalities that were shared across culture—from elites to everybody's people—were more important than the differences.

Still more, in the midst of the combinativeness, a series of identity markers could be found. Metaphysical forms of religion have privileged the mind in forms that include reason but move beyond it to intuition, clairvoyance, and relatives such as revelation and higher guidance. These mind forms of religion operate on the conviction that there is a correspondence between our present world (let us call it simply the "microcosm") and a larger reality that it replicates (the "macrocosm"). In this vision of "as above, so below," metaphysicians find a stream of energy flowing from above to below—an influx so powerful and constitutive of their reality that they discover themselves to be, in some sense, made of the same "stuff." If there are differences in this energy, they are of degree and not of kind. The influx of energy (let us now call it "divine") that enlivens their world is a healing salve for the world's ills and—in the strongest statement of their view—renders them divine and limitless. Metaphysical practice is premised on these beliefs about correspondence, resemblance, and connection. Action on one microcosmic site or piece of the world affects the larger reality. Ritual, thus, involves enacted metaphors. To say this another way, metaphysical practice is about magic. If the magic is material magic, it involves symbolic behavior using artifacts and ritual accoutrements—what is called ritual, or ceremonial, magic. If the magic is mental, it signals active use of the imagination and the powers of mind, as in forms of "mind cure."[2]

In this context, Joseph Smith and the early Mormonism that he promoted show us—more clearly than any other movement I am aware of at the time—a

sample repertoire out of which American metaphysical religion was constituted. In the mind and cultural practice of Smith, we have a dazzling display
of the ingredients and the selective combinativeness that would, in fact, be
preeminent features of a mature American metaphysical religion. From this
perspective, literary and cultural critic Harold Bloom was decidedly close to tar-
get when he pointed to the Mormonism of Smith's early production as a proto-
type for an American religion with "Gnostic, Enthusiast, and Orphic" qualities.
For Bloom, what held its principles together was the "American persuasion,
however muted or obscured, that we are mortal gods, destined to find ourselves
again in worlds as yet undiscovered."[3] He could have added, destined to find
ourselves by combining the pieces of many cultural products in a new and distinctly American synthesis.

What were the pieces as they coalesced in the life and practice of Smith and
in the emerging religious formation that he shaped? In his remarkable combination, Smith brought together a series of spiritual movements and cultural
worlds. From his youth he was fascinated by Freemasonry, and he joined a lodge
himself in 1842. He was, thus, clearly familiar with the Masonic elaboration
of biblical themes and so with the story of Enoch's hidden plates of gold and
their found-and-lost-again history in the age of the Old Testament's Solomon.
He likewise knew something of the mystical revelations of the then-celebrated
Swedish author and visionary Emanuel Swedenborg (1688–1772), who, in
Smith's nineteenth-century upstate New York environment, had become something of a Hermetic household magus. But Smith was also a cunning man in
the English country magic tradition and, in a new-country counterpart, a lover
of Indian lore. In the midst of all of this, too, he anguished as a religious seeker
struggling with the discordant messages of Christian evangelical preachers
around the era's revival fires.

Smith's exposure to Freemasonry had begun with his family's familiarity
with it from the 1790s in Vermont, where his parents then lived. Later, in New
York, Joseph Smith Sr. may have joined a lodge, and his second son, Hyrum,
surely joined one in Palmyra, where the family lived, in the 1820s. There is
evidence, as well, that the family was familiar with Masonic symbols, and—in
the time and place in which they lived—Freemasonic writings were readily
available. Moreover, although Smith early condemned secret societies and the
Book of Mormon has occasioned commentary for its anti-Masonic themes, he
was also clearly fascinated by religious secrecy, Masonic or otherwise. When
he "rose to the sublime degree" (his words) at the Nauvoo Masonic Lodge that
Mormons had begun, he gained access to the secret initiations that, in part,
helped him to shape Mormon temple ceremonies in the tradition of what was
known as Royal Arch Masonry. John Brooke, in our time, has noticed and

detailed the connections, but Brooke had plenty of earlier-twentieth-century company for the associations that he made—from S. H. Goodwin in 1924 to the tell-all Tanners (Jerald and Sandra) by at least 1964.[4]

To connect the dots between Smith and Freemasonry is well enough. But the task of historical recovery involves a deeper archaeology. In the vaults of Smith's memory and attachment were links that, as Brooke has argued, identify the Mormon founder with a broad Hermeticism that he and many who joined him inherited vernacularly. So far as the historical record can reconstruct, no early-nineteenth-century schoolmaster ever handed Smith a copy of the *Corpus Hermeticum*. But as Brooke summarized, "Smith arrived at an approximation of many of its fundamental points by a process of reassembling scattered doctrines available in dissenting and hermetic sources."[5] He fused them and extended them, even as the print culture of upstate New York helped to advance his reassembly and fusion. There, text disclosures of Freemasonic secrets fanned out into a world of other and further disclosures. Read from a metaphysical perspective, perhaps none were so significant for the Hermetic underlay of early Mormon theology as the teachings of Emanuel Swedenborg. With his doctrines of divine influx, of God as the "Divine Human" with its hints of the Father Mother God of Hermeticism, of heaven as a material place with elaborate mansions and well-appointed tables and flower gardens, and of the "conjugial love" between heavenly soulmates with their etherealized sex, the mysticizing Swede was known to many Americans. Swedenborg's notions of spirit calling and angelic communication and of heaven as a progressive place were also part of his good news, along with a gradation of three heavenly realms and reports of cryptic heavenly writing. Accounts of Swedenborg appeared in public newspapers, as at Canandaigua, New York, in 1808, and were also available in Palmyra's public library. It is not too surprising, then, that Swedenborg's theology—with the nuanced inflections and adjustments that Smith would make—was echoed in some of the major tenets of Mormon theology.

Swedenborg's anti-Trinitarianism was replaced by a tritheism in which the Father, Son, and Spirit were, and are, distinct and separate. His cryptic heavenly writing—with its echoes of hieroglyphics, secrets, Kabbalism, and Hermetic lore—found its transformation in the "reformed Egyptian" text that Smith's golden plates announced. Swedenborg's careful correspondences were refracted in a new light in which heaven was, indeed, an earthlike place and earth itself shone with the borrowed light of the heavenly world. Spirit was a form of matter in Joseph Smith's world, and the heavenly realm was inhabited by a God similar to Swedenborg's Divine Human and to the Hermetic vision in general. God, for Smith—as late as 1844—was a "man" like Mormon believers. Smith's revelation of the eternity of marriage (echoing Swedenborg's "conjugial love") affirmed a future state of glory in which those bonded for all eternity would be "Gods" with "all power" and angels "subject unto them." Meanwhile, the Mormon cosmos in which the departed found themselves existed as three worlds with differing degrees of glory. Smith's "telestial, "terrestrial," and "celestial" heavens to a certain extent recalled the Swedish seer's earlier "natural," "spiritual," and "celestial" versions.[6]

At the same time, Smith had grown up in a family with a long tradition of magical belief and practice. Vermont was what D. Michael Quinn has called a "treasure-digging mecca" when Joseph Smith Sr. lived there. In the western New York to which he eventually relocated, he found a congenial environment for magical practice, as Palmyra's local newspaper in the 1820s revealed. Even some clergy apparently carried dowsing rods, and Christianity blended seamlessly into the magic of the folk. Seer stones, astrological charts, talismans, magical daggers—all were part of the cultural milieu and used in the context of securing protection and conjuring spirits. Against this backdrop, there were, indeed, sophisticated magical artifacts in the Smith family, and it was clear that the family practiced ritual magic.[7] Joseph Smith Jr. himself was, by any standard, a cunning man, but what was new was the rapidly urbanizing and industrializing environment in which he found himself, with the Erie Canal running through one end of Palmyra. As the economy of exchange boomed in commercial venues, so it did in goods of the spirit. Given the readily available books, newspapers, and people with metaphysical knowledge, a would-be magus in Palmyra could quickly absorb a varied portfolio in the magical trade.

By the time the Book of Mormon appeared, Smith had already acquired a reputation as a local money digger and treasure hunter, employing the familiar divinatory techniques of English country magic. He used a stone to "see" what needed revealing in order to accomplish his work, and he was sought out for his seer's skill. At one time, in fact, he was part of a company of money diggers who traveled around to various places in New York and Pennsylvania seeking old Spanish and Indian treasure. When he got into trouble with the law and was tried in 1826 as a "disorderly person," he walked away as a first-time offender. But what is especially interesting about his case is how much it reveals about his magical practice, its connection with old lore about the simultaneous obstinacy and slipperiness of buried treasure, and its level and degree of magical sophistication. Michael Quinn's argument for the "apparent magical context" for Smith's earlier First Vision in 1820 suggests that the heavenly pronouncement regarding all of the sects being wrong may be construed as an endorsement for magical practice as a replacement. This line of inquiry points in a way, too, to the spiritual territory that Jan Shipps trod in her well-known reconstruction of the discovery and translation of the Book of Mormon.[8] The puzzle of the prophet could be solved with convincing ease if one followed Smith in an elision of material and spiritual treasure. One should dig for gold, yes, but—as a New World alchemist of the spirit—one should dig for gold as the philosopher's stone of a new religiosity. Here folk magic could blend with a vernacularized Hermeticism in a new and combinative version that moved beyond itself even as it was being created, laying a path for the infusion of Hebraic and Christian strands and also much more.

The Book of Mormon, which Smith testified he had unearthed and translated (with the help of biblically inflected seer stones, the Urim and Thummim), claimed to reveal the true beginnings and history of the Indian peoples who first dwelled on this and the South American continents. Three times in 1823, a "spirit" had come to Smith with the message that a record of ancient Indian history was contained in the golden plates. Such an announcement was congruent with what Dan Vogel has called the "persistent legend of a lost Indian book" abroad in the region during the early national period. When Smith was digging for Indian treasure, Indian mounds were often the sites of his labor. Nor did he and his friends have a hard time finding locations. Both the New England that Smith's father left and the New York State in which Smith himself lived during this period of his life possessed landscapes dotted with mounds and memorials of Indian provenance.[9] Americans of Smith's time and earlier had speculated, as well, on Indian origins. Were the indigenous inhabitants pre-Adamites and thereby outside a biblical framework? Were they, instead, among the descendants of Noah? More explicitly, were the American native peoples of Hebrew descent and perhaps from the lost tribes of Israel? Alternatively, were the mound builders really Indians, or did their massive and marvelous constructions suggest (in an unconscious racism) that they were of a race different from the natives encountered by Europeans in the Americas of the sixteenth and seventeenth centuries? Questions such as these about the Indians spilled over into print in vernacular media like popular books and newspapers, and descriptions of the mounds were readily available to readers in various places, including the area in which Smith was raised.

Thus, Smith and the Book of Mormon were preoccupied with the memories encrypted into the land—in its earthworks and unearthed arrowheads, in its unanswered questions and untold histories. In fact, the very title page of the Book of Mormon announced its intention "to show unto the remnant of the House of Israel what great things the Lord had done for their fathers." But there was more. The Book of Mormon had been delivered on golden plates, and its content connected the mounds to the use of metal, so that, as Vogel wrote, the "Book of Mormon's righteous Jaredites and Nephites" were presented as "advanced metallurgists." From whence did this high metallurgical ascription come? If we look to the historical and archaeological record, metallurgy was not the particular forte of mound builders.[10] And so, we must come full circle: In the received esotericism of Europe, things were different. Freemasonry's biblical Enoch had found a triangular plate of gold, and the Hermetic tradition had produced its hieroglyphics, even as the (biblical) Urim and Thummim and the ubiquitous peep stones of the cunning men and women would enable the cunning to read them.

Beyond its sheer combinativeness and prodigious religious creativity, what was so interesting about the metaphysical synthesis that Smith achieved was its corporate quality. Perhaps taking a cue from the Freemasonic lodges and brotherhoods and certainly from the models of Christian community and organization at the time, Smith's religion, which had begun as a family affair and had speedily become a family-and-friends affair, grew into a distinctly communal production. In fact, the formidable communalism of early Mormons played into the fear and hatred they generated wherever they settled. More important here, as the institutional cement for communalism was developed by Smith in his elaborate organization building, it became clear that Mormon metaphysics was not something that one did alone. The mysticism of Hermetic solitudes had given way to a larger context of corporate ritual practice in secret temple ceremonies. Mormons did metaphysical religion in community. Their production, thus, pointed toward a series of metaphysical groups, societies, and denominations that would emerge as the nineteenth century progressed. From this perspective, the usable Joseph Smith was a religious leader of extraordinary ability who charted an early path of spiritual combinativeness, embedded it in cultural practice with a seamless fusion of its theological components and practical acts, and situated it in community. Later metaphysical religion owes a mostly unacknowledged debt to Joseph Smith, and it is time for historians to take account of the debt. The acknowledgment is especially important because a full account of the major forms of religion that have characterized the American experience cannot stop at mainstream denominationalism and evangelicalism but must also include the metaphysical forms of spirituality that have pervaded our national life into the present. In that context, Joseph Smith becomes a spiritual harbinger of a distinctively American future.

6

Joseph Smith vs. John C. Calhoun: The States' Rights Dilemma and Early Mormon History

James B. Allen

On November 24, 1832, a special South Carolina convention did what U.S. President Andrew Jackson thought was unthinkable: it declared two federal tariff laws unconstitutional and forbade the collection of the tariff within the state. In attendance at the convention was the vice president of the United States, South Carolina's own John C. Calhoun. Jackson was horrified and declared the state's action both unconstitutional and treasonous. For his part, Calhoun quickly resigned the vice presidency and accepted an appointment to the United States Senate. In his view, the state had every right to do what it did, for the Constitution was only a compact between sovereign states, each of which could determine the validity of federal laws within its own borders and, as a last resort, even withdraw from the Union if its rights were violated.

In Kirtland, Ohio, meanwhile, the Mormon prophet Joseph Smith looked with dismay at what was happening, for he agreed with President Jackson that nullification smacked of treason. He even said that South Carolina had declared itself "a free and independent nation," and prophesied that this "rebellion" would lead to civil war.[1]

The issue here was states' rights, the most divisive constitutional issue in pre–Civil War America. This essay briefly examines that issue from the differing perspectives of John C. Calhoun (1792–1850), Southern statesman, national political leader, and chief architect of the philosophy that eventually led the Southern states to secede from the Union, and of Joseph Smith (1805–1844), founder and leader of The Church of Jesus Christ of Latter-day Saints (commonly called the LDS or Mormon Church).[2] It also provides an insight into the way early Mormon history was profoundly affected by the states' rights controversy.

John C. Calhoun and Joseph Smith had widely different backgrounds. Calhoun was highly educated, having graduated from Yale University and been elected to Phi Beta Kappa, while Joseph, as his followers affectionately called him, had no more than a rudimentary education. Calhoun was a slaveholding plantation owner who believed that agriculture was the chief basis for a noble society. Joseph Smith grew up as a farm boy, but was never involved in large-scale farming and did not own slaves. Calhoun began his political career as a nationalist, avidly supporting expansion of the power of the federal government so that it could build roads and canals to help bind the Union together, but he ended up as a sectionalist who would have severely limited federal power. Joseph was always a nationalist in sentiment. Calhoun considered blacks inferior and held that slavery was not only an economic necessity but also a positive good, both for the slaves and the slave owners. Joseph's early attitude toward blacks is unclear but in 1836 he ordained at least one black convert (Elijah Abel) to the priesthood, and before the end of his life he openly advocated freedom for the slaves. John C. Calhoun was well known throughout the nation and is still an important figure in the history books, but his constitutional philosophy is no longer taken seriously as a viable option. Joseph Smith, on the other hand, was not well known by the general public of his time, though today his name appears in most textbooks covering that period and his religious teachings are adhered to by millions around the world. The two men met personally only once, in Washington, D.C., early in February 1840. They also had an exchange of correspondence in late 1843 and early 1844. In both instances, states' rights was at the heart of their disagreement.

The states' rights issue appeared almost immediately after the Constitution went into effect. Its framers had left several things ambiguous, including the nature of American federalism, or "divided sovereignty," which gave some powers to the national government and reserved others to the states. But what kind of union did they really create? Was it permanent and indivisible, or was the Constitution simply a compact, or contract, between still-sovereign states? If the latter, could a state nullify within its borders a federal law that it deemed unconstitutional or, as a last resort, even leave the Union? Could sovereignty really be divided between national and state governments, as the founding fathers thought? Could the federal government reach within the borders of a sovereign state in order to put down internal unrest?

James Madison, "Father of the Constitution," was one of the first to agitate on the states' rights question. In 1798, he coauthored, with Thomas Jefferson, the controversial Virginia and Kentucky Resolutions, asserting that the states themselves had the right to determine the constitutionality of acts of Congress. The question reappeared in December 1814, when a group of New Englanders, dissatisfied with the War of 1812 and chosen by their state legislatures to do something about it, met in convention in Hartford, Connecticut. There they passed a series of resolutions calling for various constitutional amendments and clearly hinting at the possibility of secession from the Union if their concerns were ignored. John C. Calhoun, then a member of Congress, faced a cruel dilemma: he loved the Union and feared that such internal divisiveness during a war would only destroy it, but he also held strong states' rights convictions and believed that, in fact, any state could do just what the Hartford Convention had suggested. Nothing came of the convention, however, for the war was soon over.

As time went on, the states' rights controversy was fueled by a rising opposition to slavery. In 1820, in order to maintain a balance of free and slave states in the Union, Congress agreed to the Missouri Compromise, which admitted Missouri as a slave state and Maine as a free state. Equally significant, the compromise also excluded slavery from all of the Louisiana Territory north of 36°30′ N, and protected slavery in the territory south of that line. Calhoun, then a member of the president's cabinet, supported the compromise as expedient and constitutional. He changed his stance a few years later, however, arguing that the Constitution gave Congress no authority to prohibit slavery in the territories because slaves were property and Congress could not deprive people of their property without due process of law. Thomas Jefferson, meanwhile, was horrified. Fearing for the Union itself, he wrote prophetically to a friend that "this momentous question [slavery], like a firebell in the night, awakened and filled me with terror. I considered it at once as the knell of the Union."[3]

Calhoun's change of heart was a reflection of his concern not only for perpetuating slavery but also for preserving Southern economy, the Southern way of life, and Southern political unity. It seemed to him that Northern attacks on slavery were also attacks on the Southern economy, and that the only way to defend the South was to mount a more avid defense of slavery and of the rights of the states to maintain their own domestic institutions. This was also the way to preserve the Union, for if the ability of the states to control their own internal affairs was compromised, the Southern states would have no choice but to secede.

Another point of conflict was America's tariff policy. When he saw tariffs becoming so high that they were detrimental to Southern commerce, Calhoun questioned both their propriety and their constitutionality. In 1828, therefore, in response to the outrageously high "Tariff of Abominations," Calhoun, who was then vice president, secretly penned South Carolina's famous "Exposition and Protest."[4] Here he spelled out the "compact theory" of the Constitution—a theory that would infuriate Northern nationalists. If Congress should pass an unconstitutional law, he reasoned, then the states, being sovereign, had the right "to interpose to protect their reserved powers." If a state convention declared a law unconstitutional, Congress could either repeal that law or propose an amendment specifically giving it the power in question. If three-fourths of the states ratified the amendment so that it became part of the Constitution, then the nullifying state could either accept that decision or exercise its sovereignty and secede. Sovereignty was not divisible, and even though the states had delegated some of their functions to the federal government, they had not delegated their sovereignty. The states, therefore, were the final authority in interpreting the Constitution.

Andrew Jackson was elected president in 1828, with Calhoun as vice president, but there was little cordiality between the two. The rift became publicly obvious during the annual Jefferson Day dinner in 1830, where many of the toasts being offered glorified states' rights. Jackson was appalled, for even though he believed in states' rights, he also thought there was a limit. When he offered his toast, therefore, he stood and proclaimed as firmly as he knew how, "Our Federal Union. It must be preserved," with emphasis on the word *federal*. Calhoun was visibly shaken, but he quickly offered the next toast: "The Union—next to our liberty the most dear." He thus served notice that, to him, states' rights was even more important than the Union itself.[5]

Just a year later Joseph Smith sent some of his followers to settle in Jackson County, Missouri (where Independence was founded in 1827), and before long non-slaveholding Mormons were migrating in significant numbers to this slave-holding state. Since this was just at a time when the states' rights question, with its pro-slavery overtones, was becoming ever more divisive as a national issue, the move did not bode well for Mormon success.

In 1832 the states' rights controversy nearly resulted in civil war after South Carolina declared the tariff acts of 1828 and 1832 unconstitutional and forbade the collection of the tariff within the state after February 1, 1833. Outraged, Andrew Jackson minced no words in telling the people of South Carolina that their ordinance violated the Constitution and could destroy the Union. The compact theory, he said, was fallacious; disunion was treason; and if it persisted in its course, the state of South Carolina would be in rebellion. He then reinforced the federal fort in Charleston (where the first shots of the Civil War would be fired nearly thirty years later), and Congress passed a "Force Bill" authorizing him to use the military if necessary to enforce the tariff.

As Joseph Smith watched what was happening, he could hardly ignore the implications of nullification and the possibility of civil war. South Carolina, he said, had declared itself "a free and independent nation," which was not the way South Carolina put it but reflected the obvious potential. He also noticed that President Jackson had issued a proclamation "against this rebellion."[6] It was in this context that, on Christmas Day 1832, the Mormon prophet received a "revelation and prophecy on war." "Verily, thus saith the Lord concerning the wars that will shortly come to pass," it read, "beginning at the rebellion in South Carolina" (Doctrine and Covenants 87:1). Clearly, the rebellion referred to was the one Joseph Smith believed had already occurred. The revelation did not say that civil war would take place immediately, but it accurately foretold much of what would happen thirty years later.

Civil war was, of course, very predictable, for it was among the worst fears of most American statesmen, including Calhoun, who were concerned with the perpetuation of the Union. The immediate threat ended in 1833, after Congress passed a compromise tariff and South Carolina repealed its ordinance of nullification. Civil war was at least temporarily averted, but what Thomas Jefferson called a "firebell in the night" in 1820 had rung once again and would not be completely stilled.

Meanwhile, the Mormon people were facing their own problems in Missouri as the old settlers of Jackson County were determined to drive them out. The excuses were religious, economic, and political, but one of the most disturbing was the blatantly false accusation that the Mormons were attempting to encourage slave runaways and foment slave rebellions. As a result, organized mobs pillaged Mormon property, beat many Mormons, tarred and feathered others, destroyed the church's press, and eventually forced all of them from the county.

The Missouri Mormons attempted to use every legal means to regain their lands, including working with the courts and sending an appeal to President Jackson. They also petitioned Missouri's Governor Daniel Dunklin for help. The governor was disposed to help but, despite his good intentions, it was politically impossible because the bitterness in Jackson County was too intense. The Missouri Mormons had to begin again, this time in counties north of Jackson County.

Joseph Smith watched all this with mounting concern from his home in Kirtland, Ohio. Did not the Constitution afford his people some protection, he wondered as he heard tale after tale of their suffering. On December 16, 1833, he received a revelation that addressed itself directly to the problems in Missouri and gave the scattered Saints fresh hope that the Constitution would protect them. They were told to continue their appeals, for the Lord himself had established the Constitution to protect all people, including the Latter-day Saints, in their rights:

And again I say unto you, those who have been scattered by their enemies, it is my will that they should continue to importune for redress, and redemption, by the hands of those who are placed as rulers and are in authority over you—

According to the laws and constitution of this people, which I have suffered to be established, and should be maintained for the rights and protection of all flesh, according to just and holy principles.

That every man may act in doctrine and principles pertaining to futurity, according to the moral agency which I have given unto him, that every man may be accountable for his own sins in the day of judgement.

Therefore it is not right that any man should be in bondage one to another.

And for this purpose have I established the Constitution of this land, by the hands of wise men whom I raised up unto this very purpose. (Doctrine and Covenants 101:76–80)

Then, after giving a parable in which a widow who had been wronged received help from a judge only after she had wearied him through her continuous petitioning, the revelation instructed the Saints to continue their own petitioning to their judges and political authorities:

Thus I will liken the children of Zion.

Let them importune at the feet of the judge;

And if he heed them not, let them importune at the feet of the governor;

And if the governor heed them not, let them importune at the feet of the president;

And if the president heed them not, then will the Lord arise and come forth out of his hiding place, and in his fury vex the nation. (Doctrine and Covenants 101:85–89)

The Missouri Saints did just as they were told. On April 10, 1834, a second petition was sent to President Jackson, along with a reminder that even though Missouri's governor seemed willing to enforce the laws, he did not have enough power to do so. For that reason, the federal government should use its own constitutional authority to call out the militia and protect them.

As the Federal Constitution has given to Congress the power to provide for calling for the militia to execute the laws of the Union, suppress insurrections, or repel invasions; and for these Purposes the president of the United States is authorized to make the call upon the executive of the respective states; therefore, we your petitioners, in behalf of our society, which is so scattered and suffering, most humbly pray that we may be restored to our lands, houses, and property in Jackson county, and protected in them by an armed force, till peace be restored.[7]

A copy of the petition was sent to Governor Dunklin, along with a letter requesting him to write the president of the United States and ask for assistance.

The Missouri Saints thus made their appeal to both the president and the governor on constitutional grounds, but they were on shaky ground so far as their interpretation of the Constitution was concerned. Article I, Section 8, grants Congress the power to "provide for calling forth the militia to execute the laws of the Union, suppress insurrections and repel invasions." (The term *militia* had reference to state militias.) The president, according to Article II, Section 2, is commander in chief of the national military "and of the Militia of the several States, when called into the actual Service of the United States." Article IV, Section 4, says that the United States shall protect each state against invasion and, on application of the legislature or, if the legislature cannot be convened, on the application of the executive, against domestic violence. The term *insurrection*, however, meant rebellion against the government (federal or state), and *invasion* referred to the incursion of some outside military force. Federal intervention for any other purpose, such as putting down "domestic violence," could come only if requested by the legislature or the chief executive of the state. Nowhere did the Constitution give the president specific authority to "call upon the executive" of the state, but the distraught Missouri Mormons may have rationalized that the Jackson County mobs were, in fact, involved in insurrection because they were violating state law and the governor seemed unable to do anything about it.

President Jackson referred the Mormon petition to Lewis Cass, his Secretary of War. On May 2, 1834, Cass replied in a way that disappointed the Saints but should have been predictable.

I am instructed to inform you, that the offenses of which you complain, are violations of the laws of the state of Missouri, and not of the laws of the United States. The powers of the President under the constitution and laws, to direct the employment of a military force, in cases where the ordinary civil authority is found insufficient, extend only to proceedings under the laws of the United States.[8]

This was a clear statement of how the Constitution stood at the time. There was no constitutional authority for the federal government to intervene, for no federal laws were being violated. Governor Dunklin, still believing that it was a matter that must be handled internally, thus refused to write the president in support of the Mormon petition.[9]

Later in the year, acting on the governor's promise to provide state militia to help regain the lands of his Missouri brethren, Joseph Smith led an armed group of five hundred men, known in Mormon history as Zion's Camp, from Ohio to Missouri. By the time they got there, however, the governor had recognized the political impossibility of helping the Mormons militarily, and Zion's Camp had to be disbanded.[10] The Mormons would never recover their Jackson County property.

Joseph Smith had ample reason for dismay at the doctrine of states' rights but, ironically, on at least one occasion he gave it a condescending nod. In 1836 the older settlers of Clay County, Missouri, rejected the Mormons who had fled north from Jackson County but who, the Clay Countians had thought, would remain only temporarily. The complaints that piled up against the Saints almost duplicated those in Jackson County, including the charge that they were opposed to slavery. Joseph Smith, still living in Kirtland, felt compelled to make some kind of statement that would calm Missouri fears. The visit of an abolitionist to Kirtland gave him the perfect opportunity.

There was considerable antislavery sentiment in America long before this, but the extremist movement known specifically as abolitionism began about 1831. Abolitionists not only advocated direct federal intervention and the immediate, uncompensated elimination of slavery but also suggested the possible use of violence. In the April 1836 issue of the *Messenger and Advocate* the prophet not only denounced abolitionism but also went on to other points, obviously hoping to change the public image of the Mormons in the South. If slavery were really an evil, he said, perhaps unrealistically, would not the God-fearing "men of piety" in the slave states be the first to recognize it? Until they called for assistance, "why not cease the clamor, and no further urge the slave to acts of murder, and the master to vigorous discipline, rendering both miserable?" He then declared, "I do not believe that the people of the North have any more right to say that the South *shall not* hold slaves, than the South have to say the North shall." Signing abolitionist petitions was "a declaration of hostilities against the people of the South. What course can sooner divide our union?" John C. Calhoun would have applauded, for that is exactly what he was preaching. Joseph then proceeded with an argument in defense of slavery, not as a positive good in the sense that Calhoun believed, but simply as an institution supported by biblical precedent. He concluded with a word to missionaries, telling them that they had no right to interfere with slaves "contrary to the mind and will of their masters," and suggesting that they not even preach to slaves "until after their masters are converted, and then teach the masters to use them with kindness; remembering that they are accountable to God."[11] Those who may be surprised at Joseph Smith's apparent defense of slavery should remember that he did not claim divine sanction for his statement. Rather, it was a political statement intended to assure the people of the South that the Mormons were no threat to them.

Tragically, the prophet's hopes did not work out, and in the early months of 1839 the Saints were brutally expelled from the state. Meanwhile, Joseph himself languished in a filthy dungeon in Liberty, Missouri. He did not lose hope in the Constitution, however, which he extolled in a letter completed on March 25, 1839, as a "glorious standard" and a "heavenly banner."[12] Already he was planning a new propaganda assault on the nation's capital, although in this crusade the emphasis was on obtaining financial remuneration from Congress rather than military intervention.

Joseph Smith escaped from his captors in April 1839, helped select a new gathering place for the Saints at what became known as Nauvoo, Illinois, and prepared himself to lead the first delegation of Mormons to lay their case before the federal government in person. By the end of October he was on his way to Washington, where he would meet Martin Van Buren, John C. Calhoun, and other national leaders and be confronted more directly than ever before with all the implications of the doctrine of states' rights.

In preparation for the visit to Washington, the prophet asked his people to prepare statements and affidavits detailing their Missouri suffering and to gather up all the libelous publications that were afloat so they could "present the whole concatenation of diabolical rascality, and nefarious and murderous impositions that have been practiced upon this people, . . . to the heads of government in all their dark and hellish hue, as the last effort which is enjoined on us by our Heavenly Father."[13] As a result, beginning in December 1839, hundreds of affidavits were sworn out before justices of the peace, circuit court clerks, and notaries public in Iowa and Illinois. These would constitute the Saints' ammunition as they kept up an almost continuous appeal to the federal government between 1839 and 1844.

On November 28, 1839, the prophet and Elias Higbee arrived in Washington, carrying with them a long petition to Congress that recounted in great detail the Missouri abuses and concluded with a plea for redress, based on the constitutional guarantees to life, liberty, property, and religious freedom. The next day they obtained an interview with President Van Buren and presented him with letters of introduction. As soon as he finished reading one of them the president looked at the two men with "half a frown." "What can I do?" he asked. "I can do nothing for you! If I do anything, I shall come in contact with the whole state of Missouri!"[14] No doubt they expected such a response but they stood firm, and before they left, the president expressed his sympathy for the Saints and promised to reconsider his position.

Joseph then circulated in the halls of Congress, buttonholing senators and members of the House of Representatives in an effort to gain their support. He spent the last part of December and most of January in Philadelphia, but in February he was back in Washington, where he had another meeting with the president and where, for the first and only time, he met Senator John C. Calhoun.

President Van Buren had promised to reconsider his earlier position, but this time, according to Joseph, he treated the Mormon leader "very insolently" and listened to his arguments only with reluctance. "Gentlemen, your cause is just, but I can do nothing for you," he finally said. "If I take up for you I shall lose the vote of Missouri."[15]

As reported by Joseph Smith, Van Buren appeared to be worried primarily about the political fallout if he helped the Mormons, but there was more to it than that. The president was a devout, longtime states' rights advocate[16] and this, together with the fact that practically everyone in Washington told Joseph that the Mormon case did not come within the purview of the federal government, leaves little doubt that states' rights was a contributing factor to Van Buren's refusal to help. If he supported the Mormons he would be inconsistent with his own long-held views. Even providing financial aid may have been considered by some as a constitutional violation, for that would mean that the federal govern-ment had taken official cognizance of, and tried to find a solution for, a matter that everyone believed must be left up to the state.

Joseph was not only disappointed by the president's attitude, but also angered. From then on he harbored nothing but negative feelings toward Van Buren, accusing him of being little more than an office seeker and declaring that "justice and righteousness were no part of his composition." Clearly, he could not conscientiously support Van Buren, who was up for reelection that year, as the "head of our noble Republic."[17] Smith recorded in his history of the church, "On my way home I did not fail to proclaim the iniquity and in-solence of Martin Van Buren, toward myself and an injured people; . . . and may he never be elected again to any office of trust or power, by which he may abuse the innocent and let the guilty go free."[18]

The Mormon leader had a similar experience when he met Senator John C. Calhoun, though, in a way, the setting was more dramatic: Here were two fiercely determined men, each of whom saw himself in what amounted to a life-and-death struggle for his own particular view of the Constitution. Cal-houn's states' rights doctrine had become so much a part of his psyche that he simply could not listen to any other point of view. Joseph Smith's view had solidified because of his experience with Missouri lawbreakers. In his mind, if a state could not, or would not, protect the rights of the people, then the federal government must step in. In addition, since Calhoun's compact theory allowed both nullification and the possibility of secession, the nationalist in Joseph Smith could have no part of it. We do not know all that was said when these two met, except that Calhoun made it clear that, in his view, the Mormon case was not within the jurisdiction of the federal government. However he put it, Joseph Smith went away saying that his "conduct toward me very ill became his station."[19]

Meanwhile, Latter-day Saints representative Elias Higbee obtained a hearing before the Senate Judiciary Committee, but the unanimous committee report expressed the same sentiment as Calhoun's. The only appropriate place to seek relief was in the courts of Missouri or of the United States. In April, a general conference of the Mormon Church adopted a resolution saying that this report was "unconstitutional, and subversive to the rights of a free people."[20]

Joseph Smith's trip to Washington made him realize more fully than ever that his view on how far the federal government could go had little national support. He soon began to recognize openly that perhaps there was a problem with the Constitution itself, for it did not go far enough, though the remedy he proposed on one occasion seems a bit extreme. "I am the greatest advocate of the Constitution of the United States there is on the earth," he said in a Sunday sermon on October 15, 1843.

> The only fault I find with the Constitution is, it is not broad enough to cover the whole ground.
>
> Although it provides that all men shall enjoy religious freedom, yet it does not provide the manner by which that freedom can be preserved, nor for the punishment of Government officers who refuse to protect the people in their religious rights. . . . Its sentiments are good, but it provides no means of enforcing them. It has but this one fault. . . .
>
> The Constitution should contain a provision that every officer of the Government who should neglect or refuse to extend the protection guaranteed in the Constitution should be subject to capital punishment; and then the president of the United States would not say, "*Your cause is just, but I can do nothing for you.*"[21]

Still the Latter-day Saints did not give up in their quest for immediate help, hopeless as it may have seemed. In 1842 a second delegation went to Washington armed with affidavits and petitions. On November 29, 1843, several Nauvoo citizens held a meeting in the upper room of Joseph Smith's store and approved sending still another appeal to Congress. After the memorial was read aloud, Joseph uttered his strongest condemnation yet of John C. Calhoun's favorite dogma. "The State rights doctrines are what feed mobs," Smith asserted. "They are a dead carcass—a stink, and they shall ascend up as a stink offering in the nose of the Almighty."[22]

Despite his failures, Joseph Smith had one more card to play: he would run for the office of president of the United States. Practically unknown in American political affairs, with no real chance to win, the Mormon prophet nevertheless was at the point where he had no confidence in the willingness or the ability of any national political leader to pay attention to his most urgent concern: the protection of his people in their constitutional rights.

Before making his decision to throw himself on the national political stage, however, Joseph wrote to each of the five leading potential candidates: Martin Van Buren, John C. Calhoun, Henry Clay, Lewis Cass, and Richard M. Johnson, reminding them that the Latter-day Saints "now constitute a numerous class in the school politic of this vast republic" and asking, "'What will be your rule of action relative to us as a people,' should fortune favor your ascendancy to the chief magistracy?"[23] He received replies from Cass, Clay, and Calhoun. Cass denied that he would even seek the presidency but also said that he did not see what power the president of the United States had over the matter.[24] Clay simply refused to make any commitment on the question. Calhoun responded that he would try to administer the government according to the Constitution and laws of the country and would make no distinction between citizens of different religious creeds. He added, however, "candor compels me to repeat what I said to you at Washington, that, according to my views, the case does not come within the jurisdiction of the Federal Government, which is one of limited and specific powers."[25]

To Joseph Smith, Calhoun's statement was a challenge he could not ignore. On January 2, 1844, therefore, with the assistance of William W. Phelps and in what must have been one of the most indignant political statements of his lifetime, he replied to the South Carolina senator with all the political passion he and Phelps could muster. In the process he spelled out his constitutional perspective more clearly than ever before. His philosophy was not nearly as organized or well stated as that of Calhoun but a few important points stand out.[26]

Despite the fact the he had earlier recognized the weakness in the Constitution, in this letter Joseph Smith reverted to the view that the Constitution already gave the government the power it needed to intervene in the states. He asked how someone in public life could take such a fragile view of a case "fraught with so much consequence to the happiness of men in this world or the world to come." He complained that Calhoun's position really meant that a state could expel any of its citizens with impunity and the government could do nothing for them. "Go on, then, Missouri," he said in bitter sarcasm, let another set of inhabitants come into the state, then banish them, kill them, take their property, and let the legislature appropriate their goods to pay the mobs for their work. "For the renowned Senator from South Carolina, Mr. J. C. Calhoun, says the powers of the Federal Government are so *specific and limited that it has no jurisdiction of the case!*" He continued at length in the same sharp tone but finally, at the end, came to his own constitutional assumptions. Congress, he said, "has power to protect the nation against foreign invasion and internal broil," and whenever it passes an act to "maintain right with any power, or to restore right to any portion of her citizens, it is the *supreme law of the land.*" This assertion was based on Article VI of the Constitution, which states that "this Constitution, and the Laws of the United States which shall be made in Pursuance thereof . . . shall be the supreme Law of the Land." Joseph believed that this gave Congress the power to pass laws that would restore property wrongly taken from citizens and that if a state refused submission to such a law it was guilty of insurrection or rebellion. Further, he said in a reference to the Tenth Amendment, "Why, sir, the powers not delegated to the United States and the States belong to the people, and the Congress sent to do the people's business have all power." Finally, he told the senator that, before he let his *"candor compel"* him again to write upon a subject "as great as the salvation of man, consequential as the life of the Savior, broad as the principles of eternal truth, and valuable as the jewels of eternity," he should read the first, fourteenth, and seventeenth clauses in Article I, Section 8, of the Constitution. (Actually, Joseph miscounted here, for the relevant clauses are the first, fifteenth, and eighteenth.) These, he said, enumerated the specific and not very limited powers of the federal government, by which it could "protect the lives, property and rights of a virtuous people." Then, following a swipe at the politicians and bureaucrats who had failed to relieve the Mormons from their distress, he said that he anticipated a time when God "will raise your mind above the narrow notion that the General Government has no power, to the sublime idea that Congress, with the President as Executor, is as almighty in its sphere as Jehovah is in his." We have no record of how Calhoun reacted.

On January 29, 1844, Joseph began working with William W. Phelps on his "Views of the Powers and Policies of the Government of the United States," which became, in effect, his presidential platform. A nationwide campaign was soon under way, and at the April conference of the church a call was issued for volunteers to "preach the Gospel and electioneer." On May 17, a convention was held in Nauvoo at which Joseph was officially nominated, with Sidney

Rigdon as his running mate. The prophet himself did not go on the campaign trail, but over three hundred people volunteered as missionaries to preach the gospel and campaign throughout the United States for his election.[27]

It is by no means certain that Joseph Smith really believed he could win the election, but at least one good reason for his running was to help create a more positive public image for himself and the Mormon people, as his social and political views were more accurately presented by his campaign. Another was simply to fill the void created by the fact that, from among the leading candidates at the time, there were none that he could support. On February 8, 1844, after his political platform was read for the first time in public, the prophet made clear another reason for running: "I would not have suffered my name to have been used by my friends on anywise as President of the United States, or candidate for that office, if I and my friends could have had the privilege of enjoying our religious and civil rights as American citizens."[28] Tragically, his untimely murder came in June 1844, only a few short months after missionaries began preaching his political gospel around the country.

Calhoun did not run for the presidency that year. Instead, the Democrats nominated an unlikely candidate, James K. Polk, who became the first "dark horse" to win a presidential election. The Whigs nominated Henry Clay, and the tiny antislavery party, the Liberty Party, nominated James G. Birney of New York. Birney won only 2 percent of the popular vote but, in the process, deflected enough votes from Clay in New York to give that state, and hence the election, to Polk.

Joseph Smith's political tract began with an impassioned review of American history, glorifying in glowing language the administrations of all the previous presidents from George Washington to Andrew Jackson, but then, understandably, declaring that "our blooming republic began to decline under the withering touch of Martin Van Buren!" His specific proposals ran the gamut of American concerns, including demands for governmental reform, economic reform, the creation of a national bank, and prison reform.[29] He also dealt with three issues that might have been of special interest to John C. Calhoun: slavery, westward expansionism, and states' rights.

With respect to slavery, the prophet urged the people of the slaveholding states to petition their own legislators to abolish it by the year 1850. If slavery were to be eliminated, Calhoun would certainly have accepted the idea that it was up to the states, not the national government, to do so, but he would have rejected out of hand even the suggestion that it be done at all.

The most intensely debated issue of the day was expansionism. The Democrats saw America's destiny as expanding its borders from coast to coast, and called for fully occupying Oregon Territory (which, at that time, was claimed jointly by the United States and Canada) and incorporating Texas into the Union. The Whigs bitterly opposed expansionism, but in the long run this was the issue that got Polk elected. Joseph Smith went the Democrats one better. He called not only for the occupation of Oregon and the annexation of Texas but also for inviting Canada and Mexico, if they so desired, to join the Union. John C. Calhoun would have agreed with Joseph Smith's expansionism, at least with respect to Oregon and Texas, though in part for quite a different reason. The Mormon prophet, like the Democrats, saw the destiny of his country as expanding from sea to sea, and thus strengthening it not only as a Union but also against foreign threats both political and economic. Calhoun felt likewise, but he also had another reason for the annexation of Texas. This would mean adding another slave state to the Union, thus maintaining an essential balance in Congress and perpetuating slavery. In March of that year he became sec-retary of state, replacing the recently deceased Abel Parker Upshur. Calhoun reluctantly accepted the appointment only because he believed that this would put him in a position to bring about the annexation of Texas. Stunned by the Senate's rejection of his treaty of annexation in June, he finally orchestrated the acquisition through another constitutional but very unorthodox means—a joint resolution of Congress (which required only a simple majority in both houses rather than the two-thirds majority that the Senate required for trea-ties). The final documents were signed at the beginning of Polk's administra-tion, in March 1845, but Calhoun had performed the political engineering that got the joint resolution adopted. He and President Tyler signed and sent off the invitation for Texas to join the Union just hours before Tyler's presidency ended.

Perhaps, to Joseph Smith, the most important plank in his presidential platform was his direct attack on Calhoun's cherished states' rights philosophy. Smith called for a constitutional amendment that would give the president "full power to suppress mobs, and the States authority to repugn that relic of folly which makes it necessary for the governor of a state to make the demand of the President for troops, in case of invasion or rebellion."[30] Such an amend-ment would have been an abomination to Calhoun, for it would simply give too much power to the central government to intervene in state affairs.

As sectional crises continued to threaten the Union, John C. Calhoun per-sisted in his fight for what he thought was the only way to save it: a recogni-tion of states' rights, including the right to nullify acts of Congress that states deemed unconstitutional. One of his ideas, developed further in the 1840s, was the doctrine of the "concurrent majority."[31] The popular majority, he pointed out, could act in a way that was detrimental to the interests of a minority, and that was not what the founders had in mind. On the basis of his plan, the rights of the minority (that is, the rights of a particular *state*) could be protected from the tyranny of the majority (that is, the rest of the states) by such means as nullification. It really meant that the majority of the voting population within a state could protect itself against the majority of the nation, but if both majorities concurred, then the state had no problem: thus the concept of the "*concurrent* majority." An important key to Calhoun's basic concern, however, was the nature of the electorate. The voting population of South Carolina did not even approximate the total adult population of the state. Black slaves actually constituted the majority of residents, but only white male property owners could vote. What Calhoun was really trying to protect was the vested interests of white property owners, and particularly slaveholders. He honestly believed that what was in their best interest was also in the best interest of the state.

On March 4, 1850, John C. Calhoun presented his last great speech in the United States Senate. So ill that he could not deliver it himself, he had it read by his friend and colleague, Senator James Mason of Virginia. The issue was whether slavery should be allowed in the territories recently acquired from Mexico. Calhoun's speech included a melancholy rehearsal of the many cords that once bound the states together but which, one by one, had been broken. He predicted sadly, as he had many times before, that the slavery issue could cause the last cord to break and the Union to dissolve. All the North had to do to prevent this, he said, was to recognize the rights of the South in the new territories, willingly give up fugitive slaves that had escaped into the North, stop agitating the slave question, and support a constitutional amendment that would restore "the original equilibrium between the two sections." The North, everyone knew, would never agree to all these things, and Calhoun died on March 31, believing that because of this, the Union he loved so much was on the verge of destruction. Within six months, however, a series of compromise bills, engineered by Henry Clay and known in history as the Compromise of 1850, temporarily saved the Union once again.

Calhoun's overall political philosophy was much more extensive and complex than the brief comments here might suggest, and his speeches and writings on constitutional issues were extensive. Joseph Smith, on the other hand, wrote comparatively little about the Constitution. What we know of his perspective comes from gathering excerpts from various speeches and commentaries, for he never systemized his views on this matter. Both men had special axes to grind. Calhoun was concerned with protecting the Union as well as the Southern economy and slavery. This could be done only by keeping the power of the federal government to a minimum. Joseph Smith, too, was concerned with perpetuating the Union, but he was also bent on protecting the rights and liberties of the Saints. In his mind, the best way to do this was to enhance the power of the federal government and bury forever the doctrine of states' rights.

Perhaps neither of these important leaders was on completely solid constitutional ground. Calhoun's nullification theory could not be derived from any specific passage in the Constitution itself—it could only be surmised that this would be acceptable in the eyes of the founders. The compact theory was also debatable, and a few passages in the Constitution itself, including, perhaps, the "more perfect union" clause in the preamble, could be called into play to argue against it. Some of Joseph Smith's perspectives were equally questionable, at least for his time. Article I, Section 8, of the Constitution, cited by Joseph Smith as a source of unlimited power, authorizes Congress to levy taxes and collect duties in order to "provide for the common defense and general welfare" of the United States. No interpretation by the founders, however, and no court decision ever portrayed this as a grant of power to intervene militarily within a state. Joseph may have been stretching somewhat, also, when he cited the fifteenth and eighteenth clauses of this section. The fifteenth is the militia clause but, as noted earlier, it really allows the use of the militia only to put down rebellions, not to quell civil disorders within a state. Joseph used both the Whiskey Rebellion (1794) and South Carolina's 1832 tariff nullification as precedents for federal intervention, but in each of these cases the violation of *federal law* and *federal authority* was at issue. Joseph, however, interpreted the refusal of the state courts, and eventually the governor himself, to help the Mormons as an insurrection, and on that basis claimed the protection of the federal government. The eighteenth clause authorizes the government to do whatever is "necessary and proper" to carry out the powers previously enumerated, but if those enumerated powers extended only to the needs of the federal government, and did not authorize intervention in the states, then whatever was necessary to carry them into effect was likewise limited. Finally, Joseph sometimes referred to the constitutional guarantees to life, liberty, and property, as spelled out in the Fifth Amendment. At that time, however, it was clear to most people acquainted with constitutional issues that this amendment applied only to the acts of Congress, not to the states.[32]

Eleven years after Calhoun's death, the catastrophe that he, Thomas Jefferson, and Joseph Smith all feared materialized: eleven Southern states, led by South Carolina, seceded and civil war engulfed the country. Slavery was the background issue, but disagreement over states' rights was at the heart of the conflict. Did these states have the constitutional right to withdraw from the Union? Calhoun would have shouted a resounding, "Yes." Andrew Jackson and Joseph Smith would have answered with a resounding, "No." Abraham Lincoln also answered with a no. He believed that the Constitution created an indivisible union—it could not be otherwise. Tragically, this central constitutional issue was settled only by the clash of arms.

Mormon history, meanwhile, took an ironic twist. The states' rights doctrine kept the national government from intervening in behalf of the Mormons in Missouri, but after the move west and the establishment of the Territory of Utah, Brigham Young and other church leaders took another look at states' rights and did everything they could to get Congress to make the territory a state. After all, since Congress could legislate for the territories, thus allowing the federal government to intervene in almost any way it wanted, the Mormons were concerned that this could lead to undermining their control of their own domestic institutions, including the practice of plural marriage. In this situation, the states' rights doctrine would protect them from outside interference. Political reality had changed.

Postscript

John C. Calhoun was the spokesman for a dying constitutional philosophy. Joseph Smith, on the other hand, may have been ahead of his time—a harbinger of fundamental constitutional change. The Fourteenth Amendment, adopted in 1868, was not exactly what Joseph had in mind and did not give the federal government all the power he called for. But it did declare that "no State shall make or enforce any law which shall abridge the privileges or immunities of citizens of the United States; nor shall any State deprive any person of life, liberty, or property, without due process of law; nor deny to any person within its jurisdiction the equal protection of the laws." Joseph Smith, no doubt, would have approved such wording, for it had the effect of applying the Fifth Amendment to the states, not just to laws passed by Congress. At first, beginning with the Slaughterhouse Cases in 1873, the Supreme Court effectively nullified whatever restrictions the amendment may have imposed on states' rights. But in the twentieth century the courts made it a more effective protector of individual rights and freedoms. It still does not go as far as Joseph Smith may have wanted, but at least, in accord with recent interpretations, the federal government has the right to look at the actions of state governments and determine whether those governments unconstitutionally deprive a person of life, liberty, and property—the fundamental rights with which Joseph Smith was so vitally concerned.[33]

PART II

Sacred Encounters

7

Joseph Smith and Creation of the Sacred

Richard Lyman Bushman

Joseph Smith's success has always perplexed observers of the American religious scene. Why, of all the visionaries and reformers in his generation, was his movement the one to survive and flourish? Only Ellen G. White of the Adventists, Mary Barker Eddy, founder of Christian Science, and Charles Taze Russell of the Jehovah's Witnesses come close to matching Joseph Smith's achievement. He attracted followers immediately after announcing his revelations and publishing the Book of Mormon, and Mormonism has grown steadily ever since. Why this should be has baffled inquirers like Josiah Quincy Jr., the Harvard graduate and Boston Brahmin who visited Nauvoo, Illinois, in 1844, six weeks before Joseph Smith's death. Reflecting back in 1883, Quincy wrote:

> Born in the lowest ranks of poverty, without book-learning and with the homeliest of all human names, he had made himself at the age of thirty-nine a power upon earth. Of the multitudinous family of Smith, from Adam down (Adam of the "Wealth of Nations," I mean), none had so won human hearts and shaped human lives as this Joseph. His influence, whether for good or for evil, is potent to-day and the end is not yet. . . . If the reader does not know just what to make of Joseph Smith, I cannot help him out of the difficulty. I myself stand helpless before the puzzle.[1]

A multitude of answers to questions about the sources of Smith's lasting influence has been proposed. They boil down to Joseph Smith's meeting the unspoken needs of his age. In her biography of Muhammad, Karen Armstrong postulates that "the prophet who speaks on behalf of God is also in a profound sense the spokesman of his people, voicing their hopes and fears. He will share the unrest and disturbance of his time but will be able to address them at a deeper level."[2] Writing in this spirit, theorists have hypothesized a host of explanations for Mormonism's early success—sectarian divisions, republican contradictions, nascent capitalism, social dislocation, a quest for authority—all plausible and applicable. Obliquely or directly, Joseph Smith spoke to these unresolved stresses in American life. He was believed because he spoke deep truths.

I am drawn to this explanation of his success, but it is not my purpose here to explore this inquiry. Rather than sort out all these issues and begin digging for the underlying structures of American culture, I would like to take another approach, one more simple and yet, I believe, telling. I wish to explore the possibility that Joseph Smith met a human need for the sacred. I do not intend to consider the composition of the desire for the sacred. Was it a conglomerate of other needs and tensions, sociological and psychological? Was it an ideology for managing people in the service of power? Was it a form of social conditioning? All these are worthy inquiries, but I wish to begin with the fact that antebellum America was rife with religious desire. How to obtain salvation was the question of the age. People at all levels of society, from the Transcendentalists in their Boston redoubts to the camp meeting enthusiasts in Kentucky clearings, were seeking God—not as a theological idea but as a personal experience. Like Joseph Smith, they wanted contact with the divine. My question is, how did Joseph Smith appeal to this generation of seekers? In the religion he constructed, where was the sacred found?

This was not a period when Rudolph Otto's (subsequently described) terrible power of the holy best characterized what the holy was for American worshippers. Americans did not undergo feelings of terror or find awe-inspiring mystery emanating from God as Otto's subjects of study did. American evangelicals did fear the wrath of God as they passed through conversion and cowered in their sinfulness before his anger. But they came at last to the loving Jesus and the merciful God, and felt his love far more than his angry force. Far from being "wholly other," the God of these evangelical converts was their friend.[3]

In places in Joseph Smith's writing, the majestic God of power does appear. The vision of Moses in the first chapter of Smith's Book of Moses depicts a creator whose power and might exceeded all human comprehension. Moses is given a glimpse of God's glory while on a high mountain and then Moses abruptly drops back to earth. Decimated by the experience, Moses exclaims in wonder, "Now, for this cause I know that man is nothing, which thing I never had supposed." He recognizes that he cannot even look upon God without the protection of His Spirit when he says, "Now mine own eyes have beheld God; but not my natural, but my spiritual eyes, for my natural eyes could not have beheld; for I should have withered and died in his presence; but his glory was upon me; and I beheld his face." Even so, Moses is not entirely intimidated by the God of his visions. Moses asks God why he created the worlds and persists when God rebuffs him. Finally the great God yields to Moses' entreaties and explains that the divine purpose is "to bring to pass the immortality and eternal life of man" (Moses 1:9–11, 39). This God was willing to converse about his purposes.

In many respects, emergent Mormonism portrayed a God who was approachable and friendly, not unlike how the evangelicals found Jesus in the revival meetings. Mormons found the sacred in the same locations as the Protestant Christians around them did. Mormons prayed, read the Bible, partook of communion, listened to sermons, performed acts of charity. To a large extent they found God in familiar places. But Joseph Smith also reconfigured the religious world for his followers. He offered new sites for encountering the sacred, and it was the growing potency of these distinctive loci that set Mormonism apart from the rest of the Christian world. The two I would like to discuss here are, first, sacred words, and second, sacred places.

Sacred Words

The Protestants of Joseph Smith's day were all purveyors of the word. The Bible was thought of as a uniquely authentic and powerful collection of sacred words. Protestants read the Bible devotedly, that is, slowly, repeatedly, searching for guidance, comfort, and truth. Some, like young Joseph, opened the book at random and took the passages their eyes lit upon as signals from heaven. Many mined it for predictions of world history, for descriptions of the cosmos, for promises of salvation. Week after week, sermons from thousands of pulpits across the land applied the scriptures to every conceivable aspect of morality and theology.

In this milieu Joseph Smith's religious career took a peculiar direction. Unlike the army of sermonizers who drove the revivals coursing through upstate New York in his boyhood, Joseph Smith was not a devoted reader of scripture. As a young man, he was not a close student of the Bible, nor is he known to have discoursed on its meaning. There is no record of his preaching to his followers before he organized the Church of Christ in April 1830. He read the Bible in search of his own salvation like other aspiring Christians, but he is not known to have digested it for purposes of preaching.

Instead, he produced a new scripture. His place in the religious world was based on a new Bible, which he himself dictated. His claims on the loyalty of his followers and his identity as a prophet all depended on sacred words he produced. Joseph Smith had little to recommend him personally: no education, no social position, no institutional backup. Judging from early accounts, he was personally plain and unprepossessing. In the eyes of the neighbors who later signed affidavits about his character, he was lazy, mendacious, superstitious, and not particularly religious. True, they were not privy to his inner religious struggles, but they spoke about the face he presented to the world. He was not a luminous figure in Palmyra, not a favorite of the ministers, not the darling of local society. He was an indigent laborer in a struggling family. The only substantial foundation for his claims to divine inspiration was the book he published in March 1830 as the Book of Mormon, which he claimed to have translated by the gift and power of God and which he said was a religious history of ancient American Israelites.

The Book of Mormon was not his only book of scripture. As he was translating the records of an ancient people, he was also receiving revelations for himself and his followers. The organization of the church in April 1830 was commanded by one such revelation, and there were many others like it. Smith began writing revelations in 1828, when he was twenty-two, and continued to record revelations down to the last year of his life. Within six months of the Book of Mormon's appearance, he began assembling these latter-day revelations for the purpose of producing another book of sacred words—this time not so much a second Bible like the Book of Mormon but a modern Acts of the Apostles. In 1831, a year and a half after the organization of the church, plans were made to publish these revelations. On November 1, a conference of Mormons at Hiram, Ohio, voted to print 10,000 copies of the 160-page Book of Commandments, as the book was later called. The print run was subsequently reduced to a more realistic 3,000, but the first high estimate of future sales indicated the church's sense of the book's importance.[4] These many pages of scripture lay at the heart of Smith's appeal.

Other visionaries prized revealed words; seventeenth-century Quakers published their ecstatic experiences in such volume that their pamphlets at one time amounted to 13 percent of all the titles printed in England.[5] But no other nineteenth-century religious community valued their revelations more than the Mormons valued Joseph Smith's. In arranging for publication, Smith could not find words strong enough to underscore their worth. The conference affirmed that the writings "be prized by this Conference to be worth to the Church the riches of the whole Earth speaking temporally."[6]

These two writings—the Book of Mormon and the Book of Commandments, which was later called the Doctrine and Covenants—set the pattern for Joseph Smith's revealed words until the end of his life. The revealed words came in two forms: one form was found in the translations of purported historical records like the Book of Mormon, the other in the revelations directly governing the modern church. Over his lifetime, Smith produced three inspired "translations": the Book of Mormon, the Book of Moses, and the Book of Abraham, plus the "revision," of the Bible, also a form of translation. All grew out of the Bible. They centered on Moses, Enoch, and Abraham, and took place in the biblical lands of Jerusalem, Canaan, and Egypt. All of Smith's translations had the character of expansions of the Bible, enlarging a few verses in the old scriptures into lengthy accounts unknown to readers of the Bible. They are all "apocryphal" works in the sense of being uncanonized extensions of the Bible that incorporate the Bible's characters, scenes, and thinking.

The critical point for our investigation today is that the followers of Joseph Smith effectively canonized these writings—the revelations to the Mormon Church and the translations—almost as soon as they were in print, considering them to have the same authority as traditional scripture. The early Mormons instantly overthrew the principle of the lone sufficiency of the Bible, the belief that it contained a uniquely authoritative collection of God's word. The Book of Mormon even mocked those who stubbornly insisted on its monopoly of scripture.

> Because my words shall hiss forth—many of the Gentiles shall say:
> A Bible! A Bible! We have got a Bible, and there cannot be any more
> Bible. But thus saith the Lord God: O fools. . . . Know ye not that there
> are more nations than one? Know ye not that I, the Lord your God,
> have created all men, and that I remember those who are upon the
> isles of the sea; and that I . . . bring forth my word unto the children of
> men, yea, even upon all nations of the earth. (2 Nephi 29:3–4, 7)

Although for years the old Bible was preeminent in Mormon thinking and used as the main support for Mormon teachings, the Book of Mormon was scripture too, and the ongoing revelations of Joseph Smith outranked even the Bible as the chief source of direction for the young church. Anyone who denied the possibility of additional revelation, the Book of Mormon said, was a fool.

Even before they were published, Smith's revelations as prophet and seer were distinguished from his everyday words as a man. Smith's followers reacted quite differently to the two kinds of speech. When Smith asked John Whitmer to be church historian, Whitmer agreed only if the Lord would "manifest it through Joseph the Seer."[7] At first inclined to turn down the call, Whitmer complied when he was told in the voice of the Lord that "behold it is expedient in me that my servant John should write and keep a regular history" (Book of Commandments 50:1). When a new edition of the revelations was being prepared, the editor of the Mormon newspaper, William W. Phelps, an early convert and editor of the first church newspaper, wrote his wife: "The Saints must learn their duty from the Revelations. We must live by every word that proceeds from the mouth of God, and not by what is written by man or is spoken by man."[8] Smith himself held the revelations in the same high regard. Writing in 1831, he advised his brother Hyrum to come to Ohio, "for the Lord has Commanded us that we should Call the Elders of this Chur[c]h together."[9] He spoke as if the revelations coming by his voice commanded him along with everyone else.

The revelations carried authority, even though received in almost routine fashion. Smith did not fall into trances like Ellen White or withdraw into the desert like Muhammad in his early visions. Most of Smith's revelations came while he sat in council with his followers. Parley Pratt, one of Smith's early converts, described how the revelation on discerning spirits was received. John Murdock and several other elders asked Smith to inquire of the Lord. They joined in prayer in the translating room, Pratt said, and Smith dictated a revelation.

> Each sentence was uttered slowly and very distinctly, and with a pause between each, sufficiently long for it to be recorded, by an ordinary writer, in long hand. This was the manner in which all his written revelations were dictated and written. There was never any hesitation, reviewing, or reading back, in order to keep the run of the subject; neither did any of these communications undergo revisions, interlinings, or corrections. As he dictated them so they stood, so far as I have witnessed.[10]

One of his most extensive and poetic revelations, section 88 of the current Doctrine and Covenants, was interrupted while it was being received in a meeting of church leaders. The clerk noted in the minutes that the hour growing late, the revelation was halted, to be resumed the next morning when the inspired dictation took up again. Yet despite their mundane origins, once recorded, the revelations were recopied and carried around by church members.[11] Smith once said his revelations "have been snatched from under my hand as soon as given."[12]

What gave these revelations, so humbly received by so plain a man, their authority? Why did early Mormons believe the Lord was speaking to them through their prophet? A striking rhetorical feature of the revelations may partly explain their persuasiveness. Smith himself is nearly absent from the revelations; the voice in the revelations comes through as purely God's voice. In the opening lines of the 1833 Book of Commandments, for example, God's voice prevails:

> Hearken, O ye people of my church, saith the voice of Him who dwells on high, and whose eyes are upon all men; yea, verily I say, hearken ye people from afar, and ye that are upon the islands of the sea, listen together. (Book of Commandments 1:1)

That sounds like God speaking, with only the slightest human mediation. When Smith figures in the revelations, he stands among the listeners, receiving instructions. When reprimands are handed out, he is likely to receive one. The first written revelation received in 1828 chastised him for losing 116 pages of the Book of Mormon translation. The revelation was addressed to him alone, since there was yet no church and few followers. Smith stands before the Lord to receive a rebuke in words coming from his own mouth.

> Remember, remember, that it is not the work of God that is frustrated, but the work of men: for although a man may have many revelations, and have power to do many mighty works, yet, if he boasts in his own strength, and sets at nought the counsels of God, and follows after the dictates of his own will, and carnal desires, he must fall and incur the vengeance of a just God upon him. (Book of Commandments 2:2)

In this case, as in virtually all the revelations, the voice is imperious but never argumentative. The words make no appeal to reason or scripture or experience. God pronounces what is and what will be without giving evidence. Hearers must decide to believe or not without reference to outside authority— common sense, science, the Bible, tradition, anything. The hearer faces the personage who speaks, free to hearken or turn away.[13]

Smith is similarly absent from his translations. The books of Mormon, Moses, and Abraham purported to be records of another people of another time. In all these works, Joseph Smith does not introduce himself as the narrator of the story. The Book of Mormon opens with the phrase, "I, Nephi, having been born of goodly parents"; the Book of Moses begins, "The words of God which he spake unto Moses, at a time when Moses was caught up into an exceeding high mountain"; Abraham starts, "In the land of the Chaldeans, at the residence of my father, I, Abraham, saw that it was needful for me to obtain another place of residence."[14] The reader is immediately immersed in another time and place and absorbed into the narrative without the help of an intermediary.

Critics point to passages in the Book of Mormon where the text broadly hints at Joseph Smith's part in translating the Book of Mormon in the last days as a bit of self-promotion, but these are only a few such verses in hundreds of pages (2 Nephi 3:6–21). More remarkable than what the book says about him is how little he figures explicitly as a character in the book's story. In the introduction to the first edition, Smith says next to nothing about his part in making the book. "I would inform you that I translated by the gift and power of God, and caused to be written, one hundred and sixteen pages." He may not even have said that, had not the 116 pages been lost and he was worried to death they would turn up and undercut the published translation. Regarding the pages he translated and published, Smith said only, "Wherefore, to be obedient unto the commandments of God, I have, through his grace and mercy, accomplished that which he hath commanded me respecting this thing."[15] Though he signs the introduction "The Author," he is not an *auteur*.

There are strong authorial presences in the Book of Mormon—commanding presences—but they are not those of Joseph Smith. Except in the few verses where Lehi points him out, Smith remains invisible. He is a selfless writer. The authors who require our attention are powerful figures like Nephi, a pioneer and founder; Alma, a high priest and chief judge; and Mormon, a general of the Nephite armies. These writers speak with great confidence and insistence, showing us events through their eyes, but those eyes are not overtly Joseph Smith's. There is no omniscient writing in the Book of Mormon, no passages where Joseph Smith appears behind the scenes, managing the narrative. We always see the Book of Mormon's world through a specific person, Mormon or one of the other prophets. Nephi writes, "And it came to pass that after I, Nephi, had been carried away in the spirit, and seen all these things, I returned to the tent of my father" (1 Nephi 15:1). In those commonplace words, Nephi is taking us into his confidence, telling us what happened. He has the authority of a participant sharing firsthand knowledge. Joseph Smith's knowledge and authority mean nothing. It is all between Nephi and the reader. Joseph Smith does not preach the sermons or make the prophecies; his veracity and standing in the world are not on trial. His formidable authors speak for themselves—out of the dust, as Isaiah put it (Isaiah 29:4). Smith disappears and God or characters from the past do all the speaking.

There was something both grandiose and self-effacing in the Book of Mormon—and in Joseph Smith in 1829. He claimed to be undertaking a world-transforming mission, but it is all done for God and carried forward by men more powerful than Smith, men who speak from the pages of a book. Smith is the translator, not the author; he is merely obedient to God's commands.

In trying to understand the influence of religious leaders like Joseph Smith, it may be appropriate to speak of prophetic passivity. Paradoxically, in prophetic personages there is both extreme activity and extreme evacuation of self. Prophets are immensely confident, egotistical, bold historical figures who confront kings and attack whole societies. Joseph Smith was as bold as any with his proposal for a world gathering of Israel and the construction of the New Jerusalem in Missouri. And yet at the same time, these prophets present themselves as passive instruments in God's hands, saying only what they are told and doing only what God instructs. Could it be that their effectiveness partially derives from their enacting the role of agents for God so convincingly? More than anything else, religious people look for an emissary from heaven, not a man on horseback. They want to hear the words of God, not the words of a sage, a scholar, or a Napoleon. As Orestes Brownson put it in 1836, "We would hear God speak."[16] By his very passivity, by removing the traces of self from his writings, Joseph Smith presented himself as a prophet. To many ears, his revelations sounded like the words of God.

For nearly a decade, Smith was invisible in Latter-day Saint proselyting. His name was not even mentioned in missionary literature or in sermons, as far as can be told. The first hundred pages, the *Voice of Warning*, the preeminent Mormon tract of the first decade, did not mention the church, much less Joseph Smith. Finally on page 122, the author, Parley Pratt, announced that revelation had come but said nothing of the revelator. "Suddenly a voice is heard from the wilderness, a cry salutes the ears of mortals, a testimony is heard among them, piercing to the inmost recesses of their hearts." Pratt went on to say that the Book of Mormon was "brought to light by the ministering of angels, and translated by Inspiration." Pratt's descriptions of revelation were couched in the passive voice. He tells the story of finding the book and publishing it without mentioning Joseph Smith or even indicating that an actual person did the work. When people are mentioned as receiving revelation, they are a faceless group. "This manifestation was by the ministering of Angels, and by the voice of Jehovah, speaking from the heavens in plainness, unto men who are now living among you."[17] The revelations came down like rain on a company of nameless prophets. In a letter to a newspaper editor summarizing the Mormon message, Smith himself said only, "The Lord has declared to his servants some Eighteen months since that he was then withdrawing his spirit from the earth."[18]

Revelation distills on the earth like the dew without any named recep-
tacle to receive it. Could it be that this self-effacement empowered Joseph
Smith's words and made it easier for his followers to believe they were hearing from God?

Sacred Places

Speaking of the United States as a whole, Garry Wills has stated, "There is
no more defining note to our history than the total absence of a sacred city
in our myths." The only exception, he said, "is the Mormons' temple, fetched
(like Jerusalem's) from heaven."[19] In Smith's day, American Christians were
devoted to the principle of sacred time—Sabbath observance was a hot political
issue—but not, as Wills observes, to sacred space. They had political capitols, financial capitols, cultural capitols, but not religious capitols—save for Salt Lake
City. We have diffused sacred space widely across the country, into numberless
chapels and, nowadays, into storefronts with only a sign on the window. Protestants generally believe that the true God takes residence in the heart of every
believer. Spaces take on holiness only when these changed hearts assemble.
The tendency of American worship has been persistently centrifugal, scatter-
ing holy spaces ever more widely.

Joseph Smith reversed this trend within the first year of the church's organization. In the summer heat of 1831, he gathered a handful of followers on
the edge of a European settlement in western Missouri, where a revelation had
designated Independence, Jackson County, as the site for the New Jerusalem. In
the city that the Saints were to construct, also called the City of Zion or simply
Zion, there was to be a temple where the Lord could come when he returned.
This was to be the central place for the gathering of Israel from throughout the
world. The tribe of Judah was destined to return to the old Jerusalem in Palestine, but the rest of Israel was to collect in Missouri. Missionaries were to scour
the earth in search of converts and gather them to Zion. The revelation turned
the earth into a great metaphorical funnel with the City of Zion at the vortex.

The empowerment of this sacred place occurred with remarkable brevity.
The sacralization of space usually results from a succession of holy events like
repeated miracles, or from accumulated layers of worship and veneration over
centuries, in the way of Jerusalem or of Lourdes.[20] Rather than growing from
repeated sacred happenings, Smith's Zion was created in a stroke, not on a site
already laden with meaning but on an open plain at the edge of American settlement. Smith wrote on a blank slate. Yet, a few words from heaven declaring
Independence to be the site of the New Jerusalem inscribed indelible marks on

the land—forever. Though later evicted never to return, Mormons have never forgotten Jackson County. The defeat of the efforts to build a city there has not erased the site from Mormon memory.[21] In 1831 a remote location in the middle of North America became the place where Mormons believed people from around the globe were to gather, build a temple, and live for Christ. A century and three-quarters after the Mormons were evicted, Jackson County still stands for the higher society to which contemporary Mormons aspire.[22]

Into this city, Smith loaded his ideals for a righteous society. In describing an ancient holy city, one scripture said the people were called Zion "because they were of one heart and one mind, and dwelt in righteousness; and there was no poor among them" (Moses 7:18). Those simple words pointed to radical social reforms, and for the Missouri Zion, a revelation sketched in plans for the equalization of property so that every family had sufficient for its needs and great differences in wealth were erased. For two years, every Mormon migrant to Missouri was required to deed over his property to the church and each received back a stewardship suitable for his or her talents and resources. In time, these plans for radical economic reform proved impractical and were abandoned. But the ideal of consecration was not erased. It was transmuted into a requirement to donate a tithe to the church. If not required to deed over all of their property for redistribution among the poor, church members were to consider all they had a gift from God and to donate their time and money generously to the general good.

Although defeated in all of his attempts to found a city, Joseph Smith repeatedly planned for successor cities: after Independence, there was Far West, Missouri, and then Nauvoo, Illinois. Zion was his favorite topic, one follower noted in his journal.[23] After Smith's death in 1844, Brigham Young carried the idea to Utah, where Salt Lake City became the central gathering place, and as forecast by Joseph Smith, hundreds of smaller settlements, all following the original plan, were planted throughout the Great Basin.

In a sense, the replication of Smith's plans in Utah sacralized the Mormon landscape. The little Mormon villages scattered over the austere western landscape were not just settlements but cities of Zion, not only to the inhabitants but to Mormons around the world. This sacralized urban planning made migration a sacred journey, and everyday activities of home building and plowing steps toward a millennial society.

At the core of these cities of Zion, anchoring their sacred character, was the temple. Smith had included a temple in his initial plans for the city of Zion in Missouri and every subsequent city in his lifetime included a temple at its center. One of Brigham Young's first acts in the valley of the Great Salt Lake was to strike his staff in the earth and proclaim that there they would build a temple to God. The temple marks the central point from which all the streets in Salt Lake City are numbered. Not every little village had a temple, but many had smaller but still grand tabernacles, and all considered the temple cities focal points in Zion.

Although many Protestants refer to their places of worship as temples, adding an aura of the sacred to the plainest of structures, Joseph Smith's temples gradually assumed a character that sharply distinguished them from chapels. The first temple he constructed—in Kirtland, Ohio, in the mid-1830s— combined worship and ritual enactment, joining the functions of chapel and temple. But even though used for Sunday services like any New England meetinghouse, the Kirtland temple had strange features. Instead of one sanctuary where all the worshipers met, there were two matching spaces, one on top of the other, with a peculiar stack of four altars rising at each end of the two spaces.[24] On the third floor, the attic, the first phases of the temple endowment were performed. The ceremonies were derived from the Exodus instructions for consecrating priests, involving washings with water, anointings with oils, and sealings (Exodus 30:22–30; 40: 12–15). The second phase of the endowment ceremonies was instituted in Nauvoo, inspired by the rituals of Freemasonry to which Smith had recently been exposed. Over the years, as the temple ceremonies were elaborated in Utah, these rituals took over the temples. The double chapel-like spaces on the first two floors of the Nauvoo and Kirtland temples were combined into one assembly room in the Utah temples at St. George, Manti, and Salt Lake and the room placed high in the buildings. Ceremonies that in Kirtland and Nauvoo were performed in the attic were brought down to the first floors. The assembly room on top became the least used space in the temple, reserved for occasional "solemn assemblies." The real work of the temple went on in the ritual rooms.

If anything, the original conception of sacred space in Joseph Smith's religion has intensified over the years. While many Christian churches have become community centers and welfare stations as well as chapels, Mormon temples have become more austere and holy, more withdrawn from the world. With remarkable skill, Joseph Smith and his successors adopted practices that set these buildings apart from all other spaces. They achieved a separation of the sacred from the profane like the one that Mircea Eliade sees as the point of every church in the modern city.

> For a believer, the church shares in a different space from the street in which it stands. The door that opens on the interior of the church actually signifies a dissolution of continuity. The threshold that separates the two spaces also indicates the distance between two modes

of being, the profane and the religious. The threshold is the limit, the boundary, the frontier that distinguishes and opposes two worlds— and at the same time the paradoxical place where those worlds communicate, where passage from the profane to the sacred world becomes possible.[25]

Before the Manhattan temple was completed in 2003, a few score people were allowed to walk through the rooms. The spaces were still obviously a construction site, with tools on the floors and door frames and trim still missing. Carpets were not laid, no paintings were on the walls, scaffolding was still up. And yet these observers, dressed in their Sunday best as instructed, walked in silence through the rooms, many with arms folded. Already before the dedication, the temple aura was there.

After each temple's dedication, the full array of measures for sacralizing the temple spaces goes into effect. No one enters Mormon temples unless they have been interviewed by their bishop to determine their elemental worthiness. Eliade notes the importance of thresholds to sacred spaces: "They are symbols and at the same time vehicles of *passage* from the one space to the other."[26] At the thresholds of Mormon temples, a man in white clothing stands to examine each person's credentials. After entering, temple-goers change from street clothes into white temple clothing. Everywhere in the temple they speak in hushed tones. The rooms themselves are spotless, cleaned thoroughly every week. The religious scholar Jonathan Z. Smith says that "taking care" is one sign of a sacred space.[27]

Perhaps as important as anything, Latter-day Saints pledge not to speak of the temple ceremonies outside its walls. Sometimes Mormons, a little embarrassed by this prohibition, say the ceremonies are sacred, not secret. But it is probably just as true to say: the ceremonies are sacred *because* they are secret. The full temple ritual can be read on the web, like so much other information these days, but the availability of the ceremony, or lack of it, to the curious public is not the point. What matters to Mormons is that the participants in the temple ritual refrain from speaking of it. The restraint on discussion outside the temple hallows both the rituals and the spaces in which they are performed.

The temple ceremonies took hold of the Mormon imagination with amazing rapidity. Joseph Smith introduced the full endowment (temple ceremony) to a small group of Saints in the last two years of his life. Within a short time, the church membership as a whole was yearning to participate. In the final months of their time in Nauvoo, when the decree had gone forth that they must leave or face armed invasion by their hostile neighbors, the Mormons labored to complete the temple, knowing it would soon be abandoned. In the cold December and January before their departure in 1846, five thousand Mormons passed through the ceremonies in their sacred space. Then, in February they began the cold trek across Iowa on their way west. Brigham Young later said the temple ceremonies were the cord that held the people together during those difficult months.[28]

Conclusion

That December in Nauvoo can stand as an exemplary instance of the sacred contacts that Joseph Smith proffered to the first generation of Mormons. Ralph Waldo Emerson had told the Harvard Divinity School students, only eight years previously, that they needed to hear from God again. "I look for the hour," Emerson said, "when that supreme Beauty which ravished the souls of those Eastern men, and chiefly of those Hebrews, and through their lips spoke oracles to all time, shall speak in the West also."[29]

In raw, untutored form, Joseph Smith gave his followers both words from heaven and spaces in which to pledge themselves to God. Those followers believed that oracles had been pronounced and that the sacred precincts of the ancient temple had been reestablished. We may devise our own explanations for Smith's influence in antebellum America. But if we asked the early converts, they most likely would have said they heard God in their prophet's words and found God in their holy city and in their sacred temple. We can look behind and beneath their explanations for one that satisfies us, but in the end we cannot lightly dismiss their own accounts of how the sacred entered their lives.

8

Joseph Smith: Prophecy, Process, and Plenitude

Terryl L. Givens

Joseph Smith was an explorer, a discoverer, and a revealer of past worlds. He described an ancient America replete with elaborate detail and daring specificity, rooted and grounded in what he claimed were concrete, palpable artifacts. He recuperated texts of Adam, Abraham, Enoch, and Moses to resurrect and reconstitute a series of past patriarchal ages, not as mere shadows and types of things to come, but as dispensations of gospel fullness equaling, and in some cases surpassing, present plenitude. And he revealed an infinitely receding premortal past—not of the largely mythic Platonic variety and not a mere Wordsworthian, sentimental intimation, but a fully formed realm of human intelligences, divine parents, and heavenly councils.

My topic focuses first on this process of recovery, not its products. That will lead me to say a few things about the cumulative meaning for Joseph Smith of the past, of the worlds he discovered.

One of the great challenges in dealing historically with Joseph Smith has been the difficulty of meeting him on his own terms. More than anything else, Smith labored to free himself from the burdens of theological convention, intellectual decorum, and—perhaps most especially—the phobia of trespassing across sacred boundaries. Although several attempts have been made to situate Smith with respect to the paradigm shift of the early nineteenth century that we call Romanticism, these efforts have still failed to fully appreciate Smith and to meet him in the context of what we could call Romantic discourse. From Jean Jacques Rousseau's meandering "Reveries" to

Samuel Coleridge's "Kubla Khan" and other partial dream-visions, to Friedrich Schlegel's literary magazine, *Athenaeum Fragments*, the entire era was dominated (in literature but also in music and even in landscape painting) by images of the remnant, the fragment, the ruin, the shard. Such indications of tentativeness, of searching exploration, or of residual hints and vestiges reaffirmed the Romantics in their refusal to see writing as final, utterance as complete, or discursive thought as definitive. Systematization was, to Romantics, stultifying, deadening, and almost always derivative. "I must create my own system," insisted the mercurial William Blake, "or be enslaved by another man's."[1] The dynamic, active, ongoing *process* of creating meaning was primary to the Romantics—not the finality or the polish of the final product.

Like Blake, Joseph Smith almost always put himself in an agonistic, if not antagonistic, relationship to all prior systems. Consistent with other Romantic thinkers from Thomas Robert Malthus to G. W. F. Hegel to Charles Darwin, Smith believed that struggle, opposition, and contestation are not just the essence of personal probation and growth but struggle also describes an intellectual dynamic that moves us ahead in our quest for understanding. "I am like a huge, rough stone rolling down from a high mountain," Smith said, "and the only polishing I get is when some corner gets rubbed off by coming in contact with something else, striking with accelerated force against religious bigotry, priestcraft, . . . the authority of perjured executives . . . and corrupt men and women."[2] These words are not a description just of his character development, but also a delineation of his intellectual modus operandi—of his exploring the limits, challenging conventional categories, and engaging dynamically with the boundaries, all in the interest of productive provocation. Or as he said more simply, shortly before his death, "By proving contraries truth is made manifest."[3]

Let me illustrate this epistemology in the case of Joseph Smith. Smith paid as much attention to the process of true religion as to the content. I have argued elsewhere that the Book of Mormon is the prime instance of this.[4] The history of that scripture's reception clearly demonstrates that the Book of Mormon was both valued and reviled for the same reason: not for its content, but because of its dramatic enactment of the principle of continuing revelation and an open canon.

I think it is clear that Smith considered this process of revelation, not the particulars revealed thereby, as the cardinal contribution of his calling. So did his closest associates. On New Year's Day 1844, Parley P. Pratt published Mormonism's first piece of fiction in the *New York Herald*. It was a comic dialogue entitled "Joseph Smith and the Devil." In this humorous but earnest piece, the devil insists to the prophet Joseph that, contrary to popular beliefs, he, the devil, really is in favor of "all creeds, systems and forms of Christianity, of whatever name and nature; so long as they leave out that abominable doctrine which caused me so much trouble in former times, and which, after slumbering for ages, you have again revived; I mean the doctrine of direct communication with God."[5]

Certainly, what Smith revealed was important—and frequently revolutionary. A quick overview of his teachings on God and man, for instance, shows not just irruptions of novelty, but a thoroughgoing endeavor to overturn the most sacred tenets of cultural Christianity. He summarily repudiated the God of the creeds by preaching a deity who has a body, parts, and passions. Then he—almost cursorily—evaluated, dismissed, and reconceptualized answers to the three great questions of human existence. First, where do we come from? St. Augustine asked the question, "Did my infancy follow some earlier age of life? Before I was in my mother's womb, was I anywhere? Was I anyone?"[6] But Augustine gave up the answer as a great unknown. Second, what is our nature and purpose? "What could be worse pride," Augustine asks in bitter self-reproach, "than the incredible folly in which I asserted that I was by nature what You are?"[7] Contrast this attitude with Smith's emphasis on innocence, freedom, agency, accountability, liberty—words that filled Smith's mind, while other religionists were painting a portrait of "utter depravity," "corrupted nature," inherited guilt, predestination, and determinism. Not just Christendom, but as Louis Menand writes, "almost every nineteenth-century system of [Western] thought" was haunted by fatalism, by mechanical or materialist determinism.[8] Third, where are we going? In reference to the final judgment, Smith writes in the "Olive Leaf" revelation, "And they who remain shall also be quickened; nevertheless, they shall return again to their own place, to enjoy that which they are willing to receive, because they were not willing to enjoy that which they might have received" (Doctrine and Covenants 88:32). The question he poses to the human family is, what are we willing to receive? The divine potential of human destiny is limited only by our own unwillingness to receive the infinite opportunities God lays before us—even godhood itself.

Human acceptance of the serpent's invitation to "be as gods" (Genesis 3:5), according to the commentators, was the primal instance of human sinfulness. This audacity was likewise the most heinous of all human evils in Dante's catalog of evil. So profoundly wrong was it, his angelic guide explained, that "man, in his limits, could not recompense: / for no obedience, no humility, / he offered later could have been so deep / that it could match the heights he meant to reach / through disobedience."[9] As one of Dante's editors paraphrases, "Only the act of infinite humility whereby Christ became incarnate and suffered the Passion, could compensate for the infinite presumptuousness of man."[10] This fearsome presumption is what motivated an entire tradition

of indignation. Jonathan Edwards, echoing Dante's horror, found "human rebellion against such perfection [holiness that was infinitely beyond human
standards] so infinitely evil as to warrant eternal punishment."[11] Only Lucifer's
attempted emulation of the Deity ("I will be like the most High" [Isaiah 14:14,
referring literally to the king of Babylon]) can equal, even as it foreshadowed,
such titanic insolence.

I recount these examples, not to establish a basis for appraisal or a historical context, but to emphasize their common denominator: the ongoing elaboration of theological positions that stood in dramatic juxtaposition—in audacious
or brash or blasphemous opposition, some would say—to the status quo. Smith
knew that it was this collapse of sacred distance, the enunciation of the forbid-
den, the articulation of the ineffable, the concretization of the abstract, and the
invasion of sacred space that characterized both the bane and boon of his calling. In a letter to his attorney, Mr. Butterfield, Smith wrote,

> I stated that the most prominent difference in sentiment between the
> Latter-day Saints and sectarians was, that the latter were all circum-
> scribed by some peculiar creed, which deprived its members the
> privilege of believing anything not contained therein, whereas the
> Latter-day Saints have no creed, but are ready to believe all true prin-
> ciples that exist, as they are made manifest from time to time.[12]

This resistance to formal creeds, to a closed canon, and to conventional opinion are all so many versions of resistance to finality, to fixity or what he called
"circumscription"—being bound and hemmed in by orthodoxy. Elsewhere, he
declared that "the first and fundamental principle of our holy religion" is to
be free "to embrace all, and every item of truth, without limitation or without
being circumscribed or prohibited by the creeds or superstitious notions of
men, or by the dominations of one another."[13]

But Smith also recognized that the agonistic nature of his thinking was
beyond the capacity of even his followers to fully absorb:

> But there has been a great difficulty in getting anything into the
> heads of this generation. It has been like splitting hemlock knots
> with a corn-dodger for a wedge, and a pumpkin for a beetle. Even the
> Saints are slow to understand.
>
> I have tried for a number of years to get the minds of the Saints
> prepared to receive the things of God; but we frequently see some
> of them, after suffering all they have for the work of God, will fly to
> pieces like glass as soon as anything comes that is contrary to their
> traditions: they cannot stand the fire at all.[14]

At other times and places Smith similarly hinted that he was constrained by a world, and even a following, that was unwilling, or incapable, of countenancing his ever-growing audacity, heterodoxy, and innovation.

To one of his friends, he lamented that "he did not enjoy the right vouchsafed to every American citizen—that of free speech. He said that when he ventured to give his private opinion on any subject of importance, his words were often garbled and their meaning twisted, and then given out as the word of the Lord because they came from him."[15] His insistence that his pronouncements did not always carry prophetic weight was not just a safety net or a convenient means of prudent retreat. It meant that the process, the ongoing, dynamic engagement, the exploring, questing, and the provoking dialectical encounter with tradition, with boundaries, and with normative thinking should not be trammeled or impeded by clerks and scribes looking for a final word, interrupting a productive process of reflection, contestation, and creation. Sometimes, it would appear, he merely wanted the privilege of thinking out loud, but that is difficult when surrounded by scribes behaving like court stenographers. I imagine, in this regard, he would have seconded the memorable protest of Virginia Woolf: "I should never be able to fulfill what is, I understand, the first duty of a lecturer—to hand you after an hour's discourse a nugget of pure truth to wrap up between the pages of your notebooks and keep on the mantel-piece for ever."[16]

A study of Joseph Smith seems to always come back to the dynamics of the revelatory process, rather than to the finality of a polished product; to the structure of his thinking, rather than to the end result of his thought. One of these dynamics, in particular, has enormous repercussions for a philosophy of history and for Smith's recovery of both past and future worlds. I am referring to Smith's integration of the divine into the historical, and of the historical into the divine, a process that can be said to have begun when he experienced his first epiphany in the woods of upstate New York. Of course, any personal encounter with God represents a collapse of sacred distance—an intersection of the transcendent, the heavenly, and the divine with the personal, the earthly, and the human. But Smith inaugurated a pattern that would increasingly intensify the collapse of those two domains, creating in the process a radical reconceptualization of sacred history. As he translated the Book of Mormon, he found several things about the experience to be the subjects of ancient holy writ, including his own role in the process, the commencing rise of the restored church, and even the particulars of his friend Martin Harris's visit to Columbia professor Charles Anthon. Scriptural mythology became historical script. When he reached the account of Christ's visit to the Nephites inhabiting ancient America, the episode recontextualized the Incarnation itself. That divine condescension into mortality—the primary miracle of Christian history whereby the full irrupution of the divine into human history is a unique event, producing a spate of mythic reverberations—became in Joseph Smith's expanding vision only one of an extensive series of historical iterations, evidence of the complete and literal interfusion of the human by the divine.

This development pushes us in a direction opposite the dominant trend of modernity described by the religious scholar Wilfred Cantwell Smith. "With the relatively recent rise in Western consciousness . . . of the new sense of history," he writes, "and the (consequent?) careful and rigorous distinction between history and myth, . . . what happened by and large was that the West opted for history and rejected myth." Regarding a scriptural event like the earth's creation, for example, he writes, "We may recognize now that the problem . . . [is] the notion that one is dealing here with historical time, rather than mythical time."[17] With Smith, *all we have* is historical time—but it is transformed into a dimension that extends infinitely in both directions.

Smith understood the prophetic role in ways that furthered this project. We have been raised to believe that archaeologists and textual scholars recover history and the determinate and earthly past, while the future—eschatology in particular—is the province of prophets and visionaries. The Day of Judgment and millennial events are the stuff of faith and shadow. But from the day Smith relied upon prophetic authority and sacred artifacts to recover the words and deeds of Nephi, an Israelite from the sixth century B.C. who migrated to the western hemisphere and founded a civilization, Smith elided the enormous psychological and experiential distance that separated the down-to-earth world from the metaphysical.

C. S. Lewis has suggested the enormous psychological investment we have in maintaining the fundamental distinction between the human and the divine and hints at the crisis their conflation would occasion:

> [When] the distinction between natural and supernatural . . . [breaks] down, . . . one realise[s] how great a comfort it had been—how it had eased the burden of intolerable strangeness which this universe imposes on us by dividing it into two halves and encouraging the mind never to think of both in the same context. What price we may have paid for this comfort in the way of false security and accepted confusion of thought is another matter.[18]

Joseph Smith did not allow us such comfortable dichotomizing.

I want to move in another direction now and discuss the totality of his thought—conceived not exactly as system, for he was not a systematic thinker and he does not present us with enough materials to fashion a comprehensive theology. But I think we can nonetheless say something about what all of his thinking and revealing and speculating was tending toward. If we trace out briefly the evolution of Smith's prophetic career, we can mark a decisive turn sometime in 1830. When he went to that grove as a fourteen-year-old youth, he was only asking a private question in a personal prayer. And what he found was, he thought, a revelation of purely personal significance. As he said to his mother, "I have learned for myself that [such and such a church] is not true" (Joseph Smith–History 1:20). He had no clear intimation of future projects and heavenly callings. It was not until he was seventeen that he tells of an angel of light appearing in his room, telling him that God had a work for him to do. That work, as he soon learned, was the translation of the Book of Mormon. It would appear that, as he labored on that project, he still did not dream of any greater calling or mission. It was not until March 1829, just a few months before he finished that considerable task, that a revelation first mentioned to Smith "the beginning of the rising up and the coming forth of [his] church out of the wilderness" (Doctrine and Covenants 5:14).

Accordingly, in April 1830, Smith complied with that directive and organized a church. But even then he did not know that this church was not just another restorationist congregation with a few dozen members and a new revelation. He had yet to learn that this church, so-called, was to become much more. It was in December 1830, after that humble meeting of six men and onlookers in Fayette, New York, that Smith was commanded to gather his followers and actually "assemble together at the Ohio" (Doctrine and Covenants 37:3). Thus it came to pass that the "little flock" (Doctrine and Covenants 6:34) was now set on the path to become a people, the kingdom of God on earth, the rock cut without hand from a mountain that would roll forth and fill the earth.

But as his religious sphere of influence grew, so did his revelatory scope. Joseph Smith initially conceived of the Book of Mormon as "a record of a fallen people" (Doctrine and Covenants 20:9). It was presented to the world, in the first generation of the church especially, as a history of the American Indian. Its status as sacred scripture depended, first, on the fact that it was written by ancient prophets as sacred history, and second, on the fact that it bore the modern traces of the sacred, manifest through its miraculous transmission and translation. Its relationship to the Bible evolved and continues to do so. Originally, the Book of Mormon derived much of its authoritative weight *from* the Bible. But at the same time, of course, the elevation of the Book of Mormon to scriptural status challenges the supremacy, the uniqueness, and most important, the sufficiency of the Bible. The implications of that realignment deserve a second look. The principle of *sola scriptura* (the Bible as the only and sufficient ground for authority) is clearly undermined by the Book of Mormon. But that heretical affront to the Bible's status—to the Bible's function as source and guarantor of orthodoxy—may have distracted many from exploring how, in Smith's mind, that process of dethronement and realignment finished playing out.

As a youth of seventeen, when visited by the angel Moroni, Smith recorded that the heavenly messenger in his room was quoting to him passages from the Old Testament but "with a little variation from the way [they read] in our Bibles" (Joseph Smith–History 1:36). True, as all discussions of this episode suggest, Smith would have become aware at this point of the imperfection or fallibility of the King James Version. But I wonder if another seed was planted at this time, suggesting to him not just the deficiency of the known biblical text but also the possibility of an unknown text, one being quoted casually by heavenly messengers. Clearly, it would seem the angel was quoting something of which the Bible was apparently an imperfect version or derivation.

Conventional notions of a Christian apostasy—or falling away from Christian truth—began with the premise that Christ had established his true church in Palestine, only to have errors and corruptions creep in with the passage of time. In the course of the Reformation, the question was only how far those corruptions extended and how drastic the required remedies were.[19] But in the course of measuring current institutions against past incarnations of truth, those of a more liberal disposition asked how much a just God might have revealed to the ancients. Some posited that foreshadowing and fragments of the true gospel were evident among a variety of peoples scattered through time. Jonathan Edwards, like many of the Church Fathers, believed that God had, in fact, imparted to several ancient peoples essential religious truths that were subsequently lost. Much earlier, Augustine expressed a version of this idea when he wrote in his *Retractions*, "What is now called Christian religion has existed among the ancients, and was not absent from the beginning of the human race."[20] While smatterings of eternal principles emerged in the religions and philosophies of antiquity, Christian adherents of this line of reasoning held that only the Bible represented the full and complete account of God's revelation. (Speaking of the Jews, for instance, a commentator contemporary with Edwards wrote that "we have the gospel as well as they [had], and in greater purity."[21])

Prisca theologia (ancient theology), as this doctrine has been labeled, or "fulfillment theology" as variations of the doctrine are called in recent formulations, was useful both to account for prevalent archetypes (such as animal sacrifice and the idea of a divine incarnation) that could otherwise impugn the uniqueness and hence the validity of Christian doctrines, and to assert God's justice and mercy in dispensing truth to Christian, Jew, and pagan alike. But whereas previous thinkers had emphasized the fragmentary nature of prior revelation and its final consummation in modern scripture, Smith pushed the principle of *prisca theologia* in the other direction. "From what we can draw from the Scriptures relative to the teaching of heaven," he said, "we are induced to think that much instruction has been given to man since the beginning *which we do not possess now.*"[22]

Smith's production of the Book of Mormon was the most conspicuous embodiment of this challenge to biblical sufficiency; the new scripture itself hammered home the message of God's word as endlessly iterated and endlessly proliferating. As God declared in Nephi's account, "I shall speak unto the Jews and they shall write it; and I shall also speak unto the Nephites and they shall write it; and I shall also speak unto the other tribes of the house of Israel . . . and they shall write it; and I shall also speak unto all nations of the earth and they shall write it" (2 Nephi 29:12). But before Smith even finished the translation, a most enigmatic revelation suggested that Smith's paradigm was undergoing another dramatic revision. In April 1829 he produced "a translated version of the record made on parchment" by John the Beloved (Doctrine and Covenants 7, section heading). No matter that Smith never claimed to have the parchment itself, or that the content of the record was not theologically significant (except insofar as it turned the *myth* of John's reputed immortality into the *history* of John's immortality). It was, again, what this fragmentary puzzle piece was suggestive of: the incompleteness of the biblical record and the corresponding totality of something that Smith was moving toward.

Mere months after publishing the Book of Mormon, Smith even more emphatically reversed the Christian arrow of time, with its consummation in a totalizing biblical revelation and Christian dispensation, when he recast the Mosaic narrative of Adam as one in which the patriarch of the human race was the first Christian proselyte. God himself, Smith wrote in this restoration of ancient scripture,

> called upon our father Adam by his own voice, saying: . . . If thou wilt turn unto me, . . . and repent of all thy transgressions, and he baptized . . . in the name of mine Only Begotten Son, . . . which is Jesus Christ, the only name which shall he given under heaven, whereby salvation shall come unto the children of men, ye shall receive the gift of the Holy Ghost. (Moses 6:51–52)

This Book of Moses was unlike anything Smith had until then produced. In contrast to the Book of Mormon, it was not rooted in a recovered ancient record. And unlike his many other revelations, it was not God speaking to his heart and mind. It was a verbal facsimile, but of what original? At this same moment in time, Smith embarked upon a translation of the Old Testament, and later the New, but it was again a translation without any original to which he had access. He used no ancient manuscripts. Two years later, he received an elaborate revelation long honored with the simple designation "the Vision," which detailed the kingdoms of glory in the hereafter. It was, Smith wrote significantly of the document he dictated, "a transcript from the records of the eternal world."[23] One year later, in a similar manner, Smith recorded an excerpt of quotations from a first-person account written by John—yet another record that Smith quoted from that he did not possess himself (Doctrine and Covenants 93:6–17).

A few years later, Smith pushed the temporal parameters of the gospel even further back when he recounted in the writings of Abraham the foundational events that occurred in the Great Council in Heaven—a scriptural production apparently inspired by, but apparently not translated directly from, ancient papyri. The particulars of these Abrahamic writings like the recuperated Genesis material that includes an account of Enoch—and also the Zenos parable from the Book of Mormon and the previously missing writings of the apostle John— need to be evaluated on their own terms, but it is simply the grand project, the intimated master blueprint, that constitutes a major idea in its own right. The cumulative weight of these experiences seems to have created in Smith's mind a major paradigm shift, a wholesale inversion of the traditional model of biblical fullness and of *prisca theologia*. Rather than finding in the pagans and ancients foreshadowing and tantalizing hints of God's revelation, which would culminate in the Christian canon, Smith worked, with growing momentum, backward and outward. He gradually conceived of his objective as nothing less than to point us in the direction—through the assemblage of the myriad worlds he revealed—of a gospel plenitude that transcended, preceded, and subsumed any and all earthly incarnations, the Bible included. This vision or intimation of what I would call an Urtext induced him to transgress linguistic, religious, and other boundaries in its pursuit.[24]

This text was not only immanent in Smith's thought; it is, in fact, a powerful and prominent image in the scriptural canon itself. Only eleven verses into the Book of Mormon, Lehi is bidden by Christ to take a book and read, from which book he then reads and sees "many great and marvelous things" (1 Nephi 1:14), which give him a knowledge of the future, horror at human wickedness, and rejoicing in God's mercy. Likewise Ezekiel is given a book, which he is commanded to eat (Ezekiel 2:8–10) as is John the Revelator (Revelation 10). Smith's enterprise thus takes literally the implications of these scriptural images. Since the books that Lehi and Ezekiel and John are given to read or eat precede, rather than follow from, the canonical record, Smith works backward in quest of the wholeness they represent.

In this context, one begins to see why Smith's thoughts appear undisciplined and unsystematic. His major project was not the correction or enunciation of particular theological principles but the complete reconceptualization of the scope and sweep of gospel parameters themselves. The burden that he bequeathed to posterity was an array of remarkable, tantalizing texts with consistent themes, motifs, and patterns that emerge in a whole series of entire worlds recovered from the past: premortal realms, councils in heaven, Nephite and Jaredite civilizations, an Adamic gospel dispensation, Enoch's life and ministry, Mosaic epiphanies, and weeping Gods. One searches for a vocabulary adequate to such endlessly proliferating layers of time and being, beckoning us to imagine a totality in which they all share.

The remaining question is, how do the particulars of Smith's past worlds hold up? If his collapse of the sacred into the temporal is to succeed, if we are to see his project as truly historical rather than as simply mythic, then ultimately, the worlds of the Nephites and Jaredites and of Enoch—like the words of Adam, Abraham, Moses, and John that he recovered—cannot resist examination as the historical records they purport to be.

Only now, with the passage of two hundred years or more, may we have enough distance from the career of Joseph Smith to assess his contributions adequately. This is not only because of the advantages of hindsight and historical perspective, or of the development of critical tools and disciplinary sophistication. These are all important aids. But for the case of Joseph Smith, we may now have the distance needed to allow us to step back from a canvas as large as the one he painted.

9

Visions, Revelations, and Courage in Joseph Smith

Douglas J. Davies

When Joseph Smith told of divine disclosures and visitations, he was offering the essence of himself. To begin so emphatically is to emphasize the significance of visions and revelations for understanding the life of the founding Mormon prophet without either taking them for granted as a matter of faith or relegating them to some psychopathological domain. Accordingly, this essay adopts a distinctive perspective by using the notion of courage as a means of analyzing the part played by visions and revelations in the unfolding of Joseph's life. To a lesser extent, it also considers the organizational development of the Church of Jesus Christ of Latter-day Saints and the potential for what I mean by courage within its membership. In the course of so doing, we pay extensive attention to the emergence of clusters of symbolic values related to the notions of truth, goodness, evil, pain, and salvation particularly as formed within the Mormon tradition by the biblical narrative of Christ in Gethsemane. Whilst part of that account involves detailed textual comment, another is highly speculative. Finally, as a contribution to the developing interdisciplinary field of Mormon studies, this essay pursues the themes of Joseph Smith, courage, and church membership by employing the analytical insights of two quite different and long-established scholars, Paul Tillich, the theologian, and William Whyte, the sociologist.

Methodology, Courage, and Mormon Studies

In employing courage as an analytical category, I am developing a theme that I briefly raised when concluding my *Introduction to Mormonism*.[1] There I had been prompted to ponder the Smith-courage link, which comes from my friend and former colleague John Heywood Thomas's assertion that the Protestant theologian Paul Tillich (1886–1965) had, in his study *The Courage to Be*, furnished "the most penetrating theological analysis of American culture that has been written."[2] Though Mormonism was not Tillich's concern, he said much about those American religious sentiments and cultural values that relate to Latter-day Saint (LDS) cultural development within a nineteenth-century Protestant milieu and in the social changes of the first half of the twentieth century. Given current discussions on Mormonism as an "American religion," any telling insight into American life of which Mormonism might be regarded as an expression seemed worthwhile. Then, too, Tillich's work helps us theoretically to connect the existential domain of individual life with the nature of a society's cultural orientation in a way that bears significantly upon Joseph Smith as the founding leader of a distinctive American religious movement. But Tillich does not stand alone in germane cultural comment with potential LDS application—one challenging complement to his *Courage to Be*, for example, is provided by William Whyte's, *The Organization Man*. Published more than a century after Joseph Smith's 1844 death, in 1952 and 1956 respectively, these volumes by scholars unconcerned with Mormonism are sufficiently established and appropriately located in intellectual terms to help throw light upon the much-debated issue of Joseph Smith and Mormonism as typical outcomes of an American cultural dynamic.

The methodological reason for employing these volumes, one deeply theological and one sociological, alongside textual, historical, and some theological material is to foster an interdisciplinary attitude within what is increasingly identified as the field of Mormon studies: indeed, a religious founder like Joseph Smith demands multifaceted treatment. Here Sir Isaiah Berlin's careful distinction between "thin" and "thick" forms of interpretation is theoretically useful.[3] For Berlin, "thin" material, is usually single stranded and often evident in sociological, psychological, economic, or medical research; it is contrasted with "thick" materials that furnish research, especially historical analysis, with a "texture constituted by (the) interwoven strands." For Berlin, such thick material helps differentiate between the natural and the human sciences; with a distinctive element in historical work consisting in the ability to participate in past lives, to some degree at least, on the basis of our own common-sense awareness of our own day and age. More familiar than Berlin's usage is Gilbert Ryle's later, and analogous, distinction between "thick" and "thin" descriptions applied within philosophy.[4] Clifford Geertz took "thick description" further still, in an anthropological analysis that not only combined field experience with appropriate historical-cultural information in order to account for a society's emotional and symbolic disposition, but also accounted for both the observable aspects of events and the actor's intentions lying behind those actions.[5]

It is precisely such an engagement with a community's formulation of its past and with its conception of its founder that is vital for this essay. Furthermore, since interdisciplinary approaches often benefit from a concentrated focus, I have, as already intimated, located this essay in the idea of courage, aware that, despite its established roots in philosophy, ethics, and literature, courage is seldom so employed in the study of religion.[6] By adopting it as a means of approaching Joseph Smith as a visionary, I seek to provide one response to Richard Bushman's question regarding the prophet, namely, "What was the logic of his visionary life?"[7] To suggest that it was driven by courage is entirely appropriate because exploring the complexity of a prophetic figure is also a means of addressing "The Inner Joseph Smith," which, in his essay of that title, Bushman recently described as the task of "examining how personality, doctrine and society interact."[8] Accepting the complexity of this interpretative venture, this essay involves an exploration of themes that relate to aspects of courage. One of these themes is grounded in Joseph's perception of moral evil and its resolution; this essay, then, examines explicit formulations concerning deliverance from evil as expressed in Joseph Smith's First Vision. Other themes I will consider include the unique LDS emphasis upon Jesus in Gethsemane, and upon baptism for the dead.

To achieve this exploration of courage, I begin with a brief textual study of the relatively familiar biblical account of Jesus in Gethsemane; from there we will move to a much less familiar historical episode taken from the life of St. Francis of Assisi. These apparently discrete topics will be shown to possess a symbolic affinity that prepares, first, for an analysis of the LDS development of a Gethsemane spirituality, and then, more speculatively, for an interpretation of Joseph Smith's inaugural theophany or First Vision. What emerges from this discussion is a configuration of elements concerning the transcendence of despair, the birth of hope, and hope's embodiment in Joseph's courage. We then pursue his introduction of baptism for the dead, interpreted as a form of embodied conquest of despair. In the light of these achievements, we then consider the status accorded Smith in the church he founded and we will find that it is not entirely as might be anticipated, at least in terms of some sociological theory. This essay ends by considering the dynamics of courage within that church, in terms of dialectic between individual freedom and corporate obedience.

Understanding, Truth, and Lies: The Prophetic Paradox

To be a prophet is to divide a people. That ability to understand other people, which fosters social cohesion, also includes the awareness that people may lie and, through their deceit, challenge a group's integrity. This is a problem for religious institutions because, given their coinage of truth, they should not purvey lies; and this is the prophet's paradox when he speaks against churches. Though common sense supports "little white lies" as helpful in conducting everyday life, it also knows that, at its worst, deceit ends in betrayal. These profound themes bring abstract issues of truth and falsehood into sharp focus in regard to the authenticity and sincerity of individual embodiment, and truth is nowhere more critical than in a religious leader such as Joseph Smith, who reckoned to bring a truth that superseded prevailing untruth evident in other religious advocates. It was this very proclamation of truth and the counterclaim of falsehood that fired religious antagonisms surrounding Joseph Smith.

The history of assessing Joseph Smith is one of divided opinion, as advocates and enemies debate his claim on revealed truths and his apparently strange behavior. My approach assumes that Joseph Smith had experiences that he interpreted as encounters with, and communication from, the divine world. He truly saw himself as one who had been granted visions and revelations; and in communicating these to others, he was no charlatan, deceiver, or liar. Not being a Latter-day Saint, I do not make these points in order to affirm any theological or faith-based belief, nor do I seek to deploy, for example, specific psychological theories to undermine Smith's status by denaturing his claims. My limited goal is to argue that these phenomena, when interpreted as an expression of courage, afford one means of assessing Joseph Smith's religious identity.

Courage: Vision and Revelation

To treat visions and revelations as an expression of courage is, inevitably, to recognize the considerable difficulties presented by those who have shown, for example, the prevalence of visions during particular periods of history, including Joseph Smith's day,[9] or others who interpret visions through psychological interpretations of Joseph's mental status,[10] including descriptions of epilepsy.[11] Accusations of Smith's alcohol abuse or his possessing other temperamental weaknesses have also been common in anti-Mormon literature, especially that of the nineteenth century.

Certainly, a consideration of the complex field of human emotions as the most profound source of motivation and of emergent identity within cultural contexts is demanded when considering visions. Emotions are amongst the most complex aspects of existence to categorize and their historical and academic treatment in, for example, psychology and anthropology is relatively novel, making them hard to compare across cultures and time.[12] The hermeneutical challenge at cultural-historical levels increases when the focus falls upon any one individual such as Joseph Smith, who has been proved by time to be markedly influential upon others.

Emotional Correlation

Another aspect of that hermeneutical challenge involves considering the part played by faith and by faith's emotional dynamics in the interpretation of past events, especially when those reported events include visions and revelations. This affects the way in which LDS believers relate to Joseph Smith by depicting his experiences in and through their own. This is apparent in the so-termed testimony expected of each Saint, through which Saints give voice, at appropriate church services, to their personal "knowledge" that Joseph Smith was a prophet of God through whom the one true church was restored to earth. To "know" that this is the case is not regarded within the church as a mere opinion arrived at by intellectual reflection; in this sense that knowledge is not considered simply a matter of "history," but it also involves an inward sense of the truthfulness of that idea: thus it is a personal manifestation of "faithful history." Expressions such as "burning in the bosom" or some other emotional sensation reinforces the personal bond between today's believer and Joseph as the first Mormon prophet. Prayer is emphasized as the medium through which such a testimony may be gained. And that particular emphasis on prayer leading to testimony is important as a link-point for the emotional correlation of believer and prophet. This process of emotional correlation is underexplored within religious studies despite its significance as the bedrock of actual practice in religious traditions. Its theoretical significance relates to the way such traditions prioritize certain formulations of emotional moods and guide their members into a patterned experience of them. The Catholic tradition of the imitation of Christ and the Protestant models of Christ-like living, for example, furnish their own examples of schooled emotion: indeed, "religious formation" is a telling phrase that is used in Catholic traditions for processes of influenced development.

These background comments on emotional correlation serve to introduce an analysis of a distinctive portrayal of emotional experience that became highly influential in Mormon life. That portrayal aligns episodes in the life of Joseph Smith with that of Jesus Christ, and potentially, it brings that paired image to bear on the life of any Latter-day Saint. The topic focuses on the biblical image of Christ and the Garden of Gethsemane. Theoretically speaking, it shows how ideas may be developed into a particular symbolic complex within a theological and ritual scheme. By first giving a detailed account of the original biblical formulation and then offering a historical application of it outside the Mormon world, we will be able to see, all the more clearly, how the LDS formulation operates in relation both to LDS texts and doctrine regarding atonement and to Joseph Smith's First Vision. In Max Weber's terms, the Catholic and Mormon examples reveal an elective affinity between a preexisting narrative's symbolic structure and new religious contexts in need of a means of their own elaboration. To this we will return.

Gethsemane in the Gospels

We begin with a review of the biblical material following the last ritual meal Jesus takes with his disciples, when they go to the mount of Olives and a place named Gethsemane in Mark (14:26, 32) and Matthew (26:30, 36), to "the mount of Olives" and "the place" in Luke (22:39, 40), and "over the brook Cedron, where was a garden" in John (18:1; all citations from KJV).

In Mark's Gospel (Mark 14:32–51), Jesus says to disciples, "Sit ye here, while I shall pray"(v. 32). He becomes "sore amazed" and "very heavy" (v. 33) and says, "My soul is exceeding sorrowful unto death; tarry ye here, and watch." He then prays earnestly and asks that, if possible, God, whom he addresses as "Abba, Father," might "take away this cup from me: nevertheless, not what I will, but what thou wilt" (v. 36). Jesus comes back to the disciples, whom he finds asleep, and exhorts them to watch and pray, acknowledging in the memorable words that "the spirit truly is ready, but the flesh is weak (v. 38)." He goes and prays again in the same words. He returns to find them yet again asleep, and they do not know how to explain themselves. This is repeated a third time, after which he calls them all to go with him to meet his betrayer—Judas—who is "at hand (v. 42)." Judas arrives with a "great multitude with swords and staves (v. 43)," and he kisses Jesus in the often-depicted act of betrayal. Peter seeks to defend Jesus and cuts off the high priest's servant's ear. But all is in vain and the disciples "all forsook him, and fled" (v. 50)—all except a young man who follows the arresting party, some of whom try to seize him; they succeed in grabbing the young man's cloak but he escapes, naked. Jesus is taken away to be tried and his crucifixion follows.

Matthew's Gospel (Matthew 26:30–58) repeats most of Mark but makes considerable additions, including a discussion concerning betrayal, albeit before the Judas event occurs, in which Peter vows never to betray Jesus. Longer exchanges between Jesus and his captors occur, the slave's ear is severed, but Jesus disavows the use of swords. All the disciples are said to forsake him and flee, but this time it is Peter who is said to have "followed him afar off" (v. 58).

Luke's Gospel (Luke 22:39–54) contains a slightly abbreviated version of Mark, for the disciples sleep only once. But it adds that Jesus healed the severed ear and asks the arresting officers why they had not arrested Jesus during his regular presence in the temple. The explanation seems to lie in the added text, "But this is your hour, and the power of darkness" (v. 53). There is one other feature of the Lucan narrative of profound significance for Mormons, however, for, in the King James Version (KJV) of the Bible, the one in which Joseph Smith was deeply read, are found two verses that relate to Jesus in his period of anguish. They read thus: "And there appeared an angel unto him from heaven, strengthening him. And being in an agony he prayed more earnestly: and his sweat was as it were great drops of blood falling down to the ground" (Luke 22:43–44). In Luke, then, there is no account, as in Mark, of Jesus being abandoned by his disciples, and it is Peter, not some anonymous youth, who follows to see what would happen to Jesus.

John's Gospel (John 18:1–15) is, here as in many other places, quite different from the three synoptic Gospels; it works much more extensively to present material in a way that helps create a more explicit theological picture. Indeed, here the scene described is dramatically different from the synoptic versions. The focus is on Judas, on the identity of Jesus of Nazareth, and on Peter's cutting off the servant's right ear; indeed, we are told that the unfortunate servant's name is Malchus. And it is this event that gives occasion for the text in verse eleven: "Then said Jesus unto Peter, Put up thy sword into the sheath: the cup which my Father hath given me, shall I not drink it?" Much of the detail on Jesus, prayer, anguish, betrayal, and avowal of support that is focused by the synoptic Gospels on Gethsemane is distributed by John throughout the preceding chapters (thirteen through seventeen). This material includes much emphasis on divine support from the Holy Spirit (rather than from a heavenly angel) to keep the disciples from being "offended" (John 16:1), even though their abandoning of Jesus is also predicted; indeed, it is *their* hearts that are full of sorrow. For our purposes, the key feature lies in the mention of "the cup" as a metaphor for Jesus' obedient suffering about to be undergone in his passion and death.

Gethsemane and St. Francis

From these first-century biblical texts we pass to the medieval application of the Gethsemane event generated by a piety associated with St. Francis of Assisi (1181–1226). This interpretation can be seen in a single, late-fourteenth-century German woodcarving. Now in Utrecht's notable museum of religious art at the Maria Convent, its strong three-dimensional proportion brings the devotee to a highly instructive scene. On its left-hand side, as viewed, Jesus is depicted in the Garden of Gethsemane with his disciples, who are, as in the biblical narrative, asleep. He, by sharp contrast, is wide awake and, with upraised arms, is ready to take from an angel the cup that is symbolic of his awaiting destiny. In this, as in several later paintings, the cup and the supporting angel of the biblical texts come to be conflated in an angel holding the cup. This left-hand scene is divided from the right-hand side, except for an open gateway between the two, by a wicket fence. On the right-hand side, the scene is of St. Francis on Mount La Verna with its church—the site where, in September 1224, God bestowed upon Francis's body the stigmata, the signs of Christ's passion and crucifixion. In the carving, Francis is kneeling with head and arms upraised; some of his followers are depicted in the foreground and reflect the fact that he had been distinctly successful in establishing his Franciscan Order in 1209, prior to his reception of the stigmata. In fostering a piety of simplicity, devotion, service to the poor, and obedience to God, Francis's life echoed that of Jesus enough to make their parallel representations appropriate for subsequent generations of devotees and for their own correlations of emotion, including subsequent stigmatics.[13] Francis's devotion to Christ crucified made the wounds of the passion and crucifixion the medium of his desired identification with Christ. This developed in the relatively small, but not insignificant, Catholic tradition of stigmata within the spirituality of the imitation of Christ; that tradition has been reflected in our own day by Padre Pio, a much-venerated Catholic priest.[14] This case of St. Francis demonstrates the dynamic of correlated emotion in powerful symbolic associations of faith.

Gethsemane and LDS Spirituality

This Franciscan example now provides a valuable entry into the appropriation of the biblical texts of Gethsemane within the emotional correlation of faith in Mormonism. In the three synoptic Gospel accounts, which, together, constitute one of the fullest sets of parallels of events in the life of Jesus, and, in John's intricate theological reflections, we have one of the most developed theologically sculpted interpretations of that life. What is of fundamental importance as far as Mormonism is concerned is that the two verses of Luke (22:43–44) emerge in LDS texts, and are developed in Mormon theology and art, in a unique way in relation to mainstream Christianity. More than that, with time, this divergence became increasingly marked for textual-critical reasons. The 1881 Revised Version of the New Testament, for example, leaves verses 43 and 44 where they were in the King James Version, but with a marginal note that says "other ancient authorities omit" them. These very verses, however, were moved from the main body of the text and given marginal status in later translations, such as the influential New Oxford Annotated Bible, based on the Revised Standard Version (1973).

The echo of these biblical texts within the Mormon canon is strong. In Mosiah, a Book of Mormon text internally reckoned to belong to approximately 124 BC, the ancient King Benjamin addresses the people: interestingly, the text begins with an exhortation to "awake, and hear the words" that have been "made known by an angel from God" (Mosiah 3:7). In foretelling the coming of one who will be called Jesus Christ, the Son of God, the Father of heaven and earth, the Creator of all things from the beginning," and whose "mother shall be called Mary" (Mosiah 3:8), Mosiah describes the temptations, pain, hunger, and thirst that the Christ will suffer and that will culminate in a state where "blood cometh from every pore, so great shall be his anguish for the wickedness and the abominations of his people" (Mosiah 3:7). This blood will atone for those who have "fallen by the transgression of Adam" or were ignorant of divine expectations (Mosiah 3:11). The chapter does not end before reference is made to a metaphorical cup, portrayed as "the cup of the wrath of God"; that cup is intended not for Christ but for the wicked who "have drunk damnation to their own souls" (Mosiah 3:25). Here there is a potential echo of Paul's language concerning the unworthy who "eateth and drinketh damnation to himself" (1 Cor. 11:29).

There is one other biblical text that is worth recalling in associating the Gethsemane motif with LDS thought. Occurring in the Epistle to the Hebrews, it presents a rare reference to, as practically all commentators would say, Jesus and "the days of his flesh, when he had offered up prayers and supplications with strong crying and tears unto him that was able to save him from death" (Heb. 5:7). In Joseph Smith's reflection on this text, evident in his Inspired Version (which is the Joseph Smith translation of the Bible) to which we return below, he furnishes an explicit marginal note explaining that these verses "allude to Melchizedek, and not to Christ." Indeed, it is from this section that Hebrews develops the notion of the Melchizedek, or high, priesthood, which is introduced in the preceding verse and inaugurates a series of theological explorations that link Jewish religious tradition with the emergent Christianity of the first century, and which, in due course, become core concepts in the development of Mormonism. Crucially, these include the Levitical priesthood compared and contrasted with the Melchizedek priesthood (Heb. 6:20; 7:1–28).

While it is inevitably speculative to suggest that Joseph Smith's thought was deeply influenced by these associations of ideas, such a suggestion is certainly not something that can be ignored, for this cluster of ideas brings together some of the nuclear concepts that would forge a core of Mormon belief in a quite distinctive fashion, namely, atonement in Gethsemane and the Levitical and Melchizedek priesthoods. The idea of the sweated blood of Christ's anguish came to forge what later generations would call "the Gethsemane experience" and would identify, in this blood, the blood of atonement. That which mainstream Christianity located on Calvary and in the crucifixion, Latter-day Saints came to locate more especially, though not exclusively, in the garden and in Christ's inner suffering. As the LDS grammar of theological discourse is concerned, and more particularly, as far as this essay's interest in the emotional discourse on Gethsemane in LDS thought is concerned, we find the focus falling upon an intrapersonal engagement with moral evil and a disciplined application of the will to the desired goal. This leads to the role of external assailants and persecutors of Christ being redundant. Atonement is largely achieved *before* Christ's betrayal, trial, and crucifixion. This difference in dynamic led me, previously, both to speak of the "Proactive Christ" of Mormon thought rather than a passive Christ who is "led, mocked, crucified and killed," and to comment on the influence of these ideas upon Mormon use of religious art, compared with that of mainstream Christian traditions.[15]

To help substantiate the point that Joseph Smith's mind did focus upon biblical texts in ways that both influenced and were influenced by his developing theological thought, especially as evident in the church's concurrent Doctrine and Covenants, it is worth quoting some examples from what came to be called the Inspired Version of the Bible, to which reference has already been made. Working from a King James Version, largely between 1830 and 1833, Joseph produced a text that included many changes.[16] This text passed from Joseph's first wife to the RLDS Church (the Reorganized Church of Jesus Christ of Latter Day Saints, now known as the Community of Christ), which first published it as Holy Scriptures in 1867, then, in another edition of 1936 with the added title, "Inspired Version." Its presence and use in the RLDS Church is established, and though some LDS thinkers make use of it, this version has never gained status and wide currency amongst Latter-day Saints at large. I refer to it here, however, to pinpoint several texts whose changes suggest that the ideas represented in them were important to Joseph Smith, at least to some degree. I take, first, the critical case of how Luke 22:44 deals with Christ's passion. The relevant text and change between versions is as follows:

> and his sweat was as it were great drops of blood falling down to the ground. (King James Version)
> and he sweat as it were great drops of blood falling down to the ground. (Inspired Version)

This simple replacement of the noun *sweat* with its verb form makes it clear that Joseph pondered this particular text. So, too, changes in one aspect of the biblical text of Hebrews have implications, which I raise, albeit in a highly speculative fashion and with some caution, because they relate to one theory of Joseph Smith's psychological life that has, with other psychological theories, been much criticized. In Hebrews chapter 4, as it leads up to the introduction of the Melchizedek motif in chapter 5, the King James Version speaks of the "gospel" (Heb. 4:2) that has been preached, referring to it as "the word of God" that "is quick and powerful, and sharper than any two-edged sword, piercing even to the dividing asunder of soul and spirit, and of joints and marrow, and is a discerner of the thoughts and intentions of the heart" (Heb. 4:12). In Joseph's Inspired Version there is one change in text. It speaks of the "dividing asunder of body and spirit" rather than of "soul and spirit." There could hardly be a more powerful text than this to rivet the young Joseph Smith's attention on the ensuing verses, chapters, and their theological themes if, that is, there is any substance in William Morain's theory, advanced in his study *The Sword of Laban*.[17] This needs brief background explanation.

Morain, a professor of plastic surgery with a childhood association with the RLDS Church, learned in a serendipitous conversation with the dean of his medical school that the Dartmouth Medical School's founder, Dr. Nathan Smith, one of the most famous of all doctors in the United States in his day, had been the doctor called upon to conduct an excruciatingly painful operation on six-year-old Joseph Smith's leg after earlier incisions had failed.[18] The whole episode left Joseph on a blood-drenched bed "pale as a corpse" and "with large drops of sweat rolling down his face."[19] Followed by three years of convalescence and a slight lameness for life, this was no passing event. Accounts of the operation Joseph underwent without the benefit of anesthetic make it clear that this little boy knew what extremely severe pain was like. This struck a cord for Morain, whose medical experience included extensive work with severely burned children. His interpretation of the psychodynamics he believed to be associated with the immense pain and desire to transform and transcend its blocked memory led him to argue, amongst other things, that the surgical knife used by Nathan Smith in what was an innovative procedure had become transformed in Joseph's symbolic thought and emerged in his epic texts as Laban's sword. Though I cannot pursue the issues raised by Morain and his critics here, I cite his argument as part of a wider theme of Joseph's engagement with texts in the process of developing his thought in relation to his own profound life experiences.

Gethsemane and Joseph Smith: Garden and Grove

In the light of the threefold consideration of biblical, Franciscan, and LDS textual material, we are now in a position to ponder the issue of emotional correlation by asking why the Gethsemane scene of Christ's engagement with evil and achievement of atonement became so significant within the Mormon tradition. Rather than approach that question in terms of current LDS discussions over the relative place of Gethsemane and Calvary in the overall scheme of salvation, having dealt with some of these issues elsewhere, I emphasize the disposition of traditions in their selection from a spectrum of options, particular doctrinally interpreted scenes for use in religious devotion.[20] Just as the Catholic example used the biblical Gethsemane episode to express the deep and moving obedient passion of St. Francis to God, so the LDS case demonstrates an elective affinity, albeit one that takes comparison into a more complex set of interplaying themes.

This notion of elective affinity needs brief comment here, if only to stress the interplay between social and psychological factors within the traditional sociological notion that describes a process of cultural creativity in which new links are forged between existing ideas. One concept or image is seen to be appropriate to a novel situation and is adopted as a means of reflecting upon, or expressing, the significance of the new situation. Sometimes, too, preexisting and unrelated notions are brought together to form a new combination of ideas or practices, and this could be said to occur because of perceived affinities between phenomena. Certainly, when an individual or group organizes preexisting ideas into a new formulation, the outcome may be experienced as more than the sum of its parts, but what should not be ignored is the psychological domain that motivates these creative alignments. During periods of cultural creativity, when old symbols are transformed or new ones invented, the symbols' power is derived from an emotional force originating in an individual or group experience: indeed, it is important to stress the emotional dimension because the cognitive elements usually gain most attention. In theoretical terms this perceived appropriateness, which may be influenced by unspoken depths of embodied experience, is quite different from the long-standing linguistic notion of the arbitrariness of the sign. The ongoing embedding of such symbols can be expected to yield increasing depths of significance with time.

How might this relate to Joseph Smith and the development of LDS tradition? Two suggestions emerge as speculative possibilities. First, Joseph Smith identified his own experience in the woodland approach to God with Jesus' experience in Gethsemane: the affinity being grounded in a search for the way ahead during an impasse in life, a search that God alone could inform. Second, this alignment was energized by Joseph's experience of personal and bloody suffering as a child. So, to Christ in Gethsemane and Joseph Smith in the Palmyra grove, we add Joseph's own intensity of personal pain, a pain undergone whilst held in his earthly father's arms.

Such speculation demands some background description of the moods expressed in Joseph Smith's retrospective account of his own emotions relating to his visionary encounter with the divine in the woods "on the morning of a beautiful, clear day, early in the spring of eighteen hundred and twenty" (Joseph Smith–History 1:14). This was at a time when his mind was reflecting deeply upon the religious excitement of his neighborhood with "feelings . . . deep and often poignant." The experiential force of this early vision needs some careful contextual comment because it is described in close relation to a broader sense of encounter with evil. Pondering his being caught up in the contradictory arguments of different denominations, he "came to the conclusion" that he "must either remain in darkness and confusion" or else seek "wisdom" from God as the text from the Epistle of James advised (James 1: 5–6; Joseph Smith–History 1:13). Within these reflections on his religious turmoil, as formal and retrospective as they may be, the notion of darkness as an expression of Smith's mood is telling and, as likely as not, far from incidental.

Whether or not the Book of Mormon was a text composed by Joseph Smith, flowing from his previous religious knowledge under the creative capacity of his imagination and in the light of personal experience, which is the easiest and most obvious assumption for non-Mormons, the book's themes doubtless played a significant role in Smith's early thinking. One of these involves a cluster of ideas concerning darkness and light and appears in the First Book of Nephi, which begins the Book of Mormon and inaugurates the epic account of human encounters with divine figures and the obedience-disobedience syndrome that underlies its drive for salvation.

The Symbolism of Evil's Conquest

In its opening story, set in the ancient Holy Land some six centuries B.C., the Book of Mormon introduces the family of Lehi and Sariah, with sons Laman, Lemuel, Sam and the Book of Nephi's central hero, Nephi. Its grammar of discourse is radically underpinned by visions, by the status of being "a visionary man" (1 Nephi 5:4), by plates of genealogical record, and by wilderness wanderings. One of its novel stories concerns a "tree, whose fruit was desirable to make one happy" (1 Nephi 8:10). This is highly evocative of the Genesis myth concerning trees of varied destiny, as clearly recognized in First Nephi's chapter 8's subsequent editorial heading: "Lehi sees a vision of the tree of life." At the outset, however, the story is not about "the tree of life" but one of happiness, access to which is far from easy; later, however, the expanded story makes it "the tree of life" (1 Nephi 11:25; 15:22), itself a "representation of the love of God" (1 Nephi 11:25). It was accessible only by a "straight and narrow path" (1 Nephi 8:20) along the side of a river, and then only with the help of a "rod of iron," a kind of handrail that is subsequently explained as being "the word of God" (1 Nephi 15:24).

This structure was particularly important for those seeking the tree because, as various crowds pressed in its direction, some lost their way because "there arose a mist of darkness; yea, even an exceedingly great mist of darkness" (1 Nephi 8:23). Others, by contrast, "caught hold of the end of the rod of iron; and they did press forward through the mist of darkness" and achieved their arboreal goal (1 Nephi 8:24). Even some of them came to fall away and be lost when they succumbed to the "scoffing" of a crowd of unbelievers who populated a "great and spacious building" that "stood as it were in the air, high above the earth" (1 Nephi 8:26). Later accounts also draw upon the theme of this "mist" (1 Nephi 12:4) or even "vapour of darkness" (1 Nephi 12:5), explaining the "mists" as "the temptations of the devil" (1 Nephi 12:17). Such envelopments of negativity come to their full power in a later account of the crucifixion of Christ when the biblical text of a "thick darkness" covering the earth for a matter of hours becomes a "thick darkness" that could be felt as "the vapor of darkness" lasting for three days of absence of any light at all (3 Nephi 8:20–23). Darkness is also deployed in a description of people who "dwindled in belief and became a dark and loathsome, and a filthy people full of idleness and all manner of abominations" (1 Nephi 12:23).

These descriptions of darkness, its tangibility and certainly its strong negative moral attribution, serve well as a background to Joseph Smith's account of his primary encounter with supernatural forces. When the boy Joseph set himself to prayer in the woods to ask God which church was true, he tells of being "seized upon by some power" which "entirely overcame" him. The thick darkness gathering around him made him feel as though he was "doomed to sudden destruction" (Joseph Smith–History 1:15–16). Here we have an account of a form of despair, of hopelessness poignantly expressed. It holds strong echoes of the religious biographies of other religious leaders, like the Buddha's confrontation with evil in the form of Māra, or of Jesus' early temptation by the devil.[21]

Emotions of Despair and Hope

In Joseph Smith's case, it is appropriate to set this darkness motif against a readily available set of notions involving the notion of light and of white symbols. These include a figure descending from heaven with a "luster . . . above that of the sun at noon-day" (1 Nephi 1:9–10) or the fruit of the tree of life that was "white, to exceed all the whiteness that I had ever seen" (1 Nephi 8:11). One can also offset the darkness of the inaugurating vision of Joseph with his "moment of great alarm" when a "pillar of light" appeared "exactly" over his "head, above the brightness of the sun" that descended until it gradually fell upon him and delivered him from his trial, and had revealed within it "two Personages, whose brightness and glory defy all description" (Joseph Smith–History 1:16).[22] Again, to reinforce the illuminatory aspect of his vision one notes the subsequent act of prayer when his bedroom became "lighter than at noon-day" attending the manifestation of Christ in a "loose robe of most exquisite whiteness . . . beyond anything earthly" that Joseph had seen (Joseph Smith–History 1:30–31). But beyond these "white" motifs, as important as they are, stand the elements of deliverance and hope that they heralded, and in particular, Joseph's sense of having received a vision or revelation.

Just how he describes the transitional phase from despair to deliverance is telling. Had this been a clear case of a Calvinist Protestant experience, the helpless and despairing boy would have been delivered by the mighty hand of God, but it is not quite so in this case, for even amidst the "astonishing" sensation of having his tongue bound so that he could not speak, he exerts all his "powers to call upon God to deliver me out of the power of the enemy which had seized upon me." Indeed, he speaks of that point as "the very moment" when he was "ready to sink into despair and abandon" himself "to destruction." Just then he "saw a pillar of light" descend upon him. Here we are presented with an image of a boy whose calling upon God brought him first into a sphere of "enemy" attack, and whose final, concentrated effort brings him deliverance. The Father and the Son appear above him, "standing in the air" (Joseph Smith–History 1:15–17).

What basis, then, might there be for drawing any comparison between this episode—one whose telling developed in complexity in later versions that Joseph produced—and the biblical account of Jesus in Gethsemane?[23] The biblical narrative in Luke, for example, places the Gethsemane experience at nighttime, pointing to the moral situation as Jesus says to his captors, "But this is your hour, and the power of darkness" (Luke 22:53). John's stronger theological interpretation has the arresting party arrive with "lanterns and torches and weapons" (John 18:3). The Palmyra grove, by contrast, is set in the bright light of a spring morning. When the darkness gathers, what surrounds Joseph is perceived as a moral force: indeed, he speaks of it in personal terms. Any similarity between Joseph and Jesus in these contexts is, of course, relative, but in each case we are dealing with a moment of crisis and destiny and of addressing God in the face of what lies ahead. Each engages with hardship in powerfully distinctive ways. As the Mormon tradition developed, the interpretation of "the Gethsemane experience" argued that Jesus engaged internally and mentally with the sin of the whole world, the pressure of which resulted in his sweating blood, blood that would participate in atoning purposes. In the Palmyra grove, by contrast, Joseph was at the beginning and not the close of his earthly endeavors, but for him, too, there seemed to be an engagement not with "some imaginary ruin, but to the power of some actual being from an unseen world" (Joseph Smith–History 1:15–16). But both Jesus and Joseph found themselves sustained by a divine power of good. In each case, too, there is a verbal address to God. In Joseph's case this is highly significant, for his retrospective account of the event stresses that he was "determined to ask of God" and that "it was the first time in my life that I had made such an attempt, for amidst all my anxieties I had never as yet made the attempt to pray vocally" (Joseph Smith–History 1:14).[24] This exercise in vocal prayer itself became so influential in the church that later generations of missionaries, for example, would encourage prospective converts to pray aloud and ask God if the Book of Mormon is true. For both Jesus and Joseph, there seems to be a potential for destruction, and yet, the will to keep engaged with God leads each of them out of that context into the next phase of religious action.

Joseph is brought out of the "despair" on whose brink he felt poised for destruction; hope revives. The pillar of light descends and the Father and the Son come to him and begin to indicate something of his future path: he is not to join any existing church but must await new developments. Here, then, was a vision that was also a revelation of the divine mind to the teenage mind. As time went on, revelations came to stand supreme in Smith's experience and in his self-understanding, as Richard Bushman argues when rooting Joseph Smith's identity in his being "a revelatory," for whom the "signal feature of his life" was in "his sense of being guided by revelation." Tellingly, Bushman also observes that "the possibility of an imaginary revelation, erupting from his own heart and subconscious mind, seems not to have occurred to Joseph. To him the words came from heaven."[25] This is entirely intelligible, quite apart from Joseph's pre-Freudian era, given the biographical path of engagement with supernatural images in which he had come to live. At the core of Joseph's sense of identity was his active self-reflection upon the fact of having received a vision. This is strongly emphasized in the text "Joseph Smith–History," which is chosen for inclusion in the collected volume of the standard works that most Latter-day Saints possess; it is the source of quotations given above.[26] Time and again, Joseph speaks of having had a vision of the divine Father and Son, appearing in light above his head. He affirms that this occurred, that he knew it, and that he knew God knew it. Indeed, his affirmations demonstrate at least a degree of reflexive distance in his thought about his past. Joseph explained this to himself through the biblical account of Paul, who received a vision of the resurrected Christ, itself a preexisting case that helped him understand why some denied the fact and impugned his own integrity. As Smith expressed it, "I have thought since, that I felt much like Paul, when he made his defense before King Agrippa" (Joseph Smith–History 1:24). And while that is doubtless Joseph's explicit reflection, I am also suggesting that, as church tradition developed, the analogue of Gethsemane's garden and Palmyra's grove was also far from insignificant in the underlying cultural configuration of divine operation. And in this there is a real sense of hope, where hope indicates the sense of a possible future and a commitment to it, and courage bespeaks the energy summoned in forging a way ahead to make it possible.

Courage and Identity

What, then, of that way ahead, and of Joseph Smith as a religious leader forging it? While aware of Fawn Brodie's view that Joseph lacked courage amidst some episodes surrounding his death, it is, nevertheless, the case that the wide tenor of his life and its impact upon many followers provides ample evidence of a moral energy directing natural vitality to the achievement of desired goals.[27] Embedded within Smith's life is a high degree of resilience toward opposition and even toward failures within the self. Such courage helps drive the birth and growth of self-identity and of the way others view a person; in that regard it is a powerful element in the rise of a charismatic leader. Indeed, the sociology of charisma needs to include courage as an element that followers can admire and seek to emulate. The image of the teenage Joseph kneeling in the grove is well represented in LDS art and strikes a ready sentiment in its reception as a picture of faith. One feature in its dynamic composition that should not be overlooked lies precisely in his boyhood, which brings to the sense of courage an additional sense of sincerity and innocence. Tillich reminds us that, in classical literature, "the Greek word for courage, *andreia*," denotes "manliness," just as the Latin, *fortitudo*, or "strength," indicates "the military connotations of courage": the early Middle Ages, too, align courage with knightly references to nobility.[28] In Joseph's case these "manly" and "knightly" statuses are inverted or, one might even say subverted, by the individual's youthfulness. He has not been trained for this event, he is engaged in spiritual exploration, and his naïve simplicity is all the more powerful for that.

In philosophical-theological terms, Tillich is again valuable, now for his use of Thomas Aquinas in debating whether the intellect or the will takes primacy in human ontology. In developing his own position, Tillich draws from St. Ambrose the preference for courage (*fortitudo*) as that which enacts the "intention of the mind." This brings his discussion of courage into alignment with his notion of faith, enabling him to speak of courage as "the strength of the soul to win victory in ultimate danger, like those martyrs of the Old Testament who are enumerated in Hebrews 11." Tillich's desire is to "interpret faith through courage," and this is germane when considering Joseph Smith's life, not least in his first divine encounter.[29] In approaching Smith in this way, my intention is not to create an implicit hagiography, nor to suggest that Joseph Smith was without doubt, fear, or crises of confidence, but to position an analysis of identity and, behind identity, of "being," through the notion of courage: for, "Courage can show us what being is, and being can show us what courage is."[30] These great themes cannot be explored here, but they actively prevent our discussion from following the pedestrian routes of labeling Joseph Smith as "treasure digger" or the like: easy reductionism seldom fosters an understanding of religious leaders.

Courage and Vicarious Baptism

One irreducible factor needed when exploring such leaders is the alliance of courage with a desire for truth. Because it is impossible to quantify this love of truth, it is often ignored in sociological studies of religion driven by economic models of rational choice, yet it remains a cornerstone of much religious motivation, and in Joseph Smith's life, the desire for truth includes the realm of visions and revelations. Once gained, truth demanded courage for its implementation. A good example of this comes in sections 127 and 128 of the Doctrine and Covenants, pivotal texts concerning the development of Mormon thought and practice on a matter of deep concern to Joseph, namely, hope over the conquest of death.[31] Its driving rationale unites a cluster of LDS ideas focused on the belief that the living cannot be fully saved apart from the salvation of the dead. In flowing prose Joseph holds these doctrines as coming from heaven, and calls upon his followers to embrace them: "Brethren, shall we not go on in so great a cause? Go forward and not backward. Courage, brethren; and on, on to victory" (Doctrine and Covenants 128:22). To highlight courage in this text is to emphasize the fact that early followers did not always find Joseph's new doctrines immediately desirable or easy to adopt, especially when, as with plural marriage, they differed significantly from previously familiar Christian tradition. Indeed, the courage implicit in their acceptance should be pondered as a force helping to create new Mormon identities. Hope, too, was much evident and in this very text it immediately precedes courage (Doctrine and Covenants 128:21). It is this shared hope and its realization through courageous action that transforms individualistic wishes through collective action. In early Mormonism, hope took the form of belief in Christ's coming to America and in his millennial kingdom. Courage underpinned the hazardous migration of thousands of Europeans, many bereaved of kin before the trek or en route, to Utah; and all of whom were bereaved from their prophet's death in 1844. For his followers, Joseph's death was, itself, no ordinary death but was interpreted as martyrdom, a term that, in itself bespeaks an intrinsic courage.

In a previous volume, as intimated above, I was prompted by Heywood Thomas's gloss on Paul Tillich to raise the theme of courage in relation to American religion and culture; I seek to develop it further in this essay, using Tillich's definitions of kinds of courage appropriate to different relationships of an individual to God and to society. An underlying conception is that of the "courage of confidence," something "rooted in the personal, total, and immediate certainty of divine forgiveness," and this is particularly germane in the case of Joseph Smith. This orientation of the self is no simple psychological "self-acceptance." As Tillich expressed it, "It is not the Existentialist courage to be as oneself," but is "the paradoxical act in which one is accepted by that which infinitely transcends one's individual self."[32] As Bushman described the supernatural encounter with the angel Moroni, "This vision wrenched Joseph out of any ordinary track," ensuring him not only "that his sins were forgiven," but also giving him "a work unlike any envisioned in his time."[33] It is through such dynamic changes that a leader emerges and presents himself and his message to others. His courage is rooted in his sensed capacity to undertake a mission; he possesses, in Tillich's terms, "the courage to be."

Sacralizing Identity

What, then, of Smith's identity, proclaimed mission, and the status accorded him in the execution of such courage? To these issues I turn with the sociological assistance of Max Weber's notion of *charisma* and Hans Mol's theory of the sacralization of identity. Weber described charisma as "a certain quality of an individual personality by virtue of which he is set apart from ordinary men and treated as endowed with supernatural, superhuman, or at least specifically exceptional power or qualities."[34] This notion has served sociology well and is entirely applicable to Joseph Smith. A generation later, Hans Mol contributed an important complementary notion, though it is one seldom employed in relation to Weber, that of the *sacralization of identity*. This argues that those persons, events, or things that contribute substantially to our sense of identity are, in return, accorded a high sense of privilege, respect, and awe, amounting even to a sense of the divine: this could apply to a founder, a founding idea, or a rite.[35] As a group grows in significance and its members' sense of identity becomes intensified in association with that focal phenomenon, so that phenomenon or person is accorded an ever-increasing value. On this basis, for example, we could analyze the status of Jesus in Christianity, Muhammad in Islam, or Guru Nanak amongst Sikhs. For each, we would find contextual aspects that foster and constrain the ascription of high status.

What, then, of Joseph Smith? That he was, in Weber's sociological terms, a charismatic leader can hardly be doubted but, and this is the question that interests me, to what extent was he subject to a process of sacralization? Here only a sketched response is feasible. Certainly, Mol's model would anticipate that Smith would be accorded an increasingly august status as his community formed around him and grew after his death. The more the community conferred distinctive identity upon its members, the more they would confer dignity upon its founder. But this seems to have happened in a much more restrained fashion than might have been anticipated. LDS hymns such as "Praise to the Man who communed with Jehovah" or "The Seer," offer some evidence of a distinctive status accorded him, as does much other historical material, but most early Mormon hymns do not extensively develop Joseph themes.[36] Other constraints soon appear that seem to prevent large-scale sacralizing of the prophet himself, these include the Book of Mormon, endowment rites and the family emphasis, and the fact that the founding prophet was not the one and only prophet. For, in Mormonism, the office of prophet-president has continued to this day and attained a high degree of status. Unlike mainstream Sikhism, for example—the major tradition of which holds to ten historical prophets with the

spirit of Nanak, so to speak, present in them all, after which the sacred authority passes to sacred text coupled with sacred community—Mormonism did not,
as it were, close the canon of succession. The prophetic office of leader continues and it came, with time, to be an intrinsic part of an extensive hierarchical
organization. Not least significant is the fact that Brigham Young actually led
the majority of Saints westward after Joseph's death.

Another telling element concerns the fact that the very idea of deification
appears quite explicitly in core contexts of Joseph Smith's later thought and practice as something open to all worthy members. This democratization of potential
deification shifts the dynamics of sacralization from any single leader. Joseph's
introduction of the sacred ritual, especially of endowments (a ceremony in a
Mormon temple involving covenants and promises, and deemed essential preparation for inheriting the highest level of salvation), sought to initiate believers
into, and foster them within, a process of becoming divine: as the LDS dictum
has it—all men and women are gods in embryo. The fact that all dedicated Saints
should be engaged in domestic, ritual, and ethical lives leading toward a divine
status may well have militated against elevating the founding prophet too far.

Another constraint concerns the question of whether Joseph Smith was
the "founder" of Mormonism as far as believers are concerned: for obviously he
was, in the historical and sociological sense. This is where the place of Jesus in
Mormonism becomes relevant, recalling that he was one of the two personages
appearing in Joseph's early vision and that this vision was central to Joseph's accounts of his life. Also, after the successful growth of the early LDS movement,
Jesus made an appearance in the communal and institutional context of the
dedication of the Kirtland temple (Doctrine and Covenants 110).[37] Indeed, there
is both a telling symbolic equivalence and difference between the First Vision
and the Kirtland Vision—in the former, it is the Father who indicates the Son
and tells Joseph to heed him; in the latter, it is the Son who alone appears and
validates the new temple and, thereby, the church that built it. Both events reinforce each other and, in their way, reveal their own form of affinity between mo-
ments of inauguration and visions. In the First Vision Joseph's spiritual career
is launched, just as the Kirtland Vision, in a sense, launched the fuller career
of the church. In this latter vision, Moses and Elijah also appear after Jehovah
and announce what can be viewed as the single most influential textual idea
in Mormonism—the idea taken from Malachi concerning the turning of "the
hearts of the fathers to the children, and the children to the fathers" (Doctrine
and Covenants 110:1–10; Malachi 4:6).

In these events Jesus takes a priority over Joseph in a way that constrains
the possibility of the prophet being invested with an undue grandeur. The
naming of the church reinforces this point, beginning as it did in 1830 as the

Church of Christ and becoming the Church of Jesus Christ of Latter-day Saints in 1838. More recently, in 1995, the church adjusted its name to increase the textual profile of Jesus Christ and reduce that of the Church of . . . Latter-day Saints. In 2001 Elder Dallin H. Oaks, one of the Twelve Apostles, made it clear that while the full name had been given by revelation, the leadership would prefer any secondary reference to be to the Church of Christ rather than, for example, to the Mormon Church.[38] This Christological focus, along with a strong central leadership, has contributed to a restricted sacralization of Joseph Smith but with an increasing status ascribed both to the church's organization and leadership on the one hand, and to the status of Jesus on the other. Even the Book of Mormon is now, in subheadings, described as "Another Testament of Jesus Christ."

Individual and Institution

It is with this development from a single individual, and personal courage, to an enduring major religious institution with an extensive organization that we now conclude our essay. The changing context from a small group with face-to-face relations, to an international organization, inevitably demands a variety of analysis. While Jan Shipps has already reflected upon it sociologically, we add a complementary sociological perspective, one that enhances Tillich's theological account of courage as an individual attribute; this perspective comes from William Whyte's *The Organization Man*.[39] Together these scholars help interpret the American social-moral life of which Mormonism is so frequently depicted as an idealized expression. These mid-twentieth-century sociological and theological exercises engage with basic human themes and offer extensive theoretical applicability to Joseph and his church, though here I can simply allude to their combined potential.

Whyte argued that the Protestant ethic was being replaced in the United States by the social ethic, whose threefold tenets embraced "a belief in the group as a source of creativity; . . . in 'belongingness' as the ultimate need of the individual; and 'in the application of science to achieve the belongingness.' "[40] While the first two of these and, in a qualified philosophical sense, also the third, aptly reveal aspects of historical LDS culture, my point in using Whyte's idea is to accentuate the double-edged nature of his final description of the relationship between the individual and society in relation to Joseph Smith. Whyte speaks of the moral or human need to fight against "The Organization" if any kind of dynamic authenticity of the self is to be maintained, and this, it might seem, offers both a direct means of approaching Joseph's primary visionary revelations and of highlighting his intrinsic courage demanded for to carry them out.[41] "The Organization" against which Smith fought was comprised of the received religious traditions of his day—the churches then so manifest in revivalism. But there is a double-edged aspect of Whyte's analysis, for it would be improper not to ponder the question of whether the LDS Church that replaced the churches came, with time, to manifest just that social ethic that replaced the Protestant ethic. If, as is so often argued, the LDS Church does express a quintessential American form of Christianity, even an American religion, then this question becomes pertinent in the light of Whyte's reflections, and not only of Whyte's but of Tillich's, too. Indeed, these two authors almost speak with a single voice on an issue that links much of our preceding discussion, namely, the courage demanded of an individual in relation to a group. One of Tillich's most extensive streams of argument focuses on "the courage to be as a part," or "democratic conformism."[42] Whilst rooting this desire of "affirming one's being by participation in given structures of life" in a European past, and acknowledging both the American "frontier situation" and the "need to amalgamate many nationalities" in the United States, Tillich, nevertheless, identifies "the courage to be as a part" as a distinctive American trait, one that had not, in the mid-twentieth century, succumbed to the increasing European pressure of "the courage to be as oneself." There is a kind of historical irony in this analysis, for while this corporate sense constitutes the basis of the LDS Church's theology and ritual of ultimate salvation, it was born out of Joseph Smith's opposition to membership in the religious bodies of his day. Joseph's courage to be himself generated a church perfectly reflective of what Tillich saw in America as "a country whose prevailing courage is the courage to be as a part."[43] In what appears as a kind of ongoing dialectic between individualism and corporatism Whyte can then be seen as adopting a critique of that very corporate mode, of aspects of American culture as "organization," that is, of many who function "as a part."

But few things are as simple as they first appear. For while it is valuable to interpret Joseph Smith's life in terms of courage, we should not ignore Tillich's wisdom in grasping the nature of a courage grounded in a sense of being accepted by a transcendent one. And that, immediately, raises the relational nature of a person. What is more, visions and revelations are, themselves, deeply relational: they make a person into a prophet only when others heed their utterance. For Joseph Smith, this was, in all likelihood, of profound importance because, as Bushman tentatively expressed, "Joseph may have been a lonely man who needed people around him every moment."[44] His essential courage to be himself led to a search for truth that rapidly involved the courage to be accepted both by God and, later, by other people. With time, this yielded an institution that increasingly required members to possess the courage to be themselves and yet to be "as a part." Whyte's analysis highlights the paradox that we may see as inherent in the dialectic of a church requiring both independence of mind, manifest in personal testimony, and obedience, manifest in active engagement in corporate rites necessary for salvation.

10

Seeking the Face of the Lord: Joseph Smith and the First Temple Tradition

Margaret Barker (Part I) and
Kevin Christensen (Part II)

Part I

When Moses was told to build the tabernacle, the Lord said to him: "Let them make me a sanctuary, that I may *dwell* in their midst" (Exod. 25:8). When this was translated into Greek, it became: "And you shall make for me a holy place, and I shall *be seen* among you" (LXX Exod. 25:7).[1] Why the difference?

The Pentateuch was translated into Greek in Alexandria during the reign of Ptolemy II (285–247 BCE), or so the traditional story says.[2] The actual process may have been more complicated, but the Greek Pentateuch almost certainly originated in Egypt and raises the question, Why did a Jew in Egypt think that the Lord dwelling in the sanctuary meant that he was seen there? Our modern idea of the invisible presence of the Lord in the holy place cannot have been what a third-century Jew in Egypt understood by the presence of the Lord in the holy place.

Whether or not the Lord could be "seen" was a matter of some controversy. One strand in the Old Testament—and the strand that has had a disproportionate influence on reconstructions of Old Testament theology—was that of the Deuteronomists, so called because their ideals were drawn from, and expressed in, Deuteronomy. They were emphatic that the Lord could not be seen: for them, the meeting with the Lord at Sinai had been just a voice. "The Lord spoke to you out of the midst of the fire; you heard the sound of words but *saw no form*; there was only a voice" (Deut. 4:12). The people saw the Glory of God and they saw God speaking with a human being (Deut. 5:24), but there was no form. Presumably this meant a human form. The other account of the meeting at Sinai says that Moses, Aaron and his family, and the elders "saw the God of Israel; and there was under his feet as it were a pavement of sapphire stone, like the very heaven for clearness" (Exod. 24:10). God had feet; at Sinai they saw a form.

Moses asked to see the Glory of the Lord, and was told that he could see his goodness and know his Name, but he could not see the face/presence,[3] of the Lord, "for man shall not see me and live" (Exod. 33:20). The tradition is ambiguous here: the Lord used to speak to Moses face-to-face, as a man speaks to his friend (Exod. 33:11), and he spoke to him from between the two cherubim over the *kapporet* (Exod. 25:22); neither of these instances says that the Lord was actually seen. They could have been understood in the Deuteronomists' sense of sensing the presence and hearing the voice. But Aaron was told that, when he entered the holy of holies, the Lord would appear in the cloud over the *kapporet* (Lev. 16:2), so perhaps Moses did see the Lord when he stood in the same place. And Moses did see *the form* of the Lord: this was the distinction that set him apart from the other leaders of Israel. "With [Moses] I speak mouth to mouth, clearly, and not in dark speech; and he beholds *the form* of the Lord" (Num. 12:8). We shall return to this.

The Deuteronomists also show a distinct hostility toward both temple and monarchy. Samuel warned the people that a king would be a disaster (1 Sam. 8:10–18), and as their account of the monarchy unfolds, most of the kings are shown to fall far short of the people's ideal. It is remarkable to have a national history presented as a catalogue of bad kings, and where the destruction of the capital city is blamed on their behavior (2 Kgs. 23:3–4). The Deuteronomists also disapproved of the temple. It was designed by foreigners, and Solomon had to impose forced labor on his own people to build it (1 Kgs. 5:1–18); the cost was enormous, and Solomon had to sell part of his kingdom to the king of Tyre to pay the debts (1 Kgs. 9:10–14). Given that this major set of primary sources is hostile to king, temple, and the very idea of theophany, any attempt to reconstruct the situation in the first temple is fraught with difficulties.

Even the Deuteronomist description of the temple omitted certain details, which are found elsewhere. These are not random details but significant for our quest. It is as though the Deuteronomists wanted to rewrite the past and remove whatever theophany had implied. The Chronicler and the Deuteronomist both wrote accounts of Solomon's temple. The Chronicler said David had received a plan for the temple from the Lord, just as Moses had received detailed instructions on Sinai how to build the tabernacle as the place where the Lord dwelt in the midst of his people (Exod. 25:8). Deuteronomy implies that Moses did not receive any plan for the tabernacle; on Sinai he received only the Ten Commandments: "He added no more" (Deut. 5:22). The plan David received included the golden chariot throne (1 Chron. 28:18–9), but the Deuteronomist does not mention this. He had appointed temple musicians "to invoke, to thank and to praise the Lord, the God of Israel" (1 Chron. 16:4), but the Deuteronomist does not mention them. Solomon set up a veil of blue, purple, crimson, and white linen fabric to screen the cherubim of the holy of holies (2 Chron. 3:14), and the Deuteronomist does not mention this, either. All of these details are important for understanding how the Lord appeared in the temple.

King Solomon's temple dedication prayer looks as though something was added that contradicted the original words of the prayer.[4] Solomon prayed, "I have built thee an exalted house, a place for thee to dwell in for ever" (1 Kgs. 8:13), but later in the prayer we find him saying, "Will God indeed dwell on earth? Behold heaven and the highest heaven cannot contain thee; how much less this house that I have built" (1 Kgs. 8:27). The temple was to be the place of the Name: "the place of which thou hast said, 'My Name shall be there' (1 Kgs 8:29). Nobody can be sure what this meant, but the same distinction is found in the Deuteronomist's account of Nathan's warning to King David. Here the contrast is first between a permanent temple and a tent: "Would you build me a house to dwell in? I have not dwelt in a house since the day I brought up this people of Israel from Egypt to this very day, but have been moving about in a tent for my dwelling" (2 Sam. 7:6). Then there is the promise of a future house, but for the Name: "[Your son] shall build a house for my Name" (2 Sam. 7:13). We are invited to believe that the Lord was not "in" the temple, and so the purpose of building the tabernacle [and the later temple] is immediately called into question.

Since the Deuteronomists and their successors were a major influence on the formation of the Old Testament—the collection and preservation of the texts that survived the destruction of Jerusalem in 597 BCE, for example—there is a complex problem facing any attempt to reconstruct the original temple. There may be complete texts that never became canonical—1 Enoch is a good example—and there may have been earlier versions of the Hebrew text underlying the present form of biblical texts, as the Qumran fragments suggest. A reason for the exclusion and alteration of those texts is very likely to be that they were evidence for the position the Deuteronomists sought to supersede. Any reconstruction of the temple tradition that relies solely on Deuteronomist-sanctioned written evidence is therefore at a distinct disadvantage. Since conventional scholarship takes these now-canonical texts as the norm, a great deal has to be "undone" before any real progress can be made. Nevertheless, there are places in the Old Testament where the older temple is still visible, and these texts are our starting point.

The Psalms envisaged the Lord in Zion: the Lord dwelt, *yašab*, there (Ps. 9:11). His dwellings *miškanot* were on his holy hill (Ps. 43:3; also Ps. 84:1 and "The God of gods will be seen in Zion," Ps. 84:7). This was the place of his Glory: "I love the habitation of thy house, and the place where thy Glory dwells" (Ps. 26:8). The Lord was enthroned in the holy of holies that represented heaven. "The Lord is in his holy temple, the Lord's throne is in heaven" (Ps. 11:4). He was enthroned on the cherubim in the holy of holies (Pss. 80:1; 99:1), but the Deuteronomists did not mention the throne. Had we only their description of the temple, we should not know there had been a real throne there. Isaiah, however, says that in the year King Uzziah died, Isaiah saw[5] the King, the Lord of Hosts, enthroned in the temple, in the midst of the seraphim (Isa. 6:1–3). "Shout and sing for joy O inhabitant of Zion, for great in your midst is the Holy One of Israel" (Isa. 12:6).

When Isaiah saw the Lord enthroned, he learned that his Glory filled the whole earth (Isa. 6:3), but the Greek text of Isaiah 6:1 says that his Glory [rather than his train] filled the temple. The enthroned Lord gave forth a radiance, which was the Glory. The Targum here, agreeing with the Greek text, says that "the brilliance of his Glory" filled the temple, and Isaiah exclaimed that he had seen "the Glory of the Shekinah of the Eternal King." (This phrase is used also in Tg. Isa. 33:17.) The Psalmist sang, "Thou who art enthroned upon the cherubim, *shine forth*" (Ps. 80:1).[6] "O Lord . . . *shine forth*! Rise up, O judge of the earth" (Ps. 94:1–2). God *shines forth* from Zion (Ps. 50:2), and the same verb *yapa'* appears also in the blessing of Moses, an old poem attached to the end of Deuteronomy: when the Lord came from Sinai and dawned from Seir: "he shone forth" from Paran with his host of angels (Deut. 33:2). The Greek here uses the word for epiphany: "The Lord *epephanen* from Seir" (LXX Deut. 33:2). There is a clue in this ancient poem to the context of this "shining forth": it happened when the Lord became King (Deut. 33:5). Shining was the sign of the presence of the King, and his presence protected the city. "Is not the Lord in Zion? Is not her King in her?" (Jer. 8:19). Epiphany was linked to the kingdom of God.

Some key texts are hard to read. What might the original of Psalm 68:35 have been? "Terrible is God in his sanctuary, the God of Israel, he gives power and strength to his people." The Hebrew says not "in" but "from" your sanctuaries, *mimmiqdašeyka*, but the Greek read this initial *m* as *b*, thus giving "in" or "among", and then understood holy places as "holy ones,"[7] angels. "God is terrible among his angels." Several versions[8] read "sanctuary," singular. But there is another possibility; the consonants of the word for *terrible — nr'* — look very similar to n'r, glorious, shining, and so the text could have been "God shines from his sanctuary." There is a similar picture in Psalm 76:4, where God is "shining" in Zion, more majestic than the "mountains [unclear]," the final word being opaque. The Greek versions here show the same confusion between nr' and n'r: the LXX has "you shine forth," from n'r, whereas Theodotion, translating in the second century CE has "fearful," from nr'. Psalm 76:4 could therefore be describing God as shining or fearful, "greater than the [unclear] mountains" or, reading hrry as hdry,[9] as in Ps. 110:3, which has another similar context, "more glorious than the glories of the holy place." The problem in both Psalm 68:35 and Psalm 76:4 seems to be the shining of God among the angels in the holy of holies. The problem was epiphany.[10]

When David brought the ark to Jerusalem, before he made plans for the temple that was to be built by his son, he appointed musicians. Music, along with the throne and the veil, were not mentioned in the Deuteronomist's account of the first temple. We have seen the significance of the throne and the divine plan in reconstructing the older beliefs about the Lord appearing in the temple, but what of the music? The Levites were appointed to serve before the ark of the Lord, to "invoke, to thank and to praise the Lord the God of Israel" (1 Chron. 16:4). The Holy One was "enthroned on the praises of Israel" (Ps. 22:3), and the congregation praised and glorified the Lord and stood in awe of him (Ps. 22:23). "Hallelujah," usually translated "Praise the Lord," is familiar in its original form. Apart from Psalm 135:3, it always occurs at the beginning or end of the psalm, and when it occurs at the beginning, the Greek simply transliterated it: "Allelouia" (LXX Pss. 105, 110, 111, 112, 106, 134, 145, 146, 147, 148, 149, 150).[11] It must have been a significant temple term whose meaning was known to those who needed the scriptures in Greek. At the beginning of the psalm it addresses the congregation—a plural form: "Praise the Lord"—but the Hebrew root hll means not only "praise" but also "shine." Should we perhaps understand Psalm 22 as "Make Him shine, make Him glorious, stand in awe of him"? The hallelujahs at the beginning of the psalms would then be an instruction to the musicians to cause the Lord's face to shine, to invoke his presence. "Make the Lord shine forth!" This was the first duty of the Levites: "To invoke, to thank and to praise the Lord," and so they sang, "Thou who art enthroned upon the cherubim, shine forth!" (Ps. 80:1). The Levites made music when the temple was consecrated—another detail omitted by the Deuteronomist. They sang "with one voice" and then the cloud of the Glory of the Lord filled the temple (2 Chron. 5:11–4). Once the Lord had been enthroned in his temple, the music invited the Lord to shine forth from the holy of holies, to show himself as King. "For sovereignty belongs to the Lord and he rules over the nations (Ps. 22:28).[12] This would explain why the Deuteronomist did not mention the music.

The radiant Glory of the Presence was later known as the Shekinah, "the indwelling," and Kabbalah, the temple tradition as it survived and developed during the Christian era, used ritual and even magical practices to draw down the Shekinah, which had again departed into heaven. A major study of the Kabbalah suggested, on the basis of the later texts and their temple imagery, that drawing the Shekinah down into the holy of holies had been at the heart of the original temple service. "On the ground of these parallels, we can seriously consider the possibility that the Temple service was conceived as inducing the presence of the Shekinah in the Holy of Holies."[13] In the original temple, *drawing down* would not have been necessary, since the presence of the Lord was there in the midst, but calling on the Lord to appear does seem to have been at the heart of the original temple cult. Perhaps this is why the first Christians called upon the Lord to appear: "*Maranatha*": Come, Lord.

Seeing the Glory and beauty of the Lord in the temple is a recurring theme, and not only in the Psalms. Isaiah saw the Lord in the midst of the seraphim, the burning ones (Isa. 6:1–3). He must have seen through the veil to the Glory beyond. In other words, the Lord was shining forth for him; the veil between heaven and earth had been taken away. The Deuteronomist did not mention the temple veil. Isaiah promised the upright that they, too, would see "the King in his beauty," whilst sinners would fear the devouring fires of eternity (Isa. 33:14, 17)—the fires of the holy place. The Psalmist longed to see (*hazah*, so the visionary sense) the beauty, *no'am*, of the Lord and to contemplate his temple (Ps. 27:4). The *beauties* of the Lord are linked to the fullness of joy in his presence, and learning the path of life (Ps. 16:11). The Psalmist prays: "Let your work be made clear to your servants, and your Glory to their children, and may the beauty, *no'am*, of the Lord God be upon us" (Ps. 90:17, my translation). The Greek text understood this beauty as brilliant splendour, *lamprotes*. This was the King shining forth—epiphany.

Seeing the beauty could be described as seeing the face/presence of the Lord. "I shall behold thy face," sang the Psalmist (Ps. 17:15). He had prayed to the Lord in his distress, and knew that the Lord could visit him by night (Ps. 17:3). "I shall be satisfied with your form, *t'munah*, on my waking" (Ps. 17:15, my translation).[14] He expected to see *the form* of the Lord. There are several examples of these "night visions": the young Samuel at Shiloh saw and heard the Lord during the night, even though the word of the Lord was rare at the time, and there was no vision "breaking through," *nipras* (1 Sam. 3:1, 21, translating literally). Solomon went to the ancient holy place at Gibeon and saw the Lord in a dream by night (1 Kgs. 3:5–15). He saw the Lord again, after he had built the temple, but we are not told where this vision occurred (1 Kgs. 9:1). Daniel was granted a vision by night of "one like a man" (Dan. 7:2, 13), and Zechariah saw in the night a man on a red horse (Zech. 1:8).

There are no details in these texts of who was seen, what the so-called form was like. The face/presence is described as beauty and Glory, but most frequently it is light that brings prosperity and deliverance, and seeing the face of the Lord is the response to prayer. "Lift up the light of thy face upon us, O Lord" (Ps. 4:6, my translation). "Let thy face shine on thy servant, save me in thy steadfast love" (Ps. 31:16). When the Lord hid his face, there was disaster: "Thou didst hide thy face, I was dismayed" (Ps. 30:7). "Why dost thou hide thy face? Why dost thou forget our affliction and oppression?" (Ps. 44:24). "Hide not thy face from thy servant; for I am in distress, make haste to answer me" (Ps. 69:17). "Do not hide thy face from me in the day of my distress!" (Ps. 102:2). In despair, Israel felt that the Lord did not see: "My way is hid from the Lord" (Isa. 40:27). When the faithful worshipper saw the light of the Lord, he knew that he was secure: "The Lord is my light and my salvation: whom shall I fear? Thou hast said, 'Seek ye my face' My heart says to thee, 'Thy face, O Lord, do I seek.' . . . Hide not thy face from me" (Ps. 27:1, 8–9). "Blessed are the people . . . O Lord, who walk in the light of your face/presence" (Ps. 89:15).

There is a curious episode in the Infancy Gospel of James,[15] which may show one way in which the Lord revealed his face. Joachim and Anna, who were to become the parents of Mary, were childless, and Joachim was told that he could not offer gifts in the temple because he had not raised a child. As the great day of the Lord (the feast of Tabernacles?) drew near, Joachim learned that Anna was, at last, pregnant. He took his gifts to the temple, and said to himself, "If the Lord has forgiven me, the plate that is upon the high priest's forehead will make this clear to me." (This was the golden plate inscribed with the sacred Name, only worn by a high priest.) Joachim presented his offering and watched as the high priest went to the altar, "and he saw no sin in himself." "Now I know that the Lord has become propitious unto me and hath forgiven all my sins." What had Joachim seen? Did he perhaps see the golden plate shining? Since the golden plate was engraved with the Name, did it function as an oracle, and when it shone, did the worshipper know that the Lord had made his face/ presence shine on him? (Infancy Gospel of James 4.5–5.1).

Three times a year, according to the ancient calendars—at the feast of unleavened bread, at the feast of weeks, and at the feast of booths—the men of Israel had to make a pilgrimage to the temple, "to appear before the Lord" (Exod. 23:17; 34:23; Deut. 16:16). "To appear before the Lord" is the usual translation, but the Hebrew actually says that three times a year shall all your men *see the face of the Lord*. It became the custom to read the letters differently, even though the Psalms show clearly what the original meaning must have been.

- In Exodus 23:15 and 34:20, the text should be read "none shall see my face with empty hands," or it could mean, "none shall see my face in an unworthy state."[16]
- In Exodus 23:17, "each male *yr'h* to the face/presence of the Lord," the verb is read as a Niph'al form, *yera'eh* and so the verse becomes "each male shall appear before the face of the Lord." The Samaritan text, however, has the accusative particle here instead of "to" and so that the letters *yr'h* must be read as the Qal form, *yir'eh*: "each male shall see the face of the Lord." (Qal is the simple active from of the verb, and niph'al is the simple reflexive form.)
- In Exodus 34:23, the accusative particle occurs, so there is no doubt that the verb *yr'h* is to be read as a Qal form: "each male shall see the face of the Lord."
- In Exodus 34:24, the infinitive construct form of the verb, *lr'wt* is Qal; the Niph'al would be *lhr'wt*. The text must mean, "When you go up to see the face/presence of the Lord three times a year."
- In Deuteronomy 16:16, the text is like Exodus 34:23, and so a Qal form is required: "each male shall see the face of the Lord."
- In Deuteronomy 31:11, there is the Qal infinitive construct and so it means, "When all Israel comes to see the face of the Lord your God."
- In 1 Samuel 1:22, Hannah planned to take her son "to see the face of the Lord."
- In Isaiah 1:12, there is the Qal infinitive construct and so it must mean, "when you come to see my face."
- In Psalm 42:2, the Psalmist longs to see God: "My soul thirsts for God, for the living God. When shall I come and see the face of God?"

For each of these examples, the *Hebrew and English Lexicon* says that the Qal form should be read in every case. "The verbs in all these passages were originally Qal, afterwards pointed Niph'al, to avoid the expression "see the face of Yahweh."[17]

Why should this have happened? The pilgrims with clean hands and a pure heart who are worthy to make go to the holy place—"Who shall ascend the hill of the Lord, and who shall stand in his holy place" (Ps. 24:3)—are described as *seeking the face* of the God of Jacob,[18] and promised blessing and vindication (Ps. 24:5–6). They prayed, "May God be gracious to us and bless us, and make his face to shine upon us" (Ps. 67:1)—a sign of favor that would bring prosperity. The Greek here has "May the Lord *epiphanai* his face upon us" (LXX Ps. 66:1). Epiphany. The pilgrims prayed that the One enthroned on the cherubim would shine forth: "Restore us O God; let they face shine that we may be saved" (Ps. 80:1, 3, 7, 19). And the great high priestly blessing prayed that each person would see the face of the Lord: "May the Lord bless you and keep you. May the Lord make his face/presence shine upon you and be gracious to you/give you life. May the Lord make his presence rise upon you and give you peace" (Num. 6:24–26).[19] Jesus said, "Blessed are the pure in heart, for they shall see God" (Matt. 5:8), and the climax of the book of Revelation shows the servants of God and the Lamb standing before the throne and seeing his face (Rev. 22:4). *It seems that seeing the face of the Lord was also very important in early Christian teaching, one of the many elements restored from the original temple that had been suppressed or obscured in the Hebrew Scriptures. St. John began his Gospel by declaring; "We have seen his Glory"* (John 1:14).

The Targums, which cannot be dated with certainty, but which preserve ancient tradition, treat the "face" texts in various ways. All the Targums of Exodus and Deuteronomy reflect the Niph'al reading of the verb *yr'h*: they all understand that it was the people who appeared before the Lord, and not the Lord who appeared to the people. In the Targum of the Psalms, however, the Lord *does* appear, but the manner of the appearing is modified. The "face" is replaced by the Shekinah [e.g., Tg. Pss. 22:24; 27:8; 30:7; 42:2; 44:24 (which has "the Shekinah of your Glory"); 69:17; 88:14; 102:2; 143:7]; or it can be "the brightness"[20] of the face (e.g., Tg. Pss. 4:6; 11:7; 24:6; 31:16); or it can be "the splendour" of the face (Tg. Pss. 13:1; 67:1; 119:135); or it can be "the Glory" of the face (Tg. Ps. 17:15). Hiding the face becomes "removing the Shekinah" as in Tg. Ps. 22:24.[21] A key verse such as Psalm 17:15: "I shall behold thy face in righteousness; when I awake I shall be satisfied with beholding thy form" becomes: "In truth I shall see the brightness of your countenance; at the time when I awake, I shall be satisfied with the Glory of your face." Psalm 42:2b, "When shall I come and behold the face of God?" becomes, "When shall I come and see the splendour of the Shekinah of the Lord?" David M. Stec comments here, "The Targum of Psalms, in common with the Peshitta and some manuscripts of the Masoretic Text, here has an active verb, whereas most of the manuscripts of the Masoretic text point *w'r'h* as a Niph'al—appear."[22] Seeing the Lord in the temple must have been a part of the older tradition.

Philo suggests this. For him, writing in Alexandria in the first century C.E., the very name Israel meant "the one who sees God," and this "occurs twenty three times in the Philonic corpus, and is expressed or implied in some twenty six additional texts."[23] Philo does not explain it, nor does he argue for it; he assumes that this meaning is well known, presumably because his Greek version of the Scriptures said that the Lord was seen in the holy of holies (LXX Exod. 25:8). Now *'š r'h 'l* [ish ra'ah el] is an unlikely origin for the name Israel, but there is another Hebrew word that could account for it: *šwr*, meaning "behold."[24] It occurs in Job 34:29: "When he hides his face, who can behold him?" and in Job 35:14: "Although you say you do not behold him" (my translation). Job is full of archaic forms, so perhaps this is the origin of "Israel," the one who beholds God. Perhaps Philo had lost touch with the more ancient root of the name, but knew it had to mean "he who sees God" and provided his own approximation. It simply appears in his text: "for Israel means seeing God" (Preliminary Studies 51); "Israel, he that sees God" (Dreams I.171), "the nation that sees, even Israel" (Dreams II.44), "Israel means seeing God" (Dreams II.173); "Israel means seeing God" (Questions on Genesis III.49), "Israel, a name meaning one who sees" (Questions on Genesis IV.233).[25] Sometimes we see Philo reading the Hebrew scriptures in this way: "The sons of Israel" (Lev. 15:31) becomes "the sons of the seeing one" (Allegorical Interpretation III.15).

At times he gives additional explanation to set the term in a wider context. "He calls Israel, though younger in age, his firstborn son in dignity, making it evident that he who sees God, the original cause of being, is the recipient of honour" (Posterity and Exile of Cain 63). "He that sees God, drawn to Him by surpassing beauty [a reference to Isa. 33:17], has been allotted as His portion to Him whom he sees" (Posterity 92). "Ishmael means "hearkening to God." Hearing takes the second place, yielding the first to sight, and sight is the portion of Israel, the son freeborn and firstborn; for "seeing God" is the translation of Israel" (On Flight and Finding 208). Explaining Exodus 19:6, the royal priesthood and holy nation, Philo wrote, "Its high position is shown by the name; for the nation is called in the Hebrew tongue Israel, which, being interpreted is, 'He who sees God.' The sight of the mind, the dominant element in the soul, surpasses all the other faculties of the mind, and this is wisdom which is the sight of the understanding" (Abraham 57). "Israel" could apply equally to the patriarch or to his descendents: "The precious offspring of Israel who has the clear vision of God" (The Sacrifices of Cain and Abel 134). For Philo, those who lived in the knowledge of the One were rightly called "sons of God," and he quoted Deuteronomy 14:1, "You are the sons of the Lord your God," and Deuteronomy 32:18, "the Rock who begot you" (Greek: The God who begot you). They were exhorted to take their place under God's firstborn, the Logos, the chief and ruler of the angels, "the Man after his image, and he that sees, that is, Israel" (Confusion of Tongues 145–6).

Israel as "the man who sees God" appears in rabbinic texts only in one late example[26] and this is almost certainly because Christian writers favored the explanation "the man who sees God." St. Jerome, writing at the end of the fourth century, emphasized that "a man seeing God" was a forced explanation of "Israel." He said it meant "prince of God," as appears in the Targums and midrash, and so he was presumably offering the interpretation current among Jews. "He is aware of the hostility this observation will arouse among his co-religionists, some of whom were deeply suspicious of his association with Jews."[27] St. Justin Martyr, who lived in Palestine some three centuries before St. Jerome lived there ____, said the name meant "man victorious over power" (Trypho 125), a possible understanding of Genesis 32:28, and presumably another Jewish interpretation. Josephus had had something similar: "He commanded him to be called Israel, which in Hebrew means 'the one that struggled with the divine angel' " (Antiquities 1.20).[28]

"The man who sees God" was adopted by most Christian writers, all of whom could have drawn their inspiration from Philo. Seeing God always entailed understanding, an echo of the Enoch tradition that abandoning Wisdom meant losing the vision (1 En. 93.8). Israel as the one who sees God was applied in a variety of contexts to the patriarch Israel, to Jesus, or to the church. Thus Eusebius, listing heroes of the Old Testament, wrote, "Israel . . . the changed name indicates a man who sees God"; and "Israel means the one who sees God in the manner of the knowing and perceiving human mind" (Preparation of the Gospel 7.8 and 11.6). Clement of Alexandria explained that Israel had been punished by God because the people had sinned willfully. Their very name meant "he that sees God, that is, understands God" (Instructor 1.9). Elsewhere he uses the term "Israel" in another context—explaining how philosophy relates to theology. "Philosophy is the study of Wisdom, and Wisdom is the knowledge of things divine and human, and their causes. . . . He who has received previous training is at liberty to approach Wisdom, which is supreme, from which grows up the race of Israel. . . . He who is really endowed with the power of seeing is called Israel . . ." (Miscellanies 1.5). Hippolytus applied the name *Israel* to Jesus: "Having received, then, all knowledge from the Father, the perfect Israel, the true Jacob did show himself upon earth and conversed with men. And who is meant by Israel but a man who sees God?" He then links this to John 1:14 (Against Noetus 5). Origen argued that there was an Israel according to the flesh but also a spiritual Israel, and it was to those lost sheep that Jesus had been sent (Matt. 15:24), to those who saw God and who were citizens of the heavenly Jerusalem: "Israel is interpreted to mean "a mind," or "man seeing God"' (First Principles 4.1.21–2). Macarius expounded the theme of Israel leaving Egypt: "For Israel is interpreted as being the mind contemplating God, . . . set free from the slavery of darkness, from the spiritual Egyptians" (Homily 47.5). And prayers in the Apostolic Constitutions apply Israel to the church: "For by [Christ] Thou hast brought home the Gentiles to Thyself for a peculiar people, the true Israel, beloved of God and seeing God." "O God Almighty . . . who art by nature invisible and yet art known to all reasonable natures who seek Thee with a good mind and art comprehended by those that seek after Thee with a good mind; the God of Israel, Thy people which truly see, and which have believed in Christ" (Apostolic Constitutions 7.36 and 8.15).

Most famously, the name *Israel* appears in the Prayer of Joseph, quoted by Origen in his Commentary on John as "an apocryphal text presently in use among the Hebrews" (Com. John II.31). Jacob was recounting his struggle with the "man" at Penuel, a place name meaning "the face of God" (Gen. 32:22–32). "I Jacob, whom men call Jacob but whose name is Israel, am he whom God called Israel, a man seeing God, because I am the Firstborn of every living thing to whom God gives life." Jacob/Israel explained that he was the "first minister before the face of God," an angel. Since Origen was writing about 230 C.E., Israel as the man who sees God must have been known in Jewish circles well into the Christian era, since the Prayer of Joseph was "in use," presumably, in Palestine. Origen was born in Egypt, and he may well have known the early Gnostic text found in Egypt in 1945, part of the so-called Nag Hammadi library. Scholars named it "On the Origin of the World (Coptic Gnostic Library [CG] II.5), because it is an elaborate version of the Genesis creation story, peopled with heavenly beings. It describes a great chariot throne with cherubim and seraphim, surrounded by angels. On the right of the throne sat "a first born called Israel," who was also named "Jesus the Christ," and to the left of the throne sat the Virgin of the Holy Spirit.[29] Israel, the firstborn, was an angel of the Trinity.

There are examples in the Old Testament of people who saw the Lord. Abraham saw the Lord (Gen. 12:7; 17:1; 18:1), as did Isaac (Gen. 26:2, 24), and Jacob (Gen. 28:12–17; 35:1). Moses was recognized as the servant of the Lord because he had spoken directly to the Lord and seen his form (Num. 12:8, referring to Exod. 3:2 and Exod. 24:10; also Ben Sira 45:5). Gideon saw the angel of the Lord (Judg. 6:12), as did the parents of Samson (Judg. 13). The child Samuel saw the Lord at Shiloh (1 Sam. 3:21), and we learn that the more ancient name for a prophet was a seer (1 Sam. 9:9), presumably one who saw the Lord. Philo implies as much, when he comments on this verse: "He . . . is called not only the seer, but the seer of God, that is Israel" (Who is the Heir 78). The appearance of the Lord is never described. Even Isaiah's great temple vision of the King, the Lord of Hosts, does not describe the Lord (Isa. 6:1–5). Instead, we learn that his Glory fills the earth. It has been suggested that in second temple priestly texts and exegesis, the angels of the older temple, the hosts—whence the title Lord of Hosts—were described as the Glory.[30] The ancient poem about the Lord dawning and shining with his host of holy ones (Deut. 33:2), would have been understood as the Lord appearing in Glory. This is implied in Luke's account of the shepherds at Bethlehem: the *Glory* of the Lord shone around them, and they heard a *multitude* of the heavenly host (Luke 2:8–13).

Philo, a contemporary of St. Luke, explained how "seeing the Lord" was understood in his time, after centuries of Deuteronomist influence. Beginning with the story of the tower of Babel, when the Lord came to see what was happening, Philo emphasized that such anthropomorphism was a concession to the human mind. God, he said, fills all things. "He has made his powers [i.e., his angels, his Glory] extend through earth and water, air and heaven, and left no part of the universe without his presence, and uniting all with all has bound them fast with invisible bonds that they should never be loosed." He continued with a warning: "This divine nature which presents itself to us as visible and comprehensible and everywhere, is in reality invisible, incomprehensible and nowhere" (Confusion of Tongues 136–38). These ideas are perfectly compatible with the older temple tradition—that the Glory of the Lord was veiled by matter, but could shine though all the material world, and they survive in the Koran: "Whithersoever ye turn, there is the Face of Allah" (2:115). What is missing is the original belief that the "fullness of God" could be present in one human being (Col. 1:19): "We have seen his Glory" (John 1:14).

Trying to determine what was "seen" or intended by the more ancient accounts of meeting the Lord, as this was understood in the original temple, is complicated by several factors. First is the blending of the tabernacle and temple traditions.[31] When the final form of the Pentateuch was compiled, memories of the temple seeped into the ancient traditions of the tabernacle, and all these were heavily influenced by the Deuteronomists' assertion that the Lord could not be seen. The oldest Moses tradition knew the tent of meeting, located outside the desert camp, where the Lord descended in a pillar of cloud to meet with Moses at the door of the tent (Exod. 33:7–11), or to send his spirit to the seventy elders (Num. 11:14–17, 24–30), or to speak with Moses, Aaron, and Miriam and to confirm the supremacy of Moses over Aaron and Miriam (Num. 12:1–8). The Lord then left. The tent of meeting outside the camp was not part of the priestly tradition; it belonged ultimately to the Deuteronomist desert tradition, which denied that the Lord was continually present in the temple, and so had the Lord descending to meet his people and then leaving.

The other tent, the "tabernacle," was a prefiguring of the temple, but the two names (tabernacle and tent of meeting) were sometimes combined, which makes tracing the two traditions more complicated. Moses erected a tabernacle, *mškn*, "in the midst" of the camp and furnished it like the temple: veil, table, lampstand, and ark (Exod. 25:8–9). The people camped around it (Num. 2:2).

The Lord spoke from above the *kapporet* (Exod. 25:22) or appeared there (Lev. 16:2). The Glory came forth or shone forth from the holy of holies; "descend" is never used to describe the presence of the Lord in the priestly tradition.[32] The Glory "abode," *škn*, on Sinai.[33] The Glory entered the tabernacle when it was completed, and remained there (Exod. 40:34–8), but here the tabernacle is called "the *mškn* of the tent of meeting," fusing the two tents. The postexilic priestly writer in the Pentateuch "reformulated the ancient tent tradition under the influence of Jerusalemite temple theology."[34]

The Glory of the Lord entered the tabernacle to take possession and consecrate it; the Glory entered the temple (1 Kgs. 8:11); and Ezekiel had a vision of the Glory returning to take possession of the temple to be rebuilt in Jerusalem (Ezek. 43:1–5). This Glory, he said, was like the vision he had seen when Jerusalem was destroyed. Ezekiel, a priest of the original temple (Ezek. 1:3) has left us two descriptions of the Glory as he knew it, the only canonical descriptions of the Glory of the Lord. The Hebrew is, unfortunately, very difficult to read, possibly because the subject matter is so strange.[35] Several words occur only here; for example, *bzq* (Ezek. 1:14), usually translated "flash of lightning"; and *qll*, "burnished" (Ezek. 1:7), which occurs elsewhere only in Daniel 10:6, another vision of a heavenly being. Masculine and feminine forms are mixed, as are singular and plural. The vision seems to be a fiery, fourfold female figure, the Living One, above whom was the likeness of a throne where a human form was seated. The human—"*adam*," so no gender is indicated—was a fiery bronze figure surrounded by the brightness of a rainbow. This was "the appearance of the likeness of the Glory of the Lord" (Ezek. 1:28).

Ezekiel distinguishes between the likeness, *dᵉmut*, and the appearance, *mar'eh*, of the elements in the vision, but only the Authorized Version (KJV) is consistent in its translation. Other versions obscure this important distinction. The word *dᵉmut* implies the thought or concept preceding an action, a plan, whereas *mar'eh* is the visible appearance. Ezekiel uses here a distinction better, and later, known in Plato: the *dᵉmut* was the invisible aspect of the Glory and the *mar'eh* was the visible. Ezekiel saw the Glory manifested, shining forth from the invisible state. Thus the Authorized Version has: "As for the likeness of the living creatures, their appearance was like burning coals (Ezek. 1:13), and, describing the Glory: "the likeness of a throne as the appearance of a sapphire throne" (Ezek. 1:26), and "the appearance of the likeness of the Glory of the Lord (Ezek. 1:28).[36] The Glory of the Lord shone forth for Ezekiel in human form, but the implication is that the Glory could be made visible in other ways. The fiery human figure appeared to Daniel (Dan. 10:5) unnamed, but was recognized by the early Christians as the Lord. Hippolytus, writing early in the third century in Rome, said that he was "the Lord, not yet indeed as perfect man, but with the appearance and form of a man"[37] (Hippolytus Commentary on Daniel XXIV).

The Psalmist had seen the Glory of the Lord entering the temple in human form. He sang of the King of Glory entering the ancient doors (Ps. 24:7–9). He knew that the Lord was clothed with honour, majesty, and light (Ps. 104:1–2). He also sang of a great procession—singers and minstrels entering the temple with "my King, my God" (Ps. 68:24–5). What had he seen? Elsewhere in his world he might have seen a statue dressed in golden robes being taken into a temple, but Jerusalem had no statues at the time.[38] The King, the royal high priest, was God with his people, Immanuel, and so the King of Glory entering the temple was probably the human king in his role as the visible presence of the Lord. When there were no more kings in Jerusalem, the Aaronite high priest had that role, and the prescription for his vestments shows something of their original meaning. They were "for Glory and for beauty" (Exod. 28:2), and the high priest wore the Name on his forehead (Exod. 28:36–7). When Enoch stood before the throne in heaven (i.e., in the holy of holies) to be consecrated as high priest, he was anointed and then vested with the Glory of the Lord: "The Lord said to Michael, 'Go, take Enoch from out his earthly garments, and anoint him with my sweet ointment, and put him into the garments of my Glory'" (2 En. 228).[39] The meaning of the vestments was long remembered: they had been the garments of God (Exodus Rabbah XXXVIII.8); "It is because they are emanations of the supernal mysteries, and are made after the supernal pattern, that they are called residual garments, *bigde haš'rad,* inasmuch as they were made from what was left over of the supernal robes, of the residue of the ethereal celestial splendours" (Zohar Exodus 229b).[40]

If the high priest "was" the Lord, then we should expect the Lord to be depicted as a high priest, and this does happen in the Apocalypse of Abraham, a text that survives only in Old Slavonic, but it probably was written in Hebrew just after the destruction of the second temple in 70 C.E.[41] In other word, these ideas would have been available to the early Christians. The story is a longer version of Genesis 15, when Yahweh-Elohim speaks to Abraham. Genesis does not describe him, but the Apocalypse of Abraham does. Yahweh-Elohim has become Yahweh-El, the heavenly guardian of Abraham and his family (Ap. Abr. 10.16). He restrains the heavenly powers (Ap. Abr. 10.3–4), exactly what Philo says of the Logos (On Planting 10), and he is dressed as the heavenly high priest: his body like sapphire, his face like chrysolite, his hair like snow. He wears purple garments and the turban of the high priest (as in Zech. 3:5) and he has a golden staff or sceptre (Ap. Abr. 11.1–3). St. John saw the risen Lord in the temple, dressed as a high priest. His face was shining like the sun, his feet were like molten bronze, and his eyes as fire. He was wearing a long robe and the golden girdle worn only by a high priest (Josephus, Antiquities 3.159). There is no description of his robe, *poderes*, but Philo (Allegorical Interpretation II.56; Moses II.118) and Aristeas (Letter 96) both use this word to describe the colored vestment of the high priest.

The fullest description of a vested high priest in the temple is Ben Sira's picture of Simeon. He wore the garment of Glory, and, like the human figure in Ezekiel's vision of the Glory, he was like a rainbow shining in clouds of glory. He was compared to the sun shining on the temple of the Most High (Ben Sira 50:7) and made the temple court glorious by his presence (Ben Sira 50.11). The people, said Ben Sira fell prostrate to worship the Lord, the Almighty God Most High (Ben Sira 50:17), and the context implies that they were prostrated before the high priest. This is not impossible. About a century before Simeon, that is, about 300 B.C.E., a Greek visitor to Jerusalem had seen the high priest emerge from the temple and concluded that he was an angel. The Jews, wrote Hecataeus, "immediately fall to the ground and worship, *proskunein*, the high priest as he explains the commandments to them."[42] Simeon, who had just emerged in glory from "the house of the veil" (Ben Sira 50:5), had a similar reception. This was the Glory of the Lord coming forth from the holy of holies. Aristeas, a visitor from Egypt, also saw the high priest in the temple court and said of his vestments, "Their appearance makes one awe-struck and dumbfounded. A man would think he had come out of this world into another one" (Letter 99).

Given that the Glory came out into the temple as the high priest emerged from the hidden sanctuary, there may be places in the Old Testament that describe the emergence of the high priest [royal or Aaronite] from the holy of holies. Isaiah spoke of the people in darkness who had seen a great light, and then described the "birth" of a king among the angels: "Unto us a child is born" (Isa. 2, 6–7). This was the heavenly birth of the Davidic king, when he was begotten in the holy of holies, in the Glory of the holy ones (Ps. 110:3) and presumably then came forth into the temple court. The Glory of the Lord was the strength of the anointed king (Ps. 89:15–18). The Servant was appointed as a Light to the nations (Isa. 42:6; 49:6; cf. Luke 2:32); he saw the light [of the Glory] after his sufferings, and his soul was satisfied (Isa. 53:11 in the Greek and in the Qumran Hebrew 1QIs[a]).[43]

Isaiah, the great temple prophet, frequently used this imagery of light: The Holy One of Israel was a light and a fire (Isa. 10:17). "Let us walk in the light of the Lord" (Isa. 2:5; cf. Ps. 56:13). "The Lord will be your everlasting light" (Isa. 60:20). The Psalmist, too, sang of the light of the face of the Lord: "Lift up the light of thy face upon us, O Lord" (Ps. 4:6). Psalm 27 begins, "The Lord is my light and my salvation" and then describes seeing the beauty of the Lord, and seeking his face. "In thy light do we see light" (Ps. 36:90). "He will bring forth your vindication as the light" (Ps. 37:6). "Send out thy light and thy truth, let them lead me, let them bring me to thy holy hill and to thy dwelling" (Ps. 43:3). The light of the face enabled the people to triumph over their enemies (Ps. 44:3). Such use of light became proverbial: "In the light of a king's face there is life, and his favor is like the clouds that bring the spring rain" (Prov. 16:15).

Those who saw the light reflected the light. Moses' face shone when he came down from the mountain (Exod. 34:29). "Look to him and be radiant" sang the Psalmist (Ps. 34:5). Seeing the light imparted knowledge to the seer,[44] whose reflected radiance imparted this to those who saw. The unknown hymn writer at Qumran wrote, "I thank thee, O Lord, for thou hast illumined my face by thy covenant. . . . I seek thee, and sure as the dawn, thou appearest as perfect light to me" (1QH XII).[45] "My light shall shine forth in thy Glory. For as a light from out of darkness, so wilt thou enlighten me" (1QH XVII). The priests at Qumran were blessed with the words: "May you be as an angel of the presence. . . . May he make you holy among his people, and an [eternal] light [to illumine] the world with knowledge and to enlighten the face of the congregation" (1QSb IV). St. Paul explained that this radiance was part of the Christian hope: "And we all, with unveiled faces, beholding/reflecting[46] the Glory of the Lord are being changed into his likeness, from one degree of Glory to another" (2 Cor. 3:18).

The people of the restored temple looked for the light in their failing community, but Isaiah told them the light would return only when the temple and the community were fit to receive it. "They seek me daily . . . as if they were a nation that did righteousness and did not forsake the ordinances of their God" (Isa. 58:2). "Your sins have hid his face from you" (Isa. 59:2). "We look for light and behold darkness" (Isa. 59:9). Human sin had hidden the face/presence of the Lord (Isa. 59:2), which later tradition described as the Shekinah, the "dwelling" of the Lord in the temple. In the Enoch tradition, it was the sins of Enosh's generation that caused the Shekinah to return to heaven.[47] The bright image of the Shekinah had originally been on a cherub beneath the tree of life, and anyone who looked upon it was protected from all ills such as sickness, pain, demons, or insects (3 En. 5.1–5)—reminiscent of the Psalmist's plea: "Let thy face shine, that we may be saved" (Ps. 80:3). The Shekinah was the Glory seen by Ezekiel, resting above the living creatures, whose faces reflected the Glory they bore (3 En. 24.13). Isaiah's oracle of hope declared that the light and the Glory of the Lord would rise again on the truly restored city (Isa. 60:1–2), and the images in this chapter were used by St. John to describe the holy city that came down from heaven, where all the servants of the Lord saw his face in the place of everlasting light, where there was nothing accursed, no sin, (Isa. 60:19–20; cf. Rev. 21:23–6; 22:3–5,14–5).[48] The holy city of St. John's vision comes to earth after the earthly Jerusalem, the wicked city, has been destroyed. He describes it as a huge holy of holies, a golden cube (Rev. 21:16), where all the servants of the Lord not only see the vision but are taken into it (Rev. 22:3–5). This is the kingdom, where God and the Lamb, a Unity, are enthroned (Rev. 22:1). Jesus had spoken to Nicodemus about seeing the kingdom and entering the kingdom (John 3:3–5). Jesus had prayed that his disciples would be with him, to see his Glory (John 17:24), and the final scene in St. John's vision is the faithful seeing the face of the Lord who is their light. In the kingdom, they reign with him for ever.

There is reason to believe that this vision and its realisation was the original "good news" of the Gospel. The Greek word *evangelion*, gospel, became the subject of bitter word play in the second century C.E. Rabbi Meir said that it meant *aven gilyon*, the worthless revelation, and Rabbi Joḥannan said it meant *avon gilyon*, the wicked revelation (Babylonian Talmud Shabbat 116a, a line censored from many texts). There was also an anonymous ruling that the *gilyonim* and the books of the heretics did not defile the hands, meaning they were not sacred (Tosefta Yadaim 2.13).[49] *Gilyonim* usually means empty spaces or margins, but here it is likely to derive from *galah*, "reveal." Revelations, visions, were clearly an important category of Christian writing, and the rabbinic taunts suggest that vision was a key element in the meaning of *evangelion*, gospel. The gospel of the kingdom, then, was probably the vision that had been at the heart of the ancient temple cult. The Targums understood the coming of the kingdom as a revelation, and revealing the kingdom meant revealing the presence of God.[50] "Your God reigns" (Isa. 52:7), became "The Kingdom of your God has been revealed." "The Lord of Hosts will reign on Mount Zion" (Isa. 24:23) became "The Kingdom of the Lord of Hosts shall be revealed in the mountain of Zion." In Ezekiel, the day of judgment is understood as the kingdom: "Your doom has come to you, O inhabitant of the land" (Ezek. 7:7) became "The Kingdom has been revealed to you, O inhabitant of the land." "Your doom has come" (Ezek. 7:10) became "The Kingdom has been revealed."

Jesus revealed the kingdom to his disciples at his transfiguration. He told them that some would see the kingdom "come with power" before they died, and then he took Peter, James, and John up the mountain where they saw Him transfigured. They saw the Lord shining forth, as in the ancient temple visions. This was the kingdom. When Jesus said that the kingdom was in the midst (Luke 17:21), he was speaking of the original temple worldview, with the Lord enthroned as King in the holy of holies. "Build me a holy place, that I may be dwell/ be seen in their midst."

I have often wondered how this temple theophany tradition related to the experiences of Latter-day Saints, having read something of their history and scriptures, of the visions at Kirtland, and of Joseph Smith's mission to restore the temple. I have only an amateur knowledge of these matters, and so I have asked my colleague Kevin Christensen if he would offer an LDS perspective on what I have written.

Part II

As Margaret Barker rightly points out, her independent reconstruction of temple theology does, indeed, have uncanny relevance for understanding Joseph Smith's life work of restoration.[51] The debates among the Hebrews and early Christians concerning the possibility of anthropomorphic theophany and its expression in temple worship illuminate the early experience of Joseph Smith and the temple worship practiced by the LDS community. Furthermore, her discussion of the controversies of the sixth century BCE and of early Christianity has shed unexpected light on LDS scripture.

The immediate relevance of Barker's study on the controversy about whether God can be seen emerges most clearly in light of the rise of contemporary research on near-death experience. The questions belong not just to theological debates from a long ago time and from faraway places; the questions have immediate application to human experience in the here and now. In an important study comparing medieval and contemporary visionary literature, Carol Zaleski comments that "those individuals whose life has been shaped by an overwhelming visionary experience seem to be isolated from the rest of us who are trying to make sense of things without the aid of direct revelation."[52] Much of Joseph Smith's life work involved his attempts to undo the isolation via the context provided by his revealed translations and his drive to create a community centered on the temple. As Zaleski comments in her study, "Those who experience near-death visions, as well as those affected by hearing them still face the problem of finding a community and a context in which to search again for and apply the insights they have received."[53] Barker argues that the first temple is the source of both the community and context in which Jesus could apply the insights provided by his own visions.

Joseph Smith's first attempt at reporting his own "overwhelming visionary experience" led directly to a subsequent experience of isolation when his listener "treated [his] communication not only lightly, but with great contempt, saying that it was all of the devil, that there were no such things as visions or revelations in these days; that such things had ceased with the apostles and that there would never be any more of them" (Joseph Smith–History 1:21).[54] The minister who had treated Joseph Smith's initial telling "with great contempt" spoke for the Enlightenment, "which cast doubt on all the wonders of late Renaissance culture—magic, dreams, and visions—labeling them all superstition."[55]

Just as differing beliefs concerning the possibility and validity of theophanies were expressed in Old and New Testament times, so Joseph Smith also heard voices of belief beside voices of doubt. A striking example was Solomon Chamberlain, who in 1829 made himself known to Hyrum Smith by asking at the door, "Is there anyone here that believes in visions or revelations?" As Richard Lyman Bushman explains, "Chamberlain's story of meeting the Smiths, although involving only himself and half a dozen others, had implications for many more. Chamberlain's and Hyrum's mutual understanding of the word visionary implies a general category of people who were known to believe in visions. For the recognition to occur, visionary houses and visionary persons must have been a well known type."[56]

Although stories of Joseph Smith's visions of deity and angels were known in the early years of the church, several scholars have noted that Joseph's First Vision did not immediately acquire a central place for the young LDS community. Though mentions of the visions circulated among the members and rumors were printed in the press, at the beginning, the Book of Mormon and the story of its coming as an expression biblical belief were the primary missionary message. Joseph Smith formally organized the Church of Christ on April 6, 1830. When he wrote his first detailed account in 1832, he followed "a traditional form of spiritual autobiography familiar to him and those around him."[57] But as Bushman observes, "The stylistic similarities only highlight, however, the differences between Joseph and a host of now forgotten visionaries. . . . People did not flock to hear the visionaries' teachings or pull up roots to gather with fellow believers. Followers of Joseph Smith did all these things and more. They reoriented their lives to comply with his revelations. The differences were so great that we can scarcely even say Joseph was the most successful of the visionaries; taking his life as a whole, he was of another species."[58]

Commenting on the significance of modern visions, Zaleski says, "I see no justification for treating contemporary near-death testimony as though a foundation for a new eschatology or religious movement." Few of the eighteenth- and nineteenth-century conversion theophanies that Bushman discusses provide such a foundation. Indeed, he observes that the most successful denominations actively suppressed reports of visions.[59] In comparison, "The Shakers, who did not curtail their visionaries as decisively, suffered the consequences. The visionaries' contradictory and sometimes extreme revelations opened up rifts in the organization and eventually resulted in a burnout of the visionary impulse."[60]

As the young LDS movement began, the foundational context would be the biblical tradition and the revelations to the fledgling community, rather than the story of Joseph's initial theophanies. As Terryl L. Givens has shown, the Book of Mormon functioned as a sacred sign in continuity with the Bible.[61] Zaleski observes that the "medieval visions" she considered in her survey could not "stand on their own; they thrived only insofar as they exemplified a wider tradition."[62] Recall that Barker has argued that the rise of Christianity can only be understood if we recognize that Jesus' own visions drew upon and exemplified the First Temple tradition. From its first pages, the Book of Mormon invokes the wider biblical tradition directly, by starting its narrative in Jerusalem in "the commencement of the first year of the reign of Zedekiah, King of Judah" (1 Nephi 1:4), and describes how its prophets obtained a record "of the Jews from the beginning" to that time, "and also many prophecies which have been spoken by the mouth of Jeremiah" (1 Nephi 5:13). What made Joseph Smith's visions important to himself and to the earliest believers was their continuity with the Bible. Assessing his experience in his 1838 *History*, Joseph said he had followed what James 1:5 directed, and he found that God gave wisdom to those who sought it (Joseph Smith–History 1:26). In facing derisive critics, he likened his experience to that of Paul before Agrippa. "He [Paul] had seen a vision, and he knew he had. . . . I had seen a vision, and I knew it and I knew that God knew it" (Joseph Smith–History 1:24–25). Joseph embraced a biblical context for self-understanding.

Just as Joseph saw himself in a biblical context, so Joseph's growing community of followers saw themselves as the latter-day gathering of Israel, participating in the establishment of the kingdom of God. Readers of the Book of Mormon encounter several theophanies in the texts. From the start, the Book of Mormon addresses the possibility of seeing the face of the Lord. Nephi records how, in the Jerusalem of the sixth century B.C.E., his father, Lehi "saw the heavens open, and he thought he saw God sitting upon his throne, surrounded with numerous concourses of angels in the attitude of singing and praising their God" (1 Nephi 1:8). Thus, the Book of Mormon prophets immediately position themselves against the Deuteronomists and with the visionaries.

Ninian Smart and Ian Barbour offer classifications for reports of revelation that I find useful in approaching Joseph Smith's accounts. They both begin with Rudolf Otto's *The Idea of the Holy*, in which Otto studied the characteristics of a type of religious encounter that he named the numinous.[63] Smart sums up numinous experience as "a mystery which is fearful, awe-inspiring, . . . and fascinating."[64] Barbour emphasizes the "sense of otherness, confrontation and encounter" when "man is aware of his own dependence, finitude, limitation, and contingency."[65] This experience usually occurs in institutionalized worship situations involving personal models of God. The worshipper often bows to show humility, acknowledging inferiority and distance, and feels contingency and a moral demand. Worship involves sacrifice and petition.

Some of the LDS accounts, like the vision in the book of Moses, chapter 1 in *Pearl of Great Price* have a profoundly numinous quality. There is another kind of religious experience, however, that has characteristics quite different from the numinous. This is mystic's experience, as reported by such persons as the Buddha or a close contemporary of Joseph Smith, Ralph Waldo Emerson.

Smart and Barbour characterize mystical union as the experience of "joy, harmony, serenity, and peace," and a sense of the unity of all things and of the loss of identity. Separation seems illusory, differences and dichotomies of opposites are transcended. Most often, the mystic stresses the ineffability of the experience and uses impersonal models of God. This experience usually occurs in response to contemplation, meditation, discipline, and possibly asceticism.

Some kinds of mystical experience are without question foreign to Mormonism. Hugh Nibley cites such differences as the impersonal models of God, the emphasis on meditation as strict discipline requiring a teacher-guide, and the ineffable, incommunicable, and solitary aspects of the experience of mystic illumination.[66]

Differences between mystic experience and Mormonism are not the whole story, however. Numinous encounter has predominated in the West and mystical union in the East, but all the major religions have included both types of experience, and this is true of Mormonism as well. Mark Koltko's insightful essay "Mysticism and Mormonism" explores parallels between various Mormon scriptures and certain characteristics of mystical experience.[67]

For example, I see some striking parallels in the "light" passages in Doctrine and Covenants 88 (dictated by Joseph Smith in 1832) and the language Emerson uses in his 1836 essay "Nature" to describe some of his experiences. Both writers express an identical awareness of a divine spirit interpenetrating and supporting the physical world. Both speak in an identical tone, differing only in that Emerson depicts the influence of the Spirit in terms of a nature metaphor, and Smith does so in terms of a light metaphor. But even while it parallels aspects of Emerson's experience, much of Doctrine and Covenants 88 reflects numinous experience with a personal God and eschatological intent that is totally alien to Emerson's thought. These light passages do, however, resonate with Barker's observations on the Glory, particularly with her quotation from Philo.[68]

So we arrive at the point of needing to understand the relation between numinous and mystic experiences. If we think of the numinous distance and mystical identity as poles on a continuum of experience of God, we can begin to appreciate the distinctiveness of Mormonism in relation to these experiences. I see the experience of the sacred in Mormonism as bridging the numinous and the mystic. After a numinous theophany, Moses announces in the Mormon Book of Moses, "For this cause I know that man is nothing" (Moses 1:10). Yet a few verses later, changing perspectives, he makes a declaration amounting to intimate identity. "For behold, I am a son of God, in the similitude of his Only Begotten" (Moses 1:13).

The tension of distance most evidenced in Joseph Smith's first vision resolves toward a profound intimacy in Doctrine and Covenants 76, Moses 1, in Benjamin's coronation speech (Mosiah 1–5), and in Alma's conversion (Mosiah 27, Alma 36) "And then shall ye know that I have seen Jesus Christ, and that he hath talked with me face to face and that he told me in plain humility, even as a man telleth another in mine own language concerning these things" (Ether 12:39). But such intimacy in Mormon thought, even when described as Oneness, is typically associated with a personal deity. "Then shall ye know that ye have seen me, that I am, and that I am the true light that is in you, and that you are in me; otherwise ye could not abound" (Doctrine and Covenants 88:50; cf. John 15:3; 3 Nephi 19:23; Doctrine and Covenants 88:41).

These accounts occur in a context that fully embraces the biblical picture of an anthropomorphic God (Ether 3:6–16), rather than in a context that includes something like Ralph Waldo Emerson's impersonal Oversoul or the unknowable God of the Kabbalists.[69] According to Ninian Smart, the numinous and mystic poles of experience influence patterns of doctrine.

> If you stress the numinous, you stress that our salvation or liberation (our becoming holy) must flow from God the Other. It is he who brings it to us through his grace. You also stress the supreme power and dynamism of God as creator of the cosmos. If, on the other hand, you stress the mystical and non-dual, you tend to stress how we attain salvation and liberation through our own effort at mediation, not by the intervention of the Other. . . . If we combine the two, but accent the numinous, we see mystical union as a kind of close embrace with the other—like human love, where the two are one and yet the two-ness remains. If the accent is on the mystical rather than the numinous, then God tends to be seen as a being whom we worship, but in such a way that we get beyond duality.[70]

Here, I believe, is an essential distinguishing characteristic of Mormonism—the blend of the numinous and the mystic. This explains the orthodox discomfort with the Mormon idea of deification (something quite unthinkable to one caught up in a purely numinous tradition in which God must be distant and other), as well as the Eastern discomfort with our literalism and personal God (again, concepts quite unthinkable to one caught up by the incommensurable and impersonal divine of pure mysticism). In all cases, experience precedes and constrains doctrine. Joseph Smith's experiences led him to embrace the personal and anthropomorphic manifestations of God in the Bible (as seen in Ether 3:16) though with the potential for a profound oneness (as written in Doctrine and Covenants 88:67–68).

While Joseph encouraged all members to seek personal revelation, he also had to confront the challenges that tended to fragment most visionary sects.[71] In September of 1830, Hyrum Page, one of the eight witnesses of the Book of Mormon, reported revelations that conflicted with Smith's. Joseph responded with a further revelation that declared that people in the church were not to command those above them in the priesthood organization (See Doctrine and Covenants 28:6). Rather than stifle or monopolize the visionary impulse, Joseph put in place a priesthood hierarchy that bridled it in service of the community (Doctrine and Covenants 107, 84). When a few members in Kirtland accepted spiritual experiences that disrupted the community, Joseph received a revelation declaring that the spirits should be tried to see whether they edified and were understandable. The revelation warned, "That which does not edify is not of God, and is darkness. That which is of God is light; and he that receiveth light, and continueth in God, receiveth more light; and that light groweth brighter and brighter until the perfect day." (Doctrine and Covenants 50:23–24).[72]

The revelation given in the preface to the Doctrine and Covenants sets expectations for LDS revelations received by imperfect individuals as being ongoing and incomplete. Rather than promising infallibility, the text bluntly states of church leaders "that these commandments are of me, and were given to my servants in their weakness, after the manner of their language . . . inasmuch as they erred, it shall be made manifest. Inasmuch as they sought wisdom, they might be instructed; inasmuch as they sinned, they might be chastened, that they might repent" (Doctrine and Covenants 1:24–28). Indeed, Joseph Smith also presented revelation as nonexclusive to the church he organized, one Book of Mormon prophet declaring that "the Lord doth grant unto all nations, of their own nation and tongue, to teach his word, in wisdom, all that he seeth fit that they should have" (Alma 29:8). Rather than present perfection here and now, Joseph Smith offered the imperfect a path toward perfection.

And if your eye be single to my glory, your whole bodies shall be
filled with light, and there shall be no darkness in you; and that body
which is filled with light comprehendeth all things.

> Therefore, sanctify yourselves that your minds become single to God, and the days will come that you shall see him; for he will unveil his face unto you, and it shall be in his own time, and in his own way, and according to his own will. (Doctrine and Covenants 88:67–68)

The project to build a temple soon became the primary goal of the LDS community wherever it gathered. Even before the first LDS temple was built in Kirtland, the revelations promised that the temple would be a place of vision (Doctrine and Covenants 97: 10, 14–16).

In centering their communities on temples, the LDS communities followed traditions that were present throughout the Book of Mormon. Early on, the text reports that Nephi, a migrant to the New World from Jerusalem, "did build a temple; and I did construct it after the manner of the temple of Solomon save it were not built of so many precious things" (1 Nephi 5:15). Important discourses by later Book of Mormon prophets tend to be either given at the temple on significant ritual occasions or involve temple themes and imagery. The climax of the Book of Mormon in 3 Nephi, chapters 8 through 29—the account of the risen Lord—comes in a temple context. The sequence begins with the fragmented society, and the darkness and the destruction in the aftermath of cataclysmic volcanic events. These destructive events are presented in a way that recalls the most ancient creation dramas, which everywhere had been dramatized in the temple rituals.[73] After the destruction, with the survivors waiting in darkness, the voice of the Lord is heard, and the recent destruction is recast in ritual form, and redefined as a new creation, in which "old things are done away, and all things become new" (3 Nephi 12:47). Those listening are told that rather than the burnt offerings and blood sacrifices of Law, "ye shall offer for a sacrifice unto me a broken heart and a contrite spirit," and the Lord promises a baptism by fire and the Holy Ghost (3 Nephi 9:12). Why these particular sacrifices?

Joseph Campbell explains that "in temple art generally, the entrances to sacred precincts are represented as attended by two 'gate or threshold guardians' . . . which are frequently threatening of mien." They represent "physical desire and fear (the two temptations overcome by Prince Gautama Shakyamuni on the night of his attainment of Buddahood)."[74] Desire is demonstrated by the young man who would not give up his riches to follow Jesus (Luke 18:23). Fear is what we think, such as demonstrated by Peter when he rebuked the Lord for saying that Jesus would be killed and rise on the third day. "Be it far from thee, Lord: this shall not be unto thee" (Matthew 16:22). To be able to enter into the "real," we must be willing to sacrifice what we want (offer a broken heart) and what we think (offer a contrite spirit). Or as Joseph Smith expressed it, the problem with static creeds is that they "set up stakes and bounds to the work of the Almighty." Joseph wanted to be able to "come into the presence of God and learn all things," but "creeds say, Hitherto thou shalt come, and no further."[75]

In 3 Nephi 11, as the risen Jesus appears to 2,500 people gathered at the temple (3 Nephi 17:25), he comes as a man dressed in a white robe and declares, "I am he that gave the Law" (3 Nephi 15:5). It is notable that the text does not mention shining or glory at this first appearance. The light and glory had figured prominently in accounts elsewhere. For example, *Pearl of Great Price* describes how "Moses was caught up into an exceedingly high mountain, and he saw God face to face, and he talked with him, and the glory of the God was upon him; therefore Moses could endure his presence" (Moses 1:1–2).

In the 3 Nephi account, Jesus initially teaches as a temple priest, provides instruction, bestows priesthood authority to baptize, later, he confers the Holy Ghost. He provides sacraments and introduces covenants.[76] Only after a process of instruction and prayer progresses, do the participants see Jesus transfigured.

> And it came to pass that Jesus blessed them as they did pray unto
> him; and his countenance did smile upon them, and the light of his
> countenance did shine upon them, and behold they were as white
> as the countenance and also the garments of Jesus; and behold the
> whiteness thereof did exceed all the whiteness, yea, even there could
> be nothing upon earth so white as the whiteness thereof. (3 Nephi
> 19:25)

Jesus then continues his intercessory prayer that "because of their faith they may be purified in me that I may be in them as thou, Father, art in me, that we may be one, that I may be glorified in them" (3 Nephi 19:29). A witness records: "And when Jesus had spoken these words he came again unto his disciples; and behold they did pray steadfastly, without ceasing unto him; and he did smile upon them again; and behold, they were white, even as Jesus" (3 Nephi 19:30).

This completes the movement of the participants from a state of darkness and separation from God, through a transitional period of preparation at the temple, to their being brought into the divine presence, a realization of what the holy of holies in the Jerusalem temple symbolized. It is this kind of ritual movement toward theophany and literal at-one-ment that Joseph Smith sought as a communal experience in a Pentecostal-like outpouring in the Kirtland temple, and that he institutionalized in a ritual form at the Nauvoo (and later) LDS temples.

One of the hymns written for the temple dedications, "The Spirit of God," declares that "the visions and blessings of old are returning, and angels are coming to visit the earth." In the dedicatory prayer at the Kirtland temple on April 3, 1836, Joseph Smith's dedicatory prayer asked, "That thy glory may rest down upon thy people, and upon this thy house, which we now dedicate to thee, that it may be sanctified and consecrated to be holy, and that thy holy presence may be continually in this house" (Doctrine and Covenants 109:5, 10–12).

Pentecostal-like manifestations of various kinds—visions of angels or of Jesus, speaking in tongues, and prophesying—were reported by many participants in the period leading up to the Kirtland dedication.[77] The most detailed and significant vision was experienced by Joseph Smith and Oliver Cowdery on April 3, 1836. "After distributing the Lord's Supper, I retired to the pulpit [in the Kirtland temple], the veils being dropped, and bowed myself and Oliver Cowdery, in solemn and silent prayer" (Preface to Doctrine and Covenants 110). The description continues:

> The veil was taken from our minds, and the eyes of our understanding were opened.
>
> We saw the Lord standing upon the breastwork of the pulpit, before us; and under his feet was a paved work of pure gold, in color like amber.
>
> His eyes were as a flame of fire; the hair of his head was white like the pure snow; his countenance shone above the brightness of the sun; and his voice was as the sound of the rushing of great waters, even the voice of Jehovah, saying:
>
> I am the first and the last; I am he who liveth, I am he who was slain; I am your advocate with the Father. (Doctrine and Covenants 110:1–8)

Only as the community gained strength did Joseph openly discuss, publish, and distribute his more personal theophanies. Yet even then, he showed characteristic reticence. The climactic theophany in the Kirtland temple was not published during his lifetime.

The Nauvoo temple brought further developments in LDS temple worship. Bushman explains that

> In the early revelations, the word "endowment" referred to seeing God, a bequest of Pentecostal spiritual light. The use of the word "endowment" in Nauvoo implied that the goal of coming into God's presence would be realized through ritual rather than transcendent vision. . . . Ann Taves, a modern scholar of religion, has added that "direct inspiration survives only when it is supported by a sacred mythos embedded in sacred practices." The Mormon temple's sacred story stabilized and perpetuated the original enthusiastic endowment.[78]

Bushman explains the Nauvoo temple developments:

Intrigued by the Masonic rites, Joseph turned the materials to his own use. The Masonic elements that appeared in the temple endowment were embedded in a distinctive context—the Creation instead of the Temple of Solomon, exaltation rather than fraternity, God and Christ, not the Worshipful master. Temple covenants bound people to God, rather than to each other. At the end, participants entered symbolically into the presence of God."[79]

All these distinguishing aspects of the Nauvoo temple experience also characterize the temple discourses in the Book of Mormon.[80] Bushman also states that the Nauvoo endowment included women in the rituals, depicting "not male fraternity but the exaltation of husbands and wives."[81] By including women in the rituals, Joseph was again catching up to Book of Mormon precedent, where the participants in the 3 Nephi temple experiences included "men, women, and children" (3 Nephi 17:25).

The LDS community is currently set apart from other Judeo-Christian faiths by temple practices. But as Barker has shown, it does reach back to the same cultural roots in the Bible through both history and prophecy that touch on the theme of "seeking the face of the Lord" as appreciated in the First Temple period. As David Bokovoy observes:

Hence Lehi's biblical contemporary, the prophet Jeremiah, specifically identified a true messenger as one who had "perceived and heard [God's] word" (Jeremiah 23:18). In Jeremiah 23:18, "perceived" is the King James translation for the Hebrew verb *ra'ah*, which means, in its most basic sense, "to see." Therefore, according to the stipulations provided by Jeremiah, a true prophet had both *seen* and *heard* God's word.[82]

Lehi and Nephi both emphasize that they have "seen" and "heard" in many passages, evidently in a deliberate echo of Jeremiah's declaration (1 Nephi 1:6, 18–19). In subsequent chapters, the narrative reports that two of Lehi's sons begin murmuring by protesting that he is a "visionary man" (2 Nephi 2:11), which introduces the tension between those who believed in visions, and those who saw them as fraud or delusion. To those who accepted vision, the denial of such amounted to blindness. In describing conditions in Jerusalem at the end of the First Temple period in the sixth century BCE, Margaret Barker often cites passages in 1 Enoch that describe a condition of blindness that prevailed in Jerusalem in the period leading to the destruction of the temple.

And after that in the sixth week all who live in it shall be *blinded*,
And the hearts of all of them shall godlessly *forsake wisdom*. And in
it a man shall ascend; And at its close the house of dominion shall
be burnt with fire, And the whole race of the chosen root shall be
dispersed. (1 Enoch 93.7–8)

Although Enoch is outside the canon, the prophets who lived at Jerusalem also described both the blindness and the associated forsaking of wisdom. For example, Ezekiel, a priest taken as part of the first group of exiles, writes of those "which have *eyes to see, and see not*; they have ears to hear, and hear not" (Ezek. 12:2). Ezekiel credits the blindness to rebellion, which implies a willful internal enemy. Ezekiel expressly reports the opening of his own eyes in the context of anthropomorphic visions (Ezek. 40:2–4; 44:5). Jeremiah also talks about the blindness, and relates it to a loss of understanding (which implies a lack of wisdom). "Hear now this, O foolish people, *without understanding*, which *have eyes, and see not*; which have ears, and hear not" (Jer. 5:21).

Proverbs 1:2–33 also describes the forsaking of wisdom as preceding the destruction of Jerusalem. The proximity the beginning of the Deuteronomist reforms to these charges of blindness invites reconsideration of the passages in Deuteronomy that Barker cites to illustrate the group's claim that God had not been seen (Deut. 4:12), their declaration that the written law would now be wisdom (Deut. 4:6).

In the Book of Mormon, Jacob, an exact contemporary of Ezekiel, and like Ezekiel a temple priest, also provides important details about the blindness:

But behold, the Jews [that Lehi knew in Jerusalem in the period
before the destruction] were a stiffnecked people; and they despised
the words of plainness, and killed the prophets, and sought for things
which they could not understand. Wherefore, because of their blindness, which *blindness* came from *looking beyond the mark*, they must
needs fall; for *God hath taken his plainness away from them*, and delivered unto them many things which they cannot understand because
they desired it. (Jacob 4:14)

The "mark" to which Jacob refers must be the same mark mentioned in Ezekiel 9:4. Margaret Barker has shown this mark (the letter *tau*) to refer to the anointing of the first temple priests with the sign of the divine Name. She also cites traditions that the anointing oil was hidden away at the time of Josiah.[83] The anointing distinguished the priests of the first temple from those of the second, and stand directly behind the titles of Messiah and Christ, which both mean "anointed." She has shown that "Josiah's changes to the temple concerned the high priests and were thus changes at the very heart of the temple."[84]

The Book of Mormon invites us to look back at Jerusalem between the Josiah's reform and the exile as a time of controversy concerning both the possibility of *vision* and the charge of *blindness*. Here Joseph Smith's *restoration* converges on the key time, place, institutions, and issues involved in Barker's reconstruction of the first temple. As with the scriptures he produced, Smith also led his community to emulate the ancients as he prayed at the dedication of the Kirtland temple in 1836:

> For thou knowest that we have done this work through great tribulation; and out of our poverty we have given of our substance to build a house to thy name, that the Son of Man might have a place to manifest himself to his people. (Doctrine and Covenants 109:5)

PART III

Prophetic Legacy

II

Tracking the Sincere Believer: "Authentic" Religion and the Enduring Legacy of Joseph Smith Jr.

Laurie F. Maffly-Kipp

In 1902, William A. Linn published a historical work entitled *The Story of the Mormons*. That book became the most often cited treatment of the LDS Church written by a non-Mormon in the early twentieth century. Linn's exhaustive work includes more than six hundred pages of text, multiple appendices, and copious citations of the works of Joseph Smith Jr., Lucy Mack Smith, and Parley P. Pratt, as well as pro-and anti-Mormon materials that Linn gathered while conducting his research in the New York Public Library. In many respects, Linn's volume is a typical anti-Mormon exposé. Like other Gentiles who had written before him, Linn sees Mormonism as a phenomenon of inviting surfaces that gloss the evils lurking beneath. He believes the job of the historian—his job—is to unveil the deceptions, to show Mormonism for what it really is: a web of deceit spun by power-hungry leaders to ensnare the easily duped American public.

The centerpiece of Linn's debunking enterprise is his exposure of Joseph Smith as a fraud. At the very opening of his history, Linn explains that people in every time and place have been fooled by religious impostors. There is something particular about Joseph Smith's deceptions, however, Linn writes:

> It is true that the effrontery which has characterized Mormonism from the start has been most daring. Its founder a

lad of low birth, very limited education, and uncertain morals; its beginnings so near burlesque that they drew down upon its originators
the scoff of their neighbors,—the organization increased its membership as it was driven from one state to another, building up at last
in an untried wilderness a population that has steadily augmented
its wealth and numbers; doggedly defending its right to practise its
peculiar beliefs and obey only the officers of the Church.[1]

Linn's comparison of Mormonism to a theatrical production—a mocking
and unoriginal imitation of religion put forward by a man who was probably
immoral—reveals Linn's own beliefs more than it describes Joseph Smith's
following then or now. In making this claim, Linn reveals an important assumption that deserves further exploration: He assumes that Joseph Smith's
sincerity is inextricably linked to the truths of the Mormon faith. Because he
judges that Smith's intentions were not honest, the religion itself is rendered
a sham. Religious *truth* is thus linked to Smith's personal *sincerity*—defined as
genuine, honest, and free of duplicity.

This issue still haunts discussions of Smith's legacy: Are the eternal truths
of Mormonism dependent on the sincerity of Joseph Smith? And a corollary to
that question: Does contemporary Mormon faith rest on the intentions of the
first prophet?

These may seem like inappropriate or even impudent questions to ask
during the 200th anniversary of Joseph Smith's 1805 birth. After all, in an important sense, history is truth. Christianity is a religious tradition that makes
both historical and transhistorical claims: it is grounded in a historical narrative that is itself an element of its truth claim, yet Christianity is also wed-
ded to ideals and principles that are thought to be eternal. When a Christian
claims to believe, he or she is confessing to believe in both a real-life story of
Jesus' death and resurrection, and also in timeless principles about the world.
Mormons share these claims but add to them a testimony of the veracity of
Joseph Smith's revelations and of belief in a Father in Heaven who has been
revealed and is continuing to reveal himself to humanity. Joseph Smith has
to be there, in the story, for the tradition to make sense. History must be
in play.

But it bears stating, as historian Kathleen Flake and others have so ably
shown us, that the historical account of the Mormon tradition can be told
in numerous ways; the narrative is not self-evident or unchanging.[2] In other
words, the history of early Mormonism doesn't have to be told in the way it
usually is: by placing Smith's guilelessness and honesty front and center. There
may be other options, other angles of vision that reveal elements obscured by

the shadow of Joseph Smith's personal story. Even if we do linger on Smith's account, it is instructive to move away from the "sincerity box," as I want to call it, to see the Mormon prophet in other lights.

This essay attempts to do three different things. First, it explores how the notion of sincerity has been used by believers and nonbelievers alike to make claims about the truth of Mormonism. Second, it focuses on sincerity as a concept and explores why it can be a problem rather than a solution. And finally, it suggests some other possible framings for the exploration of Mormon history.

The ideal of religious sincerity is so pervasive in our day and age that we may not even realize the many ways it affects what we see and feel. Many readers may be wondering, in fact: What's the problem here? Of course religious truth is about belief, about having the right internal disposition. Like the air we breathe, our dependence on it is practically automatic.

Almost everyone before and after William Linn—believers, nonbelievers, and agnostics alike—has assumed that judging Smith's intentions will take us directly to the heart of the truth of Mormonism. At the end of the day—or at least at the end of this essay—you may still decide that judging personal sincerity is the surest way to gauge true religion. But I'd like to at least temporarily pull apart this connection, to bracket the question of the ultimate truth of Smith's work and focus instead on Smith's psychology—and thereby show how people use evidence of sincerity to judge the objective validity of the Mormon tradition. For present purposes, I'm not concerned about whether God actually revealed himself to Joseph, or whether there were golden plates in the New York hills. Instead, I want to focus on how people talk about Smith's relationship to those ancient writings. What I'm most intrigued by is the presumed clean connection between feeling and action, the importance people place on judging what Joseph thought and felt as a litmus test for the validity of Mormon origins and, by extension, for contemporary LDS faith.

So much discussion of Mormonism over the past 175 years has centered on Joseph Smith's sincerity. We might have expected that from Linn—but over a hundred years later, biographers and historians continue to engage the issue. In revisiting this terrain, I am struck not only by the vast historiography, but by the patterns of argument, the well-worn channels in which it runs. The most obvious pivot point, of course, is the issue of supernatural versus natural explanations for Smith's work and authority. Was Smith a prophet of God or a charlatan? Related to character questions, almost by necessity, is the issue of how we are to understand the content and production of the Book of Mormon. Is it chloroform in print, as Mark Twain would have it?[3] Is it the fantastic imaginings of a creative but thoroughly natural mind, as Fawn Brodie has proposed?[4] Is it Nathan Hatch's outburst of populist rant?[5] Or is it, as many believers would hold, the inspired word of God? Did Smith dig it out of a hillside? Did he *think* he dug it out of a hillside? Did he lie and tell people he dug it out of a hillside but for all the right reasons? Authors almost always weigh in on Smith's character. "Was Joseph Smith an honest man?" seems to be the underlying question for nearly every interpretation of his life.

Although this matter of Smith's sincerity may seem, on the face of it, to constitute a straightforward battle between believers and unbelievers, Saints and Gentiles, the terrain does not easily map that sincerity onto patterns of faith. Take Fawn Brodie, whose 1945 biography of Smith resulted in her being lambasted by prominent Mormon scholars and excommunicated from the LDS Church. Brodie admires Smith even as she offers thoroughly mundane explanations for his power. As I read her, Brodie thinks that Smith is a really interesting man with a forceful intellect; she argues that "faithful" scholarship has, in fact, downplayed his natural talents in order to bolster the supernatural origins of his book. Harold Bloom, no believer himself, nonetheless considers Smith a religious genius.[6]

Faithful Latter-day Saints have focused equal attention on Smith's inner state. Notice the way that the interplay of surface appearance and interior disposition shapes Marvin Hill's review of Brodie's biography:

> The Joseph Smith she depicts is a deliberate deceiver who played
> out his masquerade for personal advantage. The implication is that
> Joseph Smith was in fact skeptical as to the truths of Christianity,
> that he never underwent that moment of conversion which he details
> in his autobiography, and that he continued to enact his subterfuge
> until for so doing he was shot by a mob at the Carthage jail. She
> maintains that, to a considerable extent, his religious efforts were
> play-acting for the benefit of an appreciative audience.[7]

Hill (along with many others) was incensed by the characterization of Smith as a religious hypocrite whose inner feelings did not match his outer actions.

On the other side of the fence of faith, the less sympathetic biographer Dan Vogel acknowledges this mismatch of interior disposition and external actions but still feels a need to separate the "true" from the "false" religious experience. He theorizes insincerity as, in some cases, morally justifiable:

> Smith really believed he was called of God to preach repentance to a
> sinful world but . . . he felt justified in using deception to more fully
> accomplish his mission. Like the faith healer who uses plants or
> confederates in his congregation to create a faith-promoting atmos-
> phere in which the true miracles can occur, Smith assumed the role

of prophet, produced the Book of Mormon, and issued revelations to create a setting in which true conversion experiences could take place. It is the true healings and conversions that not only justify deception but also convince the pious frauds that they are perhaps after all real healers or real prophets.[8]

But the very vigor with which Vogel broaches the subject indicates a discomfort with it; he rationalizes Smith's insincerity. Joseph Smith, however pious, was fraudulent in his means—a fact that invalidates his ministry.

Richard Bushman's recent biography of Joseph Smith is the most exhaustive and sophisticated treatment available. He, too, stresses Smith's sincerity. Smith thought of himself as a revelator, Bushman asserts. Like the Quaker George Fox or the prophets of the Old Testament, Smith was guided by the voice of God, not the workings of his own mind. In order to "get inside the mind" of the prophet, explains Bushman, one must recognize this fact. Bushman feels that this gets around the thorny question of whether or not the revelations were *really* from God—in any case, he determines, Smith *thought* they were.[9] For Bushman, just like the others, it is Smith's veracity that is at stake.

I don't know whether Joseph Smith thought he heard the voice of God or not. Nor is my purpose to judge any of these interpretations that focus on such questions. My purpose, rather, is to call our attention reflexively to the persistence of interest, from both Mormon and non-Mormon scholars, in Smith's sincerity. Did he mean what he said? Did he feel religious inside? Did his outer actions match his inner state? Interestingly, Brodie, Hill, and Vogel all agree that Smith *must* have come to some kind of "inner equilibrium," as Brodie puts it, which allowed for a measure of "sincerity."[10]

I should point out, too, that it's not just historians who are interested in this question. The Church of Jesus Christ of Latter-day Saints itself has increasingly elevated Joseph Smith's simplicity and guilelessness as his chief virtues. Kathleen Flake tells us that it was only at the turn of the twentieth century, as the church set out to prove its "Americanness" and downplay its peculiarities, that the First Vision and the tale of the young, uneducated, and innocent boy became a hallmark of the faith.[11] The Mormon Church has its own reasons for telling the story this way: the naiveté of a young boy, in an important sense, stands in as a sign of the religious validity of the church as a whole. Current LDS literature makes this bond explicit. In his April 2002 General Conference address, Elder Carlos Amado urged newcomers to "read the testimony of Joseph Smith with an open mind and real intent. You will feel his sincerity, and you will discover the establishment of the Church, restored in a miraculous way!"[12] Through Joseph Smith's sincerity, then, new believers will come into the LDS Church. Increasingly, belief in Smith's veracity has become a signal feature of faithfulness.

Yet as a philosophical issue (I'll return to the historical question later), sincerity turns out to be a complicated matter: it can be misleading. The LDS Church teaches, on the one hand, that Mormons need sincerity (both theirs and Joseph's) to obtain true faith. They must enter into their exploration with the right heart. On the other hand, the church cautions that sincerity is not enough: "At the outset of this investigation," explains Elder John Morgan in an 1881 pamphlet, "it is deemed proper and advisable to refer to another point, so that we may have a clear understanding. The point is: Sincerity of belief does not in any way establish the correctness of a principle. Only an unimpeachable testimony can do that."[13]

This reminder that sincerity of belief is not enough to establish something's truthfulness is an important one. But what about the converse of this equation? Can insincere people express correct ideas and enact religious truths—sometimes despite themselves? It's an interesting question to which I now turn.

The church clearly has theological investments in Smith's sincerity. But why should Smith's sincerity matter to us? Of what consequence is it to both believers and nonbelievers to evaluate and judge sincerity? How are the questions we all ask of Joseph Smith—and thus the way we tell his story and the story of the church he founded—shaped by our own cultural assumptions?

It is important, first, to place ourselves in time. Sincerity, it turns out, has not always been seen as a hallmark of religious authenticity. In fact, sincerity itself—or at least the idea that one's inner thoughts and feelings had much to do with one's salvation—has been a subject of considerable dispute in the Christian tradition for at least five hundred years. As Lionel Trilling points out in his provocative essays in *Sincerity and Authenticity*, the word *sincerity* entered the English language in the first third of the sixteenth century, just at the dawn of the Reformation. And the word was connected, morally and aesthetically, to that tumultuous religious transformation: it was derived from the Latin term meaning, literally, "clean, or sound, or pure."[14] Catholics before the Reformation worried much less about intentions and much more about actions, for salvation was earned principally through the rites and sacraments of the church. For Protestants, trying to separate themselves from Catholic ritualism and ceremony, having a "clean soul" became increasingly important. Sincerity provided a convenient way to distinguish "pure" doctrine, religion, or Gospel, from the impure (Catholic) versions. Because Protestants—relying on the apostle Paul and Augustine as their guides—believed that exterior action flowed from a right interior disposition, they were deeply disturbed by any evidence that one's actions might not accord with one's faith or feelings. Unlike Catholics, who retained the conviction that deeds themselves could motivate feelings (as well as the other way around), Protestants prized purity of heart and purpose as the hallmarks of good character. *Sola fide*. Faith alone will win you heaven. It was only in subsequent centuries that sincerity came to connote an individual character trait—as in the absence of feigning or pretense.

Trilling also points out that this revolution in sensibility, this transformation to seeing good character as a matter of inner disposition rather than the performance of particular activities, prompted numerous explorations of the themes of dissemblance and dissimulation in the Elizabethan era. Think of the number of Shakespeare's plays that deal with the discrepancy between appearance and disposition: men pose as women, villains pretend to be good, and people are fooled by pretense to both comic and tragic effect. The Protestant-inspired fervor for the "pure personality" gained added force in the New World. During the religious revivals of the eighteenth century, so-called "New Light" Protestants proclaimed that one could not be a true Christian without having had a saving experience of God's grace. In turn, considerable scrutiny fell on religious leaders. Were *they* saved? If not, could they save other people? What was the relationship between salvation and inner disposition? In its most famous formulation, one New Light leader asks, "Is a dead man fit to bring others to life?"[15] In other words, those ministers who were not purified internally by God could not lead others to salvation. Unlike the Catholic priest who could serve as a sacramental medium of God despite his own personal failings, the Protestant minister was expected to be morally pure; the state of his soul affected his ability to save others.

The founding of the American nation and the disestablishment of religion lent a new urgency to moral suasion, since one could no longer compel religious behavior. Without a state church to structure and mandate religious action, fellow citizens had to *convince* one another about appropriate beliefs—an activity that they felt would, in turn, encourage moral conduct. Good behavior was thereby a sign of one's inner state of salvation. Bolstered by romantic sensibilities and the philosopher Jean Jacques Rousseau's anthropology of natural goodness, the fascination with the self and its presentation can be found everywhere in nineteenth-century art and letters—from Ralph Waldo Emerson's assertions of the primacy of loyalty to individual belief and expression to Henry and William James, both of whom, in different spheres, explored the relationship between personal feelings and behaviors and larger moral and aesthetic categories.[16]

This relationship has been explored in tales of fallen religious leaders over and over again. A brief list tells the story: Arthur Dimmesdale, the cowardly minister from the *Scarlet Letter*; Theron Ware, the eponymous fallen Methodist preacher in Harold Frederic's famous novel, who wanted only to impress his new Catholic friends; Sinclair Lewis's quack preacher, Elmer Gantry; and the brilliantly gullible and heavily mascaraed Tammy Faye Bakker. All of their sad stories raise the profound philosophical question: how do we know that what we see of a person is true, is natural, is the *real* self? And this question is premised on the idea that the real self is the self *within*, a self separable from individual behavior, rather than the sum total of one's actions.

This impulse to find the real person beneath the mask or the subterfuge, and to revere people as "good" if their inner states match their outer comportment, also leads to particular obsessions with and evaluations of the past. Two connected preoccupations offer potential reinterpretations of Smith's role in early Mormonism: the American suspicion of self-creation as inauthentic; and the unexamined assumption that personal morality ought to be marked by the transparent and consistent display of one's "innermost feelings."

Americans, shaped by this Protestant spiritual ethic, can be deeply disquieted by obvious and overt attempts at self-creation. Our culture may value the "self-made man," but that persona is a far cry from self-fashioning, from the active and deliberate creation of a personal image for public effect. The latter garners deep suspicion as being suspect or immoral. Think of the pop star Madonna, a contemporary example of someone willing to create herself over and over again (currently refashioned as a mother and housewife). Such Madonna-like flash may be entertaining, but it also elicits cynicism and derision from observers who seek the "real substance" beneath the tricks and makeup.[17] We look for sincerity.

Yet American history also offers potentially admirable models of figures that have reshaped their behavior in spite of—or even because of—a failure to feel as moral as they wanted to act. Benjamin Franklin and Dale Carnegie both offer intriguing and confounding examples of different takes on inner disposition and external behavior. Franklin, like Joseph Smith, came from humble origins. He was self-taught, an eclectic reader with deep interests in religious matters. As a youth, he engaged in "indiscrete disputations" that upset others—some of whom apparently spoke ill of him. Unhappy with being the object of scorn, Franklin determined to be seen in a different light. He chose to create a different self, much as Fawn Brodie wants to argue that Smith grew into his role as a prophet and religious leader. Indeed, in his autobiography, Franklin admits to lying and flattering in order to impress people, all to the end of having a good reputation in the world—a goal that he asserts is a deeply moral ideal.

For Franklin, a good character is formed by one's reputation, not by one's intentions. One acts not on abstract moral principles but on the pragmatic imperative to get along with others and preserve one's name. As he put it, "So convenient a thing it is to be a *reasonable creature*, since it enables one to find or make a reason for everything one has a mind to do."[18] Franklin was devoted to the art of self-presentation: He reveals his "errata," his mistakes, to his readers in such a skillful way that one is hardly aware of the masterful control he demonstrates over his own image. He puts on the guise of such sincerity that one is taken in, convinced of the essential goodness of his inner character despite his activities. But as he might well point out, the guise is what matters in the world. He made no claims to purity of heart—in fact, quite the opposite.

The example of Dale Carnegie is also potentially instructive because Carnegie believed fervently that entrepreneurship, showmanship, and self-creation are not antithetical to religious faith or purpose: they are, in fact, deeply moral acts. Like Franklin, Carnegie—who brought us *How to Win Friends and Influence People*—urges a certain kind of theatrical play-acting on his readers: "Regard this as a working handbook on human relations: whenever you are confronted with some specific problem—such as handling a child, winning a wife to your way of thinking, or satisfying an irritated customer—hesitate about doing the natural thing, the impulsive thing. That is usually wrong." He instructs readers, instead, to read his pages and follow his advice, and watch it "achieve magic for you."[19] I should point out here that scholars have felt as equally compelled to weigh in on Carnegie as they have on Smith: was he sincere or merely a charming deceiver? Yet Carnegie claims, quite straightforwardly and much like Franklin, that the art of living morally in society is *not* about personal sincerity. Theater can provoke magic, he assures us; artifice can ensure morality.

Both Franklin and Carnegie call for a lack of transparency, the obscuring of one's sincere desires for the sake of social cohesion. Their projects of self-creation, in other words, require the use of personal artifice in the service of a greater ethical good. Contemporary philosophers take this point still further. In his 1997 book *Hiding*, the philosopher Mark Taylor asserts that the mark of our postmodern condition is that we have moved beyond the modern illusion of depth into a world of surfaces. As he would have it, in an era of massive amounts of information and media bombardment, everything now is about appearances and spectacle. Image really has become substance. There is no *there* underneath the surface to unmask. As Taylor puts it in a provocative turn of phrase, "Depth is where the gods hide when they have been chased from the heavens."[20] If Taylor is right, secular scholars have chased the gods from the heavens of their scholarship, but they surreptitiously worship those gods in the guise of sincerity. They love nothing more than to debunk or delegitimate by unmasking insincerity. (I include myself here because I also relished the moral spectacle of Tammy Faye Bakker getting her comeuppance, as if this nullified all religious experience connected with her.) We *do* believe there's some essence—or ought to be one—underneath, behind, or inside the self, guiding and shaping our exterior behavior.

Artifice and showmanship are particularly sensitive subjects when we talk about religion. But they become especially difficult in talking about Mormonism. On the one hand, LDS Church leaders (especially of late) have emphasized the centrality of faith and belief in Joseph Smith. On the other hand, Mormonism is also a sacramental religion in which particular actions have efficacy not because of the power of the participants, but because of the power of God that is manifest through them. Sacramentalism requires an attention to ceremony and ritual that transcends individual character. It is no wonder that early observers compared Mormonism to Catholicism and to Islam, religious traditions in which ritual plays an essential part. Smith may in fact be understood as an advocate for renewed ceremonialism within American Christianity—in and of itself a marked turn toward materiality and surface appearance. Scholarly debunkers have delighted in pointing to the derivative nature of the church's temple rituals from Masonic tradition, but these rituals might also be explored as a radical protest against the philosophical premises of Protestant revivalism in which one had to scour one's inner feelings before one could commit to Christ. Non-Mormon scholars today have been dismissive of Mormon temple decoration and aesthetics, seeing in them a world of sentimental kitsch and excessive literalism. Dismissed as impure, unnatural, mediated by materiality, things Mormon rankle nonbelievers in part because all Americans have been shaped by a deeply Protestant sensibility of the appropriate moral relationship between belief and behavior, surface and essence.

While it is interesting that outsiders and scholars have used this Protestant lens of sincerity and purity to judge Mormonism, what about the Mormon Church itself? This is what I find most intriguing of all: by focusing matters of faith so exclusively on Joseph's testimony, Mormons are capitulating to evangelical pieties in their own self-presentation. And if one believes that salvation comes, at least in part, through sacramental observances, then why stake accounts of Mormon origins on Smith's sincerity of purpose? (I'm thinking here of the Mormon view of the necessity of receiving certain ordinances, of which LDS emphasis on vicarious temple work for the dead is a signal example.)

Another way an insider might approach this question is by asking, Why does it matter if Smith was a pious man, as long as God provided the Book of Mormon and restored the priesthood through him? Mormon salvation may be dependent on what Joseph Smith *did,* but is it dependent on what he felt? Or on what modern-day believers claim that he *felt?* This equation—Smith's sincerity equals religious legitimacy—means that any personal failing of Smith calls into question the truth of Mormonism itself.

I promised a return to history, and to the relationship between the narration of Mormon origins and the legacy of Joseph Smith. As I've already mentioned, the focus on sincere intention has shaped the way the story of early Mormonism gets told. The story of Mormon faith is told as a history of Joseph Smith and his sincere striving for God—and if you believe this story, if you *testify* to your belief in this story, then you are one of the faithful. Even church outsiders relate to the origins story in terms of believability: Personal character and history, sincerity and truth, story and faith are all intertwined in this narrative of religious conviction. But are there other potential starting points? I briefly propose several possibilities that highlight different elements of Mormonism.

One approach might be to select a different chronological starting point. In one sense, as historian Terryl Givens has recently pointed out, Joseph Smith is simply the most recent major actor in a grand and sweeping sacred drama, the full contours of which are still to be unfolded and understood.[21] In this larger framework, then, the Restoration is not the beginning point; it merely marks a *replacement*, the rightful settling of temporal affairs from the wayward course of Christian history. America is only the final stage for the unfolding of the last dispensation of a sacred drama. In this frame of reference, starting with the First Vision is like beginning the story of traditional Christianity with the founding of the United Methodist Church. It's an important piece of the picture, clearly, but it is hardly the only way to set out. Moreover, thinking of the First Vision as the narrative starting point focuses the story more on the organization of the restored church and its leaders and less on the sacred drama of which it is the final act.

A second alternative has been broached by previous scholars but still remains to be fully explored. What if the narrative of Mormon history were conceived as a story of the experiences of ordinary believers rather than the experiences of the leaders? Focusing on leadership reinforces the validity of church authority, collective unity, and the centrality of institution building. But why focus there? Why not explore how ordinary people worked out their own religious understandings? More than twenty years ago, Davis Bitton and Leonard Arrington started down this path in *Saints without Halos: The Human Side of Mormon History*, a study of the lives of ordinary believers within the church. In their introduction, they remark:

> In Latter-day Saint history there has been a tendency to ignore what happens below the top-level of administration. The lives of those who drive the engines of history are ignored, often because they leave no

written records, but just as often because they are not considered important. Such an attitude is unfortunate, for the vitality and strength of any movement is expressed in the diversity of its experience as well as its unity of purpose.[22]

Their statement aptly captures the truth that different stories accentuate different elements of history—thus where you begin, and with whom you start—matters greatly.

What if one were to focus on *diversity* of experience rather than *unity* of purpose? Historian Jan Shipps has explored the ways that some of the earliest converts focused their attention much more on the Book of Mormon itself and less on Joseph Smith as a prophet. The saga of a New World civilization drew them in. Equally important were the manifestations of the Holy Spirit that they saw in their midst and experienced for themselves. Miracles, visions, the sighting of "wonderful lights in the air," were all means by which early believers experienced spiritual power.[23]

Family history is also religious history, something which no one knew better than Lucy Mack Smith. It, too, can be seen as the experiential focus for much of Latter-day Saint history. I bring this up, in part, because I noticed, in my research, that a wonderful tool, the *New Mormon Studies CD-ROM*, itself divides materials into two separate categories: one is "history," which includes church histories and the historical memoirs of church leaders; the other is "biography, autobiography, and family history."[24] This very division makes an important statement about what counts as religious history, equating it with ecclesiastical and therefore "authoritative" narratives. The stories of "saints without halos," in contrast, are qualified as something "other," something less significant.

Finally, I would offer the possibility that new *geographies* of Mormonism will yield different historical narratives. This example draws most extensively on my own current investigations into Mormon history. I began my work on early Mormonism by reading accounts of missionaries in the South Pacific. The Saints had reached Polynesia by the early 1840s, and I became fascinated by their experiences. Most intriguing for me was a particular image of a native convert. Louisa Barnes Pratt, the wife of Addison Pratt, had hung pictures of Joseph and Hyrum Smith on the wall in her bedroom in Tahiti. Startled by the popularity of those likenesses during evenings of fellowship, she observed that "all the People on the Island came to look at [them]." One evening, a visiting man left the gathered group to look at one of the pictures. "He kneeled before it in order that the painting might come in range with his eyes. . . . For a quarter of an hour he looked steadfastly upon it, I believe without turning his eyes." Louisa did not assume that this represented an act of worship, but she concluded that "he wished undoubtedly to imprint the lineaments of the features upon his mind."[25]

This brief sketch still captivates me. What could natives in Tahiti in 1843 possibly have seen in the Mormon story that made sense to them? I had always understood Mormonism to be the most "American" of religious traditions, and much of the scholarship on the early church explains why the Book of Mormon would have been attractive to Americans in the early national period. It was democratic, scholars argued, and it was populist. The Book of Mormon appealed to people who wanted to put the new nation at the center of the sacred landscape. But none of this helped me make sense of the Tahitian converts. They had neither met Joseph Smith nor read the Book of Mormon for themselves, and they had little chance of ever visiting a temple or gathering with the Saints in Zion. They had a picture, a material object, which mediated religious truth, transporting them to another, sacred place. I'm not discounting the talents of the missionaries or the possibility of divine inspiration, but something in the Mormon tradition resonated with the experiences and desires of native peoples in a profound way.[26]

With this mystery in mind, I subsequently toured the Museum of Church History in Temple Square, Utah. Meditating on the handcarts and tales of transcontinental suffering and pilgrimage, I again puzzled over how my Tahitian friend would have understood these relics and this account of the faith. Where was *his* story? In what ways might he have thought about the westward trek as a sacred journey? Why would it have mattered to him? I was struck again by the extent to which the authorized history of the Mormon Church is, indeed, an American story. Mormonism truly has been presented as an American religion, in which national borders are deeply problematic but nonetheless essential.

I might have been content to let go of my Tahitian converts, if not for the fact that they and their non–North American brethren now make up more than half the world's Latter-day Saints. And so I persist in proposing that this geographical variety can inform accounts of the LDS Church from its beginnings. Notice that this line of inquiry doesn't discount the centrality of Joseph Smith: we still witness natives lining up to stare at his picture. But clearly that act meant something distinctive, something that has yet to be recovered fully.

There is obviously much at stake in thinking about the founder and first prophet of the LDS Church. But I think we may see more in Joseph Smith and in Mormonism by recognizing that our focus has been relatively narrow. In responding to hecklers who continually "debunked" Mormonism by "exposing" its leader as an insincere fraud, the church increasingly devoted itself to countering those accusations by proving Smith's honorable intentions. Historians of all stripes have followed suit. By proxy, this line of argument calls into question the sincerity of each believer at every moment. And this strikes me as a Protestant interrogation that effaces other Mormon claims—specifically, a sacramental claim to a power that works through the most flawed individuals.

In a sense, Joseph Smith Jr. is both more and less than the sum of how he has been memorialized. And Mormonism as a religious tradition works outside of the "sincerity box" that has been built to contain it.

12

The Possibility of Joseph Smith: Some Evangelical Probings

Richard J. Mouw

Richard Bushman once posed an intriguing question to a group of evangelical scholars who were gathered with our Mormon counterparts for dialogue. "Is Joseph Smith *possible* for you?" he asked us. I want to engage in some probings about Bushman's question in this essay.

On the face of it, of course, most evangelical Protestants would have an easy time responding to Bushman's challenge. Of course Joseph Smith is possible, they would say; we have seen many like him in the history of religion. The only question in many evangelical minds is whether Joseph was—to put the choice crudely—a liar or a lunatic. And we are all quite familiar with religious leaders who fall under one or the other of these characterizations.

Needless to say, Bushman was not asking a question that he wanted us to answer so easily. He was presenting a somewhat different challenge. As a Mormon he was posing a question to long-time critics of the message of Mormonism's prophet: Is *our* Joseph Smith—the Joseph Smith who is honored by Latter-day Saints—is *he* possible for you?

To this question, too, of course, many evangelicals would have a ready answer, but this time a decisively negative one. We have been quick to insist that Joseph Smith, as understood by his Mormon followers, is not possible for us. For us to see him as possible in this way would require that we concede far more to Mormonism than we are inclined to do. Not only do we deny the truth of Joseph's account of the bringing forth of the Book of Mormon; we also reject those substantive beliefs that have come to be associated with the unique content of Mormon thought: a continuing postbiblical revelation mediated by a living prophet, divine corporeality, eternal progression, and the like—to say nothing of the insistence that much of what we evangelicals hold precious has now been replaced by a "restoration" of a long-lost message.

The seriousness with which we take these disagreements is what makes it difficult for me as an evangelical simply to endorse some of the efforts by other non-Mormon scholars to find an alternative to the liar-or-lunatic choice. For example, while Rodney Stark does not accept the Mormon perspective on Joseph Smith, neither does he want to be forced to choose between the "psychopathological interpretation" and the insistence that Joseph was a "conscious fraud."[1] Instead, he opts for the characterization of the Mormon prophet as a legitimate "revelator." Stark creates the space for this rubric by introducing the bare bones of "a theory of revelations," in which he lays out the conditions under which revelations—"communications believed to come from a divine being"—tend to occur. This leads Stark to speculate that Joseph Smith, like other founders of religious movements, was possessed of a "creative imagination" that led (and here Stark is borrowing a formulation from W. Montgomery Watt) to the utterance of "ideas connected with what is deepest and most central in human experience, with special reference to the particular needs of . . . [his] day and generation."[2]

In his *Prophet Puzzle* volume, Brian Waterman has collected the essays of other scholars who have explored the question of Joseph Smith's character. Many of the essayists are also looking for some conceptual space between what Dan Vogel describes as the simple choice between "pious deceiver" and "sincere fraud."[3]

All of these explorations are helpful, and in several instances quite illuminating. But I have to resist the relativizing tendencies that often seem to lurk just beneath the surface of non-Mormon efforts to offer a less-than-hostile account of Joseph's status as a religious leader. Indeed, I am convinced that in my resistance I am taking seriously Joseph's own claims regarding his mission—as well as the claims that many of my Mormon friends make on his behalf. At the core of Mormon teaching is the conviction that Joseph Smith was given something new, directly from the Godhead, that trumps all other claims to revealed truth. In the light of what he brought forth—the teachings about the continuing revelations made available to human beings by the reintroduction of living prophets into human affairs—other systems of religious thought that don't accept such teachings are now to be seen as, if not blatantly false, at least in need of serious correction and revision.

I see these claims on behalf of Mormonism as, at best, seriously mislead-ing, much in need of correction and revision in the light of the teachings of the Bible as developed and clarified by historic Christianity. In this sense, then, there is a wide chasm between the evangelical understanding of what we need to know about God's will for humankind and the perspective set forth by Joseph and his followers.

Even while I reject the key claims that Joseph made on his own behalf, though, I still struggle to find some way of explaining him—of thinking about Richard Bushman's challenge about the very possibility of a Joseph Smith—that gets beyond the simple liar-or-lunatic options. I agree with Jan Shipps's insightful observation that "the mystery of Mormonism cannot be solved until we solve the mystery of Joseph Smith."[4] Like her, I do sense that I am encoun-tering a mystery of sorts in my attempts to understand his life and mission.

I have no delusions about being able to solve the mystery of Joseph Smith. Indeed, I am content, in a sense, to live with the mystery. As the Catholic theo-logian Thomas Weinandy has helpfully commented, theology is best under-stood as "a mystery discerning enterprise" rather than "a problem solving" one. To solve a problem, he points outs, is to make all of our puzzles go away, which is not the kind of resolution that we ought to expect as a matter of course in theological exploration. But we can hope, Weinandy says, to succeed in know-ing "more precisely and clearly what the mystery is."[5]

So I will not try to "solve" the mystery of Joseph Smith here. But I do hope that I can say some things that define more clearly the outlines of the mystery. And I want to do that by offering several considerations that can serve to create for evangelicals some space between the liar-or-lunatic options. Such an exer-cise might allow us to diminish—even if only ever so slightly!—our longstand-ing unqualified hostility toward Joseph Smith, without in any way sacrificing the strong theological convictions that have fed that hostility in the past. It may even be that, in a modest attempt to clarify the contours of the mystery, we evangelicals may get an even clearer grasp of the very real disagreements we have with his perspective on matters of eternal importance.

Things Now "More Precisely Known"?

Just before beginning to write this essay, I read a translation of a theological work by Herman Bavinck, published in the late nineteenth century. Bavinck was a staunch defender of Calvinist orthodoxy, and in this work he sets forth some "prologomena" to the more specific theological topics he would treat in later volumes.

I read the Bavinck book because I had promised to review it for a theological journal and the deadline was pressing upon me. Even as I was giving a careful reading to Bavinck's arguments, however, I was thinking about how I would soon switch theological gears, turning from a systematic discussion of traditional Reformed theology to an exploration of the character and message of Joseph Smith. I was pleasantly surprised, then, to come across some comments by Bavinck that struck me as having direct application to "the prophet puzzle."

Referring specifically to Muslim thought, Bavinck insists that Calvinists should approach the claims of non-Christian religions with an open mind:

> In the past the study of religions was pursued exclusively in the interest of dogmatics and apologetics. The founders of [non-Christian] religions, like Mohammed, were simply considered imposters, enemies of God, and accomplices of the devil. But ever since those religions have become more precisely known, this interpretation has proved to be untenable; it clashed both with history and psychology.[6]

While Bavinck apparently knew little or nothing about Mormonism, the relevance of his observations about Muhammad to the case of Joseph Smith seems obvious. Like the Mormon prophet, the founder of Islam also claimed that the contents of his inspired book, the Koran, were delivered to him over an extended period of time by an angel, in his case Gabriel. And Christianity has a long history of thinkers who responded to Muhammad's claims about his new revelation with arguments designed to show that he was either a liar or a lunatic.

In his comments on the subject, Bavinck refuses to carry on in that vein. He insists that it is no longer feasible to dismiss Muhammad simply as one of many "imposters, enemies of God, accomplices of the devil"—characterizations that have been regularly applied also by evangelicals to Joseph Smith. Instead, Bavinck insists that we attend carefully to the content of Muhammad's teachings. And even more important, he suggests that we can expect to find God-given truths in those teachings.

Much of the evangelical antipathy toward Joseph Smith has taken the form of questioning his personal credibility. This project began in his own day when opponents employed a variety of strategies to discredit his claims that he had received a new revelation. The more careful of these critics have searched diligently for possible sources from which Joseph might have plagiarized the Book of Mormon. The more strident attacks on his credibility have simply insisted that his message was inspired by Satan. The application of Bavinck's suggestion for approaching Joseph Smith makes room for some interesting possibilities.

In order to pursue these possibilities, though, we would first have to pay careful attention to what Bavinck is actually offering us by way of guidance. For example, when Bavinck observes that there is "also among pagans . . . a revelation of God," is he telling us that we should expect to find, even in non-Christian perspectives, straightforward "revealed truths"? It has been common for proponents of "general revelation" to hold that, while there are revealed truths that are in some sense "available" to non-Christians, typically the non-Christians—as the apostle Paul puts it in Romans 1—"suppress the truth" because of their sinful tendencies. It is one thing, then, to acknowledge the presence of divine revelation "also among pagans"; it is another thing to see non-Christian thought as embodying straightforward revealed truths. Nonetheless, recognition of the positive workings of God beyond the borders of orthodox Christianity should be seen as providing a motivation for careful engagement with other religious perspectives.

Bavinck's observation that Islam has "become more precisely known" is even more poignant now than when he offered it in his nineteenth-century context. For one thing, we have come to understand better Islam as a system of thought. In the early days, Islam was seen primarily as a political and military threat—a circumstance wherein it is always tempting to demonize one's enemy. If, however, we are given an opportunity to study and dialogue with the other group's actual teachings in a leisurely manner, we must wrestle with the question of how those teachings have actually inspired deep commitments in the lives of sane people who sincerely accept the teachings.

The shift here is one from an agenda shaped by the question "How do we keep them from taking over our world?" to one that emerges when we ask, "What is it about their teachings that speaks to what they understand to be their deepest human needs and yearnings?" When we seriously engage the ideas embodied in another religious perspective, participating in give-and-take dialogue with proponents of that perspective, we must also take seriously their own assessment of the founder(s) of their religious community. By carefully examining Islam as a system of thought, for example, we are also forced to consider carefully the way thoughtful Muslims view the character of Muhammad. I want to commend the same sort of approach to the present-day assessment of Joseph Smith's teachings.

Careful Critique

In 1998 two evangelical scholars, Carl Mosser and Paul Owen, published a lengthy essay that portrayed evangelical anti-Mormon apologetics as "losing the battle and not knowing it."[7] For the most part, they argued, Mormon scholars have provided adequate responses to evangelical criticisms of Mormonism's historical claims, and even where the responses are not fully compelling, they observed, the Mormon thinkers have at least succeeded in showing that the situation is more complex than would appear from the evangelical critiques. In short, Mosser and Owen argued, "the sophistication and erudition of LDS apologetics has risen considerably while evangelical responses have not." And to make things worse, they reported, evangelicals have continued to repeat their standard arguments against Mormonism without even demonstrating any awareness of the relevant writings by Mormon scholars.

One option, of course, is for evangelicals to engage in serious catch-up work in historical apologetics. It is unlikely, though, that such a strategy will accomplish little more beyond the maintenance of a stalemate. Short of the proverbial "smoking gun" discovery—for example, finding a source from which the Book of Mormon was obviously plagiarized—the hope of demonstrating beyond reasonable doubt the falsity of Mormon historical claims is a vain one.

I am not willing to see us declare a moratorium on all historical investigations of "smoking gun" possibilities. But I do think a more productive strategy for evangelicals is to engage in a theological critique of the content of Mormon thought by paying considerable attention both to the historical context that gave rise to Mormonism and to the basic spiritual impulses that have guided its theological development.

The kind of thing I have in mind is illustrated nicely by Nathan Hatch, in his observations about Joseph Smith's spiritual environment. He notes that, at a time when the young Joseph's family members were experiencing serious illness compounded by financial difficulties, they "looked in vain for solace from the institutional church," which made its presence known in their lives only "in shrill and competing forms."[8] Confronted by "a proliferation of religious options," they underwent—like many of their neighbors—"a crisis of religious authority." In this context, the young Joseph became "convinced that only a new outpouring of divine revelation could pierce the spiritual darkness and confusion that gripped his own soul and that of the modern church."[9]

If we leave aside questions about Joseph's unique character and motivation, the substance of his concern is not an uncommon one. His testimony that the various denominational parties of his day "were equally zealous in endeavoring to establish their own tenets and disprove all others" has a familiar ring, as does his report that "in the midst of this war of words and tumult of opinions, I often said to myself: What is to be done? Who of all these parties are right; or, are they all wrong together? If any one of them be right, which is it, and how shall I know it?"[10] In fact, this kind of puzzlement over how to adjudicate among conflicting theological claims is regularly cited by Protestant converts to Catholicism, in support of their insistence that they have found in the papal authority an anchoring for their basic beliefs.[11]

Bringing God Nearer

Another historical factor that should be taken into account is the actual manifestation of the Christian tradition against which Joseph was reacting. An important matter in this respect is the doctrine of God that had influenced the spiritual atmosphere of his day.[12] While Joseph Smith and Mary Baker Eddy espoused very different, indeed, opposing, metaphysical systems, with Joseph arguing for a thoroughgoing physicalism and the founder of Christian Science insisting on a thoroughgoing mentalism—they each were motivated by a desire to reduce the distance between God and human beings. The founder of Christian Science, for example, would have no difficulty endorsing the Mormon claim that God and human beings are of "the same species."

Needless to say, both Smith and Mrs. Eddy were departing radically from the essential Jewish and Christian teaching that there is a vast metaphysical gap between Creator and creature. But it is one thing to make that point, and another for Christians to ask ourselves whether the early- to mid-nineteenth-century movements that reduced this metaphysical distance can, in any significant way, be seen as a corrective to weaknesses in the sort of Christian theology and practice that were common in their day.

These two reduce-the-distance theologies emerged in an environment shaped significantly by the high Calvinism of New England Puritanism. I think it can be plausibly—and rightly, from an orthodox Christian perspective—argued that New England theology, which stressed the legitimate *metaphysical* distance between God and his human creatures, nonetheless at the same time fostered an unhealthy *spiritual* distance between the Calvinist Deity and his human subjects. Thus it should not surprise us that movements arose to shrink the spiritual distance, even if we must deeply regret that they did so by also shrinking the metaphysical distance of creatures from Being, rather than by drawing on corrective teachings—such as the incarnation and the person of the Holy Spirit—that can be found within orthodox Christian theology. It is not enough for traditional Christians to condemn those movements without also acknowledging the spiritual realities that the dissenting groups were addressing.

"Thin Places"?

Attention to historical context can also reveal interesting experiential parallels between Mormon origins and episodes within the Christian community of the day—thus establishing something in the direction of innocence by association.

Again, the goal of convincing evangelicals of Joseph's *complete* innocence—of establishing that, for example, he was a true prophet from God whose message must be accepted by all—is not going to happen. But we might at least try to show that some of the features in Joseph's story to which evangelicals are most hostile are actually not unlike elements in other people's stories that evangelicals do not simply chalk up to deception or lunacy.

Here, for starters, is a case study that has some potential. Cotton Mather is a much-respected figure in the evangelical narrative of American religion. Born into a line of Puritan preacher-theologians, he outdid his forebears in the power of his preaching and the brilliance of his theological writings. He is known especially for his condemnations of witchcraft, and if he comes across negatively at all in the minds of evangelical believers it would be because he is viewed as too aggressive in his efforts to uncover any sign of what he took to be Satanic influences in his New England environs.

In this light it is interesting to note that, in the early autumn of 1693, Mather, a thirty-year-old who was still struggling to understand God's calling in his life, had an encounter with the supernatural that, he testified, had a profound impact on his spiritual development. Mather was fascinated with biblical reports of angelic interventions in human affairs, and he devoted much attention, in the form of intense spiritual struggle, to the possibility of a continuing connection of human beings with divine messengers. Then, one day, in the privacy of his bedroom, Mather experienced what he came to describe as a "strange and memorable thing":

> After outpourings of prayer, with the utmost fervor and fasting there appeared an Angel, whose face shone like the noonday sun. He was completely beardless, but in other respects human, his head encircled by a splendid tiara. On his shoulders were wings; his garments were white and shining; his robe reached to his ankles; and about his loins was a belt not unlike the girdles of the peoples of the East.[13]

Mather did not record the details of the message that the angel delivered to him, but he did testify that the angel prophesied that he, Cotton Mather, would accomplish great things, and that his intellectual influence would reach to the European continent.[14]

Kenneth Silverman, who provides this account in his biography of Mather, observes that "as a Puritan . . . Cotton Mather was born into a society that daily felt the nearness of the invisible world and wove magical and supernatural notions into the very texture of his thinking, beginning in childhood."[15] In offering this observation about the mood of the time, Silverman is giving a sympathetic portrayal of Mather's account of the angelic visitation without thereby endorsing that account as literally true. Mather lived in a time when the expectation of such experiences was not uncommon. In reporting such an encounter in his own life, he need not be seen as either a deliberate deceiver or a deluded fool. There is too much in the rest of the story of Mather's spiritual pilgrimage simply to force him into one of the two liar-or-lunatic categories. We can continue to puzzle over what "really" happened that led him to insist on the truth of his story about the angel's visit, while continuing to appreciate—and even benefit from—his overall contribution.

Silverman's observation about the spiritual influences that shaped Cotton Mather can be extended to Joseph Smith in at least this regard: in his environment, too, the expectation of supernatural visitations was not uncommon. Indeed, the worlds of Joseph Smith and Cotton Mather were not that far removed from each other, temporally and geographically. Commentators on Celtic spirituality often refer to the phenomenon of "thin places," usually linked particularly to Ireland. These are spaces or regions where, as one writer puts it, "the veil between this world and the next is so sheer that it is easy to step through."[16] To be sure, the way in which Joseph Smith made use of his testimony about the stepping-through of the veil is very different from that to which Cotton Mather put his visitation—Mather certainly saw nothing in his encounter with the angel that undercut the sole authority of the Bible. Nonetheless, perhaps something of the evangelical hostility toward Joseph could be diminished, at least to some small degree, by reflecting in more general terms on what it might mean for persons to live in times and places where the veil of "thinness" is taken to be a fact of life.

Cultivating Empathy

I said early on that I would not solve the mystery of Joseph Smith but that I hoped, at least, to offer some probings that might allow evangelicals to discern the mystery more clearly. The considerations I have set out briefly here may help some in that effort. They may allow us to make a little space for Joseph between the liar-or-lunatic poles. But the moves I have been proposing will have little real effect apart from a disposition on the part of evangelicals to *look for* that kind of space.

The problem is that some evangelicals have a tendency—especially when we are asked to assess the differences between certain worldviews—to see things in terms of stark alternatives: A perspective on life is either righteous or unrighteous. Every moral option is either right or wrong. You are either on God's side or Satan's. And a person like Joseph Smith is either a true prophet of God or he is a deceiver—with the only point worth debating being whether he was a liar or a lunatic.

This tendency to reduce the situation to simple alternatives in the case of Joseph is reinforced by a legitimate antipathy toward the Mormon teaching that humans and the members of the Godhead belong to the same order of Being. As I mentioned earlier, this claim flies in the face of the traditional understanding of biblical teaching, that God is God and we are not, and that any effort to close the metaphysical gap runs the clear risk of espousing idolatry.

Idolatry is, indeed, a very bad thing, and it is a good thing to take a strong stand against it. But there is more than one way to engage in idolatry. G. K. Chesterton offered wise counsel when he wrote, "Idolatry is committed, not merely by setting up false gods, but also by setting up false devils."[17] Wrongly to demonize a person who is not a demon is itself a terrible thing, and evangelicals have to be careful not to sin against Joseph Smith and his followers by setting up false devils.

In spelling out his own version of "just war" theory, John Calvin urged civil magistrates who were thinking about attacking an enemy to engage in serious reflection before going to war. One thing they must do, he said, is to check out their own motives, to ensure that they "not be carried away with headlong anger, or be seized with hatred, or burn with implacable severity." And they must also, he insisted, "have pity on the common nature in the one whose special fault they are punishing."[18] Calvin—as a good Calvinist!—was advocating a spiritual strategy here that is designed to compensate for our sinful tendency to put the best possible interpretation on our own motives while putting the worst possible interpretation on those of our opponents.

Evangelicals have often thought of their approach to Mormonism as a form of spiritual warfare. When this combat imagery creates an atmosphere wherein those evangelicals who want to engage in genuine dialogue with Mormons are seen as traitors to the cause, its use is regrettable. But since the encounter between Mormonism and evangelical Christianity is, indeed, one between conflicting systems of thought, something like Calvin's recommendations can be helpful. It would be a healthy spiritual exercise for us evangelicals to examine our own motives in the ways we have portrayed Joseph Smith, making sure we have not been "carried away with headlong anger" or "seized with hatred." And Calvin's recommendation about having "pity on the common nature" that we share with our opponents—as applied to dealing with serious religious differences—can be seen as a plea for empathy toward those with whom we disagree. He is suggesting that we must never lose sight of the basic features of human nature that we share, even with our worst enemies (which Mormons are not).

Indeed, it is this factor of a shared human bonding that motivates me to wrestle seriously with the ideas set forth in Joseph Smith's perspective on religious matters, even though I continue to reject his claims to have received a new revelation from the heavens. In my conversations with Mormon friends, particularly those who have studied carefully Joseph's life and teachings, I have been impressed by two things: one that gives me discomfort and another that gives me comfort. The discomfort is to be expected, given our basic disagreements: they see Joseph as a prophet and a restorer and I do not. But the factor that brings me comfort caught me up short when I first encountered it, although I have now come to expect it. It is the candor with which they empathetically treat Joseph as a very human person—"warts and all," as one of them once put it. They treat him with the kind of affection and respect that also has room for acknowledging flaws, and even serious mistakes in behavior and teaching.

It is precisely this willingness on their part to engage in a nuanced discussion of Joseph's worldview that inspires me to continue in the conversation. Like me, they see the question about how a human being can be reconciled with the Eternal as the most important issue that anyone can face. The fact is that Joseph Smith articulated a perspective on this topic that has captured the imaginations of millions of people who have become his followers. However we might assess the question of the "possibility" of a Joseph Smith, then, there is no doubt in my mind that the ideas that he set forth can serve as an important springboard for the ongoing conversation about matters that have eternal importance.

13

The Prophethood of Joseph Smith

Wayne Hudson

In this essay I argue that there are grounds for construing Joseph Smith as a genuine prophet of world historical importance. More work needs to be done, however, on what kind of prophet Joseph was. Specifically, a comparative typology of prophethood needs to be developed which allows Joseph to be compared with a wide range of other prophets, many of whom also received revelations and founded major movements. Work is also needed on the prophethood of all believers, and on the difficult question of how that prophethood applies in the case of a great covenantal prophet such as Joseph. Finally, criteria need to be developed for evaluating the work of a prophet, criteria that do not reduce what a prophet reveals to historical context.

Joseph Smith was an outstanding American religious leader and visionary who has still not received the universal recognition he deserves, partly because sectarian and secular prejudices have prevented many scholars from grasping the religious reality that manifests in Joseph and his revelations—above all, in the Book of Mormon. It is not adequate to treat Joseph, as Alexander Campbell did in the nineteenth century, and as the distinguished historian of Jacksonian democracy Robert Remini has more recently done, as merely the product of his context and his times.[1] Joseph transcended the contexts that shaped him, but as Richard Bushman among others argues, his revelations were not part of an American civil religion. Nor will it do to interpret Joseph as an American gnostic, as Harold

Bloom famously did, although there was perhaps a gnostic side to his achievement.[2] What are we to make of Joseph, then?

In the existing literature there is much discussion of the so-called "Prophet Puzzle" outlined by Jan Shipps in 1974.[3] How is it possible to reconcile Joseph the money digger and possible fraud of anti-Mormon legend with Joseph the great religious leader and organizer? The answer I suggest is that the prophethood of Joseph Smith is not a puzzle any more than Joseph himself is a puzzle. In my view, *Joseph was a prophet of God*, and accepting this is the beginning and not the end of our investigations.

Those who deny the prophethood to Joseph deny it to themselves. Those who would confine prophethood to Joseph have not read the Mormon scriptures carefully enough. Those who reduce Joseph's prophethood to automatic writing, religious genius, or folk occultism do not do justice to singular historical facts. Joseph's prophethood is not simple or unitary or straightforward—to understand it we may need to revise and expand our understanding of prophethood as both a religious and a sociological concept.

The great and striking fact about Joseph, which secularists tend to deny, is that he became caught up in a communication process that was utterly beyond his own capacities and powers. I believe it is possible to discern this much about Joseph by reading the evidence with an open mind, a mind that is not closed in advance to a spiritual perspective. Of course, my own discernment is limited. I am not a Mormon, and I thus approach Joseph Smith with deep reverence, but only partial knowledge. However, even a limited discernment suggests how recognition of authentic spiritual realities can be combined with a rational and scientific outlook. Today we need to celebrate the spiritual depth and pertinence of the prophethood of Joseph without lapsing into an irrationalism that refuses to use reason and science to explain whatever they can. Joseph's prophethood is important in the context of worldwide multifaith dialogue because it forces us to accept the possibility that revelation is not closed, but continuing. Joseph also compels us to consider how, and under what conditions, the distance between the sacral and the secular can be closed.[4] Finally, there is a profound question of how neglected peoples and geographies can be brought within the processes of revelation, an issue that restates the "Americanness" of Joseph in its theological reality. All of these issues can be advanced by a more historically sophisticated approach to Joseph's prophethood.

In this essay I want to suggest that Joseph the Mormon prophet was an ordinary human being possessed by extraordinary *charisms*, where a charism is a gift and, in more theological contexts, an empowerment to undertake an important task. In Joseph's case, we can observe and evaluate his charisms but not entirely explain them. This hypothesis deserves some expansion because it involves a conception of prophethood with which many people are not familiar. In my view, the fact that Joseph possessed specific and delimited charisms, beyond which he was not inspired, is the key to understanding the complexities of his history without trivialising the sense in which he really was the bearer of revelations. Modernist or secularist approaches to Joseph that concentrate on immanentist perspectives will not suffice because they abolish the problem instead of accounting for it. To account for the problem we have to recognise both the reality of Joseph's revelations and his own role as the person through whom they were revealed. A properly historical approach will recognise both that there are genuine revelatory experiences and that actual cases depend on singular historical facts, which we must learn to take as they are, and which we must not reduce to our preexisting schemes and conceptions. Joseph was not perfect, and his inspiration varied in quality and reliability, and this can be said even by someone who has a testimony about the truth of his revelation. Joseph was a sincere and honest man, although not without guile and not unwilling to resort on occasion to deception. He did not, however, in my view, always understand what was revealed to him, and he sometimes interpreted what was revealed in ways that reflect the limited knowledge of his time and period. For example, his understanding of the apostasy of the early Christian church can be, and to some extent has been, refined in the light of later evidence about the actual course of church history.[5]

Similarly, to insist that Joseph was a genuine prophet of world historical importance does not imply that he was always right, or that all his prophecies were unambiguously confirmed. Here we need to remember that Old Testament prophets frequently made prophecies that failed. Sometimes prophets may say too much, as Brigham Young arguably did when he declared that the sun was inhabited by living beings. Nor does it imply that all of Joseph's activities were manifestations of his prophethood, that he was always "acting as a prophet," as Joseph himself conceded. Only time and accumulated wisdom will help us to understand when Joseph was "acting as a prophet."

Clearly, we need rational criteria in order to evaluate the teachings and the work of a prophet. We cannot accept the proposition that we must believe X because prophet Y has revealed it, and that prophet Y is a prophet because he has revealed X. There are false prophets as well as human prophets who speak and write beyond their brief. Criteria that can be used to evaluate prophethood include *intelligibility* (not merely acceptability to current beliefs), *sincerity* (not the same as exception from the weaknesses of human nature), *charismatic force* (not merely enthusiasm), *cognitive complexity* (more than obscurity or difficulty), and *effectivity* (more than the fact that many people have believed the prophet). Joseph was a genuine prophet by these criteria and his revelations were characterised by intelligibility, sincerity, charismatic force, cognitive complexity, and effectivity in the relevant senses.

If, however, Joseph was a genuine prophet, what kind of prophet was he? To answer this question, we need to go beyond the familiar view of a prophet as one who foretells the future and to locate Joseph instead, in comparative terms and by reference to *a typology of prophethoods.*

In the ancient Near East, prophets were of many different kinds. They also varied from society to society. At the most basic level, a prophet was *one who spoke for another.* Depending on the culture, they might speak for one or many gods. In Israel it might be for Yahweh, although it is dangerous to identify Yahweh with "God" in a modern sense. Ancient prophets could be seers, revelators, healers, oracles, writers, and so forth. They characteristically engaged in ecstatic trances, divining, oracles, and the interpretation of dreams and omens. There were seer prophets and writing prophets, court prophets and temple prophets, prophets who warned of destruction and prophets who gave hope. Prophets might also, in extreme cases, announce new covenantal relations between a god and a people.[6]

Joseph, however, is not reducible to any Near Eastern type of prophet, just as he resists reduction to Max Weber's famous account of prophecy.[7] Joseph combines several prophet types, and has other attributes as well. He was a covenantal prophet, a restorer of past worlds, and a translator and a healer, as well as a person who predicted future events. Equally, however, he was not every type of prophet. For example, he was not one who primarily denounced the moral conduct of rulers or who "spoke truth to power." However, he was an inspired orator, a social utopian, and an organisational genius, as most Near Eastern prophets were not.

Invoking a comparative approach here does not reduce Joseph to a deluded religious leader or to a case study for the secular sociology of religion. It does not *explain him away,* but it does imply that account needs to be taken of the world historical record pertaining to prophets and prophethood, and that Joseph's own history may sometimes be clarified by resorting to this record. It remains to be seen, to take a harder case, whether comparative studies can help resolve the question of what belongs to the core of Joseph's message and what does not. This is generally conceded to be a difficult issue. For example, Joseph himself did not preach from the Book of Mormon and this work was only elevated to a status equivalent to that of the Bible after his death. Again, Joseph was a millenarian who believed that the end of the world was at hand, but in this he was presumably mistaken. Yet again, Joseph's King Follett Sermon advanced substantially new theological ideas, but it is not clear to what extent these ideas can be regarded as part of Joseph's own personal theology, as some leading Mormon scholars now suggest. Clearly this is a matter for the church to decide, but it is also a matter about which judgements are likely to be made in the light of available evidence.[8]

A comparative approach to Joseph's prophethood also has transformative ethical implications for Christians generally, including Mormons, especially in the contemporary context of multifaith dialogue. In my view, Mormons need to study prophets of other traditions, including some minor prophets, in order to gain a better sense of what is new in their own movement. For example, they might choose to study the Pakistani prophet Mirza Ghulam Ahmad (1835–1908), who founded a restoration movement in Islam, the Ahmadiyya movement, which now has millions of members. They would find some interesting parallels with Joseph as well as striking differences, which make it easier to explain what is historically original in Joseph's prophethood. Such a comparative approach implies, of course, that Mormon thought should include *a theory of religious learning*, whereby religious communities seek to learn from their own experience and arrive, in their later phases, at types of cognition that were not always predominant at an earlier time.

Some are concerned that a comparative analysis will reduce Joseph to a recurrent type of religious enthusiast, but I would argue, on the contrary, that the comparative study of prophets does not reduce them to figures in a humanist drama, although it does emphasise the natural and social scientific dimensions of their achievements. Muhammad is not less a prophet because we understand to some extent what he did. Nor is it the case that understanding him as a prophet reduces the importance of his revelation. If anything, the genuine dimension of this prophethood stands out even more plainly. Others may be concerned that a comparative approach will make Joseph seem less important. Again I think this is incorrect. Some older Mormon approaches to Joseph's prophethood tend to exaggerate his uniqueness and then make equally precipitate claims for the singularity of the Church of Jesus Christ of Latter-day Saints. But this is misleading. Joseph may not have been unique in the sense of absolutely without precedent—as a seer, as a prophet of future events, as a restorer of the past, or as a translator—even though he was uniquely addressed by specific celestial beings. His revelation was not outside historical Christianity, and he did not seek to establish a new religion. Unlike other thinkers of the period concerned to revive primitive Christianity, he attempted to restore the ancient religion of Israel, including polygamy and a form of temple worship. Joseph attempted to establish Zion, as Enoch did. He sought to restore the primitive apostolic church after the apostasy. He rebuilt the temple, and he made known the books of Moses and Enoch. He restored the keys of the kingdom. These are extraordinary achievements by any standard.

Taking Joseph's prophethood seriously does not imply, however, adopting an uncritical attitude toward more controversial aspects of his career, or an unwillingness to undertake forms of inquiry that may not immediately benefit his reputation. By what criteria did he judge the prophethood of some of his closest followers inauthentic? What was his reliance on astrology? How is his sexuality to be understood? Matters of this kind will have to be openly discussed eventually, and we should be prepared for surprises in both directions. The evidence for the reality of Joseph's charisms is stronger than secular scholars have imagined, but there may also be more evidence for Joseph's humanity than some Mormon scholars have envisaged. Attempts to reduce the Book of Mormon to Joseph's own biography are absurdly insensitive to the greatness and range of the book, and it is wholly inadequate to interpret his achievements by reference to his alleged narcissism, vanity, and ambition, even if he was not, perhaps, entirely free of such characteristics. Serious study means it will not be possible to ignore Joseph's own development as a prophet, including his own changing understandings of what was being revealed.

To further advance our appreciation of Joseph's prophethood, we need to relate Joseph's special or exceptional prophethood to *the universal prophethood of all believers.*[9] The notion that all can be prophets has precedent in Latter-day Saint doctrine. It is also crucial to understanding Joseph's *agency.* Agency is a major theme in Mormon theology but, strangely, an undeveloped category where Joseph is concerned. Some writers discuss Joseph as if he were entirely passive, as if revelation came down on him like a seal, but this is as implausible as attempts to explain Joseph's revelations as if they were his own inventions. Instead, we need to explain Joseph's exercise of his agency in the context of his universal prophethood. It is probable, I think, that Joseph exercised his universal prophethood in negotiating and mediating his special prophethood. Some may not accept this, just as some secular scholars may reject the notion that Joseph had a prophethood of any kind. Those who allow no role for Joseph's universal prophethood run the risk of not really accepting Joseph's humanity; they may also want to argue that only Joseph could do X, whereas a more informed view might include some variants of X within a model of universal prophethood. Of course, Joseph's special prophethood, his bringing of a new dispensation, cannot be reduced to his universal prophethood. It is something exalted and sublime, to which the rest of us cannot aspire. Still, there is already evidence, in the case of Joseph's retranslations of the Bible, that his universal prophethood played a role, in at least some cases, in helping his special prophethood to take effect. This is a vast theme, and I leave it to Mormon scholars whose knowledge of Joseph is vastly greater than mine to address it in due course.

It may also be useful to rethink Joseph's prophethood in the light of *contemporary studies of esotericism*. This is quite different from loose assertions that Joseph's religious teachings and practice can be reduced to a wider pattern of folk occultism or from the claim that Hermeticism or Freemasonry provide the background to Joseph and the early church.[10]

It is now generally conceded that there were such elements in Joseph's background, although this may not be as important as hostile writers suggest. The question of esotericism more generally, however, is of the first importance because it goes to what is included within the prophethood of every believer. Traditional Christianity has repressed esoteric forms of spirituality and practice and also concealed the degree to which Christianity's own origins and traditions were, in part, esoteric. Once we attend to esotericism as a worldwide phenomenon, however, as Antonie Faivre in France is attempting to do,[11] then some features of Joseph's prophethood may become more intelligible, including how his revelations can be both objective and culturally mediated. Joseph the seer may have "read" what he saw in spiritual worlds. The issue is not clear-cut, and it is striking that esotericism has actually been conspicuously lacking in the bulk of Mormon experience. Indeed, many Mormon scholars are relatively unfamiliar with major contemporary esoteric movements such as Anthroposophy.

Assuming that we play down the Hermetic and Freemasonry background, Joseph's involvement with esotericism may be relevant to his exceptional cognitional powers, even if such influences do not really illuminate the content of his revelations. I am not suggesting that Joseph's prophethood can be explained by reference to occultism or magic. Quite the contrary. I think that he may have drawn on dimensions of spiritual reality that the traditional Christian churches tend to ignore. Again, this is a matter for future research. The crucial methodological point is that there is no contradiction between an approach that accepts as fact that spiritual realities did irrupt into Joseph's life and an approach that investigates the conditions of the possibility of such occurrences.

In this essay I have prepared the ground for another reading of the prophethood of Joseph Smith. Obviously, this reading needs to be pursued elsewhere at greater length. My discussion is exploratory and tentative, but even the few remarks I have been able to offer here suggest that we have yet to come to terms with Joseph and his revelations, and that doing so may well involve changing our ideas about what prophets and prophethoods are.

14

Joseph Smith and Nineteenth-Century Mormon Mappings of Asian Religions

Reid L. Neilson

It is unlikely that Joseph Smith, the founder of the Church of Jesus Christ of Latter-day Saints, ever meaningfully encountered a Buddhist, a Hindu, a Sikh, or a practitioner of Confucianism, Taoism, or Shinto during his life. Born in 1805, Smith, like many Americans of his day, spent his childhood and youth on farms in Vermont, New Hampshire, and New York, isolated from the larger world of Pacific Rim commerce and travel. It is possible, however, that he passed by Chinese sailors working along the seaport docks of Salem, Massachusetts. Smith's parents sent him there, to his uncle Jesse's, when he was eight years old, to convalesce after a leg operation. By the early nineteenth century, Salem was a major hub of Chinese trade with North America.

In 1799, six years before Smith's birth, Salem's residents established the East India Marine Society and began collecting Asian artifacts and curiosities, which they housed in a renovated bank building, the forerunner of today's celebrated Peabody Essex Museum.[1] As a curious young boy, Smith likely visited the fascinating museum, by that time one of Salem's leading attractions, to pass the time while his leg healed. If so, he was gently exposed to Asian culture through its treasures and relics. Smith's only other youthful encounter with the Pacific Rim would have been through his father, who disastrously attempted to sell Vermont ginseng to a Chinese trading company, whose customers prized it for its medicinal properties.[2]

Even as a grown man in rural antebellum America, the Mormon prophet would have had extremely limited, if any, opportunities to learn about the Far East. Smith spent his life in the interior of New England, on the landlocked Western Reserve, and on the western American frontier in Missouri and Illinois. He never traveled across the Atlantic or the Pacific oceans. An 1833 missionary journey to Toronto, Canada, proved to be the extent of his international experience. Nevertheless, twenty-five years after first visiting Salem as a boy on crutches, Smith returned to the maritime town in 1836. This time he was accompanied by a number of ecclesiastical associates with whom he hoped to discover buried treasure to help pay off church debts (Doctrine and Covenants 111).

Smith and his associates tarried in Salem for about three weeks that summer. They visited the newly constructed East India Marine Hall, an imposing columned edifice, which by then housed several thousand objects from the Orient, as it was then called. "The objects that were collected and exhibited by this society helped define the early American vision of Eastern cultures," one historian suggests.[3] Latter-day Saints Sidney Rigdon and Oliver Cowdery signed the museum's guest ledger on August 6, 1836, and Smith left his signature two days later.[4] But early Mormon interests clearly centered not on Asia but on the past, present, and future of the Americas (which they believed to be the ancient site of the Book of Mormon, the gathering place for Latter-day Saints, and the building location of the New Jerusalem). Nevertheless, Smith and his nineteenth-century successors, along with various American Protestants, participated in the mapping of Asians and their religions during the nineteenth century.

Religious studies scholars Thomas A. Tweed and Stephen Prothero suggest a number of spatial themes to interpret the ongoing religious and social encounter of Americans and Asians, including *mapping*. They claim that, "in one sense religion itself is a spatial practice, a cultural process whereby individuals and groups map, construct, and inhabit worlds of meaning." Mapping can refer "to the ways that individuals and groups orient themselves in the natural landscape and social terrain." Like other nationalities, Americans have constructed mental maps of the world. They have sought to "orient themselves in relation to Asia," as well as to understand Asians who have come to the United States. Americans and Asians have met each other at various sites or "contact zones" around the globe, especially in the Pacific world.[5]

Nineteenth-century trans-Pacific contacts and exchanges resulted in differing American attitudes toward the Chinese and Japanese, as well as their religions. Like other religious Americans, the Latter-day Saints encountered East Asians and their traditions both at home and abroad. I will argue that the nineteenth-century LDS theological mapping of Asian religions was both similar to and different from that of American Protestants. To document this variance and the evolution of LDS religious thought, I employ various typologies to compare how Mormon and Protestant leaders imagined their religious traditions in relation to those from Asia. I conclude by documenting major trajectories of Mormon thought regarding Eastern traditions.

Protestantism Maps the Religions of the East

Before American Protestants personally encountered the peoples and traditions of Asia, they "mapped" them from afar.[6] Hannah Adams, a New England Protestant dissatisfied with existing eighteenth-century surveys of world religions, lived a full generation before Joseph Smith and the advent of Mormonism. Frustrated by existing accounts of non-Christian religions, she began compiling her own survey in 1778, which she published in 1784 as *Alphabetical Compendium of the Various Sects Which Have Appeared from the Beginning of the Christian Era to the Present Day.* Over the next three and a half decades, Adams expanded and refined her study as new materials became available. In 1817, three years before Joseph Smith's First Vision, she published an updated edition, *A Dictionary of All Religions and Religious Denominations: Jewish, Heathen, Mahometan, Christian, Ancient and Modern.*[7] Although "some residue of incredulity, condescension, even hostility, can be found in Adams's accounts of Asian peoples and religions," it was the most complete one-volume treatment of Asian religions to date, Tweed argues. She offered an evenhanded treatment of Asians and their religions to a public who knew little about the subject.[8]

Although Adams's study of the world's religions was a milestone in religious scholarship, it "did not alter significantly the basic map of the religious world that she inherited," Tweed concludes. "In fact, the most basic contours of that map had changed little since the voyages of discovery. New peoples and religions were added here. New boundaries were drawn there." But Westerners, including Adams, still envisioned a world easily divided into religious categories of Christians, Jews, Muslims, and "Pagans." (This type of thinking is echoed in how the hegemonic West divided the twentieth-century nations into first-, second-, and third-world countries.) Not surprisingly, mainline Protestants both constructed and occupied the highest rung of the resulting hierarchy of this religious mapping. Jews stood on the second step and Muslims, also monotheists, crouched on the third rung. Finally, most antebellum Protestants, including Adams, grouped those traditions that did not affirm Western mono-theism ("pagans") and placed them on the lowest tread.[9]

Adams's spiritual cartography remained the standard American Protestant view of non-Christian, non-Western religions during the antebellum era.[10] By the second half of the nineteenth century, however, religious scholarship was flourishing, resulting in a flood of knowledge about non-Christian religions. Emerging academic disciplines such as cultural anthropology and comparative religion seemed to reduce Christian teachings and ordinances until they "began to bear an uncanny resemblance to the forms of other major religions." While Christians could contextualize other faiths, the opposite was also true. Biblical higher criticism further eroded Christian faith.[11] Granted, a small number of Euro-American scholars, writers, and theologians sympathized with and ad-hered to Asian religions like Buddhism, beginning in 1844. That year Elizabeth Peabody translated a Buddhist text for *The Dial*, an American Transcendental-ist periodical, and Edward Salisbury lectured on Buddhism to the American Oriental Society.[12] Nevertheless, most Americans who dabbled in Eastern tra-ditions were intellectuals, not average Protestants. The vast majority of North American Christians did not have meaningful exposure to non-Christian reli-gions, with the exception of Judaism, until the World's Parliament of Religions in 1893. As such, Asian religions were theologically unthreatening to the West until the late nineteenth century.[13]

This theological encounter, however, along with a number of social, eco-nomic, and cultural forces, soon undermined what historian Grant Wacker calls the "Christian fortress" in America after the Civil War. Modernization, urbanization, and industrialization resulted in "smokestacks elbow[ing] out steeples" and the diminuendo of the divine in daily life. Scientific progress, especially the development of evolution and geology, directly challenged Judeo-Christian creationism. Scientists and laboratories began replacing clergy and churches as the ultimate authorities of knowledge. Technological progress in travel and communication multiplied intercultural and interreligious contacts. Cultural and geographical boundaries no longer circumscribed religions. The increasing number of encounters with Asian religions demanded that Protes-tants grapple with a number of theological issues that Hannah Adams never considered. Some questioned, Was the "theological difference between Christi-anity and other religions [was] absolute or . . . one of degree?" Was Christianity truly superior and the only way to salvation? others wondered.[14] Or, as one theo-logian probes, "Is the presence of God to be found only within one commu-nity of faith? Or is he more chameleon-like than that, dancing through history, enticing men and women into faith irrespective of the cultural shape of their response?"[15] Many nineteenth-century Protestants also struggled to explain the fate of the "heathen" nations and to account for Christian truths in religions predating Christianity. In short, the challenge of pluralism rattled Christian belief. American Protestants were no longer culturally or religiously isolated. Pacific Rim faiths had roused them from their insulated sleep of absolutism.[16]

Not all American Protestants reacted the same way theologically to the peoples and religions of Asia. Contemporary scholars have constructed a three-planked intellectual scaffolding—exclusivism, pluralism, and inclusivism—that helps us map the nineteenth-century Protestant reaction. The *exclusivist position* maintains that non-Christian "religions are marked by humankind's fundamental sinfulness and are therefore erroneous, and that Christ (or Christianity) offers the only valid path to salvation."[17] William C. Wilkinson, a leading proponent of the Chautauqua movement and the consummate exclusivist, argued, "The attitude, therefore, of Christianity towards religions other than itself is an attitude of universal, absolute, eternal, unappeasable hostility." Consequently, the "erring religions of mankind" do not even represent "pathetic and partially successful, gropings after God."[18] Non-Christian religions do not help; they only hinder the future of Christianity, according to exclusivists. The *pluralist position*, asserts that all religions are "equally salvific paths to the one God, and Christianity's claim that it is the only path (exclusivism), or the fulfillment of other paths (inclusivism), should be rejected for good theological and phenomenological reasons." Diametrically opposed to Wilkinson, literary critic and abolitionist Thomas Wentworth Higginson advocated religious toleration and suggested that all men and women can find God, but only as they "pass through their own doors," not just Christianity's, until "all will come at last upon the broad ground of God's providing, which bears no man's name."[19]

Most American Protestants choose to stand somewhere between the exclusivist and pluralist rafters. Such a choice can place them in the *inclusivist position*, which confirms "the salvific presence of God in non-Christian religions while still maintaining that Christ is the definitive and authoritative revelation of God."[20] John Henry Barrows, a noted Congregational clergyman, exemplified inclusivism when he advocated the supremacy of Christianity while allowing for heavenly light and truth in non-Christian religions. "Cherishing the light which God has given us and eager to send this light everywhither, we do not believe that God, the eternal Spirit, has left himself without witness in non-Christian nations. There is a divine light enlightening every man." He further asked, "Why should not Christians be glad to learn what God has wrought through Buddha and Zoroaster—through the sage of China, and the prophets of India and the prophets of Islam?"[21] Some scholars have further delineated the inclusivist position. Diana Eck explains that what she terms the *fulfillment inclusivist position* accepts that "non-Christians are genuine seekers of truth found fully in Christ." Other religions are more incomplete than evil or misguided, "needing the fulfillment of Christ." Advocates of this position acknowledge that God and Christ are active in the lives and beliefs of non-Christian believers. This was, and still is, the most popular Christian response to an increasingly pluralistic world.[22]

Mormonism Maps the Eastern Religious World

Eventually isolated in America's Great Basin, the LDS community found their theological responses to Asian religions, like those of their Protestant counterparts, changing over time. While the exclusivist, pluralist, and inclusivist typology works well to describe the American Protestant response to non-Christian, non-Western traditions, we need to expand and revise our interpretive categories to judiciously explicate the Mormon response to Eastern faiths. At first glance, one might erroneously categorize nineteenth-century Latter-day Saints as fulfillment inclusivists, given the similarity of their descriptions of non-Christian faiths. A more careful observer, however, would conclude the opposite: Mormons believe that their gospel was as old as eternity, a unique Christian theology.[23] Therefore, I propose the construction and fastening of an additional theoretical plank, the *restoration inclusivist position*. World religions scholar Spencer J. Palmer proposes several ways Latter-day Saints have accounted for Christian parallels in non-Christian religions. I believe that two of his theories, *the light and spirit of Christ* and *diffusion*, are nineteenth-century Mormon responses, while the remaining three are twentieth-century reactions.[24]

From Mormonism's 1830 founding, Joseph Smith and subsequent LDS leaders generally employed the light and spirit of Christ theory to account for Christian parallels in non-Christian religions. According to this early explanation, "the spiritual influence which emanates from God is not confined to selected nations, races, or groups. All men share an inheritance of divine light. Christ himself is the light of the world. Even those who have never heard of Christ are granted the spirit and light of Christ." As such, God inspired the founders of Buddhism, Islam, Hinduism, Taoism, Confucianism, Shinto, Jainism, Sikhism, Zoroastrianism, and other Asian faiths, in order to bless all of his earthly children.[25]

While Smith was almost certainly ignorant of Asians and their religions, as described above, the Mormon prophet did bring forth a number of new scriptures that provided a theological framework for mapping non-Christian, non-Western religions, such as Buddhism and Shinto. According to the Book of Mormon, "The Lord doth grant unto all nations, of their own nation and tongue, to teach his word, yea, in wisdom, all that he seeth fit that they should have" (Alma 29:8), and "the Spirit of Christ is given to every man, that he may know good from evil" (Moroni 7:16; see also Doctrine and Covenants 93:2; John 1:9). In 1832, Smith further revealed that "the Spirit enlighteneth every man through the world, that hearkeneth to the voice of the Spirit. And every one that hearkeneth to the voice of the Spirit cometh unto God, even the Father" (Doctrine and Covenants 84:45–47).

As one who experienced the wrath of religious intolerance, Smith lamented that the "great designs of God in relation to the salvation of the human family are very little understood" by humankind. Muslims condemn the heathens, Jews, and Christians as infidels; the Jews view the uncircumcised as damned "gentile dogs"; the heathens "are equally as tenacious about their principles"; and Christians relegate all others to perdition. "But while one portion of the human race are [sic] judging and condemning the other without mercy," the Mormon prophet continued, "the great parent of the universe looks upon the whole of the human family with a fatherly care, and paternal regard; he views them as his offspring." He taught that all of mankind would be given the opportunity to embrace Mormonism in this life or the next.[26]

Other Mormon leaders reiterated Smith's teachings in succeeding years. Apostle Parley P. Pratt authored *Proclamation! To the People of the Coasts and Islands of the Pacific; of Every Nation, Kindred and Tongue* while presiding over the LDS Pacific Mission in the early 1850s. Printed in 1851 by Mormon missionaries in Australia, his tract announced the beginning of systematic Mormon evangelism in the Pacific basin frontier. Pratt declared the advent of a new Christian gospel dispensation. Despite the universality of the gospel message, Pratt, like Smith, mapped the peoples of the Pacific world into four groups: (1) non-Mormon Christians, (2) non-Christian "pagans," (3) Jews, and (4) "Red Men of America." Pagans (or heathens), according to Pratt, were "those who are not Christians, but who worship the various Gods of India, China, Japan, or the Islands of the Pacific or Indian Oceans."[27] Pratt was not alone in mapping the religions of the Pacific world as one pagan category.

Most nineteenth-century American Protestants likewise plotted the contours of world religions according to traditional (Protestant-centered) guidelines: they were Christians (and therefore saved) while everyone else was a Jew, Muslim, or "pagan" (and therefore damned). This order also suggests the level of descending theological esteem most Protestants had for different types of non-Christians. Coming out of the American Christian tradition, Latter-day Saints also parsed the Jews and Muslims into traditional Protestant categories but viewed the heathen nations through a different theological lens: the "prophetic telescope" of the Book of Mormon. According to Pratt, the

Mormon scripture, together with the Bible, helped explain "the fate of nations; the restoration of Judah and Israel; the downfall of corrupt churches and religious institutions; the end of Gentile superstition and misrule; the universal prevalence of peace, and truth, and light, and knowledge; the awful wars and troubles which precede those happy times; the glorious coming of Jesus Christ as king over all the earth."[28] By the end of the nineteenth century, Mormons viewed so-called pagan Asian religions as equal to, if not superior to, post-third-century Christianity.

Joseph Smith was assassinated by a mob in 1844, just as Americans were beginning to meet Asians and their religions. Nevertheless, subsequent church leaders echoed his claim: God had enlightened all mankind, in every land and in every age, through the light and spirit of Christ. John Taylor, a member of the Quorum of the Twelve Apostles, acknowledged in 1853 that "the Catholics have many pieces of truth; so have the Protestants, the Mahometans, and Heathens."[29] And Brigham Young, Mormonism's second president, declared, "I do not believe for one moment that there has been a man or woman upon the face of the earth, from the days of Adam to this day, who has not been enlightened, instructed, and taught by the revelations of Jesus Christ." He explained that even the "ignorant heathen," "Hindoos," "Hottentots," and "cannibals" had benefited from divine inspiration to "teach them right from wrong." Like Smith, Young believed that "No matter what the traditions of their fathers were, those who were honest before the Lord, and acted uprightly, according to the best knowledge they had, will have an opportunity to go into the kingdom of God."[30]

LDS leaders were still employing Smith's views during America's Gilded Age to contextualize Asian religions. Moses Thatcher, another member of the Quorum of the Twelve Apostles, admitted in 1887 that he was "struck by the profound philosophy, pure morality, and the comprehensiveness exhibited in the writings of Confucius and Mencius and the Chinese sages" and considered them as "divinely inspired, far-reaching and heavenly doctrines."[31] In 1888, Orson F. Whitney, the presiding bishop of the LDS Church, declared the Latter-day Saints "a people who are not ashamed to pick truth from the dust, to acknowledge truth wherever found, in the religions of all men. . . . The doctrines of Buddha? Yes, they have truth." As a result, the heathen nations "who have not the fullness [of truth], but only retain it in a measure, knowing no better, and live up to the light they have, are justified in the sight of God and will stand guiltless before him." But once exposed to Mormonism or "the fullness of truth" all were accountable.[32] Thus, the light and spirit of Christ theory became the leading LDS explanation for the existence and value of Asian religions during the nineteenth century.

While LDS leaders spoke in revelatory terms regarding Eastern traditions, no other nineteenth-century leader spoke on the subject as often as George Q. Cannon. Cannon, first a member of the Quorum of the Twelve Apostles (1860–1873) and later a councilor in the First Presidency (1873–1901), consistently advocated the light and spirit of Christ theory *until* attending the 1893 Parliament of Religions. "We believe that God is the same yesterday, to-day and for ever," Cannon taught in 1869, and "he is a God of revelation." Although God had largely closed the heavens for centuries, he had "bestowed his Holy Spirit" on "millions" of his children, "although not in its fulness."[33] During the 1870s and 1880s, Cannon continued to teach that "faithful men in all nations" were endowed with great light, including Eastern teachers such as Confucius. Even Muslims, "fire-worshipers," and "idolaters" had "lived up to the best knowledge they had." But they "had not the keys of the Holy Priesthood nor the power and authority thereof to guide them in their teachings; hence, they ran into errors, and this gave rise to a great variety of views and doctrines and to schools of divinity that have existed and that still exist among the children of men." He later asserted that the Latter-day Saints were not "so cramped in their feelings" as to believe they are the only children of God who receive His revelations and blessings. Echoing Brigham Young, Cannon taught that "there is no son or daughter of Adam that has ever lived upon the face of the earth who has not the right and who has not obtained at some time or other in his or her life, revelations from God, but who may not have understood what those revelations were." Even "the heathen philosophers" who were ignorant of Christianity still received truth from God.[34]

When his Latter-day Saints were feeling the weight of the American Protestant campaign against plural marriage in the 1880s, Cannon lashed out. He declared that modern Christianity "is but little, if any, better than many forms of paganism. . . . There have been millions of people, probably, whom the Christians call pagans, whose lives have been as acceptable to the true God as the lives of the same number of so-called Christians," he exclaimed. Until the late nineteenth century, LDS leaders consistently used the light and spirit of Christ theory to theologically map Asian religions, despite formal encounters of their own.[35] This changed almost overnight.

The World's Parliament of Religions

In the late summer of 1893, the LDS first presidency—Wilford Woodruff, George Q. Cannon, and Joseph F. Smith—traveled with Brigham H. Roberts to Chicago to participate in the Columbian Exposition. They also attended several sessions of the auxiliary World's Parliament of Religions.[36] More than any other encounter between Latter-day Saints and Asians, this experience radically altered the Mormon mental map of Asia and its religionists. Like other Christian attendees, the Mormon leaders were awed by the exposition's international spectacle and astonished by the richness of the Asian religions they encountered.[37] Upon his return to Utah, Cannon observed that "some things . . . are going to puzzle this parliament," at least the Christian contingent, who believed that Jesus Christ had taught novel doctrines during his mortal ministry. "But here come the Buddhists and the followers of Confucius," he mocked, "and they prove that long before the Savior was born many of the truths which He proclaimed were taught by their leading men." Cannon correctly surmised that this anachronistic Christian worldview was "likely to furnish good ground for infidelity and for men thinking that after all there is not so much in this Christian religion as those who advocate it assume; because if Buddha and Confucius knew these truths, where are the claims of the Christians that the Savior was the first to introduce them in His sermon on the Mount?" But Christian parallels in the religions of Asia would not shake the Latter-day Saints, he argued, for they believed that the restored gospel had its roots in the beginning of time.[38]

Like other Christians formally introduced to non-Christian traditions at the Parliament, Mormon leaders reformulated their theological response to Eastern religions. Previously they only had to explain how truths existed in other religions. Now they had to account for striking Christian parallels in those same faiths. In other words, the Parliament prompted an LDS rhetorical shift from the light and spirit of Christ theory to a diffusionary hypothesis: a theology better suited to account for Christian parallels in non-Christian religions.

The diffusion theory proposes that all religions can trace their beginnings to the Christian gospel as originally taught to Adam and Eve by God. Rather than advocating an evolutionary "fulfillment" model, which was quite in vogue in the late nineteenth century, Latter-day Saints viewed the gospel of Jesus Christ in an antievolutionary framework. They rejected the developmental claims characteristic of fulfillment inclusivists that suggested that Christianity was the pinnacle of human religious progress. Instead, they advanced a "declension" model, asserting that God had revealed the saving mission of Jesus Christ to Adam and Eve who had taught it to their children and children's children. But their descendants had apostatized, resulting in spiritual darkness until God had seen fit to restore that spiritual light. Thus, humanity experienced a number of dispensations of gospel truth followed by apostasy and hopes for future renewal. In short, Mormons dated Christianity at least four thousand years earlier than other Christians and thereby believed they had cut the Gordian knot of American Protestantism. By moving back the origins of the gospel of Jesus Christ to the time of Adam and Eve, they were able to avoid the timing issue of Christian parallels found in non-Christian religions.[39]

Having just experienced religious pluralism firsthand, Cannon adjusted his earlier rhetoric to match his post-Chicago realities. "The Buddhists and the Shintovists [sic] and the believers in Confucius have a great many truths among them, and they are not so imperfect and heathenish as we have been in the habit in this country of believing them to be." More important, when Cannon explained non-Christian religions, he no longer employed the light and spirit of Christ theory. Rather, he taught that "God has revealed unto us that Adam himself was taught the Gospel in the same purity and with the same power and gifts that it was taught to the Twelve apostles whom the Lord chose as His disciples." In brief, the Parliament prompted Cannon to shift rhetorically from the light and spirit of Christ theory to the diffusion theory.[40]

Although Cannon, a restoration inclusivist, highlighted the positive aspects of various systems of belief, he became concerned with the growing popularity of Asian religions in America. In November 1893, just months after the Parliament ended, he published an editorial in a church periodical and denounced the Eastern doctrine of reincarnation as "strange" and "utterly foreign to every principle which God has revealed in the last days to His Church." Every man and woman is given but one "grand opportunity" to appear in the flesh and experience this probationary state of existence in preparation for their future estate. Cannon also commented that since the 1830 restoration of the gospel, "there has been a great disposition manifested by many people to investigate the oriental religions and to appropriate from them strange ideas entirely foreign to those that have been believed in by the people of Christendom." He thought it was an "itching for something new" that prompted some "to adopt strange views and to announce beliefs that are antagonistic to Christianity" such as Buddhism.[41]

Brigham H. Roberts also advocated diffusion theory after attending the Parliament. In 1896 he argued that Mormonism, like mining quicksilver, is the force that can unite and blend all truth. The blacksmith orator recalled his own experience in Chicago, where he had the "opportunity of listening to an explanation of the religion of Brahma, of the Buddhist religion, of the Philosophy of Confucius and Zoroaster, and of the Mohammedan religion, and in short, of nearly all the religions." Like Cannon, Roberts admitted to being "very much astonished at the amount of truth to be found in all these systems of religion." He related how writers including Robert Ingersoll, David Hume, and Voltaire "have undertaken to prove that Christianity was not an original religion with Jesus Christ, that is, they insist that Jesus Christ copied his precepts, his ordinances, and the religious and fundamental truths of his religion from the religions of the orient." At the Parliament, the similarities between Christianity and Asian religions puzzled many Protestant theologians, according to Roberts. Like Cannon, Roberts employed diffusion theory to account for these Christian parallels. The Mormon leader contended that LDS scriptures, including the Bible, the Book of Mormon, and Pearl of Great Price "teach the antiquity of the Gospel" and explain the "fragments of Gospel truth held by the religions of the Orient, of India, Persia, Egypt and some portions of Japan and of China."[42] Neither Cannon nor Roberts used the light of Christ theory to map Asian religions after their "close encounters" with those religions in Chicago in 1893. In brief, the post-Parliament rhetoric of Cannon and Roberts evidences the LDS rhetorical shift from the light and spirit of Christ rationalization to a diffusionary explanation.

Conclusion

The nineteenth-century Mormon encounter with Asians and their religions was significant, perhaps not in scope but certainly in results. The LDS theological mapping of the East was somewhat reminiscent of American' Protestantism's spiritual cartography. Both Joseph Smith and his associates plotted all Asians as "heathens" and their traditions as "pagan," like other Americans. But the Latter-day Saints viewed the Asian nations through the prophetic telescope of the Book of Mormon and modern-day revelation, which rendered non-Christians as capable of salvation and partakers of divine light. Mormon leaders employed a light and spirit of Christ theory to account for truth in Asian religions until the 1893 Parliament of Religions.

But when the Asian proponents of Buddhism, Confucianism, and Hinduism demonstrated in Chicago that their belief systems predated traditional Christianity, the unfazed Latter-day Saints reformulated their theological response and began to employ a declension model of diffusion. As restoration inclusivists, the Latter-day Saints were theologically driven to eventually evangelize the peoples of Asia, despite the truths they found in the teachings of the Buddha, Confucius, Mencius, and other Eastern founders. Ironically, the Mormons likewise evangelized the Christians of North America and Western Europe under the same worldview, believing that only their unique brand of restoration Christianity enjoyed a fulness of truth.

15

Studying Joseph Smith Jr.: A Guide to the Sources

David J. Whittaker

Manuscripts

All studies of Joseph Smith (1805–1844) must begin with the original manuscripts which document his life. For a guide to the archival holdings relating to Joseph Smith Jr. owned by the Church of Jesus Christ of Latter-day Saints, the main repository of Joseph Smith manuscripts, see Jeffery O. Johnson, *Register of the Joseph Smith Collection in the Church Archives* (Salt Lake City: Historical Department of the Church of Jesus Christ of Latter-day Saints, 1973). Scans of the texts of the Joseph Smith papers have been made available on DVD-ROM: *Selected Collections from the Archives of the Church of Jesus Christ of Latter-day Saints*, edited and produced under the direction of Richard E. Turley Jr. (Provo, Utah: Brigham Young University Press, 2002). The current effort by the LDS Church to assemble and publish in a multivolume edition the papers of Joseph Smith continues to turn up documents relating to his life; thus, no listing can hope to be definitive. The Web site www.josephsmith. net can keep readers informed about the most recent developments on the Joseph Smith Papers project. A useful "Chronology of the Life of Joseph Smith," appears in *BYU Studies* 46, no. 4 (2007).

Journals

Joseph Smith's ten extant journals total about 1,600 manuscript pages. About 85 percent of the entries are work of the scribes and clerks, and only thirty-one pages contain Joseph Smith's own handwriting. Most of the journals depended upon the work of twelve clerks, including James Mulholland, Warren Parrish, George W. Robinson, William Clayton, with Willard Richards being the main contributor. The journal sets are listed below.

> *Two Ohio Journals*
> November 27, 1832–December 5, 1834, with long gaps between December
>   1832 and October 1834
> September 22, 1835–April 3, 1836
> *Two Missouri Journals*
> March 13 to September 1838
> September 3–October 6, 1838
> *Six Illinois Journals*
> April 16–October 15, 1839
> December 13, 1841–December 17, 1842
> December 21, 1842–March 10, 1843
> March 10, 1843–July 14, 1843
> July 15, 1843–February 29, 1844
> March 1, 1844–June 22, 1844, with a significant gap from October 1839 to
>   December 1841

The Smith journals, as summarized by Dean C. Jessee, cover 1832–44, with entries beginning on November 27, 1832 and ending on June 22, 1844. Entries exist for only about 25 percent of the days lived between these dates, thus leaving large gaps in Joseph Smith's personal record. All are in the LDS Church Archives. The journals from 1832 to 1842 are printed in Dean C. Jessee, ed., *The Papers of Joseph Smith*, vol. 2 (Salt Lake City: Deseret Book, 1992). The article, "Extracts from the Private Journal of Joseph Smith, Jr.," *Times and Seasons* 1, no. 1 (July [reprinted in November] 1839):2–9 was a mistitled printing of Joseph Smith's own Petition for Redress, relating his losses in Missouri, dated June 4, 1839; the manuscript for most of it is in the church archives.

Sermons and Discourses

Joseph Smith scholar Dean Jessee has stated that:

> During the last eighteen months of his life, Joseph Smith is known
> to have given seventy-eight public addresses, or an average of a little
> more than one a week. Assuming conservatively that he averaged
> thirty speeches a year during earlier years, the total discourses of
> his public ministry (1830–44) would number about 450. Available
> sources, however, identify only about 250 discourses, and his

published history gives reasonably adequate summaries of only about one-fifth of these. Not until the last eighteen months of his life were Joseph's speeches reported with reasonable consistency. Of the fifty-two addresses reported in some detail in his history, thirty-five date from that time period. The remaining seventeen average about two a year between 1834 and 1842. These figures suggest that probably not more than 10 percent of Joseph Smith's discourses were recorded, and that most of these come from the last three years of his life. [Dean C. Jessee, *BYU Studies* 31 (Spring 1991): 23]

Of the fifty-two extant reports, Willard Richards and Wilford Woodruff recorded forty. Because none of those who kept these records used shorthand, all the accounts suffer from the incompleteness and limitations that such a process involves. The best compilation of the Nauvoo discourses is Andrew F. Ehat and Lyndon W. Cook, eds., *The Words of Joseph Smith* (Provo, Utah: Religious Studies Center, Brigham Young University, 1980).

Revelations

There are about one hundred extant manuscripts that record the revelations received through Joseph Smith, in addition to documents relating to the Book of Mormon, the Book of Moses, the Book of Abraham, and Joseph Smith's revisions to the King James Version of the Bible. The extant revelations date from July 1828 to November 1843.

There are, in addition to the revelations published in the Doctrine and Covenants, about sixty other known revelations, of which about thirty are extant in texts. A useful, but now incomplete, compilation of these is H. Michael Marquardt, comp., *The Joseph Smith Revelations: Text and Commentary* (Salt Lake City: Signature Books, 1999).

Correspondence

There are 308 extant letters written by Joseph Smith and 380 written to him. Because these letters cover his whole ministry, they treat a broad range of subjects. They include letters to his wife Emma, to his colleagues and co-workers, and to friends and strangers; they cover such subject matter as business, ecclesiastical affairs, family concerns, doctrine, and other topics. They convey his strength of leadership, his prophetic mantle, his deep religiosity, and his concerns over his family and his people. But they also reveal his doubts, his loneliness, and his tendency toward melancholy. A few have been published in the

Doctrine and Covenants. See the valuable selection in Dean C. Jessee, comp. and ed., *The Personal Writings of Joseph Smith*, rev. ed. (Salt Lake City: Deseret Book, 1984, and Provo, Utah: Brigham Young University Press, 2002).

"History of Joseph Smith"

On the day the Mormon Church was organized (April 6, 1830), a revelation commanded that "a record shall be kept" (Doctrine and Covenants 21:1). The attempts of Joseph Smith to keep records of both his own life and of the church over which he presided date from that commandment. The call and counsel to individuals to keep the history can be seen in additional revelations (Doctrine and Covenants 47; 69; 85; 123; 124). The first attempts were fitful, but following the early efforts by Joseph Smith and those he assigned to write biography and history, Joseph Smith directed the preparation of what became the multivolume *History of the Church*. Begun on April 27, 1838, it would eventually run to 2,300 pages in six manuscript volumes. It was finished on November 6, 1856, twelve years after Joseph Smith's death, but it is still very dependent upon the Joseph Smith journals kept by Willard Richards. Eleven principal scribes and clerks worked on what was essentially a documentary scrapbook of the early church history, gathering into its pages all kinds of documents that presented the chronological story of the foundational years of the church. It was published in serialized form in early Mormon newspapers, and was finally gathered into a multivolume edition by B. H. Roberts and published as the *History of the Church . . .* , *Period I*, by the LDS Church from 1902–12. By Roberts's time, the methodology that had been used to create the *History* was lost, and Roberts added to the confusion (understandably, given the *History*'s heavy dependence, for both its chronology and text, upon the Joseph Smith journals that were kept by Willard Richards) by placing a note on the title page that the work was by Joseph Smith himself. For more detail, see Dean C. Jessee, "The Writing of Joseph Smith's History," *BYU Studies* 11 (Summer 1971): 439–73; and Howard C. Searle, "Early Mormon Historiography: Writing the History of the Mormons, 1830–1858" (PhD diss., University of California at Los Angeles, 1979), esp. 200–336.

Administrative Records

The institutional growth of the church under the direction of Joseph Smith created a variety of records that help reveal the great administrative and leadership capacity of the Mormon prophet. In the minute books, researchers can find material on Joseph Smith as he organized and directed the various affairs of the emerging organizations. Most are in the LDS Church Archives. Among the more important, in addition to the manuscript volumes containing scribal copies of his revelations, are:

Far West Record [Conference Minutes and Record Book], 1830–44
Kirtland Council Minute Book, 1832–37
Kirtland Elder's Quorum Record, 1836–41
Nauvoo High Council Minute Book, 1839–45
Nauvoo Municipal Court Docket, 1841–45
Record, Proceedings of the City Council of the City of Nauvoo, 1841–44
The Nauvoo Legion Minute Book, 1841–44
Record of the Organization and Proceedings of the Female Relief Society
    of Nauvoo, 1842–44

At the heart of Joseph Smith's leadership was his emphasis on missionary work. Beyond the obvious spiritual benefits of this work, there were also more practical effects. Historically, missionary work served to revitalize church membership at critical periods of stress and strain. The history and development of the various conferences and missions of the church were often the testing grounds for church leaders as well as for official programs and publications. The mission experience was an important instrument of socialization and testimony building, and problems of government and administration that arose very early in the various missions required Joseph Smith and his associates to deal more comprehensively with matters of organization, licensing, discipline, publication, immigration, and financial management. Useful studies of this formative period include Ronald E. Romig, "The Lamanite Mission," *John Whitmer Historical Association Journal* 14 (1994): 24–33; Davis Bitton, "Kirtland as a Center of Missionary Activity, 1830–1838," *BYU Studies* 11 (Summer 1971): 497–516; James B. Allen, Ronald K. Esplin, and David J. Whittaker, *Men With a Mission, 1837–1841: The Quorum of the Twelve Apostles in the British Isles* (Salt Lake City: Deseret Book, 1992). The best overview is S. George Ellsworth, "A History of Mormon Missions in the United States and Canada, 1830–1860," (PhD diss., University of California at Berkeley, 1951).

Legal Documents/Judicial History

Between 1826 and 1844 about two hundred known legal actions named Joseph Smith as a witness, a defendant, or a plaintiff. Because court cases generate lots of paperwork they can provide additional information on Joseph Smith's activities, relationships with other people, concerns, and financial and legal history. Because local and county court records are so scattered today (if they have managed to survive at all), the work of researching the legal history of Joseph Smith and early Mormonism is a truly monumental task. Examples of recent published research include Marvin S. Hill, "Joseph Smith and the 1826 Trial: New Evidence and New Difficulties," *BYU Studies* 12 (Winter 1982): 223–33; Gordon A. Madsen, "Joseph Smith's 1826 Trial: The Legal Setting," *BYU Studies* 30 (Spring 1990): 91–108; David W. Grua, "Joseph Smith and the 1834 D. P. Hurlbut Case," *BYU Studies* 44, no. 1 (2005): 33–54; M. Scott Bradshaw, "Joseph Smith's Performance of Marriages in Ohio," *BYU Studies* 39, no. 4 (2000): 23–69; Gordon A. Madsen, "Joseph Smith and the Missouri Court of Inquiry: Austin A. King's Quest for Hostages," *BYU Studies* 43, no. 4 (2004): 92–136; Stephen C. LeSueur, "'High Treason and Murder': Examination of Mormon Prisoners at Richmond, Missouri, in November, 1838," *BYU Studies* 26 (Spring 1986): 3–30; Dallin H. Oaks, "The Suppression of the Nauvoo *Expositor*," *Utah Law Review* 9 (Winter 1965): 862–903; and Dallin H. Oaks and Joseph I. Bentley, "Joseph Smith and the Legal Process: In the Wake of the Steamboat *Nauvoo*," *BYU Studies* 19 (Winter 1979): 167–99. An important study of the legal proceedings against the accused assassins of Joseph and Hyrum Smith is Dallin H. Oaks and Marvin S. Hill, *Carthage Conspiracy* (Urbana: University of Illinois Press, 1975).

Early Mormon Publications

Early Mormons, under Joseph Smith's direction, established printing offices wherever they established communities. These publications helped members communicate with each other and also carried accounts of conferences, printed revelations, published letters of missionaries; in addition, they provided information of local and national interest, and regularly carried the counsel of Joseph Smith and other church leaders. These presses published the early editions of the Mormon scriptures as well as the earliest defenses of the faith. Thus, the pages of *The Evening and the Morning Star* (Independence, Missouri, and Kirtland, Ohio), the *LDS Messenger and Advocate* (Kirtland, Ohio), the *Elder's Journal* (Kirtland, Ohio, and Far West, Missouri), the *Times and Seasons* (Nauvoo, Illinois), the *LDS Millennial Star* (Liverpool, England), the Nauvoo *Wasp*, and the *Nauvoo Neighbor*, to mention only a few, are important sources for students of Joseph Smith. In addition, there were single publications such as *General Smith's Views on the Powers and Policy of the Government of the United States* (Nauvoo, Ill.: John Taylor, 1844); *General Joseph Smith's Appeal to the Green Mountain Boys* (Nauvoo, Ill.: Taylor and Woodruff, 1843); *Correspondence between Joseph Smith, the Prophet, and Col. John Wentworth* . . . (New York: John E. Page and L. R. Foster, J. W. Harrison, Printer, 1844); and *The Voice of Truth*

(Nauvoo, Ill.: Printed by John Taylor, 1844), which reprinted some of the items that had been printed earlier. For a bibliographical guide to the early Mormon print culture, much of it shaped during Joseph Smith's lifetime, see Appendix A, "Mormon Imprints as Sources for Research: A History and Evaluation," in Ronald W. Walker, David J. Whittaker, and James B. Allen, *Mormon History* (Urbana: University of Illinois Press, 2001), 199–238.

The Papers of Joseph Smith's Associates

The journals and papers of individuals close to the prophet are important sources. See especially those of Wilford Woodruff, Heber C. Kimball, Parley P. Pratt, Orson Pratt, William Clayton, Hyrum Smith, Willard Richards, Brigham Young, and John Taylor, to mention only the best known. Many of these collections are described in Davis Bitton, *Guide to Mormon Diaries and Autobiographies* (Provo, Utah: Brigham Young University Press, 1977). A sampling of the records (mostly letters) of early women converts is in Janiece Lyn Johnson, " 'Give it all up and follow your Lord': Mormon female religiosity, 1831–1843" (master's thesis, Brigham Young University, 2001), some of which appears in *BYU Studies* 41, no. 1 (2002): 77–107.

The Accounts of Contemporaries

The accounts of people who met with, interviewed, or left accounts of their visits to Joseph Smith and early Mormon communities are also valuable sources. A sampling is in William Mulder and A. Russell Mortensen, eds., *Among the Mormons: Historic Accounts by Contemporary Observers* (New York: Knopf, 1958).

Published Sources

Bibliographical Guides and Sources

Alexander, Thomas G. "Joseph Smith." In *Research Guide to American Historical Biography*, edited by Robert Muccigrosso, vol. 3, 1404–11. Washington, D.C.: Beacham Publishing, 1988.

Allen, James B., Ronald W. Walker, and David J. Whittaker. *Studies in Mormon History, 1830–1997: An Indexed Bibliography.* Urbana: University of Illinois Press, 2000. This is available online at http://mormonstudies.byu.edu. The index will lead researchers to more than 1,400 published sources on Joseph Smith.

Berrett, LaMar C., ed. *Sacred Places: A Comprehensive Guide to Early LDS Historical Sites.* 6 vols. Salt Lake City: Deseret Book, 1999–2007. The first four volumes cover the Joseph Smith period, each devoted to a geographical area, and include essays, maps, and photographs with each volume edited with other specialists in early Mormon history.

Bitton, Davis. "Selected Bibliography." In *Images of the Prophet Joseph Smith,* by Davis Bitton, 171–96. Salt Lake City: Aspen Books, 1996.

Crawley, Peter. *A Descriptive Bibliography of the Mormon Church.* Vol. 1, *1830–1847.* Provo, Utah: Religious Studies Center, Brigham Young University, 1997.

Flake, Chad J., and Larry W. Draper, eds. *A Mormon Bibliography, 1830–1930: Books, Pamphlets, Periodicals, and Broadsides Relating to the First Century of Mormonism.* 2nd rev. ed. 2 vols. Provo, Utah: Religious Studies Center, Brigham Young University, 2004.

Holzapfel, Richard Neitzel, and T. Jeffrey Cottle. *Old Mormon Kirtland and Missouri: Historic Photographs and Guide.* Santa Ana, Calif.: Fieldbrook Productions, 1991.

———. *Old Mormon Nauvoo, 1839–1846: Historic Photographs and Guide.* Provo, Utah: Grandin Book, 1990.

———. *Old Mormon Palmyra and New England: Historic Photographs and Guide.* Santa Ana, Calif.: Fieldbrook Productions, 1991.

Holzapfel, Richard Neitzel, T. Jeffrey Cottle, and Ted D. Stoddard, eds. *Church History in Black and White: George Edward Anderson's Photographic Mission to Latter-day Saint Historical Sites: 1907 Diary, 1907–8 Photographs.* Provo, Utah: Religious Studies Center, Brigham Young University, 1995.

Jessee, Dean C. "Sources for the Study of Joseph Smith." In Whittaker, *Mormon Americana,* 7–28.

———. "Writings of Joseph Smith." In *Encyclopedia of Mormonism,* edited by Daniel H. Ludlow and others, vol. 3, 1343–46. 5 vols. New York: Macmillan Publishing, 1992.

Vogel, Dan, comp. and ed. *Early Mormon Documents.* 5 vols. Salt Lake City: Signature Books, 1996–2003.

Whittaker, David J. "Joseph Smith in Recent Research: A Selected Bibliography." In Whittaker, *Mormon Americana,* 29–44.

———, ed. *Mormon Americana: A Guide to Sources and Collections in the United States.* Provo, Utah: BYU Studies Monographs, 1995.

Diaries and Personal Writings

Faulring, Scott, comp. and ed. *An American Prophet's Record: The Diaries and Journals of Joseph Smith.* Salt Lake City: Signature Books, 1987.

Jessee, Dean C., comp. and ed. *The Papers of Joseph Smith.* 2 vols. Salt Lake City: Deseret Book, 1989, 1992. A new, multivolume edition is currently in preparation.

———, ed. *The Personal Writings of Joseph Smith.* 1984. Revised edition, Salt Lake City: Deseret Book, 2002.

Sermons/Discourses/Writings

"Articles of Faith." These thirteen concise statements of the basic beliefs of the Latter-day Saints were included in the letter Joseph Smith sent to John Wentworth, first published in the *Times and Seasons* 3 no. 9 (March 1, 1842): 706–10, and eventually canonized as part of the Pearl of Great Price in 1880. For a closer look at their textual history, see David J. Whittaker, "The 'Articles of Faith' in Early Mormon Literature and Thought," in *New Views of Mormon History: Essays in Honor of Leonard J. Arrington*, ed. Davis Bitton and Maureen Ursenbach Beecher (Salt Lake City: University of Utah Press, 1987), 63–92.

Cannon, Donald Q. "Words of Comfort: Funeral Sermons of the Prophet Joseph Smith." In *The Disciple as Witness, Essays on Latter-day Saint History and Doctrine in Honor of Richard Lloyd Anderson*, edited by Stephen D. Ricks, Donald W. Parry, and Andrew H. Hedges, 87–104. Provo, Utah: Foundation for Ancient Research and Mormon Studies, Brigham Young University, 2000.

Clark, James R., comp. *Messages of the First Presidency*, vol. 1, 1–231. 6 vols. Salt Lake City: Bookcraft, 1965–75. These are reprints of documents from Joseph Smith's presidency.

Dahl, Larry H. and Donald Q. Cannon, eds. *Encyclopedia of Joseph Smith's Teachings*. Salt Lake City: Deseret Book, 2000. Originally published as *Teachings of Joseph Smith* in 1997.

Ehat, Andrew F., and Lyndon W. Cook, eds. *The Words of Joseph Smith: The Contemporary Accounts of the Nauvoo Discourses of the Prophet Joseph*. 1980. Reprint, Provo, Utah: Religious Studies Center, Brigham Young University, 1990.

General Smith's Views of the Powers and Policy of the Government of the United States. Nauvoo, Ill.: John Taylor, 1844. This was issued in pamphlet form in February 1844 as an official statement of Joseph Smith's views as a recently nominated candidate for the upcoming campaign for the office of president of the United States. Initially drafted by William W. Phelps, Joseph approved its contents. For more information on these matters, see G. Homer Durham, *Joseph Smith, Prophet Statesman* (Salt Lake City, Bookcraft, 1944); Richard D. Poll, "Joseph Smith and the Presidency, 1844," *Dialogue: A Journal of Mormon Thought* 3 (Autumn 1968): 17–21; James B. Allen, "Was Joseph Smith a Serious Candidate for the Presidency of the United States . . . ?" *Ensign* 3 (September 1973): 21–22; Andrew F. Ehat, " 'It Seems Like Heaven Began on Earth': Joseph Smith and the Constitution of the Kingdom of God," *BYU Studies* 20 (Spring 1980): 253–79; and Timothy L. Wood, "The Prophet and the Presidency: Mormonism and Politics in Joseph Smith's 1844 Presidential Campaign," *Journal of the Illinois State Historical Society* 93, no. 2 (2000): 167–93.

Hill, Marvin S., ed. *The Essential Joseph Smith*. Salt Lake City: Signature Books, 1995.

Jessee, Dean C. "Priceless Words and Fallible Memories: Joseph Smith as Seen in the Effort to Preserve His Discourses." *BYU Studies* 31 (Spring 1991): 19–40.

————. "Joseph Smith's 19 July 1840 Discourse." *BYU Studies* 19 (Spring 1979): 390–99.

Madsen, Truman G., ed. *The Concordance of the Doctrinal Statements of Joseph Smith*. Salt Lake City: I. E. S. Publishing, 1985.

Millet, Robert L., ed. and comp. *Joseph Smith: Selected Sermons and Writings*. Sources of American Spirituality Series. New York: Paulist Press, 1989.

Smith, Joseph. "King Follett Discourse." Joseph Smith's last General Conference
discourse, delivered April 7, 1844. The discourse was first published in *Times
and Seasons* 5, no. 15 (August 15, 1844): 612–17, and then added as an appendix to
Voice of Truth (1844), 59–64. The discourse presented an expansive view of the
nature of God and the eternal possibilities of mankind. Several articles on it are in
BYU Studies 18 (Winter 1978). See also Donald Q. Cannon and Larry E. Dahl, *The
Prophet Joseph Smith's King Follett Discourse: A Six Column Comparison of Original
Notes with Introduction and Commentary* (Provo, Utah: Brigham Young University
Printing Services, 1983).

Smith, Joseph, and Sidney Rigdon. "Lectures on Faith." Lectures presented to the
School of the Prophets, 1834–35, in Kirtland, Ohio. They were included in every
edition of the Doctrine and Covenants, beginning with the 1835 edition; they were
removed from the 1921 edition and all subsequent printings. For essays assuming Joseph Smith's authorship, see *The Lectures on Faith in Historical Perspective*,
ed. Larry E. Dahl and Charles D. Tate (Provo, Utah: Religious Studies Center,
Brigham Young University, 1990). For a study that questions that these lectures
represent Joseph Smith's thought, see Noel B. Reynolds, "The Authorship Debate
Concerning *Lectures on Faith*: Exhumation and Reburial," in *The Disciple as
Witness: Essays on Latter-day Saint History and Doctrine in Honor of Richard Lloyd
Anderson*, ed. Stephen D. Ricks, Donald W. Parry, and Andrew H. Hedges (Provo,
Utah: Foundation for Ancient Research and Mormon Studies, Brigham Young
University, 2000), 355–82.

Smith, Joseph Fielding, comp. *Teachings of the Prophet Joseph Smith*. Salt Lake City:
Deseret Book, 1938. This has had many printings.

Van Orden, Bruce A. "William W. Phelps's Service in Nauvoo as Joseph Smith's Political Clerk." *BYU Studies* 32 (Winter/Spring 1992): 81–94.

"History of Joseph Smith"

Jessee, Dean C. "Joseph Smith and the Beginning of Mormon Record Keeping." In *The
Prophet Joseph: Essays on the Life and Mission of Joseph Smith*, edited by Larry C.
Porter and Susan Easton Black, 138–60. Salt Lake City: Deseret Book, 1988.

———. "The Reliability of Joseph Smith's History." *Journal of Mormon History* 3
(1976): 23–46.

———. "Return to Carthage: Writing the History of Joseph Smith's Martyrdom." *Journal of Mormon History* 8 (1981): 3–19.

———. "The Writing of Joseph Smith's History." *BYU Studies* 11 (Summer 1971):
439–73.

Searle, Howard C. "Authorship of the History of Joseph Smith: A Review Essay." *BYU
Studies* 21 (Winter 1981): 101–22.

Smith, Joseph. *History of the Church of Jesus Christ of Latter-day Saints*, edited by James
Mulholland, Robert B. Thompson, William W. Phelps, Willard Richards,
George A. Smith, Wilford Woodruff, and later, B. H. Roberts. 6 vols. Salt Lake
City: Deseret News Press, 1902–1912. Revised edition, 1956. This history was

initially serialized in the *Times and Seasons*, the *LDS Millennial Star*, and the *Deseret News*. In 1932 Roberts added a seventh volume, the *Apostolic Interregnum*, to cover the years between Joseph Smith's death in 1844 and 1847, when Brigham Young was sustained as the second president of the church.

Revelations

Allen, James B. "Emergence of a Fundamental: The Expanding Role of Joseph Smith's First Vision in Mormon Religious Thought." *Journal of Mormon History* 7 (1980): 43–61.

_____. "The Significance of Joseph Smith's First Vision in Mormon Thought." *Dialogue: A Journal of Mormon Thought* 1 (Autumn 1966): 28–45. See also James B. Allen, "Eight Contemporary Accounts of Joseph Smith's First Vision—What Do We Learn from Them?" *Improvement Era* 73 (April 1970): 4–13; and James B. Allen and John W. Welch, "The Appearance of the Father and the Son to Joseph Smith in 1820," in *Opening the Heavens, Accounts of Divine Manifestations, 1820–1844*, ed. John W. Welch with Erick B. Carlson (Provo, Utah: Brigham Young University Press, and Salt Lake City: Deseret Book, 2005), 35–75.

Anderson, Richard Lloyd. *Investigating the Book of Mormon Witnesses*. Salt Lake City: Deseret Book, 1981.

Backman, Milton V. Jr. *Joseph Smith's First Vision: The First Vision in Historical Context*. 1971. Revised edition, Salt Lake City: Bookcraft, 1980.

Barlow, Philip L. *Mormons and the Bible: The Place of the Latter-day Saints in American Religion*. New York: Oxford University Press, 1991.

Bushman, Richard L. "The Book of Mormon and the American Revolution." *BYU Studies* 17 (Autumn 1976): 3–20.

Cannon, Brian Q. and the staff of *BYU Studies*. "Priesthood Restoration Documents." Based on the research of Ronald O. Barney, *BYU Studies* 35, no. 4 (1995–96): 162–207.

Clark, James R. *The Story of the Pearl of Great Price*. Salt Lake City: Bookcraft, 1955.

Cook, Lyndon W. *The Revelations of Joseph Smith: A Historical and Biographical Commentary of the Doctrine and Covenants*. 1981. Reprint, Salt Lake City: Deseret Book, 1985.

Faulring, Scott H., Kent P. Jackson, and Robert J. Matthews, eds. *Joseph Smith's New Translation of the Bible, Original Manuscripts*. Provo, Utah: Religious Studies Center, Brigham Young University, 2004.

Gee, John L. *A Guide to the Joseph Smith Papyri*. Provo, Utah: Foundation for Ancient Research and Mormon Studies, Brigham Young University, 2000.

Givens, Terryl L. *By the Hand of Mormon: The American Scripture That Launched a New World Religion*. New York: Oxford University Press, 2002.

_____. *People of Paradox: A History of Mormon Culture*. New York: Oxford University Press, 2007.

Howard, Richard P. *Restoration Scriptures: A Study of Their Textual Development*. 1969. Second revised and enlarged edition, Independence, Missouri: Herald Publishing House, 1995.

Jackson, Kent P. *The Book of Moses and the Joseph Smith Translation Manuscripts*. Provo, Utah: Religious Studies Center, Brigham Young University, 2005.

Jessee, Dean C. "The Earliest Documented Accounts of Joseph Smith's First Vision." In *Opening the Heavens, Accounts of Divine Manifestations, 1820–1844*, edited by John W. Welch with Erick B. Carlson, 1–33. Provo, Utah: Brigham Young University Press, and Salt Lake City: Deseret Book, 2005.

———. "The Original Book of Mormon Manuscript." *BYU Studies* 10 (Spring 1970): 259–78.

Marquardt, Michael. *The Joseph Smith Revelations: Texts and Commentary*. Salt Lake City: Signature Books, 1999.

Matthews, Robert J. *"A Plainer Translation": Joseph Smith's Translation of the Bible, A History and Commentary*. Provo, Utah: Brigham Young University Press, 1975.

Nibley, Hugh W. *The Message of the Joseph Smith Papyri: An Egyptian Endowment*. 1975. Revised edition, Provo: Foundation for Ancient Research and Mormon Studies, and Salt Lake City: Deseret Book, 2006.

Porter, Larry C. "The Restoration of the Aaronic and Melchizedek Priesthoods." *Ensign* 26 (December 1996): 30–47.

Skousen, Royal. *Analysis of Textual Variants of the Book of Mormon*. Part One. *Title Page, Witnesses Statements, 1 Nephi 1–2 Nephi 10*. Provo, Utah: Foundation for Ancient Research and Mormon Studies, Brigham Young University, 2004. Also: Part Two, *2 Nephi 11–Mosiah 16* (Provo, Utah 2005); Part Three, *Mosiah 17–Alma 20* (Provo, Utah 2006); Part Four, *Alma 20–Alma 63* (Provo, Utah 2007).

———. *The Original Manuscript of the Book of Mormon: Typographical Facsimile of the Extant Text*. Provo, Utah: Foundation for Ancient Research and Mormon Studies, Brigham Young University, 2001.

———. *The Printer's Manuscript of the Book of Mormon: Typographical Facsimile of the Entire Text in Two Parts*. 2 vols. (Provo, Utah: Foundation for Ancient Research and Mormon Studies, Brigham Young University, 2001).

Van Wagoner, Richard, and Steven C. Walker. "Joseph Smith: 'The Gift of Seeing.'" *Dialogue: A Journal of Mormon Thought* 15 (Summer 1982): 49–68.

Welch, John W., with Erick B. Carlson, eds. *Opening the Heavens: Accounts of Divine Manifestations, 1820–1844*. Provo, Utah: Brigham Young University Press; and Salt Lake City: Deseret Book, 2005.

Whittaker, David J. "'That Most Important of All Books': A Printing History of the Book of Mormon." *Mormon Historical Studies* 6 (Fall 2005): 101–34.

Woodford, Robert J. "The Historical Development of the Doctrine and Covenants." PhD diss., Brigham Young University, 1974.

Biographical Studies

Alexander, Thomas G. "The Place of Joseph Smith in the Development of American Religion: A Historiographical Inquiry." *Journal of Mormon History* 5 (1978): 3–17.

Allen, James B. "Second Only to Christ: Joseph Smith in Mormon Piety." In *The Disciple as Witness, Essays on Latter-day Saint History and Doctrine in Honor of Richard*

Lloyd Anderson, edited by Stephen D. Ricks, Donald W. Parry, and Andrew H. Hedges, 1–35. Provo, Utah: Foundation for Ancient Research and Mormon Studies, Brigham Young University, 2000.

Anderson, Devery S. and Gary James Bergera, eds. *Joseph Smith's Quorum of the Anointed, 1842–1845.* Salt Lake City: Signature Books, Smith-Pettit Foundation Book, 2005.

Anderson, Richard Lloyd. "The Alvin Smith Story: Fact and Fiction." *Ensign* 17 (August 1987): 58–72.

———. "Joseph Smith's Brothers: Nauvoo and After." *Ensign* 9 (September 1979): 30–33.

———. "Joseph Smith's Home Environment." *Ensign* 1 (February 1971): 15–19.

———. "Joseph Smith's Journeys." In *2006 Church Almanac,* 131–58. Salt Lake City: Deseret Morning News and the Family and Church History Department, Church of Jesus Christ of Latter-day Saints, 2005. This article surveys the 18,000 miles Joseph Smith traveled during his lifetime.

———. *Joseph Smith's New England Heritage: Influences of Grandfathers Solomon Mack and Asael Smith.* (1971; Second revised edition, Salt Lake City: Deseret Book, and Provo, Utah: BYU Press, 2003).

———. "Joseph Smith's New York Reputation Reappraised." *BYU Studies* 10 (Spring 1970): 283–314.

———. "The Mature Joseph Smith and Treasure Searching." *BYU Studies* 24 (Fall 1984): 489–560.

———. "The Reliability of the Early History of Lucy and Joseph Smith." *Dialogue: A Journal of Mormon Thought* 4 (Summer 1969): 12–28.

———. "What Were Joseph Smith's Sisters Like, and What Happened to Them after the Martyrdom?" *Ensign* 9 (March 1979): 42–44.

Anderson, Robert D. *Inside the Mind of Joseph Smith: Psychobiography and the Book of Mormon.* Salt Lake City: Signature Books, 1999.

Andrus, Hyrum L. *Joseph Smith: The Man and the Seer.* Salt Lake City: Deseret Book, 1960.

Andrus, Hyrum L., and Helen Mae Andrus. *They Knew the Prophet.* Salt Lake City: Deseret Book, 1974.

Ashurst-McGee, Mark. "A Pathway to Prophethood: Joseph Smith Junior as Rodsman, Village Seer, and Judeo-Christian Prophet." Master's thesis, Utah State University, 2000.

Baker, LeGrand L. *Murder of the Mormon Prophet, Political Prelude to the Death of Joseph Smith.* Salt Lake City: Eborn Books, 2006. This book makes extensive use of contemporary newspapers.

Baugh, Alexander L. "Parting the Veil: The Visions of Joseph Smith." *BYU Studies* 38, no. 1 (1999): 22–69.

Beardsley, Harry M. *Joseph Smith and His Mormon Empire.* Boston: Houghton Mifflin, 1931.

Bernauer, Barbara Hands. "Still 'Side by Side'—The Final Burial of Joseph and Hyrum Smith," *John Whitmer Historical Association Journal* 11 (1991): 17–33. This article treats the 1928 exhumation and reburial.

Bitton, Davis. *Images of the Prophet Joseph Smith*. Salt Lake City: Aspen Books, 1996.

———. "Joseph Smith in Mormon Folk Memory." *Restoration Studies* 1 (1980): 75–94.

———. *The Martyrdom Remembered: A One Hundred-fifty Year Perspective on the Assassination of Joseph Smith*. Salt Lake City: Aspen Books, 1994.

Black, Susan Easton, and Andrew C. Skinner, eds. *Joseph: Exploring the Life and Ministry of the Prophet*. Salt Lake City: Deseret Book, 2005.

Black, Susan Easton, and Charles D. Tate, Jr., eds. *Joseph Smith: The Prophet, the Man*. Provo, Utah: Religious Studies Center, Brigham Young University, 1993.

Brodie, Fawn M. *No Man Knows My History: The Life of Joseph Smith, the Mormon Prophet*. 1945. Revised edition, New York: Alfred A. Knopf, 1978.

Bushman, Richard L. *Joseph Smith and the Beginnings of Mormonism*. Urbana: University of Illinois Press, 1984.

———. "Joseph Smith and Culture." In *Believing History: Latter-day Saint Essays*, edited by Reid L. Neilson and Jed Woodworth, 143–278. New York: Columbia University Press, 2004. This is a collection of essays on various aspects of Joseph Smith's life and thought.

———. *Joseph Smith: Rough Stone Rolling, A Cultural Biography of Mormonism's Founder*. With the assistance of Jed Woodworth. New York: Alfred A. Knopf, 2005.

Cannon, Donald Q. "Topsfield, Massachusetts: Ancestral Home of the Prophet Joseph Smith." *BYU Studies* 14 (Autumn 1973): 56–76.

Cannon, George Q. *The Life of Joseph Smith, the Prophet*. Salt Lake City: Juvenile Instructor, 1888. There are many reprints of this work.

Carmer, Carl. *The Farm Boy and the Angel*. Garden City, N.Y.: Doubleday, 1970.

Caswell, Henry. *The Prophet of the Nineteenth Century*. London: J. G. F. and J. Rivington, 1843.

Chase, Daryl. *Joseph Smith the Prophet: As He Lives in the Hearts of His People*. Salt Lake City: Deseret Book, 1944.

Compton, Todd. *In Sacred Loneliness: The Plural Wives of Joseph Smith*. Salt Lake City: Signature Books, 1997. See also the valuable review essay by Richard Lloyd Anderson and Scott H. Faulring, "The Prophet Joseph Smith and His Plural Wives," *FARMS Review of Books* 10, no. 2 (1998): 67–104. For the larger context, see Kathryn M. Daynes, *More Wives than One, Transformation of the Mormon Marriage System, 1840–1910* (Urbana: University of Illinois Press, 2001).

Cook, Lyndon W. *Joseph Smith and the Law of Consecration*. Provo, Utah: Grandin Book, 1985.

Cottle, Thomas D., and Patricia C. Cottle. *Liberty Jail and the Legacy of Joseph*. Portland, Oregon: Insight, 1998.

Derr, Jill Mulvay, and Susan Staker Oman. "The Nauvoo Generation: Our First Five Relief Society Presidents." *Ensign* 7 (December 1977): 36–43.

Ehat, Andrew F. " 'It Seems Like Heaven Began on Earth': Joseph Smith and the Constitution of the Kingdom of God." *BYU Studies* 20 (Spring 1980): 253–79.

———. "Joseph Smith's Introduction of Temple Ordinances and the 1844 Succession Question." Master's thesis, Brigham Young University, 1982.

Esplin, Ronald K. "The Emergence of Brigham Young and the Twelve to Mormon Leadership, 1830–1841." PhD diss., Brigham Young University, 1981.

———. "Joseph, Brigham and the Twelve: A Succession of Continuity." *BYU Studies* 31 (Summer 1981): 301–41.

Evans, John Henry. *Joseph Smith: An American Prophet.* New York: Macmillan, 1933.

Fischer, Norma J. *Portrait of a Prophet.* Salt Lake City: Bookcraft, 1960.

Gibbons, Francis M. *Joseph Smith: Martyr, Prophet of God.* Salt Lake City: Deseret Book, 1977.

Green, Arnold H., and Lawrence P. Goldrup. "Joseph Smith, an American Muhammad? An Essay on the Perils of Historical Analogy." *Dialogue: A Journal of Mormon Thought* 6 (Spring 1971): 46–58.

Gregg, Thomas. *The Prophet of Palmyra.* New York: John B. Alden, 1890.

Hansen, Klaus J. *Quest for Empire: The Political Kingdom of God and the Council of Fifty in Mormon History.* East Lansing: Michigan State University Press, 1967.

Hatch, Ephraim. *Joseph Smith Portraits: A Search for the Prophet's Likeness.* Provo, Utah: Religious Studies Center, Brigham Young University, 1998. See also Marba C. Josephson, "What Did the Prophet Joseph Smith Look Like?" *Improvement Era* 56 (May 1953): 311–15, 371–75; Lavina Fielding Anderson, "139-Year-Old Portraits of Joseph and Emma Smith," *Ensign* 11 (March 1981): 62–64; Ephraim Hatch, "What Did Joseph Smith Look Like?" Ibid., 65–73; and Robert A. Rees, "Seeing Joseph Smith, The Changing Image of the Mormon Prophet," *Sunstone* (December 2005): 18–27.

Hill, Donna. *Joseph Smith: The First Mormon.* Garden City, N.Y.: Doubleday, 1977.

Hill, Marvin S. "Joseph Smith the Man: Some Reflections on a Subject of Controversy." *BYU Studies* 21 (Spring 1981): 175–86.

Huntress, Keith, ed. *Murder of an American Prophet.* San Francisco, Calif.: Chandler Publishing, 1960.

Jenson, Andrew. "Joseph Smith, the Prophet." *Historical Record* (Salt Lake City) 7, nos. 1–3 (January 1888): 353–576.

Jessee, Dean C. " 'Walls, Grates and Screeking Iron Doors': The Prison Experience of Mormon Leaders in Missouri, 1838–39." In *New Views of Mormon History: Essays in Honor of Leonard J. Arrington,* edited by Davis Bitton and Maureen Ursenbach Beecher, 19–42. Salt Lake City: University of Utah Press, 1987.

Johnson, Joseph D. " 'To Lie in Yonder Tomb': The Tomb and Burial of Joseph Smith." *Mormon Historical Studies* 6 (Fall 2005): 163–80.

Madsen, Truman G. *Joseph Smith the Prophet.* Salt Lake City: Bookcraft, 1989.

McConkie, Mark L. *Remembering Joseph: Personal Recollections of Those Who Knew the Prophet Joseph Smith.* Salt Lake City: Deseret Book, 2003.

Morain, William D. *The Sword of Laban: Joseph Smith, Jr., and the Dissociated Mind.* Washington, D.C.: American Psychiatric Press, 1998.

Newell, Linda King, and Valeen Tippetts Avery. *Mormon Enigma: Emma Hale Smith, Prophet's Wife, "Elect Lady," and Polygamy's Foe, 1804–1879.* Garden City, NY: Doubleday, 1984.

Nibley, Preston, *Joseph Smith: The Prophet.* Salt Lake City: Deseret Book, 1944.

Oaks, Dallin H., and Marvin S. Hill. *Carthage Conspiracy: The Trial of the Accused Assassins of Joseph Smith*. Urbana: University of Illinois Press, 1975.

O'Driscoll, Jeffrey S. *Hyrum Smith: A Life of Integrity*. Salt Lake City: Deseret Book, 2003.

Orton, Chad M., and William W. Slaughter. *Joseph Smith's America: His Life and Times*. Salt Lake City: Deseret Book, 2005.

Poll, Richard D. "Joseph Smith and the Presidency, 1844." *Dialogue: A Journal of Mormon Thought* 3 (Autumn 1968): 17–21.

Porter, Larry C., and Susan Easton Black, eds. *The Prophet Joseph: Essays on the Life and Mission of Joseph Smith*. Salt Lake City: Deseret Book, 1988.

Quinn, D. Michael. "The Council of Fifty and Its Members, 1844 to 1945." *BYU Studies* 20 (Winter 1980): 163–97.

———. *Early Mormonism and the Magic World View*. 1987. Revised edition, Salt Lake City: Signature Books, 1998.

———. *The Mormon Hierarchy: Origins of Power*. Salt Lake City: Signature Books in association with Smith Research Associates, 1994.

Remini, Robert. *Joseph Smith*. Penguin Lives series. New York: Penguin Books, 2002.

Riley, I. Woodbridge. *The Founder of Mormonism: A Psychological Study of Joseph Smith, Jr.* New York: Dodd, Mead, 1902.

Rothman, Norman. *The Unauthorized Biography of Joseph Smith, Mormon Prophet*. Salt Lake City: Norman Rothman Foundation, 1997.

Shields, Steven L. *Divergent Paths of the Restoration: A History of the Latter-day Saint Movement*. 4th ed. Los Angeles, Calif.: Restoration Research, 1990. A guide to the various religious movements that trace their origin to Joseph Smith.

Shipps, Jan. "The Prophet Puzzle: Suggestions Leading toward a More Comprehensive Interpretation of Joseph Smith." *Journal of Mormon History* 1 (1974): 3–20.

Smith, Lucy Mack. *Biographical Sketches of Joseph Smith the Prophet, and His Progenitors for Many Generations*. London: Published for Orson Pratt by S. W. Richards, 1853. The most recent scholarly edition is *Lucy's Book: A Critical Edition of Lucy Mack Smith's Family Memoir*, edited by Lavina Fielding Anderson. Salt Lake City: Signature Books, 2001.

Smith, T. Michael, Kirk B. Henrichsen, and Donald L. Enders. "The Birthplace Home of Joseph Smith, Jr." *Mormon Historical Studies* 6 (Fall 2005): 19–67.

Stewart, John J. *Joseph Smith: The Mormon Prophet*. Salt Lake City: Hawkes, 1966.

Swinton, Heidi. *American Prophet: The Story of Joseph Smith*. Salt Lake City: Shadow Mountain, 1999.

Taylor, Mark W., ed. and comp. *Witness of the Martyrdom: John Taylor's Personal Account of the Last Days of the Prophet Joseph Smith*. Salt Lake City: Deseret Book, 1999.

Tullidge, Edward W. *Life of Joseph the Prophet*. New York: Tullidge and Crandall, 1878.

Van Wagoner, Richard S., and Steven Walker. "Joseph Smith: 'The Gift of Seeing'." *Dialogue: A Journal of Mormon Thought* 15 (Summer 1982): 49–68.

Vogel, Dan. *Joseph Smith: The Making of a Prophet*. Salt Lake City: Signature Books, 2004.

Walker, Kyle R. "The Joseph Sr. and Lucy Mack Smith Family: A Family Process Analysis of a Nineteenth-century Household." PhD diss., Brigham Young University, 2001.

————, ed. *United by Faith: The Joseph Sr. and Lucy Mack Smith Family*. American Fork, Utah: Covenant Communications, 2006.

Walker, Ronald W. "Joseph Smith: The Palmyra Seer." *BYU Studies* 24 (Fall 1984): 461–72.

Waterman, Bryan, ed. *The Prophet Puzzle: Interpretive Essays on Joseph Smith*. Salt Lake City: Signature Books, 1999.

Welch, John W., ed. *The Worlds of Joseph Smith*. Papers presented at the Bicentennial Conference at the Library of Congress. *BYU Studies* 44, no. 4 (2005). The entire issue is dedicated to these papers..

Wicks, Robert S., and Fred R. Foister. *Junius and Joseph: Presidential Politics and the Assassination of the First Mormon Prophet*. Logan: Utah State University Press, 2005.

Wirthlin, LeRoy S. "Joseph Smith's Boyhood Operation: An 1813 Surgical Success." *BYU Studies* 21 (Spring 1981): 131–54.

Wood, Gordon S. "Evangelical America and Early Mormonism." *New York History* 61 (October 1980): 359–86.

Zucker, Louis C. "Joseph Smith as a Student of Hebrew." *Dialogue: A Journal of Mormon Thought* 3 (Summer 1968): 41–55.

Notes

CHAPTER I

1. Arun Joshi, "Mormon Ways of Family Life Can Resolve Conflicts in World" (paper presented at "The Worlds of Joseph Smith: An Academic Symposium," National Taiwan University, Taipei, Taiwan, August 2005).

2. Josiah Quincy Jr., *Figures of the Past: From the Leaves of Old Journals* (Boston: Roberts Brothers, 1883), 376. See Richard Lyman Bushman, *Joseph Smith: Rough Stone Rolling* (New York: Alfred A. Knopf, 2005), 3–7.

3. James Gordon Bennett, *New York Herald*, August 4, 1842.

4. Catherine L. Albanese, *American Religious History: A Bibliographic Essay* (Washington, DC: United States Department of State, Bureau of Educational and Cultural Affairs, 2002), 4. See also Henry Warner Bowden, "The Historiography of American Religion," in *Encylopedia of the American Religious Experience*, Charles H. Lippy and Peter W. Williams, eds. (New York: Scribners, 1988), 1, 3–16.

5. For an excellent treatment of how nineteenth-and twentieth-century Mormon and non-Mormon biographers have written about Joseph Smith, see Richard Lyman Bushman, "A Joseph Smith for the Twenty-first Century," in *Believing History: Latter-day Saint Essays*, ed. Reid L. Neilson and Jed Woodworth (New York: Columbia University Press, 2004), 262–78. See also Richard Lyman Bushman, "Joseph Smith's Many Histories," *BYU Studies* 44, no. 4 (2005): 3–20, for an overview of Joseph Smith in American religious historiography.

6. Albanese, *American Religious History*, 5; and Bowden, "Historiography of American Religion," 4.

7. Baird, *Religion in America*, 286.

8. Albanese, *American Religious History*, 5; and Bowden, "Historiography of American Religion," 4.

9. Philip Schaff, *America: A Sketch of Its Political, Social, and Religious Character*, ed. Perry Miller (1855; Cambridge, Mass.: Belknap Press of Harvard University Press, 1961), 198–204.

10. Albanese, *American Religious History*, 5; and Bowden, "Historiography of American Religion," 4–5.

11. Daniel Dorchester, *Christianity in the United States: From the First Settlement Down to the Present Time*, rev. ed. (1888; New York: Hunt and Eaton, 1895), 538–42.

12. Leonard Woolsey Bacon, *A History of American Christianity* (1897; New York: Charles Scribner's Sons, 1930), 335.

13. Albanese, *American Religious History*, 5–6; and Bowden, "Historiography of American Religion," 5–7.

14. William Warren Sweet, *The Story of Religion in America*, rev. ed. (1930; New York: Harper and Brothers, 1939), 397–401.

15. Sidney E. Mead, *The Lively Experiment: The Shaping of Christianity in America* (New York: Harper and Row, 1963), 124–25.

16. Sydney E. Ahlstrom, *A Religious History of the American People* (New Haven, Conn.: Yale University Press, 1972), 508.

17. Albanese, *American Religious History*, 5–7.

18. The handful of reprint essays in this volume first appeared in Mormon scholarly journals such as *BYU Studies, Journal of Mormon History*, and *Sunstone*, all of which are all well regarded within the LDS (Latter-day Saint) intellectual community but often fail to reach the larger academic community and discourse.

19. This essay was presented as the Obert C. Tanner Lecture at the annual meeting of the Mormon History Association, May 2002, Tucson, Ariz. It was then first published in the *Journal of Mormon History* 29 (Spring 2003): 43–65.

20. This essay was presented at the College of Humanities "Literature and Belief Colloquium," Brigham Young University, Provo, Utah, 1998. It was then first published in *BYU Studies* 38, no. 1 (1999): 151–69.

21. This previously unpublished essay was presented during a panel at the American Historical Association, to mark the Joseph Smith Bicentennial, Seattle, Wash., January 2005. She draws on and adapts material from her book *A Republic of Mind and Spirit: A Cultural History of American Metaphysical Religion* (New Haven, Conn.: Yale University Press, 2007), esp. 136–50.

22. This previously unpublished essay was presented at the lecture series and exhibit "Remembering Joseph Smith Jr., 1805–2005," L. Tom Perry Special Collections, Harold B. Lee Library, Brigham Young University, Provo, Utah, March 2006.

23. This previously unpublished essay was presented at "Joseph Smith and the Prophetic Tradition: A Comparative Inquiry," Claremont Graduate University, Claremont, Calif., October 2005.

24. This essay was presented at "The Worlds of Joseph Smith: A Bicentennial Conference," Library of Congress, Washington, D.C., May 2005. It was then first published in *BYU Studies* 44, no. 4 (2005): 55–68.

25. This previously unpublished essay was presented at the "Joseph Smith Bicentennial Symposium," Parliament House, New South Wales, Sydney, Australia, May 2005.

26. This essay was presented as the Smith-Pettit Lecture at the "Salt Lake Sunstone Symposium," Salt Lake City, Utah, July 2005. It was then first published in *Sunstone* 140 (December 2005): 28–36.

27. This previously unpublished essay was presented at the Mormon-Evangelical Dialogue Luncheon during the annual meeting of the American Academy of Religion, Washington, D.C., November 2006.

28. This previously unpublished essay was presented at the "Joseph Smith Bicentennial Symposium," Parliament House, New South Wales, Sydney, Australia, May 2005.

29. This previously unpublished essay was presented at "The Worlds of Joseph Smith: An Academic Symposium," National Taiwan University, Taipei, Taiwan, August 2005.

30. This previously unpublished essay was presented at the lecture series and exhibit "Remembering Joseph Smith Jr., 1805–2005," L. Tom Perry Special Collections, Harold B. Lee Library, Brigham Young University, Provo, Utah, March 2006.

CHAPTER 2

1. *The Confessions of Nat Turner, the Leader of the Late Insurrection in Southampton, Va., as Fully and Voluntarily Made to Thomas R Gray* (Baltimore, Md.: Lucas and Deaver, 1831). Page numbers following quotations from *The Confessions* are from the reprint of *The Confessions* in *The Southampton Slave Revolt of 1831: A Compilation of Source Material*, ed. Henry Irving Tragle (Amherst: University of Massachusetts Press, 1971). I offer a fuller reading of Nat Turner's version of prophecy in "Millennium, Prophecy, and the Energies of Social Transformation: The Case of Nat Turner," in *Imagining the End: Visions of Apocalypse from the Ancient Middle East to Modern America*, ed. Abbas Amanat and Magnus T. Bernhardsson (London: I. B. Tauris, 2002), 212–33.

2. Lance S. Owens notes the coincidence of Smith's visions with the autumnal equinox in his "Joseph Smith: America's Hermetic Prophet," in *The Prophet Puzzle: Interpretive Essays on Joseph Smith*, ed. Bryan Waterman (Salt Lake City: Signature Books, 1999), 164.

3. I am quoting the 1839 manuscript of Joseph Smith's "History of the Church" in Dean C. Jessee, ed., *The Papers of Joseph Smith*, vol. 1, *Autobiographical and Historical Writings* (Salt Lake City: Deseret Book, 1989), 271.

4. Quoted in Terryl L. Givens, *By the Hand of Mormon: The American Scripture that Launched a New World Religion* (New York: Oxford University Press, 2002), 28.

5. Oiiver Cowdery, 1834 manuscript "History of the Church," in Jessee, *Papers*, 1:31.

6. Ibid., 1:290.

7. James B. Allen, "Joseph Smith's 'First Vision' in Mormon Thought," in *The New Mormon History: Revisionist Essays on the Past*, ed. D. Michael Quinn (Salt Lake City: Signature Books, 1992), 37–52. For a full consideration of issues of authorship and

authenticity in *The Confessions of Nat Turner*, see Eric J. Sundquist, *To Wake the Nations: Race in the Making of American Literature* (Cambridge, Mass.: Harvard University Press, 1993), 36–56. See also Richard Brodhead, "Energies of Social Transformation," 219–20. Newer work adding further uncertainty to the subject is surveyed in Tony Horwitz, "Untrue Confessions," *New Yorker* (December 13, 1999): 80–89.

8. On Wilkinson, see Herbert A. Wisbey Jr., *Pioneer Prophetess: Jemima Wilkinson, the Publick Universal Friend* (Ithaca, N.Y.: Cornell University Press, 1964). The career of Handsome Lake is considered in Anthony F. C. Wallace, *The Death and Rebirth of the Seneca* (1969; reprint, New York: Random House Vintage Books, 1972). The best source on the Shakers is Stephen J. Stein, *The Shaker Experience in America* (New Haven, Conn.: Yale University Press, 1992). The Dylks cult is described in R. H. Taneyhill, ed., *The Leatherwood God: An Account of the Appearance and Pretensions of Joseph C. Dylks in Eastern Ohio in 1828* (Cincinnati: Robert Clarke, 1870). Evidence of early confusion of Joseph Smith with Dylks (and possibly also Ann Lee) can be found in "Mormonism," *Wayne Sentinel* (Palmyra, N.Y.), August 23, 1831, the final day of the Nat Turner rebellion.

9. Karl R. Arndt, "George Rapp's Harmony Society," in *America's Communal Utopias*, ed. Donald E. Pitzer (Chapel Hill: University of North Carolina Press, 1997), 57–87; see esp. 57, 75–76. Arndt notes (69) that the Harmony Society gave financial assistance to the Mormons, as well as to other communitarian movements.

10. On William Miller's 1831 emergence see David L. Rowe, *Thunder and Trumpets: Millerites and Religious Dissent in Upstate New York 1800–1850* (Chico, Calif.: Scholars Press, 1985), chap. 1. The prophetic career of Robert Matthews is reconstructed in Paul E. Johnson and Sean Wilentz, *The Kingdom of Matthias: A Story of Sex and Salvation in 19th-Century America* (New York: Oxford University Press, 1994); the quotations are on 79. Joseph Smith's 1835 account of the First Vision to "Joshua, the Jewish Minister," is reprinted in Jessee, *Papers*, 1:124–27. After Joshua's identity as Matthias was revealed, Smith eventually informed him that "his God was the Devil" and made him leave, but his reception of Matthias was not unambivalently hostile. Matthias was invited to "deliver a lecture to those present" even after he had "confessed that he was really Matthias" (Jessee, *Papers*, 1:128–32).

11. Original source in Spencer Klaw, *Without Sin: The Life and Death of the Oneida Community* (1993; reprint, New York: Penguin Books, 1994), 26.

12. Original source in Henry Mayer, *All on Fire: William Lloyd Garrison and the Abolition of Slavery* (New York: St. Martin's Press, 1998), 326.

13. The strongest recent version of this argument, which is quite familiar from Mormon historiography, is Johnson and Wilentz, *The Kingdom of Matthias*.

14. Nell Irwin Painter, *Sojourner Truth: A Life; A Symbol* (New York: W. W. Norton, 1996).

15. The relation of Brown's paramilitary tactics to his biblical fundamentalism and sense of personal appointment is clear, for instance, in his fantasy of the United League of Gileadites, a guerilla army modeled on Gideon's army in the book of Judges. Stephen B. Oates, *To Purge This Land with Blood: A Biography of John Brown*, 2nd ed. (Amherst: University of Massachusetts Press, 1984), 72–75. The role of Nat Turner's Rebellion in the planning of the Harper's Ferry raid is evident in the June 1858 interview with John

Brown and John Henrie Kagi by Richard Hinton, in Richard Warch and Jonathan F. Fanton, eds., *John Brown* (Englewood Cliffs, N.J.: Prentice Hall, 1973), 56. In this interview, Brown correctly remembers the special possibilities for the creation of terror that Nat Turner had located in the fear of slave revolt, but he mistakenly recalls that "Nat Turner with fifty men held a portion of Virginia for several weeks" (56), an exaggeration of Turner's success.

16. Ralph Waldo Emerson, *Ralph Waldo Emerson: Essays and Lectures*, ed. Joel Porte (New York: Library of America, 1983), 80. Subsequent Emerson quotations are from this edition, cited parenthetically in the text.

17. Jessee, *Papers*, 1:273.

18. Ibid., 1:273–74

19. Ibid., 1:274.

20. Jan Shipps, *Mormonism: The Story of a New Religious Tradition* (Urbana: University of Illinois Press, 1985), esp. 67–86, has explored how Joseph Smith moved to appropriate the status of the Chosen People through his literalizing recapitulations of biblical marks of chosenness: the Aaronic priesthood, the exodus, the temple, the twelve apostles, and so on. See also Harold Bloom's apt remark, "Had they met in their lifetimes, the Transcendental sage and the Mormon prophet could not have talked to one another. Smith's visions and prophecies were remarkably literal; the subtle Emerson, master of figurative language, knew that all visions are metaphors, and that all prophecies are rhetorical." Bloom, *The American Religion: The Emergence of the Post-Christian Nation* (New York: Simon and Schuster, 1992), 53.

21. I think of Martin Luther King: "He's allowed me to go up to the mountain. And I've looked over. And I've seen the promised land." King said this in his last sermon, delivered in Memphis, Tennessee, April 3, 1968, on the eve of his assassination. James M. Washington, ed., *A Testament of Hope: The Essential Writings and Speeches of Martin Luther King Jr.* (1986; reprint, New York: HarperCollins, 1991), 286. For an excellent discussion of King's identification with Moses and other biblical prophets, see Richard Lischer, *The Preacher King: Martin Luther King Jr. and the Word That Moved America* (New York: Oxford University Press, 1993), 172–94. Lischer's understanding of the psychological and rhetorical operation of such identification is highly relevant to the study of Joseph Smith (as to many other prophets); but King's deployment of this identification as a figure, not as a literally claimed identity, marks an important difference from Smith.

22. In early Mormonism the monopolization of vision by the prophet was not quite total, as the second of these revelations suggests. One of the less egotistical prophets, Joseph Smith was willing to share the prophetic prerogative on occasion with close associates (e.g., Oliver Cowdery and Sidney Rigdon), though these licensing moves were offset by countermoves of containment or subordination. Later Mormonism, Shipps (*Mormonism*, 137–38) explains, allows all church members access to that degree of revelation appropriate to their church position—a move that democratizes revelation in a somewhat Emersonian way while also subordinating such access to the structures of church hierarchy. But it is not envisioned that believers will have church-founding revelations of the order of Joseph Smith's. The way Mormons partake of revelation in

that strong or primary form is by participating in the church the prophet founded, the institution his vision restored in which the divine is felt to be continuingly embodied.

23. Givens, *By the Hand of Mormon*, esp. 72–88.

24. Jessee, *Papers*, 1:30.

25. Ibid., 1:290

26. Ibid.

27. Ibid.

28. The classic reading of the nature and meaning of Smith's act on this occasion is Mario S. De Pillis, "The Quest for Religious Authority and the Rise of Mormonism" (1966), in Quinn, *New Mormon History*, 13–35.

CHAPTER 3

1. Karen Armstrong, *The Great Transformation: The Beginning of Our Religious Traditions* (New York: Alfred A. Knopf, 2006); Karen Armstrong, *From Abraham to the Present: The 4,000-Year Quest for God* (London: Heinemann, 1993); Karl Jaspers, *The Origin and God of History* (Westport, Conn.: Greenwood Press, 1977).

2. Max Weber, *Gesammelte Aufsaetze zur Religionssoziologie* (Tuebingen: Mohr, 1922–23); *The Protestant Ethic and the Spirit of Capitalism* (London: Allen and Unwin, 1930).

3. Harold Bloom, *The American Religion: The Emergence of the Post-Christian Nation* (New York: Simon and Schuster, 1992), 95.

4. John S. Rigdon, *Einstein 1905: The Standard of Greatness* (Cambridge, Mass.: Harvard University Press, 2005).

5. Cited in Klaus J. Hansen, *Mormonism and the American Experience* (Chicago: University of Chicago Press, 1981), 16.

6. Hansen, *Mormonism and the American Experience*, 17–18.

7. Bloom, *The American Religion*, 127.

8. Thomas Carlyle, "The Hero as Prophet," *Heroes and Hero Worship* (1840), in Terryl L. Givens, "'Lightning Out of Heaven': Joseph Smith and the Forging of Community," *BYU Studies* 45, no. 1 (2006): 19. In this essay, however, I wish to pass on the controversy that Carlyle ignited and that has not been resolved to this day: whether it is history that makes a great man, or the other way around.

9. Alexander Campbell, *Delusions: An Analysis of the Book of Mormon* (Boston: Benjamin H. Greene, 1832).

10. Fawn M. Brodie, *No Man Knows My History: The Life of Joseph Smith the Mormon Prophet* (New York: Alfred H. Knopf, 1945), 69.

11. Givens, "Lightning Out of Heaven," 8.

12. It seems to me that much of Richard Lyman Bushman's pathbreaking biography, *Joseph Smith: Rough Stone Rolling* (New York: Alfred A. Knopf, 2006) is in that vein. On the dust jacket, the book is identified as "a cultural biography of Mormonism's founder," but this phrase is not on the title page. Also moving beyond Fawn Brodie, albeit from a secular perspective, is Dan Vogel, *Joseph Smith. The Making of a Prophet* (Salt Lake City: Signature Books, 2004), covering the prophet's early formative years to 1831. According

to historian Daniel Walker Howe, Vogel locates Smith "within a broader framework of American history and religion, providing an insightful treatment of the Mormon prophet's complex personality." (Vogel, *The Making of a Prophet*, back cover).

13. Jan Shipps, "The Prophet Puzzle: Suggestions Leading Toward a More Comprehensive Interpretation of Joseph Smith," *Journal of Mormon History* 1 (1974): 3–20.

14. Marvin S. Hill, *Quest for Refuge: The Mormon Flight from American Pluralism* (Salt Lake City: Signature Books, 1989).

15. Jay Fliegelman, *Prodigals and Pilgrims: The American Revolution Against Patriarchal Authority, 1750–1800* (Cambridge, U.K.: Cambridge University Press, 1982), 6.

16. Richard L. Bushman, *From Puritan to Yankee: Character and the Social Order in Connecticut, 1690–1765* (Cambridge, Mass.: Harvard University Press, 1967).

17. Bushman, *Puritan to Yankee*, 288.

18. Alexis de Tocqueville, *Democracy in America*, trans. Henry Reeve, ed. Phillips Bradley, 2 vols. (New York: Alfred A. Knopf, 1978), 205–6.

19. The literature on this transformation is enormous. Among the works I have found useful are Rowland Berthoff, *An Unsettled People: Social Order and Disorder in American History* (New York: Harper and Row, 1971); Stuart M. Blumin, *The Emergence of the Middle Class: Social Experience in the American City, 1760–1900* (Cambridge, U.K.: Cambridge University Press, 1989); Lawrence Frederick Kohl, *The Politics of Individualism: Parties and the American Character in the Jacksonian Era* (New York: Oxford University Press, 1989).

20. Although I still find useful James A. Henretta, *The Evolution of American Society, 1700–1815: An Interdisciplinary Analysis* (Lexington, Mass.: D.C. Heath, 1973), it should be supplemented by the more recent, more in-depth study by Gordon S. Wood, *The Radicalism of the American Revolution* (New York: Alfred A. Knopf, 1992). A veritable tour de force, the work traces the transformation of American politics, society, and culture from monarchy to republicanism to democracy, effectively contextualizing the world into which Joseph Smith was born, and in which he became the founder of a new religion. Even as this essay is about to go to press a brilliant new book has come to my attention that picks up where Gordon Wood's chronology leaves off (1815): Daniel Walker Howe, *What Hath God Wrought. The Transformation of America, 1815–1848* (New York: Oxford University Press, 2007). A Pulitzer Prize-winning, magisterial synthesis and interpretation of the enormous literature covering the political, social, economic, cultural and religious history of the period, it is a work all serious students of Mormon history should read to better understand the America in which Joseph Smith carried out his mission. As it is, I have relied on an updated and revised version of my own work, "Mormonism and American Culture," chapter 2 (pp. 45–83), in *Mormonism and the American Experience*.

21. Fliegelman, *Prodigals and Pilgrims*, 5.

22. William McLoughlin, "Revivalism," in *The Rise of Adventism: Religion and Society in Mid-Nineteenth-Century America*, ed. Edwin Scott Gaustad (New York: Harper and Row, 1974), 129–30; William McLoughlin, *Revivals, Awakenings, and Reform: An Essay on Religion and Social Change in America, 1607–1977* (Chicago: University of Chicago Press, 1978).

23. Kenelm Burridge, *New Heaven, New Earth: A Study of Millenarian Activities* (New York: Schocken Books, 1969).

24. Alice Felt Tyler, *Freedom's Ferment: Phases of American Social History from the Colonial Period to the Outbreak of the Civil War* (Minneapolis: University of Minnesota Press, 1944); John Higham, *From Boundlessness to Consolidation: The Transformation of American Culture, 1848–1860* (Ann Arbor, Mich.: William L. Clements Library, 1969).

25. Lawrence Foster, *Religion and Sexuality: Three American Communal Experiments of the Nineteenth Century* (New York: Oxford University Press, 1981), 3–20.

26. Gordon Wood, "Evangelical America and Early Mormonism" (April 1980), in *The Mormon History Association's Tanner Lectures: The First Twenty Years*, ed. Dean L. May and Reid L. Neilson (Urbana and Chicago: University of Illinois, 2006), 9–28. A striking parallel to Wood's comment is one by Terryl Givens: "[Joseph] . . . was . . . born to his hour in human history." Givens, "Lightning Out of Heaven," 19.

27. Wood, "Evangelical America and Early Mormonism," 21.

28. Brodie, *No Man Knows My History*, 297.

29. Lawrence Foster, "Between Two Worlds: The Origins of Shaker Celibacy, Oneida Community Complex Marriage, and Mormon Polygamy" (PhD diss., University of Chicago, 1976), 265.

30. Ralph Waldo Emerson, "Self-Reliance," in *Essays and Other Writings* (London: Cassell & Co., 1911), 51. See also Daniel Scott Smith and Michael Hindus, "Premarital Pregnancy in America, 1640–1971: An Overview and an Interpretation," *Journal of Interdisciplinary History* 5 (Spring 1975): 538; Mary Beth Stevens, *Stray Wives: Marital Conflict in Early National New England* (New York: NYU Press, 2005); George M. Fredrickson, *The Black Image in the White Mind: The Debate on Afro-American Character and Destiny, 1817–1914* (New York: Harper and Row, 1971); Klaus J. Hansen, "The Millennium, the West, and Race in the Antebellum American Mind," *Western Historical Quarterly* 3 (October 1972): 384–385; William J. Rorabaugh, *The Alcoholic Republic: An American Tradition* (New York: Oxford University Press, 1979); Ronald D. Walters, *American Reformers, 1815–1860* (New York: Hill and Wang, 1978).

31. Bushman, *Rough Stone Rolling*, 445; Foster, "Between Two Worlds," 226; Doctrine and Covenants 132:7.

32. McLoughlin, *Revivals, Awakenings and Reform*; Perry Miller, "The Evangelical Basis," in *The Life of the Mind in America: From the Revolution to the Civil War* (New York: Harcourt, Brace and World, 1965), 3–95; Wood, "Evangelical America and Early Mormonism," 16.

33. Paul E. Johnson, *A Shopkeeper's Millennium: Society and Revivals in Rochester, New York, 1815–1837* (New York: Hill and Wang, 1978).

34. Anthony F. C. Wallace, *Rockdale: The Growth of an American Village in the Early Industrial Revolution* (New York: W. W. Norton, 1978), 243–474.

35. Ray Allen Billington, *The Protestant Crusade: A study of the origins of American nativism* (New York: Rinehart, 1938); emphasizing a common Protestant paranoia is David Brion Davis, "Some Themes of Counter-subversion: An Analysis of Anti-Masonic, Anti-Catholic, and Anti-Mormon Literature," *Mississippi Valley Historical Review* 47 (1960): 205–24.

36. Bloom, *The American Religion*, 107.

37. Alexis deTocqueville, *Democracy in America*, trans. and ed. Harvey C. Mansfield and Delba Winthrop (Chicago: University of Chicago Press, 2000), ii, 419–20.

38. Herbert Butterfield, *The Whig Interpretation of History* (London: Bell, 1931). Clyde R. Forsberg Jr. makes a perceptive comment in his often controversial *Equal Rites: The Book of Mormon, Masonry, Gender, and American Culture* (New York: Columbia University Press, 2004), xvi: "Whether the Mormon prophet should be seen as a threat to the American way depends entirely on whether . . . one ought to take with a grain of salt the history of the Great Republic as imparted by a decidedly victorious Protestantism."

39. Bushman, *Rough Stone Rolling*. Jan Shipps (an outsider) pioneered a scholarly approach of writing the history of Mormonism "as perceived from the inside" in her influential *Mormonism: The Story of a New Religious Tradition* (Urbana: University of Illinois Press, 1985), xii. Shipps, however, also acknowledged that " 'facts' . . . do not necessarily speak for themselves," and that the historian has to evaluate a particular account in the context in which it is presented. Shipps, *Mormonism*, 4.

40. Bushman, *Rough Stone Rolling*, 18–19; Tocqueville, *Democracy in America*, 528. The contemporary work that has been at the center of the discussion focusing on the concept of the market revolution in antebellum America is Charles Sellers, *The Market Revolution. Jacksonian America, 1815–1846* (New York: Oxford University Press, 1991). If I have any disagreements with the work, it is that Sellers' treatment of religion seems to be somewhat reductive, such as his discussion of Mormons and evangelicals (pp. 217–25). In my own work I have attempted to keep in mind that correlation is not causation.

41. W. Jackson Bate, *Samuel Johnson* (New York: Harcourt Brace Jovanovich, 1975), 115–29; the text's quotation is on 129.

42. Richard Hofstadter, "Abraham Lincoln and the Self-Made Myth," in *The American Political Tradition and the Men Who Made It* (New York: Alfred A. Knopf, 1948), 93–136.

43. Doris Kearns Goodwin, *Team of Rivals: The Political Genius of Abraham Lincoln* (New York: Simon and Schuster, 2005), 53.

44. Bushman, *Rough Stone Rolling*, 55.

45. Ibid., 444.

46. Joseph Fielding Smith, comp., *Teachings of the Prophet Joseph Smith* (Salt Lake City: Deseret Book, 1972), 39.

47. Forsberg, *Equal Rites*, xiii–xxii.

48. W. B. Yeats, "Among School Children," in *The Poems: A New Edition*, ed. Richard J. Finneran (London: Macmillan, 1983), 217.

CHAPTER 4

1. Herman Melville to Evert A. Duyckinck, March 3, 1849, in *Correspondence*, vol. 14, *The Writings of Herman Melville*: Northwestern-Newberry Edition, ed. Harrison Hayford and others (Evanston and Chicago: Northwestern University Press and The Newberry Library, 1993), 121, emphasis in original. All subsequent references to Melville's personal letters or published works are to this multivolume edition.

2. Herman Melville, "Hawthorne and His Mosses," in *The Piazza Tales and Other Prose Pieces, 1839–1860*, vol. 9, *Writings of Herman Melville*, 249.

3. James G. Bennett, as quoted in Dean C. Jessee, ed., *The Papers of Joseph Smith*, 2 vols. (Salt Lake City: Deseret Book, 1989–1992), 1:xiv.

4. Josiah Quincy Jr., as quoted in Jessee, *Papers*, 1:xiv.

5. R. W. B. Lewis, *The American Adam: Innocence, Tragedy, and Tradition in the Nineteenth Century* (Chicago: University of Chicago Press, 1955), 127.

6. Harold Bloom, *The American Religion: The Emergence of a Post-Christian Nation* (New York: Simon and Schuster, 1992), 96–97.

7. Herman Melville to Nathaniel Hawthorne, April 16?, 1851, in *Correspondence*, 186.

8. Stan Goldman, *Melville's Protest Theism: The Hidden and Silent God in "Clarel"* (DeKalb: Northern Illinois University Press, 1993), 73.

9. Joseph Smith to L. Daniel Rupp, June 5, 1844, in Joseph Smith Jr., *History of The Church of Jesus Christ of Latter-day Saints*, ed. B. H. Roberts, 2nd ed., 7 vols. (Salt Lake City: Deseret Book, 1962), 6:428.

10. Laurie Robertson-Lorant, *Melville: A Biography* (New York: Clarkson Potter, 1996), 83. Traveling past Nauvoo on steamship is also assumed in Hershel Parker, *Herman Melville: A Biography, Volume 1, 1819–1851* (Baltimore and London: Johns Hopkins University Press, 1996), 178.

11. Melville, *Pierre; or, The Ambiguities*, vol. 7, *Writings of Herman Melville*, 291.

12. Robert A. Rees, "Melville's Alma and the Book of Mormon," *Emerson Society Quarterly* 43 (II Quarter 1966): 41–46.

13. Melville, *Pierre*, 291.

14. Melville, *Mardi, and a Voyage Thither*, vol. 3, *Writings of Herman Melville*, 348.

15. Herman Melville to Evert A. Duyckinck, February 2, 1850, in *Correspondence*, 154.

16. Melville, *The Confidence-Man: His Masquerade*, vol. 10, *Writings of Herman Melville*, 7.

17. Ibid., 50.

18. Ibid., 9.

19. Walter E. Bezanson, "Historical and Critical Note," in Melville, *Clarel: A Poem and Pilgrimage in the Holy Land*, vol. 12, *Writings of Herman Melville*, 514.

20. Philip Young, *The Private Melville* (University Park: Pennsylvania State University Press, 1993), 141.

21. Joseph Fielding Smith, comp., *Teachings of the Prophet Joseph Smith* (Salt Lake City: Deseret Book, 1972), 38–39.

22. Herman Melville to Nathaniel Hawthorne, June 1?, 1851, in Melville, *Correspondence*, 193.

23. Melville, *Moby-Dick; or, The Whale*, vol. 6, *Writings of Herman Melville*, 112.

24. Melville, *Clarel*, 25.

25. Ibid., 26.

26. Malcolm Cowley, ed., *The Portable Hawthorne*, 2nd ed. (New York: Viking Press, 1969), 651.

27. J. F. Smith, *Teachings*, 342.

28. Merton M. Sealts Jr., *Melville's Reading, rev ed.* (Columbia: University of South Carolina Press, 1988); Mary K. Bercaw, *Melville's Sources* (Evanston: Northwestern University Press, 1987); Melville, *Moby-Dick*, 136.

29. Joseph Smith Jr., *History of The Church of Jesus Christ of Latter-day Saints*, ed. B. H. Roberts, 2d ed., rev., 7 vols. (Salt Lake City: Deseret Book, 1971); Joseph Smith Jr., *Personal Writings of Joseph Smith*, comp. and ed., Dean C. Jessee, rev. ed. (Salt Lake City: Deseret Book, 2002).

30. Melville, "Hawthorne and His Mosses," 246, 244.

31. Ibid., 250.

32. As cited in Leon Howard and Hershel Parker, "Historical Note," in *Pierre*, 380.

33. Melville, *Clarel*, 69.

34. Herman Melville, "I and My Chimney," in Melville, *Piazza Tales*, 352–77.

35. Melville, *Pierre*, 362.

36. J. F. Smith, *Teachings*, 361; J. Smith, *History of the Church*, 6:317.

37. J. Smith, *History of the Church*, 6:291.

38. Herman Melville to Evert A. Duyckinck, December 14, 1849, in Melville, *Correspondence*, 149.

39. Melville, *Redburn*, vol. 4, *Writings of Herman Melville*, 11; Melville, *Moby-Dick*, 3.

40. Melville, "Hawthorne and His Mosses," 243.

41. Donald Yannella and Hershel Parker, eds., *The Endless, Winding Way in Melville*, ed. with new charts by Kring and Carey (Glassboro, N.J.: Melville Society, 1981), 37.

42. Melville, *Pierre*, 169.

43. Herman Melville, "The Piazza," in *Piazza Tales*, 12.

44. Herman Melville, "The Encantadas, or Enchanted Isles," in *Piazza Tales*, 130.

45. J. F. Smith, *Teachings*, 69–70.

46. Ibid., 95.

47. Melville, *Pierre*, 182.

48. Paul Brodtkorb Jr., *Ishmael's White World: A Phenomenological Reading of "Moby-Dick"* (New Haven, Conn.: Yale University Press, 1965), 84.

49. Melville, *Moby-Dick*, 423.

50. Ibid., 424.

51. Ibid., 423.

52. Jessee, *Papers*, 1:87. Compare Matthew 6:23.

53. In *Confidence-Man*, Melville ironically says, "Life is a pic-nic *en costume*; one must take a part, assume a character, stand ready in a sensible way to play the fool. To come in plain clothes, with a long face, as a wiseacre, only makes one a discomfort to himself, and a blot upon the scene" (133). Here Melville presents a view he assumed others would have had when he appeared without a costume at a local costume party in the Berkshires (Watson Branch and others, "Historical Note," in Melville, *Confidence-Man*, 295). For an extensive treatment of Melville's maskless men, see James Edwin Miller Jr., *A Reader's Guide to Herman Melville* (Syracuse, N.Y.: Syracuse University Press, 1998).

54. Herman Melville to R. H. Dana Jr., May 1, 1850, in *Correspondence*, 162.

55. Melville to Hawthorne, June 1?, 1851, 191.

56. J. F. Smith, *Teachings*, 139.

57. Melville, *Pierre*, 339.

58. For critical explorations of Melville's religious struggles, see William Braswell, *Melville's Religious Thought: An Essay in Interpretation* (New York: Octagon Books, 1973); Stan Goldman, *Melville's Protest Theism*; Walter Donald Kring, *Herman Melville's Religious Journey* (Raleigh, N.C.: Pentland, 1997); Vincent Kenny, *Herman Melville's "Clarel": A Spiritual Autobiography* (Hamden, Conn.: Archon Books, 1973); Lawrance Thompson, *Melville's Quarrel with God* (Princeton, N.J.: Princeton University Press, 1952); and William Hamilton, *Melville and the Gods* (Chico, Calif.: Scholars Press, 1985).

59. Melville, *Clarel*, 347.

60. Melville, *Moby-Dick*, 374.

61. Melville, *Mardi*, 339.

62. Melville, *Moby-Dick*, 492

63. J. F. Smith, *Teachings*, 192.

64. J. Smith, *History of the Church*, 6:50.

65. J. F. Smith, *Teachings*, 107.

66. Ibid., 137.

67. Melville, *Redburn*, 10.

68. Melville, *Mardi*, 594.

69. Ibid., 557.

70. Melville, *Moby-Dick*, 425.

71. Ibid., 185–86.

72. Ibid., 414.

73. Melville, *Clarel*, 347.

74. Melville, *Mardi*, 556.

75. Melville, *Moby-Dick*, 107.

76. Melville, *Moby-Dick*, 311.

77. Ibid., 572.

78. Ibid., 111.

79. Ibid., 573.

80. Jessee, *Papers*, 2:456. Compare Doctrine and Covenants 127:2.

81. Melville, *Moby-Dick*, 423.

82. Melville, *Pierre*, 204.

83. Ibid., 208.

84. Ibid., 262, 207–8.

85. The different uses of silence in the arts and in religion have been explored in Jon D. Green, "The Paradox of Silence in the Arts and Religion," *BYU Studies* 35, no. 3 (1995–96): 94–131.

86. Melville, *Clarel*, 498.

87. Ibid., 499.

88. Melville, *Pierre*, 288–89.

89. Melville, "Hawthorne and His Mosses," 242.

90. As quoted in Braswell, *Melville's Religious Thought*, 27.

91. J. F. Smith, *Teachings*, 51.

92. Ibid., 346–47.

CHAPTER 5

1. Richard Bushman, preparatory remarks for participants in a panel at the American Historical Association to mark the Joseph Smith Bicentennial, Seattle, Wash., January 2005.

2. Here and in what follows, I draw on and adapt material from my book *A Republic of Mind and Spirit: A Cultural History of American Metaphysical Religion* (New Haven, Conn.: Yale University Press, 2007), esp. 136–50.

3. Harold Bloom, *The American Religion: The Emergence of the Post-Christian Nation* (New York: Simon and Schuster, 1992), 35, 103.

4. See, for example, John L. Brooke, *The Refiner's Fire: The Making of Mormon Cosmology, 1644–1844* (New York: Cambridge University Press, 1994), 220, 249, 253; S. H. Godwin, *Mormonism and Masonry* (Washington, D.C.: Masonic Service Association of the United States, 1924), 34–36, 50, 54–59; Jerald Tanner and Sandra Tanner, *Mormonism: Shadow or Reality?* (Salt Lake City: Modern Microfilm, 1964), and Jerald Tanner and Sandra Tanner, *The Changing World of Mormonism: A Condensation of Mormonism: Shadow or Reality?* (Chicago: Moody Press, 1980), 535–47.

5. Brooke, *Refiner's Fire*, 204.

6. See Sterling M. McMurrin, *The Theological Foundations of the Mormon Religion* (1965; reprint, Salt Lake City: University of Utah Press, 1974), 17–18; Joseph Smith, *The Doctrine and Covenants of the Church of Jesus Christ of Latter-day Saints*, ed. Orson Pratt (1880: reprint, Westport, Conn.: Greenwood Press, 1971), 131:7, 132: 20, 76: 50–98; Joseph Smith, Funeral Oration for King Follett, as recorded by Wilford Woodruff, quoted in Brooke, *Refiner's Fire*, 235, 199–200; D. Michael Quinn, *Early Mormonism and the Magic World View* (Salt Lake City: Signature Books, 1987), 175.

7. See Quinn, *Early Mormonism and the Magic World View*, 22, 25, 111, 78–79.

8. Ibid., 27; Jan Shipps, "The Prophet Puzzle: Suggestions Leading Toward a More Comprehensive Interpretation of Joseph Smith," *Journal of Mormon History* 1 (1974): 3–20.

9. Dan Vogel, *Indian Origins and the Book of Mormon: Religious Solutions from Columbus to Joseph Smith* (Salt Lake City: Signature Books, 1986), 18, 24–27; on New England, see James W. Mavor Jr. and Byron E. Dix, *Manitou: The Sacred Landscape of New England's Native Civilization* (Rochester, Vt.: Inner Traditions, 1989).

10. See Vogel, *Indian Origins*, 66, 33, 29.

CHAPTER 6

1. Joseph Smith Jr., *History of The Church of Jesus Christ of Latter-day Saints*, ed. B. H. Roberts, 2d ed., rev., 7 vols. (Salt Lake City: Deseret Book, 1971); 1:301.

2. See Margaret L. Coit, *John C. Calhoun: American Portrait* (Boston: Houghton Mifflin, 1950); and Richard L. Bushman, *Joseph Smith: Rough Stone Rolling* (New York:

Alfred A. Knopf, 2006). For a general overview of Mormon history, see James B. Allen and Glen M. Leonard, *The Story of the Latter-day Saints*, 2nd ed. (Salt Lake City: Deseret Book, 1992).

3. Thomas Jefferson to John Holmes, April 22, 1820. This letter can be found online by going to http://teachingamericanhistory.org/library, then following the links to Founding Era, Thomas Jefferson, Letter to John Holmes.

4. This document may be found online at http://en.wikisource.org/wiki/South_Carolina_Exposition_and_Protest.

5. Glyndon G. VanDusen, *The Jacksonian Era* (New York: Harper and Row, 1959), 44–45.

6. Smith, *History of the Church*, 1:301. Readers of this work should be aware that much of it is not Joseph Smith's own work. It was compiled, at his instruction and initially under his direction, by various scribes who garnered from his writings as well as from the writings of others who were with Smith at the time. For a discussion of how this history was written, see Dean C. Jessee, "The Writing of Joseph Smith's History," *BYU Studies* 11 (Summer 1971): 439–73.

7. Smith, *History of the Church*, 1:485.

8. Smith, *History of the Church*, 1:493. Cass continued:

> Where an insurrection in any state exists, against the government thereof,
> the President is required on the application of such state, or of the executive
> (when the legislature cannot be convened), to call forth such number of the
> militia, as he may judge sufficient to suppress such insurrection.
>
> But this state of things does not exist in Missouri, or if it does, the fact
> is not shown in the mode pointed out by law. The President cannot call out a
> militia force to aid in the execution of the state laws, until the proper requisi-
> tion is made upon him by the constituted authorities.

9. On April 24 Dunklin replied to those who had asked him to write the president by telling them of his doubts that the president had the power to do as they asked. Further, he said, "I could no more ask the President—however willing I am to see your society restored and protected in their rights—to do that which I may believe he has no power to do, than I could do such an act myself." He also told them of his hope to have a federal arsenal established in the state that, he thought, might be of help to the Saints. J. Smith, *History of the Church*, 1:488–89.

10. For an important treatment of Zion's Camp, see Peter Crawley and Richard Lloyd Anderson, "The Political and Social Realities of Zion's Camp" *BYU Studies* 14 (Summer 1974): 406–20.

11. For the entire letter, see *Messenger and Advocate* 2 (April 1836): 289–301. See also J. Smith, *History of the Church*, 2:436–40. This was consistent with a statement in the official declaration of beliefs regarding government and laws, adopted in August 1835:

> We believe it just to preach the gospel to the nations of the earth, . . . but
> we do not believe it right to interfere with bondservants, neither preach the

gospel to, nor baptize them contrary to the will and wish of the masters, nor to meddle with or influence them in the least to cause them to be dissatisfied with their situations in this life, thereby jeopardizing the lives of men; such interference we believe to be unlawful and unjust, and dangerous to the peace of every government allowing human beings to be held in servitude. (Doctrine and Covenants 134:12)

12. Smith, *History of the Church*, 3:289–305.

13. Ibid., 3:302.

14. Ibid., 4:40.

15. Ibid., 4:80.

16. During his service in the United States Senate (1821–1829) and as Secretary of State (1829–1831) Martin Van Buren consistently opposed any extension of federal power.

17. Smith, *History of the Church*, 4:80.

18. Ibid., 4:89.

19. Ibid., 4:80.

20. Ibid., 4:107. The Saints knew that it was impossible to obtain redress in the courts of Missouri, for they had already tried. There is no evidence that they ever tried through the federal courts. But since they were living in Illinois, this may have been impossible anyway because of the strictures of the Eleventh Amendment to the Constitution: "The Judicial power of the United States shall not be construed to extend to any suit in law or equity, commenced or prosecuted against one of the United States by citizens of another state, or by citizens or subjects of any foreign state."

21. Smith, *History of the Church*, 6:56–57; italics in original.

22. Ibid., 6:95.

23. Ibid., 6:64–65. To former President Van Buren's letter he added a biting postscript: "Also whether your views or feelings have changed since the subject matter was presented to you in your official capacity at Washington, in the year 1841, and by you treated with a coldness, indifference, and neglect, bordering on contempt." Notice that he should have said 1840 instead of 1841.

24. Lewis Cass to Joseph Smith, December 9, 1843, as reproduced in Edward George Thompson, "A Study of the Political Involvements in the Career of Joseph Smith" (master's thesis, Brigham Young University, 1966), Appendix G.

25. Smith, *History of the Church*, 6:155–56.

26. The letter may be found in J. Smith, *History of the Church*, 6:156–60. The full correspondence may also be found in Joseph Smith Jr., *Correspondence between Joseph Smith, the Prophet, and Col. John Wentworth, Editor of "The Chicago Democrat," and Member of Congress from Illinois; Gen. James Arlington Bennett, of Arlington House, Long Island, and the Honorable John C. Calhoun, Senator from South Carolina* (New York: John E. Page and L. R. Foster, 1844).

27. For treatment of Joseph Smith's presidential campaign, see James B. Allen, "Was Joseph Smith a Serious Candidate for the Presidency of the United States . . . ?" *Ensign* 3 (September 1973): 21–22; Arnold Garr, "Joseph Smith: Candidate for President of the United States," *Regional Studies in Latter-day Saint Church History: Illinois*, ed.

H. Dean Garrett (Provo, Utah: Department of Church History and Doctrine, Brigham Young University, 1995), 151–68; Martin B. Hickman, "The Political Legacy of Joseph Smith," *Dialogue: A Journal of Mormon Thought* 3 (Autumn 1968): 22–27; Richard D. Poll, "Joseph Smith's Presidential Platform," *Dialogue: A Journal of Mormon Thought* 3 (Autumn 1968): 17–21; and Margaret C. Robertson, "The Campaign and the Kingdom: The Activities of the Electioneers in Joseph Smith's Presidential Campaign," *BYU Studies* 39, no. 3 (2000): 147–80.

28. Smith, *History of the Church*, 6:210.

29. His proposal for prison reform was unusually radical for the time: to let all the prisoners go, except murderers, telling them to "go thy way and sin more," then to have the states punish felons by making them work on roads, public works, or any other place where they could learn wisdom and virtue and become more enlightened. In addition, Smith proposed that penitentiaries be turned into "seminaries of learning, where intelligence, like the angels of heaven, would banish such fragments of barbarism." Such proposals may seem strange today but, as Martin Hickman points out in his brilliant analysis of Joseph's platform, they at least reflect the prophet's sensitivity to the social problems of his day. Most prisons of the day were filthy, unhealthy, poorly managed, and did little if anything to facilitate personal reform. Joseph knew, because he had spent time in some. Hickman, "Political Legacy of Joseph Smith," 23. Smith's political platform, "Views of the Powers and Policy of the Government of the United States" appears in full in Smith, *History of The Church*, 6:197–209.

30. Smith, "Views of the Powers."

31. See Calhoun's 1848 "Disquisition on Government." It may be found online at http://www.constitution.org/jcc/disq_gov.htm.

32. In the case of *Barron v. City of Baltimore* (1833), for example, the Supreme Court ruled that the Bill of Rights limited the actions of the federal government only, not those of state governments. *Barron v. City of Baltimore*, 32 U.S. 243.

33. As Keith Melville has observed,

The substantive rights of the First and Fifth Amendments have now been applied to the states, protecting the freedoms of religion, press, speech, and assembly, and those of life, liberty, and property against violations of these rights from any officials or instrumentalities of the states. Similar incorporation of the procedural protections found in the Fourth, Fifth, Sixth, and Eighth Amendments has brought the criminal justice systems of the states a long way toward the ideals of fairness and justice implied in the notion of "due process of law."

This important national function of protecting individual rights, which Joseph Smith considered appropriate under the Constitution, should not be lost sight of in an age clamoring for new checks on federal power. [J. Keith Melville, "Joseph Smith, the Constitution, and Individual Liberties," *BYU Studies* 28 (Spring 1988): 73–74.]

CHAPTER 7

1. Josiah Quincy Jr., *Figures of the Past: From the Leaves of Old Journals* (Boston: Roberts Brothers, 1892), 400.

2. Karen Armstrong, *Muhammad: A Western Attempt to Understand Islam* (London: Victor Gollancz, 1991), 74.

3. Rudolph Otto, *The Idea of the Holy: An Enquiry into the Non-rational Factor in the Idea of the Divine and Its Relation to the Rational*, tr. John W. Harvey, 2nd ed. (London: Oxford University Press, 1950 [orig. pub. 1917]); and Mircea Eliade, *The Sacred and the Profane: The Nature of Religion*, tr. William R. Trask (New York: Harcourt, Brace, 1959 [orig. pub. 1957]). On Jesus as friend to American Christians, see Harold Bloom, *The American Religion: The Emergence of the Post-Christian Nation* (New York: Simon and Schuster, 1992).

4. Donald Q. Cannon and Lyndon W. Cook, eds., *Far West Record: Minutes of the Church of Jesus Christ of Latter-day Saints, 1830–1844* (Salt Lake City, Utah: Deseret Book, 1983), 27 and n. 2 (November 1, 1831). The process of compiling the revelations began in July 1830. After receiving sections 25–27 of *A Book of Commandments: For the Government of the Church of Christ, Organized according to the Law, on the 6th of April, 1830* (Zion, Mo.: W. W. Phelps, 1833) [hereafter Book of Commandments], Joseph Smith began to arrange and copy the revelations. H. Dean Garrett, "The Coming Forth of the Doctrine and Covenants," in *Regional Studies in Latter-day Saint Church History: Ohio*, ed. Milton V. Backman (Provo, Utah: Department of Church History and Doctrine, Brigham Young University, 1990), 90. On the publishing history, see Peter Crawley, *A Descriptive Bibliography of the Mormon Church*, vol. 1, *1830–1847* (Provo, Utah: Religious Studies Center, Brigham Young University, 1947), 37–42.

5. David D. Hall, *Cultures of Print: Essays in the History of the Book* (Amherst: University of Massachusetts Press, 1996), 143–45.

6. Cannon and Cook, *Far West Record*, 26–28, 31–32 (November 1–2, 12–13, 1831). On the resulting Book of Commandments, see Crawley, *Descriptive Bibliography*, 37–42.

7. John Whitmer, *From Historian to Dissident: The Book of John Whitmer*, ed. Bruce N. Westergren (Salt Lake City: Signature Books, 1995), 55.

8. William Phelps to Sally Phelps, ca. January 1836, in Bruce Van Orden, "Writing to Zion: The William W. Phelps Kirtland Letters (1835–1836)," *BYU Studies* 33, no. 3 (1993): 578.

9. Joseph Smith to Hyrum Smith, March 3, 1831, in Joseph Smith Jr., *The Personal Writings of Joseph Smith*, ed. Dean C. Jessee (1984; reprint, Salt Lake City: Deseret Book, and Provo, Utah: Brigham Young University Press, 2002), 257.

10. Parley Pratt, *The Autobiography of Parley Pratt*, ed. Parley P. Pratt Jr. (New York: Russell Brothers, 1874), 65–66.

11. Levi Hancock, Diary, L. Tom Perry Special Collections, Harold B. Lee Library, Brigham Young University, 45.

12. Joseph Smith to William W. Phelps, July 31, 1832, in Smith, *Personal Writings*, 273.

13. The voice is reminiscent of the distinction Søren Kierkegaard made in his essay on the difference between an apostle and a genius. "An apostle has no other evidence than his own statement, and at most his willingness to suffer everything joyfully for the sake of that statement." Søren Kierkegaard, "The Difference between a Genius and an Apostle," in *Without Authority*, ed. and tr. Howard V. Hong and Edna H. Hong (Princeton, N. J.: Princeton University Press, 1997), 105.

14. Joseph Smith, *Joseph Smith's New Translation of the Bible: Original Manuscripts*, ed. Scott H. Faulring, Kent P. Jackson, and Robert J. Matthews (Provo, Utah: Religious Studies Center, Brigham Young University, 2004), 591 (Moses 1:1); 1 Nephi 1:1; *Times and Seasons* 3 (March 1, 1842), 704 (Abraham 1:1).

15. Joseph Smith Jr., trans., *The Book of Mormon: An Account Written by the Hand of Mormon, upon Plates Taken from the Plates of Nephi* (Palmyra, N.Y.: E. B. Grandin, 1830), iii, iv.

16. Quoted in David F. Holland, "Anne Hutchinson to Horace Bushnell: A Take on the New England Sequence," *The New England Quarterly* 77 (June 2005): 194.

17. Parley Pratt, *A Voice of Warning and Instruction to All People: Containing a Declaration of the Faith and Doctrine of the Church of the Latter Day Saints, Commonly called the Mormons* (New York: W. Sandford, 1837), 122, 125, 128–29, 140.

18. Smith, *Personal Writings*, 296

19. Garry Wills, *John Wayne's America: The Politics of Celebrity* (New York: Simon and Schuster, 1997), 304, 349 n. 9.

20. David Chidester and Edward T. Linenthal, eds., *American Sacred Space* (Bloomington: Indiana University Press, 1995), 5–19.

21. The temple lot, like contested sacred space in Jerusalem, has been the source of endless conflict over the years. See, for example, Ronald Romig, "The Temple Lot Suit After 100 Years," *John Whitmer Historical Association Journal*, 14 (1994): 3–15; and Courtney S. Campbell, "Images of the New Jerusalem: Latter Day Faction Interpretations of Independence, Missouri, 1830–1992 " (PhD diss., University of Kansas, 1993).

22. On the significance of settling and possessing sacred space, see Eliade, *The Sacred and the Profane*, 29–42.

23. J. Smith, *Personal Writings*, 217.

24. On temples, see Laurel B. Andrew, *The Early Temples of the Mormons: The Architecture of the Millennial Kingdom in the American West* (Albany: State University of New York Press, 1978); Elwin C. Robinson, *The First Mormon Temple: Design, Construction, and Historic Context of the Kirtland Temple* (Provo, Utah: Brigham Young University Press, 1997).

25. Eliade, *The Sacred and the Profane*, 25.

26. Ibid., 25; emphasis in original.

27. Jonathan Z. Smith, speaking at the "Sacred Space in the Modern City" conference, Auburn Theological Seminary, New York, New York, May 4, 2004.

28. David John Buerger, *The Mysteries of Godliness: A History of Mormon Temple Worship* (San Francisco: Smith Research Associates, 1994), 75.

29. Ralph Waldo Emerson, "An Address Delivered Before the Senior Class in Divinity College, Cambridge, Sunday Evening, 15 July, 1838," in *The Collected Works of*

Ralph Waldo Emerson, ed. Robert E. Spiller and Alfred E. Ferguson (Cambridge, Mass.: Belknap Press of Harvard University Press, 1971), 1: 92.

CHAPTER 8

1. William Blake, *Jerusalem* (London: Allen and Unwin, 1964 [originally published 1804]).

2. Joseph Smith Jr., *History of the Church of Jesus Christ of Latter-day Saints*, ed. B. H. Roberts, 2nd ed., 7 vols. (Salt Lake City: Deseret Book, 1971), 5:401. (Hereafter cited as *History of the Church*.)

3. Smith, *History of the Church*, 6:428.

4. Terryl L. Givens, *By the Hand of Mormon: The American Scripture That Launched a New World Religion* (New York: Oxford University Press, 2003). See especially pages 66–82.

5. Parley P. Pratt, "A Dialogue between Joseph Smith and the Devil," *New York Herald* (January 1, 1844), reprinted in Richard H. Cracroft and Neal E. Lambert, *A Believing People: Literature of the Latter-day Saints* (Provo, Utah: Brigham Young University Press, 1974), 34.

6. Augustine, *Confessions*, trans. F. J. Sheed, rev. ed. (Indianapolis: Hackett, 1993), 1:vi.

7. Ibid., 4:xv.

8. Louis Menand, *The Metaphysical Club* (New York: Farrar, Straus and Giroux, 2001), 371.

9. Dante Alighieri, *Paradiso*, trans. Allen Mandelbaum (New York: Bantam, 1984), Canto 7:97–101.

10. Mandelbaum, in Ibid., 335.

11. George M. Marsden, *Jonathan Edwards: A Life* (New Haven, Conn.: Yale University Press, 2002), 112.

12. Smith, *History of the Church*, 5:215.

13. Joseph Smith Jr., *The Personal Writings of Joseph Smith*, ed. Dean C. Jessee (Salt Lake City: Deseret Book, 1984; repr., Provo, Utah: Brigham Young University Press, 2002), 458.

14. Smith, *History of the Church*, 6:184–85.

15. Jesse W. Crosby, cited in Mark L. McConkie, ed., *Remembering Joseph: Personal Recollections of Those Who Knew the Prophet Joseph Smith* (Salt Lake City: Deseret, 2003), 99.

16. Virginia Woolf, *A Room of One's Own* (New York: Harcourt, Brace, Jovanovich, 1989), 4.

17. Wilfred Cantwell Smith, "The Study of Religion and the Study of the Bible," in *Rethinking Scripture: Essays from a Comparative Perspective*, ed. Miriam Levering (Albany: State University of New York Press, 1989), 26.

18. C. S. Lewis, *Perelandra* (New York: Macmillan, 1965), 11.

19. It became imperative, for instance, "to distinguish between corrupt Churches & false Churches," since, as the non-separating Puritans would argue, "the corruption of

a thing doth not nullify a thing." Francis J. Bremer, *John Winthrop: America's Forgotten Founding Father* (New York: Oxford University Press, 2003), 199.

20. Augustine, *Retractions*, 1.13, cited in Gerald R. McDermott, "Jonathan Edwards, John Henry Newman, and Non-Christian Religions" (paper delivered at the American Society of Church History Meeting, Yale University, New Haven, Conn., March 31, 2001).

21. *Matthew Henry's Commentary* (Grand Rapids, Mich.: Zondervan, 1961), 1914. The glossed verse is Hebrews 4:2. A board of Nonconformist ministers wrote the commentary on the epistles after Henry's death in 1714.

22. Joseph Fielding Smith, comp., *Teachings of the Prophet Joseph Smith* (Salt Lake City: Deseret Book, 1972), 61; emphasis added.

23. Smith, *History of the Church*, 1:252.24. Hugh Nibley has used this term in the context of temple rituals, when he referred to "a God-given Urtext which has come down to the present day in many more or less corrupt forms." See his "What Is a Temple?" in *The Prophetic Book of Mormon*, volume 8 of the Collected Works of Hugh Nibley (Salt Lake City: Foundation for Ancient Research and Mormon Studies, Deseret Book; Provo, Utah: 1989), 215.

CHAPTER 9

1. Douglas J. Davies, *Introduction to Mormonism* (Cambridge, U.K.: Cambridge University Press, 2003), 252.

2. John Heywood Thomas, introduction to *The Boundaries of Our Being*, by Paul Tillich (London: Collins, 1973), 291.

3. Isaiah Berlin, "The Concept of Scientific History," [1960] *The Proper Study of Mankind: An Anthology of Essays* (London: Pimlico, 1997), 47.

4. Gilbert Ryle, *The Thinking of Thoughts: What is 'Le Penseur' Doing* [1968], Collected Papers, vol. 2 (London: Hutchinson, 1971), 480–496.

5. Clifford Geertz, *The Interpretation of Cultures* (1993; New York: Basic Books, 1973), 6–10.

6. Aristotle, *Ethics* (London: J. M. Dent and Sons, 1963), 57–63

7. Richard Lyman Bushman, *Joseph Smith: Rough Stone Rolling* (New York: Alfred A. Knopf, 2005), xx.

8. Richard Lyman Bushman, "The Inner Joseph Smith," *Journal of Mormon History* 32 (Spring 2006): 81.

9. Ann Taves, *Fits, Trances, and Visions: Experiencing Religion and Explaining Experience from Wesley to James* (Princeton, N.J.: Princeton University Press, 1995).

10. Bushman, *Rough Stone Rolling*, 41; Taves, *Fits, Trances, and Visions*.

11. See, for example, Woodbridge Riley, *The Founder of Mormonism: A Psychological Study of Joseph Smith, Jr.* (London: William Heinemann, 1903), 73.

12. See John Corrigan, *Religion and Emotion: Approaches and Interpretations* (Oxford, U.K.: Oxford University Press, 2004); and Kay Milton and Maruska Svasek, eds., *Mixed Emotions: Anthropological Studies of Feeling* (Oxford, U.K.: Berg, 2005).

13. Michael Freze, *They Bore the Wounds of Christ: The Mystery of the Sacred Stig-mata* (Huntington, Ind.: Our Sunday Visitor Publishing Division, 1989).

14. Mary F. Ingoldsby, *Padre Pio: His Life and Mission* (Dublin: Veritas, 1978).

15. Douglas J. Davies, *The Mormon Culture of Salvation: Force, Grace, and Glory* (Aldershot, U.K.: Ashgate, 2000), 49.

16. Robert J. Matthews, "Joseph Smith Translation of the Bible," in *Encyclopaedia of Mormonism*, ed. Daniel H. Ludlow, 4 vols. (New York: Macmillan, 1992), 2:763–69.

17. William D. Morain, *The Sword of Laban: Joseph Smith, Jr. and the Dissociated Mind* (Washington, D.C.: American Psychiatric Press, 1998).

18. Leroy S. Wirthlin, "Joseph Smith's Boyhood Operation: An 1813 Surgical Success," *BYU Studies* 21 (Spring 1981): 131–54.

19. Bushman, *Rough Stone Rolling*, 21.

20. See Davies, *Mormon Culture of Salvation*, 29–64; and Davies, *Introduction to Mormonism*, 144–70.

21. W. James Boyd, *Satan and Māra: Christian and Buddhist Symbols of Evil* (Leiden: Brill, 1975).

22. There is extensive artistic representation of this First Vision, see Richard G. Oman, "'Ye Shall See the Heavens Open': Portrayal of the Divine and the Angelic in Latter-day Saint Art," *BYU Studies* 35 (1995–96): 113–41.

23. Bushman, *Rough Stone Rolling*, 39–40.

24. See Dean C. Jessee, "The Writing of Joseph Smith's History," *BYU Studies* 11 (Summer 1971): 439–73.

25. Bushman, *Rough Stone Rolling*, xx, 438.

26. See Oman, "'Ye Shall See the Heavens Open'."

27. Fawn Brodie, *No Man Knows My History: The Life of Joseph Smith* (New York: Vintage Books, [1947] 1995), 377.

28. Paul Tillich, *The Courage to Be* (New Haven, Conn.: Yale University Press, 1952), 17.

29. Ibid., 20.

30. Ibid., 14.

31. Davies, *Introduction to Mormonism*, 206–11. Richard Bushman has recently emphasized the significance of death in Smith's thought. See Bushman, "The Inner Joseph Smith," 77–79.

32. Tillich, *The Courage to Be*, 218.

33. Bushman, *Rough Stone Rolling*, 44.

34. Max Weber, *The Theory of Social and Economic Organization* (New York: Free Press, 1947), 358.

35. Hans Mol, "Identity and the Sacred: A Sketch for a New Social Scientific Theory of Religion," *Sociological Analysis* 38.4 (Winter 1977): 420–22.

36. Kurt F. Kammeyer, *The Harp of Nauvoo* (Highlands Ranch, Colo.: Able Printing and Graphics, 2001); and Kurt F. Kammeyer, *A Collection of Sacred Hymns for the Church of the Latter Day Saints Selected by Emma Smith* (Highlands Ranch, Colo.: Able Printing and Graphics, 2003).

37. Jesus is equated with Jehovah in Mormon thought.

38. Gustav Niebuhr, "Adapting 'Mormon' to Emphasize Christianity," *New York Times*, February 17, 2001, 8.

39. Jan Shipps employed Ferdinand Tönnies' contrast between gemeinschaft and gesellschaft to distinguish the smaller, communal movement from the later bureaucratic organization. See Jan Shipps, *Sojourner in the Promised Land: Forty Years Among the Mormons* (Urbana and Chicago: University of Illinois Press, 2000), 379–80.

40. William H. Whyte, *The Organization Man* (Harmondsworth, U.K.: Penguin Books, [1956] 1960), 11.

41. Ibid., 372.

42. Tillich, *The Courage to Be*, 105.

43. Ibid., 143.

44. Bushman, *Rough Stone Rolling*, 473.

CHAPTER 10

1. Unless otherwise indicated, I cite the chapter and verse numbers of the English versions of the Bible.

2. As told in *The Letter of Aristeas*, 172–181, 301–311. In *The Old Testament Pseudepigrapha*, ed. J. H. Charleswporth, vol. 2 (New York: Doubleday, 1985).

3. *Face* and *presence* are the same word in Hebrew: *panim*.

4. This addition occurs also in the Chronicler's account, 2 Chron. 6:18.

5. He saw, *ra'ah*—not *ḥazah*, which implies a visionary experience, since related nouns mean seer and vision. It must have been customary to use the word *ra'ah* for a vision of the LORD.

6. The Targum here shows that losing sight of the face was being in exile. "You whose Shekinah dwells among the cherubim . . . restore us from our exile and make the brightness of your countenance shine upon us." In D.M. Stec, The Targum of Psalms, London: T&T Clark, 2004, ad. loc.

7. Some MSS have *hagiois*, others *hosiois*. The meaning is the same.

8. Thus Syriac, Targum, and St. Jerome.

9. The letters *d* and *r* look similar in Hebrew and are often confused.

10. The Targum here has "You are awesome O God, Praised in the house of your sanctuary."

11. At the end of the psalms there is either translation, paraphrase, or nothing: LXX Pss. 104, 105, 112, 114, 115, 134,145, 146, 147, 148.

12. This pattern appears at the climax of the book of Revelation. The multitude in heaven sing, "Hallelujah," and then the LORD appears on earth, riding forth from heaven with his angels (Rev. 19:1, 3, 7, 11–16).

13. M. Idel, *Kabbalah: New Perspectives* (New Haven, Conn.: Yale University Press, 1988), 168.

14. The Greek has "I shall be satisfied by seeing your Glory."

15. An early Christian text attributed to James, the first bishop of Jerusalem.

16. *reyqam* can mean either.

17. F. Brown, S. Driver, and C. Briggs, *A Hebrew and English Lexicon of the Old Testament* (Oxford: Clarendon Press, 1962), 811, 908.

18. The Hebrew is literally "those who seek your face, Jacob."

19. The Syriac translator read *wyhnk*, "and be gracious to you," as *wyhyk*, "and give you life," but the Hebrew letters *y* and *n* are similar and so the confusion is understandable. The question is, which is the original? The covenant with the priests was a "covenant of life and peace" (Mal. 2:5). One of Zechariah's symbolic staves was named "beauty," *no'am*, and breaking that staff was the sign that the covenant had been broken (Zech. 11:7, 10). Perhaps Zechariah's sign of the broken staff related to losing the vision of the beauty of the LORD, or perhaps to losing the presence of the LORD in the temple. Both would have been consequences of the Deuteronomists' programme. Proverbs 29:18 warns that losing the vision results in social chaos. The text says, literally, where there is no prophetic vision, the people unravel. The Apocalypse of Weeks, an enigmatic history incorporated into 1 Enoch, described the Deuteronomists' purge as the time when the people in the temple lost their sight and godlessly forsook Wisdom (1 En. 93.8).

20. *sbr*, which usually means "hope."

21. See D. M. Stec, *The Targum of Psalms* (London: T and T Clark/Continuum, 2004).

22. Ibid.

23. Origen, quoted in J. Z. Smith, "The Prayer of Joseph," in *Religions in Antiquity: Essays in Memory of E. R. Goodenough*, ed. J. Neusner (Leiden: Brill, 1970), 253–94, 265.

24. Ibid., 266 n. 2.

25. Also Leg. All. II.34; III.186, 212; Conf. 56,72,148; Migr. 113,125,201.

26. Midrash on Hosea 9:10 in Seder Eliyyahu Rabbah 27; see J. Z. Smith, "The Prayer of Joseph," 267.

27. C. T. R. Hayward, *Interpretations of the Name Israel in Ancient Judaism and Some Early Christian Writings* (Oxford: Oxford University Press, 2005), 311.

28. For a fuller discussion see Hayward, *Interpretations of the Name Israel*, 330–51.

29. This description of the Trinity—the One enthroned, the firstborn called Israel, and the Holy Spirit, is very like that in the Ascension of Isaiah, an early Christian text reworked from a Jewish original. Isaiah ascended to heaven and saw the Great Glory, God Most High, enthroned, and on the right he saw Jesus the LORD, and on the left he saw the angel of the Holy Spirit (Asc. Isa. 10.7; 11.32–33).

30. See T. N. D. Mettinger, *The Dethronement of Sabaoth* (Lund: CWK Gleerup, 1982), 80.

31. Ibid., 80–115.

32. Ibid., 86.

33. Thus the Authorized Version (or KJV).

34. Mettinger, 85, summarizing the work of R. Schmitt.

35. A comparison of modern translations, which differ quite widely, will show the difficulties of these passages.

36. For detail, see my book *The Great High Priest* (London: T and T Clark, 2003), 179–184.

37. "*Dominum videt, non quidem perfecte hominem, sed in habitu hominis apparentem.*"

38. A. L. Oppenheim, "The Golden Garments of the Gods," *Ancient Near Eastern Studies* 8 (1949): 172–93. For a detailed study, see C. H. T. Fletcher-Louis, *All the Glory of Adam. Liturgical Anthropology in the Dead Sea Scrolls* (Leiden: Brill, 2002), 68–84.

39. Translation in R. H. Charles, *Apocrypha and Pseudepigrapha of the Old Testament*, 2 vols. (Oxford: Clarendon Press, 1968), 2:443.

40. The passage continues: "R Simeon said: 'All the priestly robes were emblematic of the supernal mystery, having been made after the celestial pattern.'" Zohar Exodus 231a.

41. Scholars have detected Hebrew forms and idioms in the sometimes very literal translation. There is an allusion to the Apocalypse of Abraham in Clementine Recognitions 1133. This reference is Clementine Recognitions I.33

42. Quoted in Diodorus of Sicily XL 3.5–6.

43. Jesus expounded on the version of this text found at Qumran to the disciples on the road to Emmaus in Luke 24:26. Nothing else in the Hebrew Scriptures fits.

44. Another echo of 1 En. 93.8, the link between Wisdom and the vision.

45. Quotations from G Vermes, *The Complete Dead Sea Scrolls in English*, London: The Penguin Press, 1997.

46. *Katoptrizo* can mean looking into a mirror or reflecting like a mirror.

47. Another version of this tradition appears in Gen Rab XIX.7: the Shekinah left by seven stages of sin—Adam, Cain, Enosh, Noah's generation, the builders of Babel, the Sodomites, and the Egyptians in the time of Abraham—and it returned through seven righteous men—Abraham Isaac, Jacob, Levi, Kohath, Amram, and Moses.

48. The alternative way to read Psalm 37:29 was "The righteous shall take possession of the land and cause the Shekinah upon it for ever," thus R. Isaac, Genesis Rabbah XIX 7, reading *wayyaškinu*, they will cause the Shekinah to dwell, instead of MT *wayyiškenu*, and will they dwell.

49. The *gelyana* of Jesus Christ is how the Syriac version of the book of Revelation begins.

50. See B. D. Chilton, *The Glory of Israel: The Theology and Provenance of the Isaiah Targum, Journal for the Study of the Old Testament* Supplement no. 23 (Sheffield, U.K.: JSOT Press, 1983), 77–81.

51. See Margaret Barker, *Temple Theology: An Introduction* (London: SPCK, 2004).

52. Carol Zaleski, *Otherworld Journey: Accounts of Near-Death Experience in Medieval and Modern Times* (New York: Oxford University Press, 1987), 204.

53. Ibid., 204.

54. The Pearl of Great Price: A Selection from the Revelations, Translations, and Narrations of Joseph Smith (Salt Lake City; Church of Jesus Christ of Latter-day Saints 1979 edition).

55. Richard Lyman Bushman, "The Visionary World of Joseph Smith," *BYU Studies* 37, no. 1 (1997–98): 184.

56. Ibid., 184–5.

57. Lambert and Cracroft, "Literary Form and Historical Understanding: Joseph Smith's First Vision," *Journal of Mormon History* 7 (1980): 31–33.

58. Bushman, "The Visionary World of Joseph Smith," 193.

59. Richard Lyman Bushman, *Joseph Smith: Rough Stone Rolling* (New York: Knopf, 2005), 148.

60. Ibid., 593, note 31.

61. Terryl L. Givens, *By the Hand of Mormon: The American Scripture That Launched a New World Religion* (New York: Oxford University Press, 2002), 63–64.

62. Zaleski, *Otherworld Journeys*, 204.

63. Rudolf Otto, *The Idea of the Holy*, trans. John Harvey, 2nd ed. (New York: Oxford University Press, 1950).

64. Ninian Smart, *Worldviews: Crosscultural Explorations of Human Beliefs* (New York: Scribners, 1983), 63–64.

65. Ian Barbour, *Myths, Models, and Paradigms* (New York: Harper & Row, 1974), 54.

66. Hugh Nibley, "Prophets and Mystics," in *The World and the Prophets: Collected Works of Hugh Nibley*, ed. John W. Welch, Gary P. Gillum, and Don E. Norton (Salt Lake City: Deseret Book, 1987), chap. 12.

67. Mark E. Koltko, "Mysticism and Mormonism: An LDS Perspective on Transcendence and Higher Consciousness," *Sunstone* 13, no. 2 (April 1989): 14–19.

68. Philo, Confusion of Tongues, 136–38. Quoted in Barker, Temple Themes in Christian Worship (London: T&T Clark, 2007), 159

69. Carl Bode and Malcolm Cowley, eds., *The Portable Emerson* (Viking Penguin, New York, 1981), 215. As an exact contemporary of Joseph Smith, likewise a New Englander, only two years older, Ralph Waldo Emerson provides many interesting points of comparison and contrast. On the Kabbalist's view of God as unknowable, see Bushman, *Rough Stone Rolling*, 451. The desire for unity with God is shared, but the view of God as personal and knowable diverges.

70. Smart, *Worldviews*, 71–72.

71. Bushman, *Rough Stone Rolling*, 151.

72. Ibid., 150–51.

73. Mircea Eliade, *The Myth of the Eternal Return: or, Cosmos and History* (Princeton, N.J.: Princeton University Press, 1954), 67–69.

74. Joseph Campbell, *The Inner Reaches of Outer Space: Metaphor as Myth and as Religion* (New York: Harper and Row, 1986), 79.

75. Joseph Smith, *History of the Church of Jesus Christ of Latter-day Saints 1805–1847*, ed. B. H. Roberts, 7 vols. (Salt Lake City: Deseret Book, 1978), 6:57.

76. John W. Welch, *Illuminating the Sermon at the Temple and the Sermon on the Mount* (Provo, Utah: FARMS, 1999). For the temple context, see pages 14–17.

77. See Steven C. Harper, "'A Pentecost and Endowment Indeed': Six Eyewitness Accounts of the Kirtland Temple Experience," in *Opening the Heavens: Accounts of Divine Manifestations 1820–1844*, ed. John W. Welch (Provo, Utah and Salt Lake City: BYU Press and Deseret Book, 2005), 326–71.

78. Bushman, *Rough Stone Rolling*, 450.

79. Ibid., 450

80. Welch, *Illuminating the Sermon at the Temple*, 24.

81. Bushman, *Rough Stone Rolling*, 451.

82. David E. Bokovoy, "The Bible vs. the Book of Mormon: Still Losing the Battle" in *FARMS Review of Books* 18 (Provo, Utah: FARMS, 2006), 8.

83. Margaret Barker, *The Revelation of Jesus Christ, Which God Gave Him to Show to His Servants What Soon Must Take Place: Revelation 1.1* (Edinburgh: Clark, 2000), 162.

84. Margaret Barker, "What Did King Josiah Reform?" in *Glimpses of Lehi's Jerusalem*, ed. John W. Welch, David Rolph Seely, and Jo Ann H. Seely (Provo, Utah: FARMS, 2004), 526.

CHAPTER 11

1. William A. Linn, *The Story of the Mormons* (New York: Macmillan, 1902), 1.

2. Kathleen Flake, *The Politics of American Religious Identity: The Seating of Senator Reed Smoot, Mormon Apostle* (Chapel Hill: University of North Carolina Press, 2005), chapter 5.

3. Mark Twain, *Roughing It* (Hartford, Conn.: American Publishing Company, 1872), 111.

4. Fawn McKay Brodie, *No Man Knows My History* (New York: Alfred A. Knopf, 1945).

5. Nathan O. Hatch, *The Democratization of American Christianity* (New Haven, Conn.: Yale University Press, 1989).

6. Harold Bloom, *The American Religion: The Emergence of the Post-Christian Nation* (New York: Simon and Schuster, 1992).

7. Marvin S. Hill, "Brodie Revisited: A Reappraisal," *Dialogue: A Journal of Mormon Thought* 7, no. 4 (Winter 1972): 74.

8. Dan Vogel, "'Prophet Puzzle' Revisited" (paper presented at the Mormon History Association annual meeting, Snowbird, Utah (May 18, 1996).

9. Richard Lyman Bushman, *Joseph Smith: Rough Stone Rolling* (New York: Alfred A. Knopf, 2005), xxi.

10. Brodie, *No Man Knows My History*, 85.

11. Flake, *Politics of American Religious Identity*, 117–28.

12. Carlos H. Amado, "Some Basic Teachings from the History of Joseph Smith," *Ensign* (May 2002): 80.

13. John Morgan, *Plan of Salvation* (1881). Full text available at: http://www.geo cities.com/danforward/Plan_of_Salvation.htm, accessed July 10, 2005.

14. Lionel Trilling, *Sincerity and Authenticity* (London: Harvard University Press, 1971), 12.

15. Gilbert Tennent, *The Danger of an Unconverted Ministry* (1740).

16. See, for example, Ralph Waldo Emerson, Address Delivered before the Senior Class in [Harvard] Divinity College, Cambridge, Sunday Evening, July 15, 1838; Henry James, *Portrait of a Lady* (1881) and *The Ambassadors* (1903); and William James, *The Varieties of Religious Experience* (1902).

17. The array of responses elicited by news in the spring of 2007 that Madonna wanted to open an orphanage in Malawi indicates a deep and pervasive suspicion of her

motives. One representative blogger responded that "Madonna will do whatever it takes to stay in the public eye, while using and exploit [sic] anyone in the process." In feedback to the article "Madonna to take over Malawi orphanage?" at http://www.sfgate.com/cgi-bin/blogs/sfgate/detail?blogid=7&entry_id=15545, accessed 10/31/07.

18. *Autobiography of Benjamin Franklin*, Harvard Classics, vol. 1 (New York: P. F. Collier and Son, 1909), 36.

19. Dale Carnegie, *How to Win Friends and Influence People* (1936). This citation is from the section "Nine Ways to Get the Most Out of This Book," of which this is method number 6.

20. Mark C. Taylor, *Hiding* (Chicago: University of Chicago Press, 1997). This quotation is not from Taylor's book, but from an online interview he gave after its publication entitled "Mark C. Taylor in Conversation with Buck Tampa, www.press.uchicago.edu/Misc/Chicago/791599.html, accessed July 10, 2005.

21. Terryl L. Givens, *The Latter-day Saint Experience in America* (Westport, Conn.: Greenwood Press, 2004), 2.

22. Leonard J. Arrington and Davis Bitton, *Saints without Halos: The Human Side of Mormon History* (Salt Lake City: Signature Books, 1981), vii.

23. Jan Shipps, *Sojourner in the Promised Land: Forty Years Among the Mormons* (Urbana and Chicago: University of Illinois Press, 2000); the mention of "wonderful lights in the air" is from John Corrill, *A Brief History of the Church of Christ of Latter Day Saints (Commonly Called Mormons)* (St. Louis: self-published, 1839), 17.

24. *New Mormon Studies CD-ROM: A Comprehensive Resource Library* (Salt Lake City: Smith Research Associates, 1998).

25. S. George Ellsworth, ed., *History of Louisa Barnes Pratt* (Logan: Utah State University Press, 1998), 128. Grant Underwood discusses similar resonances among the Maori of New Zealand in his "Mormonism, the Maori and Cultural Authenticity," *Journal of the Pacific* 35, no. 2 (September 2000): 133–46.

26. The now-common LDS teaching that Polynesians are descendents of Book of Mormon peoples was not preached until the 1850s. For more on the appeal of Mormonism to Polynesian peoples, see Laurie F. Maffly-Kipp, "Looking West: Mormonism in the Pacific World," *Journal of Mormon History* 26, no. 1 (Spring 2000): 40–63.

CHAPTER 12

1. Rodney Stark, *The Rise of Mormonism*, ed. Reid L. Neilson (New York: Columbia University Press, 2005), 32.

2. Ibid., 56.

3. Dan Vogel, "'The Prophet Puzzle' Revisited," in *The Prophet Puzzle: Interpretive Essays on Joseph Smith*, ed. Bryan Waterman (Salt Lake City: Signature Books, 1999), 50.

4. Jan Shipps, "The Prophet Puzzle," in Vogel, *The Prophet Puzzle*, 43.

5. Thomas G. Weinandy, O.F.M., Cap., *Does God Suffer?* (Notre Dame, Ind.: University of Notre Dame Press, 2000), 32–34.

6. Herman Bavinck, *Reformed Dogmatics*, vol. 1, *Prologomena*, trans. John Vriend (Grand Rapids, Mich.: Baker Academic, 2003), 318.

7. Paul Owen and Carl Mosser, "Mormon Apologetic, Scholarship, and Evangelical Neglect: Losing the Battle and Not Knowing It?" *Trinity Journal* 19 no. 2 (1998): 179–205.

8. Nathan O. Hatch, *The Democratization of American Christianity* (New Haven, Conn.: Yale University Press, 1989), 113.

9. Ibid., 114.

10. Joseph Smith Jr., *History of the Church of Jesus Christ of Latter-day Saints*, ed. B. H. Roberts, 2nd ed. 7 vols. (Salt Lake City: Deseret Book, 1971), 1:4.

11. See, for example, the conversion narratives at http://www.chnetwork.org/journals/authority/authority_1.htm.

12. My comments on this subject in the next several paragraphs are a restating of my discussion of this topic in my "Joseph Smith's Theological Challenges: From Revelation and Authority to Metaphysics," in *The Worlds of Joseph Smith: A Bicentennial Conference at the Library of Congress*, ed. John W. Welch (Provo, Utah: Brigham Young University Press, 2006) 218–19.

13. Mather did not record this in his diary but in a separate document, and he described the visitation in Latin. The translation here is by Kenneth Silverman, *The Life and Times of Cotton Mather* (New York: Harper and Row, 1984), 127–28.

14. Silverman, *Cotton Mather*, 128.

15. Ibid., 129.

16. C. Wayne Hilliker, "Seeing God As God Is," *The Chalmers Pulpit*, http://www.chalmersunitedchurch.com/sermons/oct17s99.htm.

17. G. K. Chesterton, *Illustrated London News*, September 11, 1909; http://www.chesterton.org/discover/quotations.html.

18. John Calvin, *Institutes of the Christian Religion*, 2 vols., ed. John T. McNeill, trans. Ford Lewis Battles, Library of Christian Classics, vols. 20–21 (Philadelphia: Westminster Press, 1960), iv, xx, 12.

CHAPTER 13

1. Robert V. Remini, *Joseph Smith* (New York: Penguin, 2002), 36–37.

2. Harold Bloom, *The American Religion: The Emergence of a Post-Christian Nation* (New York: Simon and Schuster, 1992).

3. Jan Shipps, "'The Prophet Puzzle': Suggestions Leading Toward a More Comprehensive Interpretation of Joseph Smith," *Journal of Mormon History* 1 (1974): 3–20.

4. See Terryl L. Givens, *By the Hand of Mormon: The American Scripture that Launched a New World Religion* (New York: Oxford University Press, 2002).

5. Latter-day Saint scholarship is gradually absorbing the more complex readings of church history that contemporary scholarship has now made available. See Eric Dursteler, "Inheriting the 'Great Apostasy': The Evolution of Mormon Views on the Middle Ages and the Renaissance," *Journal of Mormon History* 28 (Fall 2002): 23–59.

6. For detailed discussion of the scholarly literature abounding in useful distinctions, see Ben Witherington, *Jesus the Seer: The Progress of Prophecy* (Peabody, Mass.: Hendrickson Publishers, 1999).

7. Weber argued that the Old Testament prophets turned away from magic and esotericism and helped to create the moral rationalism of Western civilisation. He emphasised that they responded to the challenge of the political events of the day. See Max Weber, *Ancient Judaism*, ed. and trans. Hans H. Gerth and Don Martindale (Glencoe, Ill.: Free Press, 1952).

8. The living prophets of the LDS Church have, in fact, taken activist approaches to the issue of what, at any particular point in time, should be regarded as central; accordingly, they have relativized as *obiter dicta* many statements by Brigham Young that earlier generations regarded as authoritative, for example, the Adam-God theory.

9. James L. Adams, *The Prophethood of All Believers*, ed. George K. Beach (Boston: Beacon Press, 1986).

10. See D. Michael Quinn, *Early Mormonism and the Magic World View* (Salt Lake City: Signature Books, 1987).

11. For relevant discussion, see Antonie Faivre and Jacob Needleman, eds., *Modern Esoteric Spirituality* (New York: Crossroad, 1992); Antonie Faivre, *Access to Western Esotericism* (Albany: State University of New York Press, 1994); and Antonie Faivre, *Theosophy, Imagination, Tradition: Studies in Western Esotericism*, trans. Christine Rhone (Albany: State University of New York Press, 2000). Faivre is a distinguished French scholar whose efforts to bring esotericism within a critical scholarly purview have modified our understanding of the field.

CHAPTER 14

1. Thomas A. Tweed and Stephen Prothero, *Asian Religions in America: A Documentary History* (New York: Oxford University Press, 1999), 51. See also East-India Marine Society of Salem, *By-laws and regulations of the East India Marine Society, Massachusetts: An association of masters and commanders of vessels, and of such persons as may be hereafter described, who have been, or are, engaged in the East India trade from the town of Salem* (Salem, Mass.: Thomas C. Cushing, 1800).

2. Dan Vogel, ed., *Early Mormon Documents*, 6 vols. (Salt Lake City: Signature Books, 1996), 1:243–47; Richard L. Bushman, *Joseph Smith and the Beginnings of Mormonism* (Urbana and Chicago: University of Illinois Press, 1984), 1:30.

3. Daniel Finamore, "Displaying the Sea and Defining America: Early Exhibitions at the Salem East India Marine Society," *Journal for Maritime Research* (May 2002).

4. David R. Proper, "Joseph Smith and Salem," *Essex Institute Historical Collections* 100 (April 1964): 94. See also Donald Q. Cannon, "Joseph Smith in Salem (Doctrine and Covenants 111)," in *Studies in Scripture*, vol. 1, Doctrine and Covenants, ed. Kent P. Jackson and Robert L. Millet (Salt Lake City: Deseret Book, 1989), 432–36.

5. For an overview of the concepts of contacts, exchanges, and encounters, see Thomas A. Tweed, "Introduction: Narrating U.S. Religious History"; and Laurie F. Maffly-Kipp, "Eastward Ho! American Religion from the Perspective of the Pacific Rim," in *Retelling U.S. Religious History*, ed. Thomas A. Tweed (Berkeley: University of California Press, 1997), 17–19, 127–48.

6. Tweed and Prothero, *Asian Religions in America*, 5–6.

7. Thomas A. Tweed, "Introduction: Hannah Adams's Survey of the Religious Landscape," in Hannah Adams, *A Dictionary of All Religions and Religious Denominations: Jewish, Heathen, Mahometan, Christian, Ancient and Modern* (Atlanta: Scholars Press, 1992), vii–ix.

8. Ibid., xxiv–xxv.

9. Ibid., xiv–xv, xxv.

10. See Sydney E. Ahlstrom, *The American Protestant Encounter with World Religions* (Beloit, Wisc.: Beloit College, 1962); Tweed, *The American Encounter with Buddhism, 1844–1912: Victorian Culture and the Limits of Dissent* (Chapel Hill: University of North Carolina Press, 2000); Robert S. Ellwood, *Alternative Altars: Unconventional and Eastern Spirituality in America* (Chicago: University of Chicago Press, 1979); Carl T. Jackson, *The Oriental Religions and American Thought: Nineteenth-Century Explorations* (Westport, Conn.: Greenwood Press, 1981); and George Hunston Williams, "The Attitude of Liberals in New England toward Non-Christian Religions, 1784–1885," *Crane Review* 9 (Winter 1967): 59–89.

11. Grant Wacker, "A Plural World: The Protestant Awakening to World Religions," in *Between the Times: The Travail of the Protestant Establishment in America, 1900–1960*, ed. William R. Hutchison (Cambridge, U.K.: Cambridge University Press, 1989), 256.

12. Tweed, *American Encounter with Buddhism*, 2.

13. Tweed, *American Encounter with Buddhism*; and Wacker, "A Plural World," 253–56.

14. Wacker, "A Plural World," 257.

15. Alan Race, *Christians and Religious Pluralism: Patterns in the Christian Theology of Religions* (London: SCM Press, 1983), 1.

16. Wacker, "A Plural World," 253–57; Race, *Christians and Religious Pluralism*, 1–3.

17. Gavin D'Costa, *Theology and Religious Pluralism: The Challenge of Other Religions* (New York: Basil Blackwell, 1986), 22, 52.

18. William C. Wilkinson, "The Attitude of Christianity to Other Religions," in *The World's Parliament of Religions*, ed. John H. Barrows, 2 vols. (Chicago: Parliament Publishing Company, 1893), 2:1249; and Richard Hughes Seager, ed., *The Dawn of Religious Pluralism: Voices from the World's Parliament of Religions, 1893* (La Salle, Ill.: Open Court, 1993), 70–74. There was some variety in this movement.

19. Thomas Wentworth Higginson, "The Sympathy of Religions," in *The World's Parliament of Religions*, 1:780–84; and Seager, *The Dawn of Religious Pluralism*, 321–22.

20. D'Costa, *Theology and Religious Pluralism*, 80.

21. John Henry Barrows, "Words of Welcome," in *The World's Parliament of Religions*, 1:72–79; and Seager, *The Dawn of Religious Pluralism*, 23–31.

22. Diana L. Eck, *Encountering God: A Spiritual Journey from Bozeman to Banaras* (Boston: Beacon Press, 1993), 179.

23. Some eighteenth-century deists advanced their own version of "primitive monotheism" or "original monotheism," although it differed from the later Christ-centered LDS theological position. See Samuel Shuckford, *The Sacred and the Profane History of the World Connected*, vols. 1 and 2, 3rd ed. (London: Printed for J. and R. Tonson, 1743).

Peter Harrison describes primitive monotheism in his book *"Religion" and the Religions in the English Enlightenment* (Cambridge, U.K.: Cambridge University Press, 1990), 139–46. Wilhelm Schmidt, a non-LDS critic of evolutionism, argued a similar original monotheism theory, but not until the first decades of the twentieth century. According to Eric Sharpe, Schmidt's "overriding concern was to demonstrate that the older stratum of human culture, the more clearly can one discern in it clear evidence of the worship of a Supreme Being." Eric J. Sharpe, *Comparative Religion: A History* (New York: Charles Scribner's Sons, 1975), 182–84. See also Wilhelm Schmidt, *The Origin and Growth of Religion: Facts and Theories* (London: Methuen, 1930).

24. Spencer J. Palmer, *Religions of the World: A Latter-day Saint View* (Provo, Utah: Brigham Young University, 1988), 191–96. The remaining three theories are as follows: His *primordial images theory* posits that "human predispositions of thought and feeling may be viewed as 'echoes of eternity,' since all men lived together under common conditions with God in a premortal spirit world." His *devil invention theory* speculates that "the devil has exerted a powerful influence upon men in counterfeiting the true principles and ordinances of the gospel . . . in an effort to lull mankind into satisfaction with partial truths and to weaken the appeal of divinely appointed teachers." The *common human predicament theory* argues "certain experiences are fundamental to all human beings." Therefore, "common beliefs and practices arise from the common predicaments faced by man."

25. Ibid., 197.

26. Joseph Smith, "Baptism for the Dead," *Times and Seasons* 3 (April 15, 1842): 759. Smith writes in this same editorial:

> To say that the heathens would be damned because they did not believe the Gospel would be preposterous, and to say that the Jews would all be damned that do not believe in Jesus would be equally absurd; for "how can they believe on him of whom they have not heard and how can they hear without a preacher, and how can he preach except he be sent."
>
> See David L. Paulsen, "The Redemption of the Dead: A Latter-day Saint Perspective on the Fate of the Unevangelized," in *Salvation in Christ: Comparative Christian Views*, ed. Roger R. Keller and Robert L. Millet (Provo, Utah: Religious Studies Center, Brigham Young University, 2005), 263–97.

27. David J. Whittaker, "Parley P. Pratt and the Pacific Mission: Mormon Publishing in 'That Very Questionable Part of the Civilized World,'" in *Mormons, Scripture, and the Ancient World: Studies in Honor of John L. Sorenson*, ed. Davis Bitton (Provo, Utah: Foundation for Ancient Research and Mormon Studies, 1998), 51, 55; *The Essential Parley P. Pratt* (Salt Lake City: Signature Books, 1990), 152, 156.

28. Tweed, *American Encounter with Buddhism*, xxix–xxx; *The Essential Parley P. Pratt*, 161.

29. George D. Watt and others, eds., *Journal of Discourses*, 26 vols. (Liverpool, U.K.: F. D. Richards et al., 1854–86): 1:155, June 12, 1853.

30. Brigham Young, Sermon of December 3, 1854, *Journal of Discourses*, 2:140.

31. Moses Thatcher, "Chinese Classics," *Contributor* 8 (June 1887): 301.

32. Brian H. Stuy, ed., *Collected Discourses Delivered by Wilford Woodruff, His Two Counselors, the Twelve Apostles, and Others*, 5 vols. (Burbank, Calif.: B. H. S. Publishing, 1987–1992): 1:162, June 24, 1888.

33. George Q. Cannon, sermon given August 15, 1869, *Journal of Discourses* 14:54–55.

34. George Q. Cannon, editorial dated February 1, 1877, *Juvenile Instructor* 12:30; George Q. Cannon, sermon given October 5, 1879, *Journal of Discourses* 21:74–75. Cannon later taught that Muhammad, "whom the Christians deride and call a false prophet and stigmatize with a great many epithets, was a man raised up by the Almighty and inspired to a certain extent by Him." George Q. Cannon, sermon given September 2, 1883, *Journal of Discourses* 24:371.

35. George Q. Cannon, "Editorial Thoughts," *Juvenile Instructor* 21 (August 15, 1886): 248. See also George Q. Cannon, "Topics of the Times," *Juvenile Instructor* 22 (October 1, 1887): 291.

36. I am currently writing a monograph on the Mormon representation at the 1893 Chicago World's Fair, including the Parliament of Religions, tentatively titled *Exhibiting Mormonism: The Latter-day Saints at the 1893 Chicago World's Fair* (New York: Oxford University Press, in progress). See also Davis Bitton, "B. H. Roberts at the World Parliament of Religion, 1893," *Sunstone* 7 (January/February 1982): 46–51; and Richard Hughes Seager, *The World's Parliament of Religions: The East/West Encounter, Chicago, 1893* (Bloomington: Indiana University Press, 1995).

37. See Judith Snodgrass, *Presenting Japanese Buddhism to the West: Orientalism, Occidentalism, and the Columbian Exposition* (Chapel Hill: University of North Carolina Press, 2003).

38. Stuy, *Collected Discourses*, 3:356–59.

39. Palmer, *Religions of the World*, 194.

40. Stuy, *Collected Discourses*, 3:359–56.

41. George Q. Cannon, *Juvenile Instructor* 28 (November 1, 1893): 675–76.

42. Stuy, *Collected Discourses*, 5:155.

Index